# Forests and Forestry

*Fourth Edition*

# Forests and Forestry

**I. I. HOLLAND, Ph.D.**

Former Head, Department of Forestry
University of Illinois at Urbana-Champaign


**G. L. ROLFE, Ph.D.**

Head, Department of Forestry
University of Illinois at Urbana-Champaign


**DAVID A. ANDERSON, M.S.**

Former Head, Information and Education
 Department
Texas Forest Service
Texas A&M University

**INTERSTATE PUBLISHERS, INC.**

Danville, Illinois

*Library of Congress Catalog Card No. 89-80062*

3
4 5 6
7 8 9

ISBN 0-8134-2854-8

# Preface

"Grow timber as a crop" was the rallying cry of foresighted state, federal, and private forest conservationists for many years. Actually, the intensity of forest management on small holdings has varied considerably over time. Some forest owners have managed their forest lands for long-term timber production; others have not. Those who did are benefiting from high timber prices today, as well as from the other values which forests provide when properly managed. The reasons why some woodland owners manage their forest holdings for the production of timber and other values, while others do not, are complex. Despite much study of this problem over the years, we still have much to learn about how better forest management can be encouraged on the nation's very large area of small, privately owned woodlands.

We are in a period when the term "biomass" has entered the vocabulary of forest landowners. The use of forest biomass as a source of energy is in its infancy, and much progress is being made. It is evident that we shall see the development of more complete tree utilization in the years ahead. The forest industry and government are taking leading roles in this development.

With rising costs of fossil fuels, wood from the nation's forests is being viewed as a potential source of energy, and there is evidence to indicate that much progress is being made toward the greater use of wood in meeting part of the nation's demand for energy.

Overall, the future looks bright for forest landowners who practice intensive forestry. In our industrialized society, with increasing population, demand for all types of wood products is rising. Today, as a net importer of timber, our nation is no longer self-sufficient in this resource.

There are in the continental United States 481 million acres of timberlands, a large proportion of which is suitable for the production of timber crops. Annually there are drains on these forests for the construction of dams, highways, roads, preserves, and other land uses. Thus, it is necessary that more intensive management practices be applied to the forest land remaining. To some extent, our standard of living is dependent upon the care given to this forest land in the production of timber and other forest values, including water, wildlife, grazing, and recreation.

Obviously, the forests must be protected from fire, insects, and diseases. Idle or unproductive lands must be reforested. And, the forests must be properly managed and harvested to meet the increasing wood needs of our society.

This text was developed to provide teachers and students of agriculture and forestry, as well as forest landowners, with information on forestry and the problems to be encountered in its practice. The subject is presented in a simplified manner. References are also provided at the close of each chapter for those who wish to devote further study to certain subjects.

The Appendices contain much useful information. The reader should become acquainted with their contents.

Many chapters in this text have been revised and expanded to include recent developments in forestry that are of interest to forest landowners. Taken into consideration were comments by book reviewers and others so as to make this edition as applicable as possible. While emphasis continues to be placed on the South, the reader will note that the information presented has application to all regions of the continental United States.

The authors hope that this book will prove profitable to the reader and that it will provide a better understanding of forestry and the need for management of the nation's forest resources.

I. I. HOLLAND
G. L. ROLFE
DAVID A. ANDERSON

# Acknowledgments

This text has, over the years, been expanded, revised, and updated. The authors are greatly indebted to a very large number of individuals and organizations who graciously supplied information, pictures, or materials in the production of the earlier editions.

In producing this latest edition, the authors are especially indebted to the following individuals who supplied the critical data needed in updating much of the tabular and other information:

David Darr, of the U.S. Forest Service, who provided the latest forest resource information. Other Forest Service contributors are Mel Bellinger and Karen Hanson. Lester De Coster of the American Forest Council provided needed private forest sector information. Tim Blechl, a graduate student in the Forestry Department, University of Illinois, did important work in locating information needed in the extensive revision of several chapters of the book. Several faculty members of the Forestry Department were also helpful in supplying new information, including Gene Campbell, Poo Chow, Ann Dennis, and George Gertner. The authors are also indebted to Joyce Canaday and her secretarial support staff for the typing of revised tabular and text material.

Finally, the authors express grateful appreciation to Ronald L. McDaniel and the editorial staff of Interstate Publishers, Inc., for their helpful suggestions and cooperation in producing this text.

# Table of Contents

CHAPTER I

# Introduction to Forestry

In every land, and in all ages, trees have had an influence on the progress and welfare of humans. The progress from primitive cave dweller to the present civilized state cannot be told without frequent reference to trees and their products. Trees provided these early inhabitants with food, medicines, fuel, shelter, protection, shade, tools, and other needs. Today, over 10,000 products are reportedly made of and from wood. It is the raw material from which forest industries manufacture countless products for the home, factory, and office.

A forest is a living, complexly interrelated community of trees and associated plants and animals. Within the community, plants and animals grow old and die. From the soil, trees take moisture and nutrients, and with the aid of sunlight, they manufacture wood and other products used by humans.

## *WHAT IS FORESTRY?*

Forestry is the art and science of managing forests so as to yield, on a continuous basis, a maximum in quality and quantity of forest products and services. It is, in a broad sense, the handling of forest lands to satisfy people's needs. It includes the logging, manufacturing, marketing, and use of wood products.

Forests can be managed for single or multiple purposes, to include protection of watersheds, production of timber, provision of wildlife habitat and recreation, regulation of stream flow, control of erosion, and general aesthetics.

It would be impossible for our country to maintain the standard of living it enjoys without the products and services which forests provide. History teaches that the more prosperous nations are those which have productive forests. Forests will play an increasing social and economic role in the United States in the future.

### Forestry as a Profession

Technical forestry education in the United States commenced in 1898 when the New York State College of Forestry at Cornell University and the Biltmore Forestry School on the Vanderbilt Estate near Asheville, North Carolina, opened their doors to interested students. By 1914, schools of forestry were in operation in various parts of the United States.

Following World War II there was a growing demand for professional foresters, brought on by the need to more intensively manage forest lands for multiple purposes. The need today is much greater due to the growing population and land-use problems.

While there is need for some students to specialize in one phase of the forestry profession or another, it has become necessary for most students to acquire a strong, well-rounded general education in forestry; specialized graduate work is becoming more essential.

As of March 1988, there were 47 accredited institutions in the United States and 31 institutions offering recognized technical forestry programs approved by the Society of American Foresters.

A list of colleges and universities offering forestry instruction is found in Appendix I.

## IMPORTANCE OF FORESTS TO THE NATION

The 481 million acres of timberlands (Table 1-1) in the United States are being called upon to meet a rapidly increasing demand for wood. This is attributed, in a large measure, to the increase in population and to an increased per capita demand.

To fulfill the country's needs and to process the raw material, in 1985 there were 12,000 logging camps, 7,500 sawmills, 215 plywood plants, 315 pulp mills, and thousands of other operations that convert the wood into fiberboard, particleboard, millwork, furniture, adhesives, preservatives, and a host of other products such as feed molasses, fodder yeast, and oil-well drilling additives.

Lumbering operations and plywood, pulp and paper, and furniture production employ more than 1.6 million persons earning some $24 billion a year. Adding to this wealth and job production are those individuals gainfully employed as carpenters, lumber yard operators, printers, and book manufacturers, to name but a few.

Coupled with the nation's demand for increasing amounts of wood has been the growth in demand for social benefits, such as rec-

TABLE 1-1

TIMBERLAND IN THE UNITED STATES
BY OWNERSHIP AND REGION, 1987

| Region[1] | All Owners | Total Public | Public Federal | Public Indian | Public State | Public County & Municipal | Private |
|---|---|---|---|---|---|---|---|
| . . . . . . . . . . . . . . . . . . . . . . (thousand acres). . . . . . . . . . . . . . . . . . . . . . . | | | | | | | |
| Northeast | 78,674 | 9,373 | 2,714 | 123 | 5,665 | 871 | 69,301 |
| North Central | 74,649 | 21,194 | 7,968 | 841 | 7,504 | 4,881 | 53,455 |
| Great Plains | 3,524 | 1,221 | 990 | 83 | 137 | 11 | 2,303 |
| Southeast | 84,594 | 8,772 | 6,983 | 60 | 1,434 | 295 | 75,822 |
| South Central | 109,938 | 10,875 | 8,903 | 56 | 1,466 | 450 | 99,063 |
| Pacific Northwest | 54,359 | 31,620 | 22,087 | 1,712 | 7,475 | 346 | 22,739 |
| Pacific Southwest | 17,412 | 9,595 | 9,051 | 99 | 431 | 14 | 7,817 |
| Rocky Mountains | 57,611 | 42,905 | 37,709 | 2,652 | 2,428 | 116 | 14,706 |
| Total U.S. | 480,761 | 135,555 | 96,405 | 5,626 | 26,540 | 6,984 | 345,206 |

[1]States for each region are listed in Table 1-2.

(Source: U.S. Forest Service, Preliminary RPA Review Draft, 1988)

reation, wilderness areas, wildlife habitat, and the use of forests to improve the quality and quantity of water yields. These social benefits have helped initiate restraints in traditional timber production and harvesting practices.

Until the year 1940, the nation's forest lands could be depended upon to fulfill all U.S. wood needs. Such is not the case today, however. In 1986, imports of wood reached 4.4 billion cubic feet. This was equal to over 25 per cent of the total production of wood that year (17.8 billion cubic feet). Considering our exports for the same period (2.3 billion cubic feet), the net imports amounted to 2.1 billion cubic feet, about 13 per cent of the industrial wood consumed in the United States. Thus, our nation is today heavily dependent upon wood imports.

Overall, the timberlands of the United States (Tables 1-1 and 1-2) are producing only about one-half of their biological potential.

TABLE 1-2

**TIMBERLAND AREA IN THE UNITED STATES
BY OWNERSHIP, REGION, AND STATE 1987**

| Region and State | Total Land Area | Forest Land Area | Federal | Indian | State | County & Municipal | Private |
|---|---|---|---|---|---|---|---|
| | | | ...(thousand acres)... | | | | |
| Northeast | | | | | | | |
| Connecticut | 3,112 | 1,777 | 16 | 0 | 156 | 74 | 1,530 |
| Delaware | 1,268 | 388 | 0 | 0 | 14 | 0 | 374 |
| Maine | 19,789 | 17,175 | 76 | 118 | 331 | 88 | 16,561 |
| Maryland | 6,330 | 2,461 | 22 | 0 | 236 | 22 | 2,182 |
| Massachusetts | 5,009 | 3,010 | 40 | 0 | 292 | 142 | 2,536 |
| New Hampshire | 5,777 | 4,189 | 426 | 0 | 96 | 104 | 3,563 |
| New Jersey | 4,813 | 1,914 | 246 | 0 | 224 | 63 | 1,380 |
| New York | 30,612 | 15,799 | 123 | 0 | 899 | 193 | 14,583 |
| Pennsylvania | 28,778 | 16,186 | 552 | 0 | 2,879 | 113 | 12,642 |
| Rhode Island | 671 | 368 | 3 | 4 | 68 | 7 | 286 |
| Vermont | 5,931 | 3,609 | 140 | 0 | 219 | 65 | 3,186 |
| West Virginia | 15,405 | 11,799 | 1,070 | 0 | 250 | 0 | 10,479 |
| North Central | | | | | | | |
| Illinois | 35,679 | 4,030 | 292 | 0 | 55 | 42 | 3,641 |
| Indiana | 23,102 | 4,296 | 329 | 0 | 177 | 29 | 3,761 |
| Iowa | 35,802 | 1,459 | 43 | 0 | 52 | 7 | 1,357 |
| Michigan | 36,364 | 17,342 | 2,498 | 22 | 3,581 | 187 | 11,053 |
| Minnesota | 50,745 | 13,571 | 1,825 | 465 | 2,654 | 2,334 | 6,293 |
| Missouri | 44,157 | 11,996 | 1,390 | 0 | 242 | 25 | 10,339 |
| Ohio | 26,224 | 7,229 | 171 | 0 | 173 | 79 | 6,806 |
| Wisconsin | 34,857 | 14,727 | 1,419 | 355 | 569 | 2,179 | 10,204 |
| Great Plains | | | | | | | |
| Kansas | 52,344 | 1,207 | 37 | 4 | 7 | 2 | 1,157 |
| Nebraska | 48,949 | 536 | 29 | 9 | 22 | 4 | 473 |
| North Dakota | 44,335 | 337 | 12 | 31 | 22 | 2 | 271 |
| South Dakota | 41,732 | 1,443 | 912 | 39 | 86 | 3 | 403 |
| Southeast | | | | | | | |
| Florida | 34,618 | 15,238 | 1,577 | 6 | 542 | 41 | 13,072 |
| Georgia | 37,167 | 23,383 | 1,421 | 0 | 118 | 70 | 21,775 |
| North Carolina | 31,231 | 18,359 | 1,365 | 53 | 332 | 80 | 16,529 |
| South Carolina | 19,344 | 12,179 | 913 | 1 | 233 | 27 | 11,005 |
| Virginia | 25,459 | 15,436 | 1,707 | 0 | 209 | 77 | 13,442 |
| South Central | | | | | | | |
| Alabama | 32,453 | 21,659 | 950 | 0 | 147 | 63 | 20,498 |
| Arkansas | 33,245 | 16,673 | 2,659 | 0 | 311 | 41 | 13,662 |
| Kentucky | 25,376 | 11,908 | 856 | 0 | 34 | 0 | 11,019 |
| Louisiana | 28,755 | 13,873 | 833 | 0 | 330 | 168 | 12,542 |
| Mississippi | 30,269 | 16,673 | 1,488 | 5 | 100 | 132 | 14,949 |

(Continued)

**TABLE 1-2 (Continued)**

| Region and State | Total Land Area | Forest Land Area | Federal | Indian | State | County & Municipal | Private |
|---|---|---|---|---|---|---|---|
| | | | *(thousand acres)* | | | | |
| **South Central** | | | | | | | |
| Oklahoma | 44,021 | 4,748 | 464 | 46 | 115 | 7 | 4,116 |
| Tennessee | 26,449 | 12,839 | 958 | 0 | 373 | 29 | 11,480 |
| Texas | 167,766 | 11,566 | 694 | 6 | 56 | 12 | 10,797 |
| **Pacific Northwest** | | | | | | | |
| Alaska | 362,516 | 15,763 | 4,936 | 22 | 4,622 | 20 | 6,163 |
| Oregon | 61,558 | 21,749 | 12,126 | 315 | 827 | 102 | 8,379 |
| Washington | 42,605 | 16,848 | 5,025 | 1,376 | 2,025 | 225 | 8,197 |
| **Pacific Southwest** | | | | | | | |
| California | 100,071 | 16,712 | 9,051 | 99 | 95 | 12 | 7,455 |
| Hawaii | 4,112 | 700 | 0 | 0 | 336 | 2 | 362 |
| **Rocky Mountains** | | | | | | | |
| Arizona | 72,587 | 3,789 | 2,515 | 1,219 | 12 | 0 | 43 |
| Colorado | 66,410 | 11,740 | 8,144 | 50 | 274 | 46 | 3,226 |
| Idaho | 52,913 | 14,534 | 10,310 | 38 | 1,036 | 51 | 3,099 |
| Montana | 93,175 | 14,737 | 8,742 | 622 | 638 | 2 | 4,733 |
| Nevada | 70,329 | 221 | 106 | 0 | 3 | 0 | 112 |
| New Mexico | 77,704 | 5,180 | 2,893 | 581 | 112 | 0 | 1,594 |
| Utah | 52,541 | 3,078 | 2,314 | 30 | 150 | 17 | 567 |
| Wyoming | 69,210 | 4,332 | 2,685 | 112 | 203 | 0 | 1,332 |

(Source: U.S. Forest Service, Preliminary RPA Review Draft, 1988)

Through improvement of forest management practices on the part of timberland owners, the United States can become less dependent on other nations for its wood resources.

## IMPORTANCE OF FORESTS TO THE SOUTH[1]

The South has been blessed with a warm climate, abundant rainfall, a long growing season, and soils which make for rapid tree growth. Less time is required to raise a tree crop in the South than in any other region of the nation. Only 12 to 15 years following the planting of seedlings, a post or pulpwood thinning can be made.

The South is a fast-growing area, and within this region (Figures 1-1 and 1-2) is found 38 per cent of the nation's timberland. Its 536 million acres of land support almost 75 million people, about one-

---

[1]Includes the Southeastern and South Central States of Tables 1-1 and 1-2.

third of the total U.S. population. By the year 2000, the population is expected to reach 100 million people.

The region's 195 million acres of timberland (Table 1-2) support about 5,000 primary industries, such as sawmills, pulp mills, and plywood plants. In addition there are thousands of secondary manufacturing plants, such as furniture manufacturers and wood novelty industries. The South has a vast furniture industry and is the world center for naval stores production.

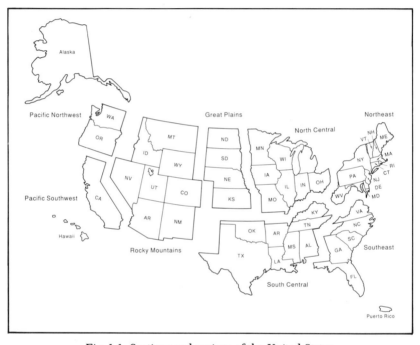

Fig. 1-1. Sections and regions of the United States.

Over 90 per cent of the timberland in the South is in state and private ownership (Table 1-1). For the United States as a whole, 77 per cent is in state and private ownership. Three-fourths of the private lands in the South are owned by about 1.6 million small landowners.

The South is in a period of industrial expansion which calls for more wood products in construction and other home and business needs. The pulp industry, which produces over half the nation's pulp from southern trees, is still expanding.

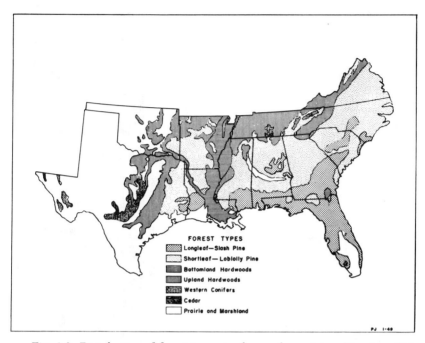

Fig. 1-2. Distribution of forest types in the southern states. (Courtesy U.S. Forest Service)

In 1987, the Pacific Northwest and Southwest produced 38 per cent of the harvest of sawlogs and veneer logs. The South produced 32 per cent of all sawlogs and veneer logs and 74 per cent of the total pulpwood harvest (Table 1-3). The strength and versatility of wood-pulp from southern pines, plus the historic advantage of low production costs and ready access to eastern and foreign markets have contributed to the South's dominance of the U.S. pulp and paper industry.

## REVIEW OF FORESTRY IN THE UNITED STATES

When the first white settlers came to America, they found extensive forests that were both a help and a hindrance to them. From the forests they secured material to build their log cabins and sheds for their livestock and the wood with which to keep warm. Blockhouses and stockades, to which they fled in times of danger, also came from material in the forest. Much of their food, clothing, and medicine were supplied by this source.

**TABLE 1-3**

**FOREST HARVEST PRODUCTS FROM THE FOREST REGIONS OF THE UNITED STATES, 1987**

*(million cubic feet)*

| Species Group and Products Produced | Total | North-east | North Central | Great Plains[1] | South-east | South Central | Douglas Fir Sub-region | Ponderosa Pine Sub-region | Alaska | Pacific Northwest Total | Pacific Southwest | Rocky Mountains |
|---|---|---|---|---|---|---|---|---|---|---|---|---|
| *Softwoods* | | | | | | | | | | | | |
| Sawlogs | 5,723 | 298 | 46 | 23 | 1,065 | 1,108 | 1,273 | 620 | 37 | 1,930 | 669 | 584 |
| Pulpwood | 2,748 | 264 | 114 | — | 1,149 | 1,058 | 100 | — | 20 | 120 | 4 | 39 |
| Veneer logs | 1,557 | 9 | 1 | — | 221 | 516 | 573 | 124 | 8 | 697 | 35 | 78 |
| Fuelwood | 546 | 86 | 39 | 3 | 43 | 10 | 140 | 51 | 8 | 199 | 84 | 82 |
| Other industrial[2] | 1,042 | 21 | 23 | 1 | 48 | 84 | 770 | 1 | 34 | 805 | 17 | 43 |
| Total | 11,616 | 678 | 223 | 27 | 2,526 | 2,776 | 2,856 | 796 | 99 | 3,751 | 809 | 826 |
| *Hardwoods* | | | | | | | | | | | | |
| Sawlogs | 1,723 | 324 | 402 | 9 | 344 | 558 | 81 | — | — | 81 | 2 | 3 |
| Pulpwood | 1,717 | 246 | 352 | — | 434 | 642 | 35 | — | — | 35 | 8 | — |
| Veneer logs | 117 | 19 | 14 | — | 49 | 22 | 13 | — | — | 13 | — | — |
| Fuelwood | 2,569 | 891 | 750 | 56 | 358 | 335 | 88 | — | 6 | 94 | 61 | 24 |
| Other industrial[2] | 220 | 32 | 149 | — | 15 | 20 | 1 | — | — | 1 | — | 3 |
| Total | 6,346 | 1,512 | 1,667 | 65 | 1,200 | 1,577 | 218 | — | 6 | 224 | 71 | 30 |
| *All Species* | | | | | | | | | | | | |
| Sawlogs | 7,446 | 622 | 448 | 32 | 1,409 | 1,666 | 1,354 | 620 | 37 | 2,011 | 671 | 587 |
| Pulpwood | 4,465 | 510 | 466 | — | 1,583 | 1,700 | 135 | — | 20 | 155 | 12 | 39 |
| Veneer logs | 1,674 | 28 | 15 | — | 270 | 538 | 586 | 124 | — | 710 | 35 | 78 |
| Fuelwood | 3,215 | 977 | 789 | 59 | 401 | 345 | 228 | 51 | 14 | 293 | 145 | 106 |
| Other industrial[2] | 1,262 | 53 | 172 | 1 | 63 | 104 | 771 | 1 | 34 | 806 | 17 | 46 |
| Total | 17,962[3] | 2,190 | 1,890 | 92 | 3,726 | 4,353 | 3,074 | 796 | 105 | 3,975 | 880 | 856 |

[1]Includes Kansas, Nebraska, North Dakota, and east and west South Dakota.
[2]Includes roundwood used for cooperage, piling, poles, posts, shakes, shingles, boardmills, charcoal, export logs, etc.
[3]Excludes the figures for the Pacific Northwest total.

(Source: U.S. Forest Service, Preliminary RPA Review Draft, 1988).

Nonetheless, forests in this period were a hindrance to crop production and defense. Therefore, some of the reasons for clearing land occupied by trees were to grow crops, to provide grass for livestock, to rid areas of wild beasts, and to eliminate a hiding place for Indians. There was no economic justification for sparing them. They were an obstacle to progress.

The development of the English colonies in the seventeenth century marked the beginning of the commercial utilization of our forest resources. What is believed to be the first sawmill in the United States was in operation at Jamestown, Virginia, in 1625. Subsequently, sawmills became essential in every colony, supplying local needs for lumber and providing a surplus for export to all parts of the world.

The industrial development of the South was influenced by the invention of the first steam-powered circular sawmill in 1803 at New Orleans. Mills of this type later sprang up in other areas of the South. It was not, however, until 1895 that lumbering developed into a major industry due to a rapid increase in population and a tremendous demand for construction material.

Fig. 1-3. Pulpwood being piled at a Lake States pulpmill. (Courtesy Omark, Inc.)

The peak of lumber production was reached in 1909, when 50,000 mills were in operation in the nation. They employed 500,000 workers and cut an estimated 46 billion board feet of lumber.

The United States has made and will continue to make significant contributions to the world's needs for wood.

## Beginning of Federal Forestry

The first appropriation for the acquisition of timberland by the federal government was made in 1799. Congress appropriated $200,000 to buy reserves of live oak along the coasts of South Carolina and Georgia to provide the growing nation with a reserve supply of desirable ship timbers and masts. Some years later the President was authorized to buy additional public lands bearing live oak and cedar in Florida, Alabama, and Louisiana, and to conduct experiments in the planting and cultivation of live oak. This was the start of the first federal forest research in the United States.

With the passing years, exploitation of the nation's forest resources was accelerated and was encouraged by the federal government through policies which encouraged the disposition of public domain.

At a meeting of the American Association for the Advancement of Science at Portland, Maine, in 1873, a report on "The Duty of Governments in the Preservation of Forests" was presented by Dr. Franklin B. Hough. It was very favorably received and was subsequently presented to Congress and to the state legislatures. President Grant was favorably impressed with the recommendations and urged action by Congress in 1874. It was not until 1876, however, that this body made the first appropriation for forestry. It provided for the appointment of an agent in the Department of Agriculture to conduct forestry investigations. Dr. Hough's investigations included the first survey of the nation's timber resources.

In 1881, a Division of Forestry was created in the Department of Agriculture. In 1901, it was known as the Bureau of Forestry and in 1905, it became the Forest Service. Gifford Pinchot became the first chief of the Forest Service.

Primarily through the efforts of the American Forestry Association, the first law to establish forest reserves from the public domain was enacted by Congress in 1891. These forest reserves were changed to national forests in 1907.

In 1986, there were 190,832,179 acres within the national forests of the United States where principles of sustained yield and multiple use are carried out (Appendix II).

## Beginning of State Forestry

On March 3, 1885, the state of California established the first forest agency in the United States. It was followed, in the same year, by Colorado, Ohio, and New York.

In the South, only Virginia, Louisiana, Texas, and North Carolina had forestry agencies prior to 1921. Other states set up such agencies as follows: Alabama in 1923, Georgia in 1924, Oklahoma in 1925, Mississippi in 1926, Florida in 1927, South Carolina in 1927, and Arkansas in 1931. While state forestry was slow in getting started in the South, it has progressed rapidly.

The forestry agencies within the various states in the South are organized as a division of a state department of conservation, a commission, a state board, or as a part of a university. All state and federal forestry agencies and their addresses are found in Appendices III and IV.

While there are variations in the activities performed by the several state forestry agencies, each state has the responsibility for the development of forest policy as it relates to state and private forest lands within its boundaries. Programs generally include forest fire control, operation of tree nurseries, assistance to small woodland owners in timber management problems, research, operation of state forests, and general education of the public.

Much of the progress shown by state forestry agencies has been made possible through cooperation of the federal government. One important enactment was the Weeks Law of 1911 which authorized financial aid to states in forest fire protection. The Clarke-McNary Law of 1924, subsequently amended in 1949, provided additional help for fire protection, for the production and distribution of nursery stock, and for cooperative assistance in farm forestry.

The McSweeney-McNary Law of 1928 provided for a national program of forest research and the nationwide survey of forest resources, important to state forestry agencies.

Other federal legislation which strengthened state agencies was the Emergency Conservation Work Program, later called the C.C.C. or Civilian Conservation Corps. Established in 1933 and abolished in 1942, it contributed much in reforestation, road construction, fire control, and other activities. The Norris-Doxey Cooperative Farm Forestry Act of 1937, superseded by the Cooperative Forest Management Act of 1950, authorized federal financial assistance to provide technical service to farmers and other forest landowners in the management, harvesting, marketing, and processing of forest products. In 1973 the Forest Incentive Program was created by Congress to share the cost of tree planting and forest management with small forest landowners.

## Other Forestry

The state extension services, through their forestry specialists, are important public organizations working diligently to advance forestry in the United States. Extension programs are carried on in all states by the land-grant colleges in cooperation with the federal government. In addition to working with other forest landowners, a task in which county agents also play a large part, the forestry specialists work cooperatively with public agencies and private industry in promoting forestry.

The Soil Conservation Service works with soil conservation districts. To these districts this agency assigns technical staffs to provide landowners with technical services for planning an integrated soil, water, and forest conservation program on their lands. The Soil Conservation Service employs foresters to help arrive at sound decisions concerning the use and treatment of forest resources. This agency coordinates its efforts with other state, federal, and private organizations.

The Federal Land Banks are contributing to forestry by providing long-term loans to forest landowners. Equally, the U.S. Department of Agriculture, through its Agricultural Stabilization and Conservation Service, known as A.S.C.S., provides cost-sharing programs in many forestry practices.

While only concerned with parts of seven states, the Tennessee Valley Authority, an agency of the federal government, has responsibility for 22.2 million acres of forest land. Its activity in forestry is carried out largely with forestry agencies, forest industries, and landowners.

The Bureau of Land Management, with land holdings in the Northwest, including Alaska, carries on an intensive forest management program. It employs foresters to work on its varied programs.

The nation's schools of forestry carry on much forest research, contributing to our knowledge of forestry.

The various state forestry associations, industrial and consulting foresters, forest industry trade associations, vocational agriculture divisions of the various state departments of education, and others have made and are making notable contributions to forestry in the United States.

## BENEFICIAL INFLUENCES OF TREES

Aside from the direct benefits which forests provide in the way of products, other values are derived from trees. Some of the beneficial influences are often overlooked and their value underestimated. A few of these are related here.

### Influence on Climate

Forests do not affect the climate over an extended area. They are the result rather than the cause of climate. However, they do have effect in a localized area. Due to the denseness of the crowns of the trees, the forest is cooler in summer and warmer in winter than are open areas. The same variations hold true in the daily fluctuations. Within a forest the air is more moist than on the outside. This is due to the fact that the force of wind is broken and there is less evaporation from forest soils. During the winter, the soil in a forest area is less subject to frost because of the insulating effect of the litter and humus on the forest floor. Snow has a tendency to stay longer in a forest than on an open area.

### Control of Runoff

During a rainstorm the leaves and branches of trees break the impact of rain, causing the moisture to drip rather than reach the earth with a force. Upon reaching the forest floor, the ground litter and humus absorb the water and reduce surface runoff. Of most importance, however, is the effect of the litter and humus in keeping the soil mellow, porous, and permeable, allowing seepage of water into the substratum where nature stores water. Much of it subsequently appears at the surface in the form of springs. Thus, forests help regulate stream flow and in the process act as natural filtering agents. In contrast, surface runoff in urban areas is high and contributes to peak flows of water.

### Retention of Snow Melt

In sections of the United States where snow occurs, forests retard snow melt which may last up to several weeks longer in forested areas than in open areas. Since the forest soil is likely to freeze less deeply, it absorbs more water from the melting snow. By delaying the melting of the snow and by the absorption of snow water in the soil, forests prolong the period of runoff. They also help, through this means, to reduce flooding and equalize stream flow in the streams and rivers.

### Environment for Fish

Forest vegetation that shades water courses from the full heat of the sun contributes toward the prevention of excessive stream temperatures. In certain areas of the nation the removal of trees from creeks and streams resulted in warm water that was undesirable for the continued existence of eastern brook trout. Forests also help to produce clear streams most desirable for fish life.

### Flood Prevention and Water Flow

In forested watersheds where management is carefully practiced, extremes of water flow in winter and summer are avoided, thus aiding in flood control. In contrast, where poor land management is practiced (Figure 1-4) and forests are depleted on the headwater basins, the resulting discharge following a rain carries topsoil downstream in flash floods, affecting aquatic life and reducing the productivity of streams and rivers for many years. Forest streams usually have a minimum amount of sediment, even during periods of high stream flow.

### Wildlife Habitat

Many kinds of wildlife are found in the forests where they obtain shelter and food. Some kinds of wildlife disappear when forest trees are removed. Other kinds of wildlife dependent on shrubs, weeds, and young trees may occupy the area where the

Fig. 1-4. Forest denudation, followed by wildfires, resulted in serious soil erosion on this area. It will take years to heal this scar and make the forest productive.

tree habitat is restored. The original kinds of habitat may return. When trees and other forest vegetation are destroyed, all wildlife may disappear for a long time.

### Prevention of Soil Erosion

On bare soil the amount of water that can be absorbed from a heavy rainfall is less than in a forested area. The result is rapid runoff over the land surface. In the process, soil particles are picked up by the water as it travels. The result is a quick accumulation of muddy water in streams and rivers. In contrast, water that moves through forested soils does so more slowly and stays free of sediment.

### Reduction of Wind Erosion

In treeless areas, such as in western Oklahoma and western Texas, windbreaks are established to reduce the harmful effects of the wind in drying out and blowing the soil, as protection against drifting snows, and to protect crops, livestock, homes, and barns from cold or hot winds. In other regions of the South plantings of this nature have been made, to some extent, where wind exposure is a problem.

Wind in treeless areas removes fertile topsoil, results in an increase in evaporation, and blows sand over fertile soil. Research has shown that properly established windbreaks reduce wind speed in relation to the height of the trees. The area over which wind is reduced can be expressed by the ratio of 1 to 20. That is, a row of trees 20 feet in height with dense foliage will reduce the speed of wind as far as 400 feet.

### Habitat for Songbirds

Songbirds are not found in dense forests. Rather, they prefer open spaces as are found in rural areas. Their desirable habitat is one that includes forests and open areas. At one time they were common in our smaller tree-lined cities with their diversity of trees and other smaller plants. However, with urban sprawl, in which trees and plants are replaced with concrete and stone, the number of songbirds has diminished in central city areas.

### Removal of Gas Pollutants

While the role of trees in cleansing the air is not yet fully understood, there seems to be no doubt that trees do take in pollutants from the air during their normal gas exchange. Small amounts of sulfur dioxide, for example, could possibly be taken in and used in metabolism by the trees. There is also the view that trees may take up various soil and water pollutants through the roots and thus aid in cleaning soil and water.

### Removal of Particulates

The leaves of trees aid in the removal of particulate matter. When such material is deposited upon leaves, particularly hairy leaves, the leaves usually hold onto the particles until the particles are washed to the ground by a rain. Additionally, trees can also reduce the velocity of wind in a given area, allowing the dust particles in the air to settle to the ground by gravity.

### Noise Abatement

There can be no doubt that noise can be abated through the proper use of trees and other plants. Even a few trees can be effective if placed between the noise source and people. However, hardwood trees which drop their leaves are not much help in winter. Trees, to be effective in noise abatement, should be close to the source of the noise. Particularly is noise a problem in urban areas.

### Temperature Differences in City Areas

Trees play a role in the temperature differences that are often reported between the downtown and the residential areas of a city on hot summer days. In the residential areas, trees are usually more prevalent. It is not only cooler in the shade of the trees, but the heat absorbed in the transpiration process also cools the air in the immediate vicinity of the cities.

### Greenbelts for Moisture Storage Zone

Greenbelts, made up of trees and other plants, are becoming increasingly important in urban planning. Aside from the aesthetic and social values which greenbelts provide, their recognition as moisture storage zones is becoming evident. Water diverted from streets is directed into these storage zones which do affect the quality and quantity of runoff. A single full-grown oak tree transpires 50 gallons of water on a hot summer day. Trees pump water from the soil allowing storage for additional runoff.

### Effect on Property Values

There can be no doubt that property values are enhanced if trees are growing on a city lot or a city "ranch."

### *Barriers to Reduce Glare and Reflection*

In urban areas in particular, trees are being utilized effectively as barriers against excessive glare and against reflection from high albedo surfaces such as concrete and glass.

## *SOCIAL VALUES OF FORESTS*

The better-known values of forests are the social benefits which they provide for outdoor recreation. Hunting, fishing, bird watching, nature study, camping, picnicking, hiking, and scenic or aesthetic value are but a few. With an increasing population in the United States, its forested areas are becoming of greater importance for these purposes.

## *ECONOMIC VALUE OF FORESTS*

One cannot deny the fact that the greatest contribution forests make is the forest products derived from trees. Too frequently their value is overlooked. Ours is a wood-oriented society. Wood is a most important part of houses, and wood is also important in the construction of apartment buildings and many commercial and industrial structures. There is wood in the morning paper, in cereal boxes, in sports equipment, and in furniture. Wherever one looks there is a wood product.

Trees from forests are made into lumber, pulpwood, veneer, poles, railroad ties, and piling, to name but a few. Lumber is further used to produce furniture and other manufactured items. Pulpwood is used to manufacture a multitude of products, including paper. Disposable bathing suits and dresses are two items produced by paper mills. Today, through chemistry, wood is providing a variety of products, including rayon, cellophane, plastics, and other well-known products. Wood is likely to play an increasingly important role in supplying some of the nation's energy needs, through production of biomass from timber.

Not to be overlooked, but subordinate to wood production, is the value forests also provide for cattle grazing and for use as recreational areas. These subjects will be covered in other chapters.

Employment and taxes on goods produced are the end result of good forest management, especially of importance to the South.

### Some Minor Forest Values

Often overlooked is the fact that a forest is made up of all kinds of plants, some of which offer a potential for financial return. While large landowners can concentrate on one or two products, such as sawlogs and pulpwood, small forest landowners must supplement their incomes from their main products in other ways. Minor plants of the forest offer this opportunity in localized areas throughout the South.

Sassafras roots and leaves find a limited sale in some areas for tea or for use in soups. There is also an export market for sassafras roots. Ginseng, found in the mountains of Georgia and the Carolinas, is valuable for its roots and has a large export market. Spanish moss is used in some areas as a packing material. Many florists purchase fern fronds and attractive weed plants for use in bouquets. Gum, produced by the sweet gum or red gum tree, is marketable in certain areas.

During the Christmas season a market is available for Christmas trees; mistletoe; uncolored or colored pine cones of all species; branches of evergreens, such as longleaf pine and holly; and sweet gum balls. Galex, an evergreen herb, is used by florists for decoration. Pine straw and a compost pile may find a market near a city where flower and vegetable gardeners are found.

In some areas, "lighter" wood, the pitch laden wood of pines, has a market for use in starting fires in fireplaces. Basket willow shoots are of value to the basket market. The cutting and sale of barbecue wood will bring good returns. Wild fruits and berries can, in some local areas, be marketed from roadside stands. Mushrooms also offer an opportunity for financial reward. There is a limited demand for tree pollen for use by doctors in allergy treatments.

Where possible, small hardwood trees could be carefully removed from the small forest land and sold to people in the city. Live oak and water oak are but two species that are in demand.

These are only a few of the opportunities available. Of importance to small woodland owners is to find out what is growing in their forests and then seek out markets. The cooperative extension forest research specialists (Appendix V) offer sources for information on this subject.

## FORESTRY FOR SMALL TIMBER GROWERS

Forestry for small timber growers deals with the protection, management, and utilization of forests that are a part of a farm unit or of small timberland areas. As a general rule, the forests produce only a part of the owner's income.

### Condition of Small Timberlands

The forests of small timberland areas in the South, as well as elsewhere in the nation, are generally poorly managed. They are cutover, for the most part, whenever there happens to be an opportunity for a cash sale. Ordinarily, cutting is heavy, and in too many instances the forests are stripped of timber (Figure 1-5). The result is that many years must elapse between cuttings. In the intervening period the timberland does not produce enough income to jus-

Fig. 1-5. A severely cutover timberland. Many years must elapse before this land becomes productive.

tify the effort to find out how to manage it. Because it produces little income, it is a liability to the owner, to the community, and to the area.

Unfortunately, most small timber growers have acquired no knowledge of forest management. They have a tendency to believe that growing trees is something they can do nothing about. Yet, with good management, a small forest can be made to yield an owner financial returns at 5- or 10-year intervals.

## Timberlands Can Be Productive

Regardless of mistakes that may have been made, a small owner can successfully practice forestry. For some it will require some patience and practical business judgment. While it may take several years to make a forest productive, the waiting period between harvests of trees, once the forest is productive, will be lessened. Each owner must start with what he or she happens to have and gradually make desired changes over a period of years. Technical forestry assistance is available to a landowner for this purpose.

To the great majority of small woodland owners, growing trees as a crop is a new business. Especially is this so for those who live in the cities and own forest land in rural areas. Timber growing, if it is engaged in at all, is definitely a side issue. Thus, it is most important that technical forestry assistance be obtained.

## Timberland Forestry in the Farm Program

Forestry has a definite place in all small timber ownership plans. Not only will the owners earn financial returns from the sale of forest products, but they will receive their own wood-products needs from the land. It is only when the owners treat their timberlands as they would their other income-producing assets and activities that they derive benefits and profits from those lands.

Small timber tracts provide cover for steep hillsides, thus helping prevent erosion and the siltation of bottomlands. They serve as a refuge for game, providing hunting opportunities. In some instances the lands are leased during hunting season with good financial returns. Forests also shelter cattle during the cold winter weather.

The timberlands also provide for woods work, integrated with other farm activity. Forest management is definitely an asset to southern farmers and other woodland owners.

### Sources of Technical Assistance

Professional forestry assistance is available to all forest landowners who will avail themselves of the opportunity. Foresters are employed by state forestry agencies. The state agricultural extension services also employ foresters. Usually there is no charge for advice and assistance from these groups. See Appendices III and V.

Consulting foresters provide comprehensive assistance in forest management, but a fee is usually charged for their services. Many forest industries also provide technical help free of charge.

Using technical knowledge and experience, a forester develops a simple management plan geared to the owner's desire and needs. It provides for planting, thinning, fire and grazing protection, and stand improvement. The forester may help the owner to mark trees for a timber sale, estimate volume in trees, and advise on marketing.

Every small timberland owner should seek technical help in forest management. It is to the owner's benefit, financially.

### Financial Assistance

Financial assistance is available to forest landowners through the Agricultural Conservation Program (A.C.P.) in each state as administered by local A.S.C.S. committees. Included are such forestry practices as tree planting, killing of undesirable hardwoods, plowing of firebreaks, and prescribed burning. A county A.S.C.S. committee determines whether a county will adopt a practice and the amount of cost sharing for each.

Loans for the purchase of forest lands or management activities thereon are available through the Farmers Home Administration, Federal Land Banks, and some insurance companies.

### Tree Farms System

The American Forest Council is the national sponsor of the Tree Farms System. This system was organized to recognize landowners who are practicing forest management, including forest fire prevention. Its objective is to encourage the owners of small woodlands, in particular, to practice forestry. In each state, industrial groups and associations cooperate in the program. All owners of forest land in excess of 5 acres may qualify for membership. Foresters inspect the woodland property to ascertain that the owners are making an attempt to grow trees as a crop. Those owners who qualify are furnished a certificate and a Tree Farm sign (Figure 1-6) to place on

Fig. 1-6. A Tree Farm sign posted on woodland property signifies that the owner is managing the woodland to grow repeated crops of trees.

their woodlands. It is a recognition of those who are making a sincere effort to practice forestry. Information on membership is available from one's state forestry agency or extension forester. Currently, almost 90 million acres of forest land in the United States are part of the Tree Farm program (Table 1-4). There are 31,262 tree farms in the South, representing about 50 per cent of the nation's total.

## FOREST PRACTICE LAWS

Federal and state legislative bills aimed at controlling management of private forest lands in the various states are being considered by forestry, conservation, and governmental leaders. In some states it has become reality. The regulatory concept on the management of forest resources, however, is not new either in the United States or abroad. European forestry has been characterized for centuries as functioning under strict control of governmental regulations. In many nations allowable timber harvests on private forest lands are established by governmental agencies.

Early regulation in the American colonies under English rule protected certain desirable shipbuilding trees. Only in the last quarter century, however, have the more complex forest regulatory laws been considered in the United States. In more recent years management regulations on private forest lands have been stimulated in part by a desire to solve the problem of low productivity of timber on small ownerships.

Each of the 50 states has some regulation that either directly or indirectly regulates private forest practices. Some of the states have laws that are quite detailed and elaborate while other states have laws that are of a more general nature. Many of the state "forestry" laws deal only with fire, timber trespass, and pest control. Some 16 states, however, currently have legislation that controls cutting practices and other silvicultural activities. Due to pressure from a variety of sources, including federal legislation, this number is apt to grow quite rapidly in the next decade.

The current or recommended state forest practices acts have several common elements. In general the acts recommend the establishment of some type of forest practices board to be composed of agency representatives and other forestry leaders. The board would then establish standards for the management of private forest lands in that state. Landowners desiring to undertake forest

TABLE 1-4

**STATUS OF TREE FARMS PROGRAM
AS OF OCTOBER 1, 1988**

| State | Number of Tree Farms | Acreage |
|---|---|---|
| Alabama | 2,525 | 7,274,503 |
| Alaska | 24 | 1,253 |
| Arizona | 27 | 3,930 |
| Arkansas | 3,984 | 4,508,906 |
| California | 670 | 3,745,682 |
| Colorado | 199 | 72,147 |
| Connecticut | 516 | 137,248 |
| Delaware | 130 | 36,514 |
| Florida | 3,146 | 6,875,197 |
| Georgia | 3,874 | 7,497,184 |
| Hawaii | 2 | 814 |
| Idaho | 721 | 1,619,190 |
| Illinois | 805 | 73,166 |
| Indiana | 995 | 116,809 |
| Iowa | 499 | 38,753 |
| Kansas | 322 | 12,301 |
| Kentucky | 809 | 286,639 |
| Louisiana | 2,988 | 5,535,103 |
| Maine | 1,813 | 7,303,769 |
| Maryland | 1,130 | 241,092 |
| Massachusetts | 1,330 | 242,609 |
| Michigan | 1,958 | 2,202,649 |
| Minnesota | 2,162 | 901,331 |
| Mississippi | 5,366 | 3,686,533 |
| Missouri | 790 | 585,618 |
| Montana | 420 | 1,994,454 |
| Nebraska | 192 | 9,092 |
| Nevada | 3 | 13,064 |
| New Hampshire | 1,260 | 786,695 |
| New Jersey | 211 | 78,967 |
| New Mexico | 74 | 108,458 |
| New York | 1,483 | 972,950 |
| North Carolina | 3,008 | 2,544,691 |
| North Dakota | 277 | 14,080 |
| Ohio | 1,708 | 409,824 |
| Oklahoma | 296 | 1,244,291 |
| Oregon | 985 | 6,247,013 |
| Pennsylvania | 1,661 | 856,800 |
| Rhode Island | 175 | 36,185 |
| South Carolina | 1,528 | 3,323,502 |
| South Dakota | 218 | 47,662 |
| Tennessee | 1,523 | 2,216,476 |

(Continued)

TABLE 1-4 (Continued)

| State | Number of Tree Farms | Acreage |
|---|---|---|
| Texas | 3,119 | 4,203,991 |
| Utah | 5 | 11,048 |
| Vermont | 871 | 538,555 |
| Virginia | 2,215 | 2,055,877 |
| Washington | 716 | 5,140,149 |
| West Virginia | 588 | 1,393,464 |
| Wisconsin | 2,414 | 1,860,802 |
| Wyoming | 10 | 13,565 |
| Totals | 61,745 | 89,120,595 |

(Source: American Forest Council)

activities such as road building, clearing for fences or other construction, pest control, timber harvest, or a change in the form of land use, such as the clearing of timber to develop cattle pasture, would have to apply to the forestry board and receive approval for the activity to be conducted. Some forestry practice laws call for a performance bond for satisfactory work completion. In addition, most state laws call for civil penalties in the case of law violations. Preservation groups have attempted to include: provisions for wilderness set-asides on private forest lands, criminal in lieu of civil penalties, and stringent permit systems.

The second session of the 92nd Congress in the Federal Water Pollution Control Act Amendments of 1972 gave the U.S. Environmental Protection Agency (EPA) the authority to issue information on processes, procedures, and methods to control pollution resulting from silvicultural activities. EPA has issued a report on this topic. It has prepared a suggested state forest practices act for the Council of State Governments. By definition EPA has considered all forest management activities to be included under the term "silviculture."

## URBAN FORESTRY

Urban forestry has been defined as a specialized branch of forestry that has as its objective the cultivation and management of trees for their present and potential contribution to the physiological, sociological, and economic well-being of an urban society. Inherent in this function is a comprehensive program designed to educate the urban populace on the role of trees and related plants in the urban environment.

Urban forestry embraces a multi-managerial system that includes municipal watersheds, wildlife and fisheries habitats, outdoor recreational opportunities, landscape design, recycling of municipal wastes, tree care in general, and the future production of wood fiber as raw material. A significant role involves the large scale plantings of trees and shrubs for noise abatement, sight barriers, beautification, and landscape purposes.

Specialized subdivisions of urban forestry are identified as metro, metropolitan, city, municipal, environmental, and park forestry. Community, municipal, and utility arboriculture are also used. Those workers with horticultural backgrounds identify urban vegetation management with titles such as urban botany, urban agriculture, horticultural aesthetics, and therapeutics, as well as urban and environmental horticulture. All these workers are striving toward the common goal of applying sound biological and managerial principles and programs to improve the urban culture. These efforts are designed to enhance the urbanized landscape with functional and attractive trees, shrubs, and related vegetation.

A related activity to this description of urban forestry is one of providing educational forestry opportunities to the urban resident forest landowner. Some estimates are that as much as 75 per cent of all timberland owners currently reside in the nation's metropolitan areas. Traditional educational programs conducted in rural areas are ineffectual in reaching this growing audience. Special educational programs including forestry short courses, tours, and workshops have been conducted for urban tree farmers by state forestry agencies and cooperative extension services with the assistance of forest industries and other organizations.

### BIBLIOGRAPHY

There are numerous excellent references pertaining to forestry for each state and for the nation as a whole. Since it would be impractical to provide a complete list of such references, only a partial list is given. No discrimination is intended against any reference that is not listed.

*Career Profiles in Forestry, Conservation, Ecology and Environmental Management.* F.S. 308. Washington, D.C.: U.S. Forest Service, 1973.

Clepper, Henry. *Origins of American Conservation.* For the Natural Resources Council of America. New York, N.Y.: The Ronald Press Company, 1966.

*Conservation Directory.* Washington, D.C.: National Wildlife Federation, 1975.

Dana, S. T., and Johnson, E. W. *Forestry Education in America, Today and Tomorrow.* Washington, D.C.: Society of American Foresters, 1963.

Demmon, E. L. *Opportunities in Forestry Careers.* Louisville, Ky.: Vocational Guidance Manuals, Inc., 1975.

*Edible Fruits of Forest Trees.* Publication K-6. Washington, D.C.: U.S. Forest Service, 1957.

*Elements of Forestry with Special Reference to Illinois.* Springfield, Ill.: Department of Conservation, Division of Forestry, 1973.

*Highlights in the History of Forest Conservation.* Agricultural Information Bulletin 83. Washington, D.C.: U.S.D.A., 1952.

*How Paper Comes from Trees.* Atlanta, Ga.: Southern Forestry Institute, Undated.

Kummerly, Walter. *The Forest.* New York, N.Y.: Robert B. Luce Company, Inc., 1973.

*Learning About the Environment.* Washington, D.C.: U.S. Department of the Interior, Bureau of Land Management, 1973.

Little, Silas, and Noyes, John H. *Trees and Forests in an Urbanizing Environment.* Amherst, Mass.: Cooperative Extension Service, University of Massachusetts, 1971.

Loomis, Robert C., and Padgett, D. K. *Air Pollution and Trees in the East.* Upper Darby, Pa.: U.S. Forest Service, State and Private Forestry, 1974.

Maisenhelder, Louis C. *Understory Plants of Bottomland Forests.* Occasional Paper 165. New Orleans, La.: Southern Forest Experiment Station, 1958.

*The Outlook for Timber in the United States.* Forest Resource Report No. 20. Washington, D.C.: U.S. Forest Service, 1973.

Read, Ralph A. *Windbreaks.* A series of seven leaflets. Tucson, Ariz.: Rocky Mountain Forest and Range Experiment Station, 1965.

Schenck, Carl Alwin. *The Birth of Forestry in America. Biltmore Forestry School 1898-1913.* Forest History Society and Appalachian Consortium. Santa Cruz, Calif.: Big Trees Press, 1974.

Society of American Foresters. *Forest Terminology.* Baltimore, Md.: Monumental Printing Co., 1965.

Society of American Foresters. *Forestry as a Career.* Texas Chapter, College Station, Tex., 1966.

*Special Forest Products for Profit.* Agricultural Information Bulletin No. 278. Washington, D.C.: U.S. Forest Service, 1967.

*Statistical Abstract of the United States 1988.* Washington, D.C.: U.S. Department of Commerce, Bureau of the Census, 1987.

Stoeckeler, J. H. *Shelterbelt Influence on Great Plains Field Environment and Crops.* Production Research Report No. 62. Washington, D.C.: U.S.D.A., 1962.

*The Timber Owner and His Federal Income Tax.* Agricultural Handbook 274. Washington, D.C.: U.S. Forest Service, 1975.

*To Grow a Tree.* Portland, Ore.: Georgia Pacific Corporation, 1975.

U.S. Forest Service, Georgia Forestry Commission, and the University of Georgia. *Symposium on the Role of Trees in the South's Urban Environment.* Athens, GA.: University of Georgia, 1971.

U.S. Forest Service. RPA Review Draft, 1988.

U.S. Forest Service. *U.S. Timber Production, Trade, Consumption, and Price Statistics 1950-1986.* Miscellaneous Publication No. 1460. Washington, D.C.: 1988.

Widner, Ralph R. *Forests and Forestry in the American States*. A Reference Antholo-
    gy. Compiled for the Association of State Foresters. Washington, D.C., 1968.
Winters, Robert K. *The Forest and Man*. New York, N.Y.: Vantage Press, Inc., 1974.
*Wood Industry Careers*. Washington, D.C.: National Forest Products Association,
    Undated.

# CHAPTER II

# Forests and Ecology

Forests are a very important part of the environment. They cover about one-third of the earth's surface and approximately one-third of the continental United States. Unless seriously disturbed by people or altered by catastrophic events, they continue to live indefinitely on a given area of land. The contribution of forests to the stability of nature benefits many forms of life, including human beings (Chapter I).

## *ECOLOGY*

*Ecology* is the science of the interrelationships of organisms to their total environment. Forest ecology is concerned with the forest as a biological community. It deals with the interrelationships among the various trees, plants, and other living organisms comprising the community and with the interrelationships between these organisms and the physical environment in which they exist. In other words, forest ecology is the study of the forest ecosystem; a concept which combines both the living and the non-living aspects of the environment.

## *CONCEPTS OF AN ECOSYSTEM*

An *ecosystem* might be likened to an aquarium in which the water, containing a number of dissolved minerals, constitutes the physical environment. Sunlight enters the tank allowing the green plants to grow by providing an energy source. The plants give out oxygen in photosynthesis (carbon dioxide is used in this process). The fish in turn feed on the plants. Fish excrement helps feed the green plants by providing minerals back into the water. This environment survives entirely on its own for a time. A forest is similar, but on a much larger scale.

Forest ecosystems are best described by understanding various characteristics and processes which are typical of the forest environment. The characteristics of ecosystems include *stratification, zonation,* and *diversity* and *stability,* while processes include *energy flow, material cycling, succession, decomposition,* and *competition.*

*Stratification* refers to the various layers that one can observe in the forest. The upper canopy trees and trees just below the main canopy, such as saplings, seedlings, and small herbaceous plants near the forest floor, are typical layers. These many layers of leaves result in an efficient capture of sunlight (energy) for growth of the forest. Sometimes ecosystems are also *zoned;* for example, as you walk from a very wet area near a stream to a very dry area further away, you may move through several zones comprised of groups of tree species. This occurs because the various kinds of trees in the forest have different needs for moisture and nutrients, just as people like different kinds of food. *Zones* are also apparent and easily observed as you travel up a mountain.

Natural forest ecosystems are also very diverse with many kinds of trees and plants. The various layers in a forest provide a variety of habitats for both plants and animals allowing many different kinds to develop. This *diversity* results in a stable environment which does not change greatly. Consider the comparison between a diverse forest and a cornfield which has only one species. In the cornfield, if you remove one species of plant, the system can no longer function; however, in the forest, removing one kind of tree will have little impact. Other kinds of trees are available to substitute for the one removed. The trees in the forest have overlapping jobs or *niches.*

*Energy flow* is an important ecosystem process. Energy in the form of sunlight is captured by green plants which are the *producers* in the system. Green plants combine the sun's energy with water and minerals from the soil in order to grow. These non-living materials used by green plants to survive and grow are termed the "abiotic" or "non-living" part of the ecosystem. Animals or consumers in the ecosystem survive on the green plants for food. As waste from both plants and animals accumulates on the soil surface, *decomposition* becomes very important. *Decomposers* are the fungi and bacteria, primarily in the upper soil layer, which break down plant and animal matter to be recycled and used over again by the green plants.

Energy is considered a flow because it is captured by green plants as sunlight, but as it is used in the ecosystem, it is constantly converted to heat energy, which goes back to outer space not to be used again in the ecosystem. Materials, on the other hand, are used over and over again. Plants which use materials from the environment are eaten by animals, and as both plants and animals die, the waste is decomposed, returning the materials back to the environment so that they can be used again. This is a circular process, so it is called a *material cycle*.

All through this process both plants and animals are competing for the resources they need to survive. *Competition* for light, space, water, nutrients, and other materials is a constant process in ecosystems.

Forest ecosystems are also constantly changing through a very slow process called *succession*. As individuals die, they may be replaced by other kinds of plants resulting in a change in the ecosystem; for example, if you allow a bare field to develop naturally, you will observe several stages of vegetation over time. The process may take 200 years to reach a mature forest. The forest is considered in most areas to be the *climax*, or terminal stage, which is very stable and diverse, but it is also constantly changing as individuals die and are replaced.

## ECOSYSTEMS

Ecosystems can be various sizes. They range from a few acres to thousands of acres. Generally, forest ecosystems are classified into types based on the dominant tree species; for example, Table 2-1 shows types and acreages for typical forest ecosystems in the eastern United States, while Table 2-2 shows similar information for the western portion of the country.

Some ecosystems are simple in nature, while others are complex. A cotton field, an apple orchard, or a pine plantation is an example of a simple ecosystem. A true pine-hardwood forest, an oak-hickory forest, or a beech-maple forest is a complex ecosystem.

The more complex an ecosystem, the more resistant it is to either change or damage by insects, diseases, ice storms, fire, and other disasters. The reason is that the ecosystem has many plant species represented in the stand that are not similarly affected by one of these damaging factors. In a mixed hardwood ecosystem (Figure 2-1), one species of tree may be killed out by a disease, yet other plants will take its place. There will not be a total loss in the timber resource, and the ecosystem will continue to function. In contrast, a

## TABLE 2-1

### AREA OF FOREST LAND IN THE EASTERN UNITED STATES BY FOREST TYPE, ALL OWNERSHIPS, 1987

*(thousand acres)*

| Region | Total | White Pine, Red Pine, Jack Pine | Spruce, Fir | Longleaf, Slash Pine | Loblolly, Shortleaf Pine | Oak, Pine | Oak, Hickory | Oak, Gum, Cypress | Elm, Ash, Cottonwood | Maple, Beech, Birch | Aspen, Birch | Other Forest Types | Non-stocked |
|---|---|---|---|---|---|---|---|---|---|---|---|---|---|
| Northeast | 81,264 | 7,917 | 10,262 | — | 1,725 | 2,640 | 23,927 | 363 | 3,784 | 26,836 | 3,174 | — | 636 |
| North Central | 77,450 | 4,047 | 8,578 | — | 663 | 922 | 23,197 | 432 | 6,765 | 16,452 | 14,586 | — | 1,808 |
| Great Plains | 4,157 | 1,516 | 16 | — | 2 | 117 | 710 | — | 1,310 | 148 | 183 | 33 | 122 |
| Southeast | 85,740 | 480 | 18 | 11,839 | 20,813 | 9,598 | 25,440 | 12,470 | 1,422 | 236 | — | — | 3,424 |
| South Central | 110,370 | 35 | — | 3,697 | 25,428 | 18,175 | 44,897 | 15,562 | 1,493 | 640 | — | — | 443 |
| Total East | 358,981 | 13,995 | 18,874 | 15,536 | 48,631 | 31,452 | 118,171 | 28,827 | 14,774 | 44,312 | 17,943 | 33 | 6,433 |

(Source: U.S. Forest Service, Preliminary RPA Review Draft, 1988)

## TABLE 2-2

## AREA OF FOREST LAND IN THE WESTERN UNITED STATES BY FOREST TYPE, ALL OWNERSHIPS, 1987

| Region | Total | Douglas Fir | Ponderosa Pine | Western White Pine | Fir, Spruce | Hemlock, Sitka Spruce | Larch | Lodge-pole Pine | Redwood | Other Soft-woods | Western Hard-woods | Pinyon, Juniper | Non-stocked[1] |
|---|---|---|---|---|---|---|---|---|---|---|---|---|---|
| | | | | | | | (thousand acres) | | | | | | |
| Douglas Fir Subregion | 23,665 | 14,038 | 241 | 8 | 1,290 | 3,313 | 74 | 54 | 6 | 243 | 3,933 | 9 | 456 |
| Ponderosa Pine Subregion | 20,559 | 4,056 | 7,102 | 4 | 2,792 | 669 | 778 | 2,264 | — | 117 | 361 | 1,786 | 630 |
| Alaska | 121,003 | — | — | — | 71,990 | 10,927 | — | 268 | — | 18,470 | 19,344 | — | 4 |
| Pacific Southwest | 36,030 | 1,581 | 5,144 | 3 | 6,236 | 32 | — | 330 | 1,109 | 1,160 | 10,649 | 2,475 | 7,311 |
| Rocky Mountains | 121,438 | 15,500 | 15,154 | 261 | 12,758 | 1,503 | 1,781 | 11,312 | — | 2,766 | 10,947 | 45,706 | 3,750 |
| Total West | 322,695 | 35,175 | 27,641 | 276 | 95,066 | 16,444 | 2,633 | 14,228 | 1,115 | 22,756 | 45,234 | 49,976 | 12,151 |

[1]Includes Chaparral.

single pine species in a plantation could be wiped out by an attack of pine bark beetles.

In a mature forest ecosystem, the large trees grow at a slow rate. Due to mortality and tree decay, net growth in a stand is negligible or non-existent. Under good forest management, in which mature trees and those with diseases are removed, timber productivity can

Fig. 2-1. A mixed hardwood stand made up principally of sweet gum, red and white oak, hickory, magnolia, and beech.

be maintained. At the same time, the forest areas can provide social values such as recreation, while functioning as a stable ecosystem.

Because it is extremely important to manage forests for multiple values, including timber, wildlife, recreation, and water, there is a great need for a better understanding of how the different parts of the ecosystem are related. Because forest ecosystems are very complex, the relationships among the ecosystem parts are difficult to describe and quantify. The need to better understand how forests behave under different management procedures or stress has greatly encouraged research in forest ecology.

### BIBLIOGRAPHY

Colinvaux, Paul. *Ecology.* New York, N.Y.: John Wiley and Sons, Inc., 1986.

Forman, Richard T., and Godron, Michael. *Landscape Ecology.* New York, N.Y.: John Wiley and Sons, Inc., 1986.

Hocker, H. W., Jr. *Introduction to Forest Biology.* New York, N.Y.: John Wiley and Sons, Inc., 1979.

Ketchum, Richard M. *The Secret Life of the Forest.* New York, N.Y.: American Heritage Press, 1970.

Levitt, J. *Response of Plants to Environmental Stresses.* New York, N.Y.: Academic Press, Inc., 1972.

Odum, Eugene P. *Fundamentals of Ecology.* Third Edition. Philadelphia, Pa.: W. B. Saunders Co., 1971.

Rasmussen, Frederick A., Holobinko, Paul, and Showalter, Victor M. *Man and the Environment.* Boston, Mass.: Houghton Mifflin Company, 1971.

Smith, David M. *The Practice of Silviculture.* Eighth Edition. New York, N.Y.: John Wiley and Sons, Inc., 1986.

Spurr, Stephen H., and Barnes, Burton V. *Forest Ecology.* New York, N.Y.: John Wiley and Sons, Inc., 1980.

Walter, Heinrich. *Vegetation of the Earth.* London, England: The English Universities Press, Ltd., 1973.

CHAPTER III

# Tree Study

Second only to grass, trees are the most common and most widely distributed plants on earth. On the North American continent, there are about a thousand native kinds besides a large number of foreign trees that have been introduced. With the Great Plains as a dividing line, there are in the eastern United States about 600 native tree species representing 171 genera and 67 families. In contrast, the western portion of the United States is represented by 227 native tree species, made up of 76 genera and 33 families.

Forest landowners should be familiar with the names of the trees on their lands, their economic importance as a source of wood, and their responses to environmental conditions such as soil and climate. With such knowledge, the landowners can better apply forestry practices to their woodlands. It is just as important for a woodland owner to know trees as it is for a stock owner or manager to know breeds and characteristics of cattle and the methods used to care for them.

## HOW TREES GROW

### Parts of a Tree and Their Function

A tree is defined as a woody plant having one well-defined stem and a formed crown, usually attaining a height of at least 8 feet. Its three main parts are: roots, trunk (also called the stem or bole), and crown (Figure 3-1).

Roots extend deep into the ground and serve to anchor a tree against winds and other forces of nature. Large roots bear smaller roots, called *rootlets*, which in many species have fine hairlike roots called *root hairs*. It is the root hairs which extract nutrients and water from the soil which are so necessary for the growth of trees.

Pines lack root hairs. Serving in the capacity of root hairs are mycorrhiza attached to the rootlets. Dissolved plant nutrients move

# HOW A TREE GROWS

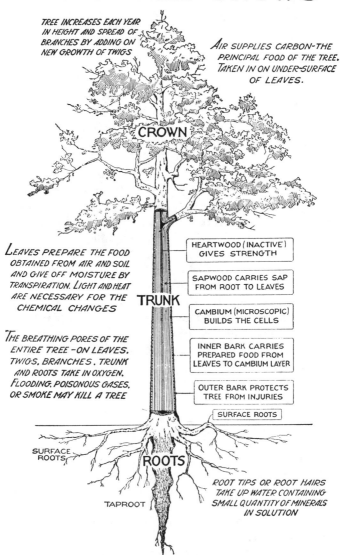

TREE INCREASES EACH YEAR IN HEIGHT AND SPREAD OF BRANCHES BY ADDING ON NEW GROWTH OF TWIGS

AIR SUPPLIES CARBON-THE PRINCIPAL FOOD OF THE TREE. TAKEN IN ON UNDER-SURFACE OF LEAVES.

CROWN

LEAVES PREPARE THE FOOD OBTAINED FROM AIR AND SOIL AND GIVE OFF MOISTURE BY TRANSPIRATION. LIGHT AND HEAT ARE NECESSARY FOR THE CHEMICAL CHANGES

THE BREATHING PORES OF THE ENTIRE TREE – ON LEAVES. TWIGS, BRANCHES, TRUNK AND ROOTS TAKE IN OXYGEN. FLOODING. POISONOUS GASES. OR SMOKE MAY KILL A TREE

TRUNK

HEARTWOOD (INACTIVE) GIVES STRENGTH

SAPWOOD CARRIES SAP FROM ROOT TO LEAVES

CAMBIUM (MICROSCOPIC) BUILDS THE CELLS

INNER BARK CARRIES PREPARED FOOD FROM LEAVES TO CAMBIUM LAYER

OUTER BARK PROTECTS TREE FROM INJURIES

SURFACE ROOTS

SURFACE ROOTS

ROOTS

ROOT TIPS OR ROOT HAIRS TAKE UP WATER CONTAINING SMALL QUANTITY OF MINERALS IN SOLUTION

TAPROOT

THE BUDS, ROOT TIPS, AND CAMBIUM LAYER ARE THE GROWING PARTS OF THE TREE. WATER CONTAINING A SMALL QUANTITY OF MINERALS IN SOLUTION IS ABSORBED BY THE ROOTS, CARRIED UP THROUGH THE SAPWOOD TO THE LEAVES AND THERE COMBINED WITH CARBON FROM THE AIR TO MAKE FOOD. THIS FOOD IS CARRIED BY THE INNER BARK TO ALL GROWING PARTS OF THE TREE, EVEN DOWN TO THE ROOT-TIPS.

Fig. 3-1. Parts of a tree.

Fig. 3-2. Shortleaf pine trees, on water-saturated soil, that were blown down by a strong wind. Such trees are called "windfalls."

into the mycorrhiza and then into rootlets to the sapwood of the tree and eventually to the crown where it is used in growth, maintenance, and reproduction.

Some trees have a shallow root system which is spread laterally from the trunk in the upper portion of the soil. Such trees are more likely to be blown down by strong winds than are deep-rooted trees. "Windfall" is the name given to a tree that has been blown down by wind.

Windfall trees are more prevalent where forest stands have been heavily cut over leaving isolated trees unprotected from windstorms. Windfalls are especially evident on shallow soils (Figure 3-2).

Isolated trees which grow naturally in open areas usually adapt themselves by having more extensive root systems and by having shorter trunks. As such, they are more wind-firm.

In general, most pine species have roots that are well-anchored in the soil. Longleaf pine, however, is less susceptible to windfall due to a taproot that extends deep into the lower soil strata. Other pine species have taproots but are more liable to windfall than is the longleaf pine.

Most hardwood trees usually have a combination of taproots and lateral roots which anchor them firmly to the soil. Oak, walnut, and hickory are noted for their deep taproots.

Among the surface-rooted species are spruce, birch, elm, western larch, hemlock, and lodgepole pine. The trunk of a tree (Figure 3-1) serves to conduct nutrients and water from the roots to the manufacturing (photosynthetic) portion of the tree represented by the crown. The trunk also produces the bulk of the useful wood in a tree.

An examination of a cross section of a tree (Figure 3-3) will show a series of rings. Under normal conditions, one ring is produced each year and thus the age of a tree can be determined by counting the number of rings.

In a large tree, the center portion is darker-colored and is known as *heartwood*. In this portion of the tree, the cells have ceased to function. It is dead wood. This core of heartwood serves only to give strength to the tree and keep it upright.

Outward from the heartwood is the lighter-colored wood known as sapwood, or *xylem*. In contrast to heartwood, it is the living portion of the tree. It is the means whereby raw nutrients and water are carried from the roots to the crown. The sapwood also serves for the storage of food synthetized in the leaves.

Around the outside of the sapwood and inside the bark is the *cambium*. It is an active layer of cells that is responsible for the growth of a tree. Each year it forms a new annual ring.

Immediately outward from the cambium are the living cells called the inner bark, or *phloem*. This living tissue serves to carry

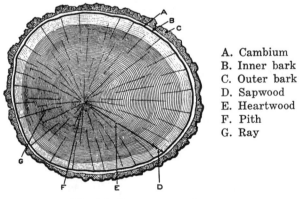

A. Cambium
B. Inner bark
C. Outer bark
D. Sapwood
E. Heartwood
F. Pith
G. Ray

Fig. 3-3. Cross section of a tree.

food made in the leaves down to the branches, trunk, and roots. This is protected by dead, non-functioning outer bark. Both the phloem and sapwood are formed by divisions of the cambium. The bark is developed from the so-called phellogen, or cork cambium. It protects the trunk of a tree.

The crown is the manufacturing plant of the tree. Composed of the branches, twigs, and leaves, the wood structure is similar to that of the trunk. From the smaller twigs, conduction cells extend to the leaves.

From the roots, through the sapwood, nutrients and water are carried to the leaves. Inside each leaf, millions of green chloroplasts are found. With the aid of sunlight (radiant energy), carbon dioxide from the air, and water from the soil, carbohydrates (starches and sugars) are produced. Oxygen is also produced as a by-product in this process called *photosynthesis*. Fats and proteins are then made from carbohydrates and certain minerals from the soil. Fats may be later reconverted to starches and finally to sugars with the aid of enzymes. Certain enzymes also produce oils, latex, resin, and alkaloids such as quinine, tannins, vitamins, and acids. Rosin from pine trees is the result of action by enzymes.

Much of the water brought to the crown is transpired as water vapor into the atmosphere. Most of this occurs through pores (stomata) (Figure 3-4) on the underside of the leaves. It is through these

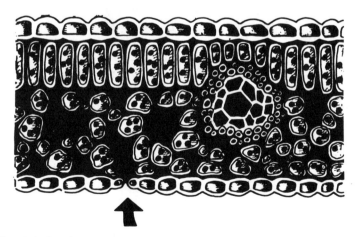

Fig. 3-4. Graphic cross section of a leaf showing stomata. Through many stomata in a leaf, there is an exchange of oxygen for carbon dioxide in the process known as photosynthesis. (Courtesy U.S. Forest Service)

stomata that air passes in and out of the leaves. As water passes through the tree, it carries dissolved nutrients along to be used in the growth process.

While a tree uses oxygen in the process of respiration, more oxygen is given off than is consumed.

After the manufacture of food by the leaves, the food is used in respiration, is converted to starch or other products and stored, or moves down through the inner bark, or phloem, to branches, trunk, and roots to the growing parts of the tree.

## Tree Growth

Each year, a tree increases in diameter as a ring of many cells of xylem is laid down by division of the cambium. A close examination of a tree's cross section will reveal that each ring is made up of a darker-colored area made up of small, dense, heavy-walled cells called summerwood and a lighter-colored area of large, thin-walled cells called springwood. It is the difference in the cell structure between these which makes up the distinctive bands of wood. From these rings it is possible to determine the age of a tree by counting them outward from the center. In some regions, however, where there is not a definite growing season, such as in the tropics, age determination is difficult.

Annual rings vary in width. Trees growing close together produce narrow rings in contrast to well-spaced trees. Drought causes slower growth, with close rings, while an overabundant rainfall will increase growth, producing wider rings. In some instances, very favorable growing conditions may occur when a tree is growing slowly, resulting in an additional ring of wood in a given year. This second ring is called a false ring and is characteristic of pines.

In determining the total age of a tree, it must be kept in mind that a ring count is most accurate only when taken low on the stump. If a ring count is made higher on the tree, fewer rings will be found.

The ability of a tree to endure shade is called "tolerance." The amount of shade that different species of trees can tolerate varies. Beech, maple, black gum, black tupelo, and many other hardwood species can grow in the shade. Pine and some hardwoods, such as black locust, tulip poplar, and black cherry, are intolerant and must receive more sunlight in which to grow. No tree can live without some sunlight.

## *HOW TREES REPRODUCE*

There are three methods by which trees reproduce: by seed, by sprouts, and by suckers. Most trees reproduce themselves by seed. Broad-leaved trees sprout profusely, while needle-leaved trees (conifers) usually do not. Shortleaf pine and bald cypress are two exceptions. Suckering is the sending up of shoots from underground roots. Black locust can reproduce itself in this manner.

### *Seed Production*

Very often the words "fruit" and "seed" are used indiscriminately; but they are not the same. In hardwood (broad-leaved) trees, a fruit is usually a ripened ovary of a flower. The ovary is the enlarged portion at the base of the pistil. This is the female reproductive part of the flower. The pistil is made up of the stigma, style, and ovary. The stigma, found at the top, is generally sticky. It holds any pollen that may reach it by wind or insects. The style is the tube through which a developing pollen grain grows downward to reach the ovary. The ovary contains one or more ovules which, if fertilized, ripen to produce seeds.

Figure 3-5 shows the complete flower. Sepals collectively are designated as *calyx*; petals collectively are designated as *corolla*; the ripened ovary comprises the fruit; and the ripened ovules of the ovary comprise the seed of the fruit. If a flower lacks a calyx, corolla, stamen, or pistil, it is an incomplete flower. If the male and female flower parts occur in separate flowers on the same tree, the species is

## THE COMPLETE FLOWER

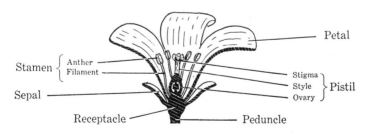

Fig. 3-5. Parts of a flower.

said to be *monoecious*. If the male and female flowers occur on separate trees, the species is said to be *dioecious*.

The type of fruit produced by a tree (Figures 3-6 and 3-7) is determined by the nature of the ovary; for example, in the locust (a legume), the entire pod with enclosed seed comprises the fruit.

Fig. 3-6. Live oak (*Quercus virginiana* Mill.). (1) Flowering branch, with drooping staminate (male) aments; tiny pistillate (female) flowers are borne among the axils of the leaves; (2) staminate flower, enlarged; (3) stamen, enlarged; the anther (large portion) contains pollen; (4) pistillate flower cluster, enlarged; (5) fruiting branch, showing mature acorns; (6) germinating acorn; (7) leaf; (8) winterbud. (Adapted from *Silva of North America*, by Charles S. Sargent)

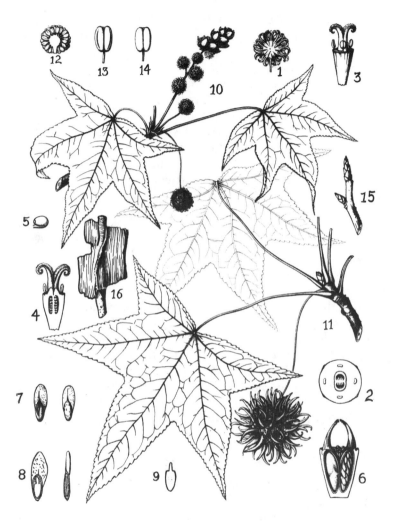

Fig. 3-7. Sweet gum (*Liquidambar styraciflua L.*). (1) Vertical section of a head of pistillate flowers; (2) transverse section of a diagrammatic pistillate (female) flower; (3) pistillate flower, enlarged; pollen adheres to the stigmas at the top; the stamens shown do not function; (4) vertical section of a pistillate flower; the ovules (potential seeds) may be seen within the ovary; (5) an ovule, magnified; (6) vertical section of a capsule showing in one cell a perfect seed, and in the other cell a mass of enlarged undeveloped ovules, one of which will develop; (7) fully developed seed; (8) vertical sections of a seed; (9) an embryo, enlarged; (10) flowering branch; (11) fruiting branch; (12) vertical section of a head of a staminate (male) flower; (13) and (14) front and rear views of a stamen showing the enlarged pollen-bearing anther; (15) winter-bud; (16) part of a young branch showing corky wings. (Adapted from *Silva of North America,* by Charles S. Sargent)

Acorns, pecans, and hickory nuts are all fruit, though not popularly called such. Each is a ripened ovary and its parts, not an individual ovule.

In most instances, the fruit of broad-leaved trees mature in one year, during the growing season in which they are fertilized. Most red oaks are an exception, requiring two growing seasons.

Reproduction in conifers (needle-leaved trees) is different from that of broad-leaved trees. The ovules of conifers are born naked on cone scales. The ovules are not enclosed in an ovary (Figure 3-8).

As an example, pine seeds are produced on the scales of the carpelate, or female cones. In the spring, pine produces clusters of staminate pollen-bearing cones, or sacs. Upon ripening, they disperse their pollen and fall to the ground. Female cones are produced on a tree about the same time. They are usually located in greater numbers on the outside of the crown. At pollination time, the female cone scales spread apart for a short period so that pollen grains can reach the stigma. After pollination, the pollen develops a tube which grows slowly toward the ovule. It takes approximately a year. Once fertilized, however, the cone grows rapidly with its developing seeds. Most pines require two years for the seed to mature.

Upon ripening, the cone dries out, the scales come apart, and the winged seeds are dispersed by wind. In general, about 85 per cent of the seed fall within 125 feet of the tree producing the seed.

A test usually employed to determine the ripeness of pine cones is to place them in the Society of Automotive Engineers (S.A.E.) 20 weight oil. If ripe, the cones will float. Those that sink are still green.

### Seed Dispersal

Wind is an important factor in the distribution of the light seed of trees such as cottonwood or catalpa. Birds, eating certain fruits such as mulberry, disseminate seed in distant places in their droppings. Animals such as squirrels and mice bury or hide nuts that may later germinate. Some seeds are carried by streams to distant locations where they germinate and grow. During flood periods in particular, many seeds are distributed by water. Heavy fruits such as pecans and walnuts fall to the ground within a few feet of the tree.

How well any tree will reproduce itself is generally based on the weight of the seeds, the number of seeds, and their viability as well as environmental factors at the time of germination.

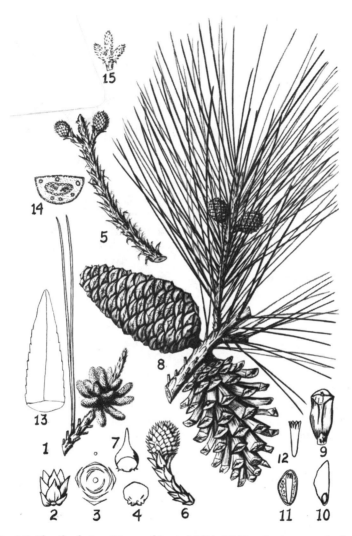

Fig. 3-8. Shortleaf pine (*Pinus echinata* Mill.). (1) Developing growth showing cluster of staminate (male) cones; (2) cluster of bracts of a staminate cone, enlarged; (3) diagram of the cluster of bracts of the staminate cone, transverse section; (4) pollen-bearing anther, front view; (5) end of a branch with carpellate (female) cones; (6) carpellate immature cone; (7) scale of a carpellate cone, lower side, with its bract enlarged; (8) fruiting branch showing immature and mature (second year) cones; (9) mature cone-scale, lower side, with its bract; (10) fully developed seed; (11) vertical section of a fully developed seed, enlarged; (12) an embryo, enlarged; (13) tip of a leaf, enlarged; (14) cross section of a needle, enlarged; (15) terminal and lateral buds. (Adapted from *Silva of North America*, by Charles S. Sargent)

## *TREE IDENTIFICATION*

The question "What kind of a tree is this?" is often difficult to answer in a given area due to a local or regional name commonly associated with it; for example, in certain areas, water oak, live oak, and willow oak are called Spanish oak. In some areas, willow oak is called pin oak. The usage of such names, rather than the correct ones, tends to confuse rather than help in tree identification.

### *Tree Names*

Trees are members of the plant kingdom and are divided into classes, orders, families, genera, and species.

There are two *classes*. One, made up of coniferous species, is called Gymnospermae. The other, the hardwood species, is called Angiospermae. The classes are in turn divided into *orders*, the names of which end in "ales." Oaks, for example, are members of the Fagales.

*Orders* are made up of one or more *families*, the names of which generally end in "aceae." For example, the oaks are members of the family of Fagaceae. Also included in this family are the chestnuts and beeches.

*Families* are made up of one or more *genera* which in turn are made up of *species*. Each individual plant, such as sweet gum, white oak, and longleaf pine, is given both a generic and a species name. Carl von Linne (Linnaeus), the Swedish botanist, was the first to use this system of classifying plants and is called the "father" of systematic botany.

In the use of scientific names for trees, the generic name is always written first and is capitalized, while the species name which follows is used in lower case, thus red maple is *Acer rubrum*; however, the scientific name of a species is, in many instances, followed by the abbreviation of or full last name of the person who described and named the species, thus black walnut is *Juglans nigra L.* The "L" stands for Linnaeus who first described the species.

Latin has been used in taxonomy because it is a so-called dead language. It is the language of no particular nation today and is not subject to change. To some extent Greek is also used in taxonomy.

There is a continuing effort on the part of taxonomists to standardize common names in the United States. Names used in this text are those most widely accepted by botanists and foresters.

It is unnecessary for forest landowners to familiarize themselves with the scientific name of every tree. They should, however, be familiar with the scientific names of the more important species in their woodlands. They should at least be aware that trees have scientific names.

## Identifying Characteristics of Trees

The most important characteristics to identify a tree are its leaves, fruit, twigs, and bark. In some instances, positive identification necessitates the study of the flower. This can be done only by one with a technical knowledge of taxonomy. Since flowers are generally of few day's duration, identification by this means is limited to a short period.

Each kind of tree has certain characteristics which make it distinctive from another species. A discussion of the major characteristics follows.

*Leaves.* Generally, most trees can be identified by type, size, shape, color, texture, and the arrangement of leaves (Figures 3-9 and 3-10). In some species, such as sassafras, the smell of crushed leaves is distinctive. During the autumn and winter season, one must resort to other means of identification, such as twig and bark characteristics. Leaf characteristics of many species found in the United States are noted in Appendix VI.

*Twigs.* Except for a short period in the spring when buds formed during the previous season are opening, and those for the present season have not appeared, twigs are a good means of identification. Major characteristics of twigs used in identification are buds, leaf scars, lenticels, and bark (Figure 3-11). Some twigs have a distinctive color, smell, or taste. Some have pith.

*Bark.* On large trees, the bark is the most important identification feature in the dormant winter period. Bark varies in thickness, roughness, type of fissures, and color, and while these characteristics change with the increasing age of a tree, they remain a means of identification. As related earlier, each year the cambium lays down an annual ring of new cork cells (bark), forcing the old bark outward. Since the outer bark cannot stretch, it fissures or cracks into plates, ridges, and scales, forming the bark characteristic of each species. Some barks have distinguishable colors and odors.

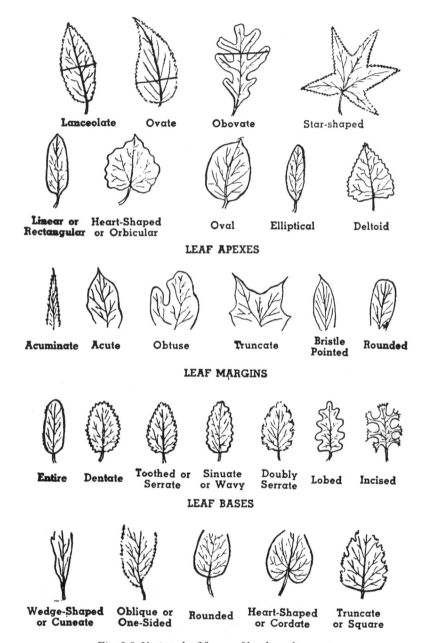

**LEAF APEXES**

**LEAF MARGINS**

**LEAF BASES**

Fig. 3-9. Various leaf forms of hardwood trees.

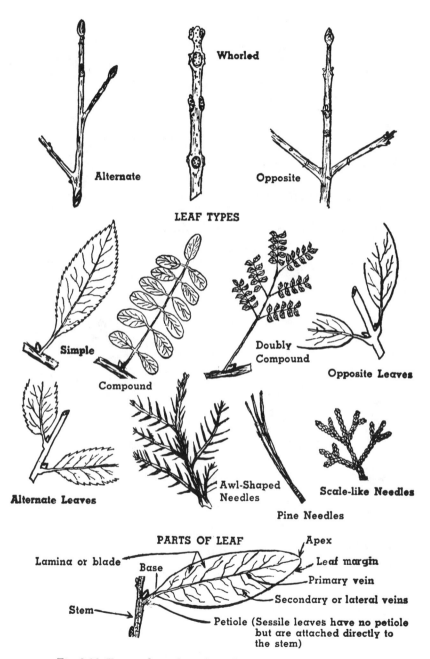

Fig. 3-10. Types of twig branching, leaf types, and parts of leaf.

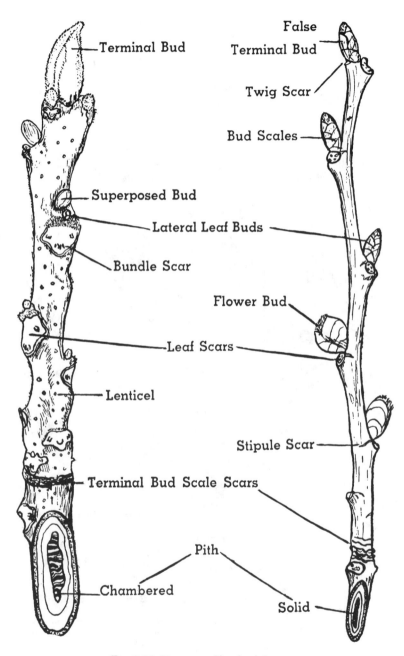

Fig. 3-11. Features of hardwood twigs.

*Fruit*. The following common types of fruit (Figure 3-12) may be found on hardwood (broad-leaved) trees:

SIMPLE FRUITS consist of a single enlarged ovary with which some other flower parts may be incorporated. They may be divided into two major groups: fleshy fruits and dry fruits.

1. *Fleshy Fruits*
    a. *Berry*. The outer and inner walls are fleshy and enclose one or more seeds. Persimmon and huckleberry are examples.
    b. *Drupe* (or stone fruit). Fruit is one-seeded and fleshy. The outer part is fleshy while the inner part is stony. Examples are black cherry, sassafras, holly, and hackberry.
    c. *Pome*. The outer portion of the fruit is fleshy while the inner portion is somewhat "papery" and forms a "core" containing numerous seeds. Examples are mayhaw, pear, and apple.
2. *Dry Fruits*
    a. *Dehiscent* (those which pop open when ripe)
        (1) *Legume*. Fruit with a true pod and one seed chamber which split along two sutures when ripe to discharge their seeds. Examples are black locust, mimosa, and redbud. However, not all legumes have dehiscent fruit; for example, mesquite and honey locust.
        (2) *Capsule*. Fruit with two or more chambers, dehiscing along two or more sutures; for example, catalpa and desert willow. The capsule of catalpa dehisces down the centers of the two sections at right angles to the partition in the center of the fruit. The desert willow dehisces parallel with the partition inside the fruit.
    b. *Indehiscent* (those which do not open when ripe)
        (1) *Achene*. Fruit is small, dry, one-seeded, and unwinged, but often hairy; for example, the sycamore, in which numerous achenes form the "ball."
        (2) *Samara*. Fruit is a winged achene. Examples are maple, elm, and ash.
        (3) *Nut*. Fruit is a hard, usually one-seeded fruit with a bony, woody, leathery, or papery wall, and usually partly or entirely enclosed in an involucre or husk. Examples are oak, walnut, pecan, beech, and chinkapin.

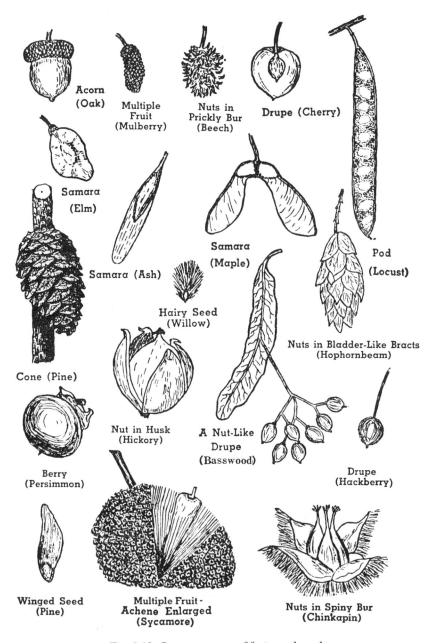

Acorn (Oak)

Multiple Fruit (Mulberry)

Nuts in Prickly Bur (Beech)

Drupe (Cherry)

Samara (Elm)

Samara (Ash)

Samara (Maple)

Pod (Locust)

Hairy Seed (Willow)

Cone (Pine)

Nuts in Bladder-Like Bracts (Hophornbeam)

Nut in Husk (Hickory)

A Nut-Like Drupe (Basswood)

Drupe (Hackberry)

Berry (Persimmon)

Winged Seed (Pine)

Multiple Fruit - Achene Enlarged (Sycamore)

Nuts in Spiny Bur (Chinkapin)

Fig. 3-12. Common types of fruits and seeds.

COMPOUND FRUITS may be divided into two major groups: aggregate fruit and multiple fruit.

1. *Aggregate fruit.* Such fruit is a cluster of ripened fruits produced from a single flower containing numerous pistils inserted on a common receptacle. Examples are magnolia and tulip tree (yellow poplar).
2. *Multiple fruit.* A cluster of fruits of separate flowers crowded together and forming what appears to be a single fruit. Examples are sycamore "balls," mulberries, "hedge apples" of osage-orange (bois d'arc), and the prickly ball of sweet gum.

### Guides to Tree Identification

Within this text, it is impractical to provide a simplified taxonomic key to the identification of all trees. Generally, such keys require a knowledge of botany. They are nonetheless important to the detailed study of the tree species and are available for review in public and school libraries. Most of the state forestry agencies have produced a tree book that may be helpful to those interested in the study of trees (see Bibliography). As an aid to the student in tree identification, a list of special guides to some of the common trees, based on characteristics discussed in this chapter, follows.

*TREES WITH EVERGREEN LEAVES*

| | |
|---|---|
| Live Oak | Yaupon |
| Southern Magnolia | Huckleberry |
| Red Bay | Baretta |
| American Holly | |

*TREES WHICH PRODUCE NUTS*

| | |
|---|---|
| The Walnuts | The Oaks |
| The Hickories | The Buckeyes |
| The Beeches | Horse-chestnut |
| Chinkapin | The Chestnuts |

*TREES WITH PODS AS FRUIT*

| | |
|---|---|
| Corkwood | Black Locust |
| Texas Ebony | Catalpa |
| Catclaw Acacia | Desert Willow |
| Leadtree (Mimosa) | Huisache (Sweet Acacia) |
| Mesquite | Guajillo |
| Redbud | Coral Bean |
| Honeylocust | Mexican Leadtree |
| Waterlocust | Kentucky Coffee Tree |

## TREES WITH SOFT BERRYLIKE FRUIT

The Hackberries
The Mulberries
Osage-orange (Bois d'Arc)
Red Bay
Sassafras
The Hawthorns
The Cherries and Plums
American Holly
Yaupon

Black Gum and Tupelo
Dogwood
Tree Farkleberry
    (Tree Huckleberry)
Gum Bumelia (Gum Elastic)
PersimmonFringe Tree
Black Hawthorn
Sourwood

## TREES WITH BRIGHT RED FRUIT

Red Mulberry
The Magnolias
The Hawthorns

Shining Sumac
American Holly
Flowering Dogwood

## TREES WITH SEEDS WINGED OR WITH PARACHUTELIKE ATTACHMENTS

The Cottonwoods
Black Willow
American Hornbeam
    (Blue Beech)
Ironwood
River Birch
The Elms
Planetree
Sweet Gum
American Sycamore
Hoptree

The Maples
The Basswoods
Silverbell
The Ashes
Catalpa
Desert Willow
Buttonbush
Alder
Tree of Heaven
Tulip Tree
Ailanthus

## TREES WITH CORKY PROJECTION ON TWIGS

Bur Oak (Mossy-Cup Oak)
Cedar Elm

Winged Elm
Sweet Gum

## TREES WITH FLOWERS IN CLUSTERS

Red Bay
The Hawthorns
The Plums and Cherries
Redbud
Black Locust
Devil's-Walking-Stick
Hercules'-Club
Hoptree
The Sumacs
Poison Sumac

Yaupon
Ohio Buckeye
Western Soapberry
The Basswoods
Flowering Dogwood
Silverbell
Fringe tree
Catalpa
Black hawthorn
Shadbush

*TREES WHOSE BLOSSOMS APPEAR BEFORE*
*OR WITH THE LEAVES*

The Walnuts
The Hickories
The Cottonwoods
Black Willow
Ironwood
Eastern Hophornbeam
River Birch

The Elms
Sassafras
Redbud
The Maples
The Ashes
Alder
Shadbush

*TREES WITH SPINES OR THORNS*

Osage-orange (Bois d'Arc)
The Hawthorns
Texas Ebony
Catclaw Acacia
Leadtree (Mimosa)
Mesquite
Honey Locust

Water Locust
Black Locust
Prickly Ash
Devil's-Walking-Stick
Huisache (Sweet Acacia)
Wild Plums
Wild Crab Apple

*TREES WHOSE BLOSSOMS APPEAR*
*AFTER THE LEAVES*

Chinkapin
Magnolia
Honey Locust
Black Locust
The Sumacs
Ohio Buckeye
Basswood
Flowering Dogwood

Persimmon
Silverbell
Fringe tree
Catalpa
Mountain Maple
Horse Chestnut
Mountain Ash
Sourwood

*TREES WHOSE LEAVES TURN RED IN AUTUMN*

Red Oak
Sweet Gum
The Hawthorns
The Sumacs
Red Maple

Black Gum
Flowering Dogwood
Sugar Maple (yellow as
   well)
Scarlet Oak

*TREES WHOSE LEAVES TURN YELLOW IN AUTUMN*

The Hickories
The Cottonwoods
Black Willow
Hornbeam (Blue Beech)
River Birch
Most of the oaks
   (except red oak)
Osage-orange (Bois d'Arc)
Southern Magnolia
Pawpaw

Mesquite
Redbud
Hercules'-Club
Red Maple
Ohio Buckeye
Devil's-Walking-Stick
The Ashes
Fringe Tree
Catalpa
Sugar Maple (red as well)

## TREES THAT PREFER WET SITES

Bald Cypress
Water Hickory
Corkwood
Cottonwood
Black Willow
Blue Beech (Hornbeam)
Ironwood (Hophornbeam)
Red Birch (River Birch)
Water Oak
Willow Oak
Bur Oak
Overcup Oak

Swamp Chestnut Oak
Sweet Bay
Sweet Gum
The Hawthorns
Water Locust
Poison Sumac
Yaupon
Black Gum (Black Tupelo)
Tupelo (Water Tupelo)
Water Ash
Swamp Privet
Alder

## TREES WITH SINGLE LARGE FLOWERS

Magnolia

Pawpaw

## TREES WHOSE TWIGS HAVE A CHAMBERED PITH

Walnut
Sugarberry

Hackberry

## TREES KNOWN BY THE COLOR AND SHAPE
## OF THE TWIG PITH

### Star-shaped in Cross Section

The Cottonwoods
The Oaks

Chestnut
Aspen

### Triangular in Cross Section

Alder

### Brown in Color

The Walnuts
The Sumacs

Mountain Maple
Striped Maple

### Red in Color

Kentucky Coffee Tree

### Greenish in Color

Shadbush

A brief description of the leaf characteristics of the major pine and hardwood trees of the United States is noted in Appendix VI.

Figures 3-13 through 3-18 provide a visual description of leaves, cones, fruit, or flowers of trees common in the various forest regions of the United States.

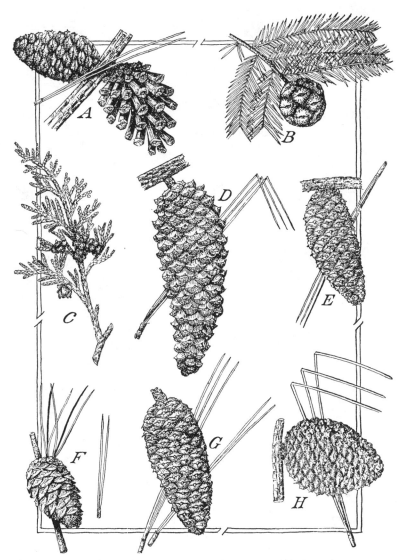

Fig. 3-13. Cones and leaves of most of the major conifers of the South: (A) spruce pine; (B) southern cypress; (C) southern white cedar; (D) longleaf pine; (E) loblolly pine; (F) shortleaf pine; (G) slash pine; (H) pond pine. (Adapted from U.S.D.A. Miscellaneous Publication 217)

Fig. 3-14. Cones and leaves of important timber trees of the western part of the United States: (A) ponderosa pine; (B) Englemann spruce; (C) western white pine; (D) western red cedar, (E) sugar pine; (F) Douglas fir; (G) coast redwood; (H) western hemlock. (Adapted from U.S.D.A. Miscellaneous Publication 217)

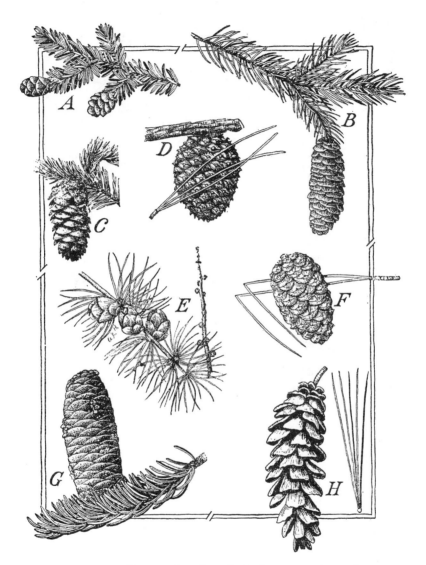

Fig. 3-15. Cones and leaves of conifers which characterize the northern region: (A) eastern hemlock; (B) white spruce; (C) red spruce; (D) pitch pine; (E) tamarack; (F) red (Norway) pine; (G) balsam fir; (H) northern white pine. (Adapted from U.S.D.A. Miscellaneous Publication 217)

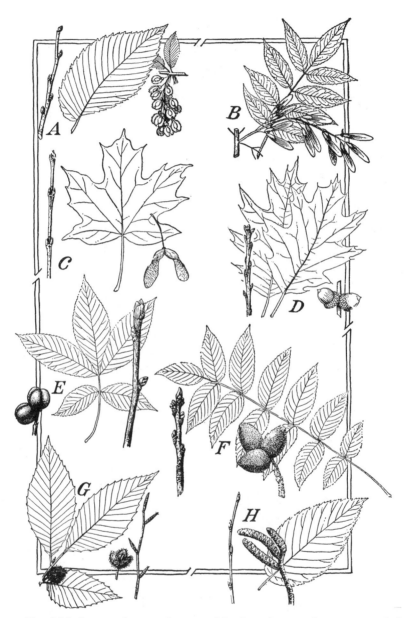

Fig. 3-16. Leaves, fruit, and twigs of hardwood trees characteristic of the northern forest region: (A) American elm; (B) white ash; (C) sugar maple; (D) northern red oak; (E) pignut hickory; (F) butternut; (G) beech; (H) sweet (or black) birch. (Adapted from U.S.D.A. Miscellaneous Publication 217)

Fig. 3-17. Leaves, fruit, and twigs of a few trees which compose the central hardwoods forest region: (A) post oak; (B) eastern red cedar; (C) silverbell; (D) shortleaf pine; (E) southern red oak; (F) black walnut; (G) white oak; (H) yellow or tulip poplar; (I) persimmon. (Adapted from U.S.D.A. Miscellaneous Publication 217)

Fig. 3-18. Leaves, fruit or flowers, and twigs of some hardwoods occurring chiefly in the southern forest region: (A) water oak; (B) live oak; (C) winged elm; (D) sweet or red gum; (E) swamp cottonwood; (F) swamp black gum; (G) tupelo gum; (H) overcup oak. (Adapted from U.S.D.A. Miscellaneous Publication 217)

## BIBLIOGRAPHY

Anderson, David A. *Trees and Woody Plants of the Bible*. Waco, Tex.: Word, Inc., 1979.

Collingwood, G. H., and Brush, W. D. *Knowing Your Trees*. Washington, D.C.: The American Forestry Association, 1984.

Fernald, Merritt Lyndon. *Gray's Manual of Botany*. New York, N.Y.: Van Nostrand Reinhold Company, 1988.

Gunn, Charles R. *Seed Collecting and Identification*. Three Volumes. New York, N.Y.: Academic Press, Inc., 1972.

Hoag, Donald G. *Trees and Shrubs for the Northern Plains*. Fargo, N. Dak.: North Dakota Institute for Regional Studies, 1965.

Johnson, Hugh. *Hugh Johnson's Encyclopedia of Trees*. New York, N.Y.: Simon and Schuster, Inc., 1984.

Ketchum, Richard M. *The Secret Life of the Forest*. New York, N.Y.: American Heritage Press, 1970.

Kummerly, Walter. *The Forest*. New York, N.Y.: Robert B. Luce Company, Inc., 1973.

Lamb, Samuel H. *Woody Plants of the Southwest: A Field Guide with Descriptive Text, Drawings, Range Maps, and Photographs*. Santa Fe, N. Mex.: The Sunstone Press, 1975.

Levitt, J. *Response of Plants to Environmental Stress*. New York, N.Y.: Academic Press, 1980.

Lewey, Helen J. *Trees of the North Central States: Their Distribution and Uses*. Technical Report NC-12. St. Paul, Minn.: Experiment Station, U.S. Forest Service, 1975.

Little, Elbert L., Jr. *Atlas of United States Trees: Conifers and Important Hardwoods*. Volume 1, Miscellaneous Publication 1314. Washington, D.C.: U.S. Forest Service, 1971.

Little, Elbert L., Jr. *Atlas of United States Trees: Minor Western Hardwoods*. Volume 3, Miscellaneous Publication 1314. Washington, D.C.: U.S. Forest Service, 1976.

Little, Elbert L., Jr. *Atlas of United States Trees: Minor Eastern Hardwoods*. Volume 4, Miscellaneous Publication 1342. Washington, D.C.: U.S. Forest Service, 1977.

Little, Elbert L., Jr. *Atlas of United States Trees: Florida*. Volume 5, Miscellaneous Publication 1361. Washington, D.C.: U.S. Forest Service, 1977.

Little, Elbert L., Jr. *Checklist of United States Trees, Native and Naturalized*. Agricultural Handbook 541. Washington, D.C.: U.S. Forest Service, 1979.

Little, Elbert L., Jr., and Honkala, Barbara H. *Trees and Shrubs of the United States: A Bibliography for Identification*. Miscellaneous Publication 1336. Washington, D.C.: U.S. Forest Service, 1976.

Neelands, R. W. *Important Trees of Eastern Forests*. Washington, D.C.: U.S. Forest Service, 1973.

Preston, Richard J. *North American Trees*. Third Edition. Cambridge, Mass.: Massachusetts Institute of Technology, 1976.

*Seeds of Woody Plants in the United States*. Agricultural Handbook 450. Washington, D.C.: U.S. Forest Service, 1974.

Spurr, Stephen H., and Barnes, Burton V. *Forest Ecology*. New York, N.Y: The Ronald Press Company, 1980.

U.S. Forest Service. *Identifying Woody Plants Valuable to Wildlife in Southern Forests.* Research Paper SO-92. New Orleans, La.: U.S.D.A., 1974.

Viereck, Leslie A., and Little, Elbert L., Jr. *Atlas of United States Trees: Alaska Trees and Common Shrubs.* Volume 2, Miscellaneous Publication 1293. Washington, D.C.: U.S. Forest Service, 1975.

Vines, R. A. *Trees, Shrubs and Woody Vines of the Southwest.* Austin, Tex.: The University of Texas Press, 1960.

Zim, Herbert S. *Trees of North America.* New York, N.Y.: Golden Press, Inc., 1968.

Zimmerman, Martin H., and Brown, Claud L. *Tree Structure and Function.* New York, N.Y.: Springer-Verlag, 1971.

### Selected State or Regional Bulletins on Tree Identification

Alabama: *Forest Trees of Alabama.* Montgomery: Department of Conservation, 1965.

Alaska: *Alaska Trees and Shrubs.* U.S.D.A. Agricultural Handbook 410. Washington, D.C.: U.S. Forest Service, 1972.

Arizona: *Easy Field Guide to Common Trees of Arizona.* Glenwood, N. Mex.: Tecolote Press, Inc., 1976.

Arkansas: *Trees of Arkansas.* Little Rock: Arkansas Forestry Commission, 1981.

California: *The Distribution of Forest Trees in California.* Berkeley: U.S. Forest Service, 1972.

Colorado: *Common Forest and Windbreak Trees of Colorado.* Fort Collins: Colorado State Forest Service, 1963.

Connecticut: *Forest Trees of Southern New England.* Hartford: Connecticut Forest and Park Association, 1974.

Delaware: *Delaware Trees: A Guide to the Identification of the Native Tree Species.* Dover: Delaware State Forestry Department, 1960.

District of Columbia: *Checklist of Trees Native to Washington, D.C.* Washington: U.S. Department of the Interior, 1960.

Florida: *Common Forest Trees of Florida.* Tenth Edition. Tallahassee: Florida Forest Service, 1972.

Georgia: Bishop, G. N. *Native Trees of Georgia.* Third Edition. Athens: School of Forestry, University of Georgia, 1965.

Idaho: *Native Trees of Idaho.* Moscow: Idaho Agricultural Extension Service, 1966.

Illinois: *Forest Trees of Illinois.* Springfield: Department of Conservation, Division of Forestry, 1986.

Indiana: *Trees of Indiana.* Indianapolis: Indiana Department of Conservation, 1953.

Iowa: *Simple Key to Iowa Trees.* Des Moines: Iowa State Conservation Department, 1970.

Kansas: *Trees, Shrubs, and Woody Vines.* Lawrence: University Press, 1969.

Kentucky: *Kentucky Forest Trees—How to Know Them.* Frankfort: Cooperative Extension Service, 1972.

Louisiana: *Commercial Trees of Louisiana.* Fourth Edition. Baton Rouge: Louisiana Forestry Commission, 1965.

Maine: *Forest Trees of Maine.* Tenth Edition. Augusta: Maine Forestry Department, 1973.

Maryland: *Leaf Key to Common Trees in Maryland.* College Park: Maryland Cooperative Extension Service, 1970.

Massachusetts: Refer to reference under "Connecticut."

Michigan: *Simple Key to Michigan Trees.* Lansing: Forestry Division, Michigan Department of Natural Resources, 1970.

Minnesota: *Woody Plants for Minnesota*. St. Paul: Minnesota Agricultural Extension Service, 1966.

Mississippi: *Mississippi Trees*. Jackson: Mississippi Forestry Commission, 1975.

Missouri: *Missouri Trees*. Jefferson City: Missouri Department of Conservation, 1973.

Montana: *Trees and Shrubs for Montana*. Bozeman: Montana State University, 1963.

Nebraska: *Handbook of Nebraska Trees: A Guide to the Native and Most Important Introduced Species*. Lincoln: The University of Nebraska, 1971.

Nevada: *Nevada Trees*. Reno: Nevada Agricultural Extension Service, 1954.

New Hampshire: *Trees and Shrubs in New Hampshire: A Guidebook for Natural Beauty Projects*. Durham: University of New Hampshire, 1967.

New Jersey: *Common Forest Trees of New Jersey*. New Brunswick: Cooperative Extension Service, 1972.

New Mexico: *Southwestern Trees: A Guide to the Native Species of New Mexico*. U.S.D.A. Agricultural Handbook 9, 1968.

New York: *Trees of New York State: Native and Naturalized*. New York: Dover Publications, Inc., 1975.

North Carolina: *Common Forest Trees of North Carolina*. Thirteenth Edition. Raleigh: State Department of Conservation and Development, Forestry Division, 1972.

North Dakota: *Common Trees and Shrubs of North Dakota*. Bottineau: North Dakota State University, 1972.

Ohio: *Ohio Trees*. Columbus: The Ohio State University Press, 1949.

Oklahoma: *Forest Trees of Oklahoma*. Tenth Edition. Oklahoma City: Oklahoma Planning and Resources Board, Division of Forestry, 1973.

Oregon: *Identification Key to the Common Native Evergreen Trees of Oregon*. Salem: Oregon State Forestry Department, 1973.

Pennsylvania: *Common Trees of Pennsylvania*. Harrisburg: Department of Environmental Resources, 1971.

Rhode Island: Refer to reference under "Connecticut."

South Carolina: *Familiar Trees of South Carolina*. Eleventh Edition. Columbia: State Commission of Forestry, 1968.

South Dakota: *Trees of South Dakota*. Brookings: Cooperative Extension Service, 1959.

Tennessee: *Common Forest Trees of Tennessee*. Tenth Edition. Nashville: Department of Conservation, Division of Forestry, 1964.

Texas: *Forest Trees of Texas*. Eighth Edition. Bulletin 20. College Station: Texas Forest Service, 1963.

Utah: *Common Native Trees of Utah*. Logan: Utah Agricultural Experiment Station, 1976.

Vermont: Refer to reference under "Connecticut."

Virginia: *Forest Trees of Virginia*. Charlottesville: Division of Forestry, 1974.

Washington: *Trees of Washington*. Pullman: State University Extension Bulletin 440, 1974.

West Virginia: *Common Trees of West Virginia: How to Know Them*. Charleston: West Virginia Department of Natural Resources, 1968.

Wisconsin: *Forest Trees of Wisconsin: How to Know Them*. Madison: Wisconsin Department of Natural Resources, 1977.

Wyoming: *Wyoming Trees*. Laramie: Wyoming Agricultural Extension Service, 1959.

CHAPTER IV

# Land and Forest
# Products Measurements

To manage forest resources properly, it is essential to know the size and nature of them. For this reason, land and forest products measurements are a basic part of forest management. The measuring of standing timber, or logs cut from it, is called forest mensuration. This topic is sometimes broadened to include other natural resources measurements and is then called biometrics. This includes related resources, such as rangelands, wildlife and fisheries, water, and outdoor recreational areas.

Timber growers must know the acreage of forest land, the volume of timber, the location of roads and property boundaries, and other factors. It is as vital for tree farmers to know the amount of timber they have for sale as it is for ranchers to know the weight of cattle they offer for sale.

Land surveying is logically a branch of forest measuring. Surveying is, however, too important to other sciences and other areas of study to be claimed entirely by forestry. The instruments of the surveyor (Figure 4-1), such as the compass, level, transit, and tape, are frequently used in measuring timberlands.

Taking land and timber measurements of a forest is comparable to taking an ordinary business inventory and audit. Several means and methods of measurement may be employed, but the accuracy or intensity will vary with differences in size or value of the individual tract and timber stand. As an example, an "average tree" estimate might be adequate for a small woodlot, especially if the trees are uniform in size and quality. In this instance, a count may be made of all trees and an average tree estimated for volume determination.

A large area of 350 acres of big timber may require an accurate survey, a 20 per cent sample of timber volume and value, and the preparation of a map. Timber stand uniformity is important. A cruise of less intensity is required in uniform timber. Generally, the value of the timber governs the amount of surveying and timber cruising that needs to be done and the degree of accuracy that is required. The size of the sample is also important for accuracy.

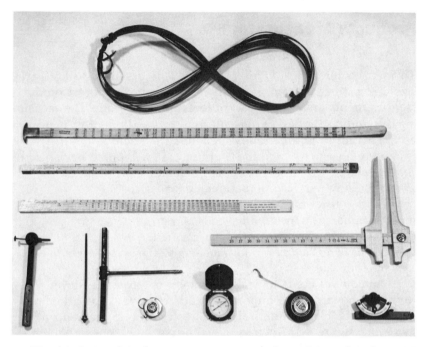

Fig. 4-1. Some of the basic equipment commonly used in making land and timber measurements. From the top: steel tape, log scale stick, Biltmore stick, tree scale stick, and tree calipers. Bottom row, left to right: increment hammer, increment borer, tally register ("tally whacker"), forestry compass, diameter tape, and topographic Abney level.

Comprehensive timber estimates, or cruises, show landowners how much timber they are growing. This is basic in determining how much timber should be marked for cutting and how much should be allowed to grow. It also gives a basis upon which to determine the timber's worth. All timber growers need a basic knowledge of forest measurements to sell for the highest returns and to manage their forest lands most profitably.

## LAND SURVEYING

Prior to making any measurement, the unit of measure must be selected. Land measurements use those units common to other types of surveys, such as feet, inches, miles, and acres, but also have some unique units such as links and chains. The units of the metric system are commonly used in forest measurements in the United States. Appendix XIII presents some of the more common measures of area, length, and volume in both English and metric terms and the factors to use in converting from one measure to the other.

Some units of measurement imply a high degree of precision. An example would be in measuring high-valued land surfaces to the nearest one-thousandth of a foot. In other instances, the measurements may be made to the nearest foot, 5 feet, or even 10 feet, depending upon the accuracy required. The mere adoption of a unit of measurement suggesting high-level precision is no assurance that the precision will be obtained. Such precision requires that the measurement be made with sufficient care and with accurate instruments. The accuracy of the methods used and the units of measurement selected should be compatible, and the selection of each should be decided upon by the needs of each problem encountered.

If the land survey is taken of a small area, the earth's curvature may be disregarded. This is called *plane surveying*. For large areas, curvature must be considered by what is called *geodetic surveys*.

### Measurements of Horizontal Distances

The length of land surfaces, or distance, may be measured in several ways. It can be measured by using a metal surveyor's chain, an engineer's tape, or a cloth tape; by stepping off the distance; or even by utilizing aerial photographs. In determining timber volume or performing a cruise, pacing is usually an acceptable method of measuring linear land distances.

A chain is a unit of land measurement 66 feet in length. It is divided into 100 links, each of which is 0.66 foot long. A surveyor's chain in the form of a steel tape is usually two chains (132 feet) in length. The chain is a convenient unit of land measurement because 10 square chains is the equivalent of an acre, and 80 chains is a mile. Distances can be measured also by cloth or metal tapes, up to 500 feet in length, which are subdivided into feet, tenths of a foot, and inches. "Engineer's tape" is the common term for the metal version.

The foot and chain (66 feet) are the basic units of linear land measurements. In some areas of the Southwest, the Spanish vara (33⅓ inches) has had general use. The basic unit of land area is the acre—that is, 43,560 square feet or 10 square chains. A larger unit of area is the section which equals a square mile, or 640 acres. A township is made up of 36 sections, or 36 square miles.

An indispensable "tool" in land surveying and timber cruising is pacing. It is, however, the least accurate means of measurement. A pace, as used here, is two steps. Pacing requires the use of a short stride which can be maintained all day. The number of paces required to measure one chain (66 feet) can be determined as follows:

1. Measure off a two-chain (132-foot) distance on ground typical of that to be mapped.
2. Pace this distance at least three times.
3. Determine the average number of paces per chain.

For example, a two-chain course is paced three times, and the total number of paces is 78. The 78 paces are divided by 6 to give an average of 13 paces per chain, and each pace is about 5.1 feet long.

More accurate measurements are made by using either a surveyor's tape or an engineer's tape. In use, the tape should be kept horizontal and free of obstructions. It should be pulled sufficiently tight to reduce errors caused by sagging.

### Slope Chaining

The slope of the ground is important in land distance measurements, since land may be measured to a horizontal plane, hence the term "plane surveying." On normal terrain, the tape is held horizontally, not with the slope of the ground. In very steep terrain, it may not be possible to hold the tape at or near the horizontal, therefore, a correction is necessary.

In this case, slope tapes may be used which are supplemented—by correction graduation for slope chaining—with a topographic Abney level. It measures the angle between the horizontal plane and the line of sight along a slope. The topographic Abney contains a scale which directly corresponds to the correction graduations on the slope tape. Slope corrections may be made also with the per cent and degree Abneys, but they require additional calculations.

### Direction Measurements

The angle, measured in degrees 1/360 of a circle or 1/90 of a quadrant, which a line makes with some reference line establishes the direction of that line. If a magnetic compass is used, the reference line is true north. Compasses may be mounted on a tripod or a staff or held by hand—in descending order of accuracy.

The bearing of a line is measured from north and south to east or west, dividing the circle into quadrants of 90 degrees each. The first reference is to either north or south, whichever is closest. The bearing is then referenced to either east or west in terms of the number of degrees variation from either north or south. A line of sight that runs halfway between north and west has a bearing of N 45° W. The absolute reverse bearing of this line would be S 45° E. A line which is 60 degrees toward the west from south has a bearing of S 60° W.

A compass needle points to magnetic north, a point some 1,300 miles from true north or the north pole. The angular variation of magnetic north from true north is referred to as the magnetic declination. Although it varies slightly from year to year, the general declination or correction varies from about 5° W on a line through Virginia and eastern North Carolina, to 10° E on a line through central Texas, to 15° E on a line through central Arizona. The current declination for any area may be obtained by contacting a local civil engineer or surveyor. Current declination may be determined by observations on the sun or Polaris.

Compass readings are generally made in terms of magnetic bearings. Compasses suitable for surveying have magnetic declination adjustments so that correct bearings may be directly read from the compass face. Failure to correct for declination will give a bearing other than the true one.

However, an allowance for declination may be made if the true bearing of a line is known. For example, if a property line's true bearing is due north, the compass needle may be pointed exactly along that line and the compass graduated degree circle turned until it points to true north. This is the most accurate means of establishing property lines with the compass.

### Elevation Measurements

Differences in elevation may be determined by various types of altimeters or clinometers, such as the aneroid barometer, the Abney level, or the more accurate Dumpy level or transit. These instruments measure either the angle or the rise from the horizontal plane to a point along a slope. Aneroid barometers may be used where a low order of accuracy is required. For most forest surveying conditions, the Abney level provides sufficient accuracy.

### Area Measurements

Most forest surveys are plotted to determine the area within certain boundaries. The area or amount of horizontal surface may either be determined by plotting or be determined by strictly mathematical methods. An instrument called a *polar planimeter* is used to accurately measure areas, whether enclosed by straight lines or curved ones, directly from maps.

Graphical methods of determining areas give suitable results with allowable limits of accuracy for most compass and tape forest surveys. The use of cross-section paper is a common graphic method of determining area. A compass is used to determine boundary bearings and angles. A surveyor's tape measures the length of the bearings or boundaries. These measurements are then transferred to or plotted on cross-section paper, using an appropriate scale. The area within each square of the cross section can be determined in relation to the scale used in plotting.

Aerial photographs of a known scale may be used also for rapid determination of areas of timberland. County aerial photographs are available from the Agricultural Stabilization and Conservation Service (A.S.C.S.) offices of the United States Department of Agriculture. These offices are located at the county or parish seat. The photographs are helpful to locate property, to reduce the amount of survey field work, and to make timber inventories. The use of aerial photographs in this fashion is a new science of measurement called *photogrammetry,* now used intensively in forest management.

### Boundary Surveys

Surveys of the boundaries of a timber tract are done (1) to establish exact property locations, (2) to make timber cutting lines, and (3) to determine the area of the tract. In establishing property or cutting lines, it is necessary to obtain the field notes of surveys of the property recorded in the county or parish surveyor's office. The notes are essential to locating established property corners or markers. In some instances, it may be necessary to run a survey line from an established survey marker off the property to locate a corner on the property.

A rough survey to determine the area for a timber tract, not associated with property lines, may be performed with a hand compass and pacing. More accurate surveys would be made with a staff compass and surveyor's tape.

An example of an area survey would begin by assuming a rectangular-shaped woodland tract with five corners. The corners will be respectively designated as A, B, C, D, and E. Starting at corner A, a hand compass bearing (foresight) is made to corner B. It is recorded on a sheet of paper similar to that shown in the example in Figure 4-2. Then the distance is paced from corner A to corner B and recorded to the nearest foot. At corner B, a bearing reading is taken back to corner A. This is called a backsight and is used to check the accuracy of the foresight in case of magnetic interferences or error in sighting or reading the bearing. Compasses must be kept away from metal objects, including wire fences, while readings are being taken.

The reading is recorded along with the foresight. If a difference between the readings exists, the bearing will be corrected at the completion of the survey. This is done by determining the actual number of degrees of interior angle in the survey and comparing it to the number of degrees of interior angle as indicated by the survey bearings. The actual sum is equal to 90 degrees multiplied by twice the number of sides (n) minus 4. In our example this would be $2n - 4 (90) = 10 - 4 (90) = 6 (90) = 540°$. Corrections of interior angles as indicated by differences of backsights to foresights are made to develop corrected bearings.

The survey from corner B through to corner D or back to the starting point is made in the same way as from corner A to corner B. Foresights, distances, and backsights are all recorded as shown in Figure 4-2. Each corner should be marked with a stake for future reference. If needed, points along the line between corners also may be marked.

In most surveys, it is not possible to make one sight from corner to corner. If this is the case, it is necessary to use two or

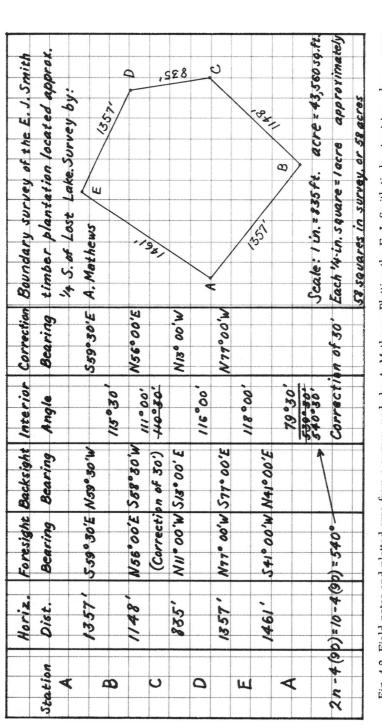

Fig. 4-2. Field notes and plotted area from a survey made by A. Mathews. Plotting the E. J. Smith timber tract to scale on cross-section paper is done to provide an estimate of the total area.

more bearings between corners. The points are adjusted to provide a straight line at the close of the survey line between corners. This technique is used also to intentionally offset lines around obstructions.

At the completion of the survey, the distances and interior angles are used to plot the timber tract on cross-section paper. Select a scale to facilitate area determination within each square of the cross section. This in turn will make it easier to determine the total area of the timber tract. Using readily divisible areas within each cross section improves the accuracy of the estimate of that portion of the square inside the plotted line for those bisected by it.

## Other Uses for Land Surveys

In addition to establishing property boundaries and timber cutting lines and determining timber areas, surveys are helpful:

1. To locate fences and firebreaks or guards.
2. To locate and survey roads, log skid trails, and log loading sites.
3. To locate and survey water drainages, culverts, bridges, and cattle guards.
4. To map plant types and soil series and to make integrated inventories in order to determine timber production, cattle and wildlife grazing capacity, watershed development, and recreational areas.

## MEASUREMENT OF TREES

Tree measurements are necessary to determine the volume of wood in each tree. The sum total of individual tree measurements and volumes provides an inventory of the whole timber stand. It is called a timber cruise. Timber and wood products have a variety of units of volume, some unique to these products and others in general use.

Some of the more common units are:

*Board foot*—a piece of rough wood 1 foot square and 1 inch thick, generally used to measure sawtimber and veneer timber. (Note—in finished or surfaced lumber, width and thickness are based upon measurements before surfacing or other finishing.) Timber and lumber are usually sold on the basis of thousand board feet, abbreviated as MBM or MBF.

*Cubic foot*—a cube of rough wood 1 foot on each side. It contains about 6 board feet and is used to measure all kinds of timber products.

*Cord*—a stack of wood, including air space between pieces, which measures 4 feet by 4 feet by 8 feet, or 128 cubic feet. This is accepted as the standard cord in the United States and Canada. A 4-foot by 8-foot stack of over-length sticks is called a long cord. When the sticks are 5 feet long to make a stack 4 feet by 5 feet by 8 feet, the stack represents one type of unit, or 160 cubic feet. Another unit contains 168 cubic feet when the pulpwood bolts are 5 feet 3 inches long. Solid wood content or actual wood, less the air space, of a cord is about 80 cubic feet, varying somewhat between softwood and hardwood. The cord or unit is used to measure pulpwood and fence posts.

*Cunit*—a stack of wood containing 100 cubic feet of solid wood. Long used by Canadian firms, the cunit is now being used by some American companies.

*Piece*—a unit of measure which refers to the number or quantity of timber products of a specified dimension.

*Linear feet*—some forest products are measured in terms of the length in feet. Length may be in 1-, 2-, 5-, or 10-foot categories.

*Basal area*—a unit of measurement for standing timber to indicate the degree of stocking. It is the cross-sectional area of trees at breast height or 4½ feet above the average ground line. Basal area is expressed in square feet and may apply to individual trees or all trees on an acre basis.

Selling timber by weight is quite common in the pulp and paper industry and is fast replacing dimensional measurements. In the measurement of standing trees, a conversion is necessary from board feet, cords, etc., to weight. Data has been gathered by industries and forest agencies for many years to develop suitable conversion factors. In the measurement of logs or bolts, called scaling, measurement by weight (1) eliminates much of the human judgment, (2) is quicker, (3) encourages prompt delivery of green wood to the mill, and (4) facilitates handling and inventorying of large quantities of wood.

The weight of wood varies by species of tree, and many times within species—depending in part upon the growing site. The principal factors influencing weight are the wood density and its moisture content. The density of the wood is related to the amount or per cent of summerwood in the tree, the rate of growth, and the position of the log in the tree. The amount of moisture in the wood or its moisture content varies between species and within species between the heartwood and sapwood.

Some softwood weight per cord, green and unbarked wood, varies from about 4,800 pounds to 6,400 pounds with an average of about 5,300 pounds. For hardwood, the per cord weight is from 5,000 pounds to 6,100 pounds, with an average of about 5,700 pounds.

A variety of studies on weight scaling sawlogs have been made across the nation. Those in the South have shown weights of from 7,000 pounds to 18,000 pounds per thousand board feet (MBF) of pine sawlogs. These vary by species, volume tables used, and states where the timber is grown. Studies in the Southeast by the Corps of Engineers, U.S. Army, using the Scribner Decimal C log volume rule, indicate an average of 15,270 pounds per MBF for pine second growth and 12,100 pounds per MBF for pine old growth. The hardwood average was 14,130 pounds per MBF. A Texas study on pine revealed an average of about 17,000 pounds per MBF using the Doyle-Scribner log rule. Western species vary from 6,465 pounds per MBF for Sitka spruce, 9,230 pounds for Ponderosa pine, 8,215 pounds for Douglas fir, and 10,260 pounds for Port Orford cedar using the Scribner log scale. Generally, sawmills buying by weight use averages from 12,100 pounds to 17,500 pounds of softwood, depending upon the size, species, and log rules used.

### Diameters

In the United States the diameter of standing trees is most commonly measured at breast height—called dbh. The dbh is usually measured at 4½ feet above the average ground level. Diameter measurements are taken outside the bark. Allowances are made for bark thickness in timber volume tables.

Tree diameters are usually recorded in even 2-inch classes to facilitate volume determination; for example, diameter classes such as 6-, 8-, 10-, 12-, 14-inch groups, etc. Trees are placed according to diameter in the nearest 2-inch class. A tree measuring 13.4 inches dbh will be considered a 14-inch tree, as an example. Diameter classes are as follows: 10-inch trees—9.1 to 11.0 inches, 12-inch trees—11.1 to 13.0 inches, 14-inch trees—13.1 to 15.0 inches, 16-inch trees—15.1 to 17.0 inches, 18-inch trees—17.1 to 19.0 inches, 20-inch trees—19.1 to 21.0 inches, etc.

A variety of instruments may be used to measure diameters. Physical measurements may be made with a Biltmore stick, diameter tape (Figures 4-1 and 4-3), or tree calipers. In recent years certain optical tree measuring devices have been developed to estimate diameters accurately at some distance from the tree. This type of device is generally referred to as a dendrometer. In addition, angle gauges have been employed to estimate the basal area of a timber stand. One such device is a wedge prism.

A diameter tape is the most accurate tool for measuring trees. It is so calibrated that each inch on the diameter side of the tape is actually 3.1416 inches in length. In this way, the diameter is read

Fig. 4-3. A student demonstrates tree diameter measurement using a metal diameter tape. (Courtesy Department of Forestry, University of Illinois)

directly from the tape which is actually measuring the tree's circumference.

A similar technique is used when roughly measuring tree diameters with a Biltmore stick (Figure 4-4). It is based upon the geometric principle of similar triangles with the scale graduated

Fig. 4-4. A diameter measurement. A Biltmore stick is held against the tree, 4½ feet above the ground and 25 inches from the eye, to directly read the diameter of the tree outside the bark.

on the stick to read directly in inches. The stick is most accurately used by following these rules:

1. Hold the stick horizontally at midpoint, at arm's length (25 inches).
2. Place it against the tree, with the left edge of the stick along one edge of the tree. Keep one eye closed.
3. Without moving the head, read the diameter along the stick.

### Basal Area

In addition to diameter, the basal area or cross-sectional area of trees at breast height expressed in square feet is commonly measured to determine (1) the degree of stocking of a stand of trees, (2) the amount of timber to remove in thinning an over-stocked stand, and (3) timber volume calculations.

Table 4-1 shows the basal area of trees ranging from 2 to 24 inches dbh.

TABLE 4-1

**BASAL AREA OF TREES BY DBH CLASSES**

| DBH (in.) | Basal Area (sq. ft.) | DBH (in.) | Basal Area (sq. ft.) |
|:---:|:---:|:---:|:---:|
| 2 | 0.022 | 14 | 1.069 |
| 4 | 0.087 | 16 | 1.396 |
| 6 | 0.196 | 18 | 1.767 |
| 8 | 0.349 | 20 | 2.181 |
| 10 | 0.545 | 22 | 2.640 |
| 12 | 0.785 | 24 | 3.142 |

Basal area may be determined by physically measuring each tree with a Biltmore stick, a diameter tape, or calipers. One of the easiest methods for estimating basal area is by the use of angle gauges in optical tree measuring devices. A wedge prism will determine which trees should be counted or tallied in a timber sample and which should not.

A prism is a thin wedge of glass that bends light rays as they pass through it. Prisms are fast, simple to use properly, and very accurate. They eliminate sample plots and individual tree measurements when determining basal area. This technique is point-sampling which selects trees to be tallied on the basis of size rather than on the frequency of occurrence in traditional cruising. However, prisms may be used also for timber cruising or for locating points at a desired distance from a target.

Prisms are ground to a specified basal area factor size. These factors generally vary from 2½ to 50, but the most common size is 10. Multiplying the basal area factor of the prism used at a given point in a timber stand times the number of trees counted with the prism will directly give the square feet of basal area per acre of the trees around that point.

The technique to determine basal area with a prism is as follows:

1. Hold the prism at eye level over the center of a point to be used to sample the timber stand.
2. Look through the prism and count the number of trees which should be tallied or recorded as shown in Figure 4-5.

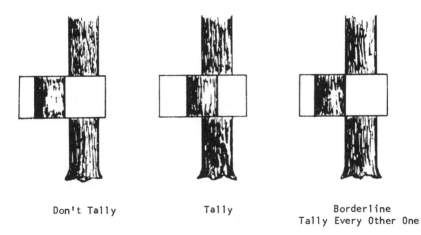

Don't Tally               Tally                    Borderline
                                           Tally Every Other One

Fig. 4-5. The wedge prism indicates the number of trees which should be counted and recorded when determining basal area per acre of a timber stand. When sighted through the prism, the tree stem covered by it appears to move off center. Where the stem remains within the vertical lines of the actual tree stem above and below the prism, the tree should be counted. Where the prism "stem" is moved outside the vertical lines, the tree is not tallied. Where the edge of the prism "stem" is directly in line with the tree stem, every other tree of this type is tallied.

3. Multiply the tree count at this point by the basal area factor of the prism to get the basal area per acre in square feet around this sampling point.

When a series of points is taken in a timber stand, average the basal area per acre from all sampling points to obtain the average basal area per acre for the entire stand. To maintain accuracy, rotate around the prism, directly over the sampling point, rather than rotate the prism around you. The face of the largest edge of the prism should be at right angles to the line of sight and the top edge should be horizontal to the level ground. The prism may be used on ground with a slope up to 15 per cent (15 feet rise in 100 feet of horizontal distance) without an adjustment.

An instrument, called a *Spiegel relascope,* is a hand-held point-sampling device. It may also be used to determine basal area per acre, upper-stem diameters, total tree heights, horizontal distances with slope corrections, and slope measurements.

### Tree Height

Tree height may be measured in terms of feet or number of logs or bolts. The tree is measured to its total height or merchantable height. The latter refers to the useable length of the tree for a specific product and is measured from the stump height to the cut-off point near the top. This point is located where the trunk diameter reaches a minimum size for the product to be harvested or where excess limbs or forks prevent closer utilization. Figure 4-6 shows a staff Abney level in use to accurately measure tree heights.

Merchantable height for sawtimber trees is determined by the number of 16-foot logs and half logs which can be cut from the tree. The 16-foot log is the standard length in the East, while 32-foot logs are frequently used in the far West. In some instances, 8-foot logs are used for hardwood. Log lengths are usually recorded to the nearest half log. For example, a sawtimber tree having a merchantable height of 40 feet would be tallied as a 2½-log tree. The cut-off point for sawtimber trees varies from 6 to 10 inches, depending upon the type of utilization.

Merchantable height for pulpwood trees is usually tallied to the nearest pulpwood bolt of a given length. This will be 4 feet, 5 feet, or 5 feet 3 inches, depending upon pulp mill specifications.

For example, a 24-foot merchantable height pulpwood tree would have 6 bolts of 4-foot pulpwood and 5 bolts of 5-foot pulpwood. In some instances, total tree height is used to measure pulpwood, with an allowance in the volume table for unmerchantable tree tops. The cut-off point for pulpwood is generally 4 inches.

Fig. 4-6. A forester cruises timber by the use of a staff Abney level to accurately measure tree heights. (Courtesy American Forest Institute)

Figure 4-7 illustrates the use of the *hypsometer* (graduated in log length) on the tree scale stick for measuring merchantable height.

Most tree scale sticks also have volume tables printed on one of the wide sides. These make it convenient to determine immediately the number of board feet in a tree.

5 INCHES - INSIDE BARK

4 LOGS
(64 FEET)

LINE OF SIGHT

TREE SCALE STICK

LINE OF SIGHT

STUMP HEIGHT

66 FEET

Fig. 4-7. Merchantable tree heights are measured using the hyposometer on the tree scale stick. The hypsometer is graduated in log lengths, usually 16 feet, so the observer can directly read the number of logs in a tree. Working on the principle of similar triangles, the stick must be held at the proper distance from the eye (usually 25 inches) when the observer is standing 1 chain, or 66 feet, from the tree. For accurate readings, the observer must also be standing on the same general elevation as the tree base. This illustration uses a 5-inch inside bark cut-off point rather than the 6- to 8-point suggested for sawtimber and the 4-inch point for pulpwood.

## TREE VOLUMES

Tree volume tables are available to facilitate estimating the number of board feet, cubic feet, or cords in standing trees. Conversion tables are also available from basal area to these measurement units. The volume tables are designed to indicate a specific volume for a tree of a certain dbh and height. In addition to these dimensions, some tables necessitate an estimate of the amount of taper in the stem.

The amount of taper in the tree trunk affects the yield in board feet, cubic feet, etc. A short, stubby tree will make less lumber than a tall, cylindrical tree of the same diameter. Taper is expressed as a per cent and is commonly called "form class." The primary one in use in the United States is the *Girard form class*. It is expressed as the percentage ratio of the dbh, outside bark, of a tree and the diameter, inside bark, at the top of the first 16- or 32-foot log. Form class may be accurately estimated by the use of optical tree measuring devices or by measuring felled timber in an area near to the one to be cruised. An ocular estimate is sometimes used in the field by experienced timber cruisers. As the tree stem approaches the form of a cylinder, its form class approaches 100.

An example of form class is a tree 14 inches dbh that is 11 inches in diameter inside bark at the top of the first 16-foot log. These statistics are substituted into the formula below.

$$\text{Form class} \quad = \quad \frac{\text{dia., inside bark, top of first log}}{\text{dbh}} \times 100$$

$$= \frac{11}{14} \times 100$$

$$= 78\%, \text{ or } 78 \text{ form class}$$

Form class volume tables have been worked out for a wide variety of tree species throughout the United States. In some instances, trees are categorized for ease of table use because of similar growth characteristics; for example, southern pines, Douglas fir, eastern hardwoods, etc. The principal advantage in the use of form class tables is the ease with which they can be accurately adapted for local use.

An average form class for second-growth softwood is 78. For old-growth softwood, it may run as high as 84. The form class for hardwoods will vary more widely, from a low of 70 to 80 or more.

### Types of Volume Tables

Tree volume tables which give the merchantable content of the standing timber are generally derived from log rules or tables developed to measure the volume of individual logs. Volumes indicated by log rules are derived by formulas or graphic means.

Some 50 different log rules are in use in the United States, and the values assigned to trees or logs vary considerably. The more common rules are the Doyle, Scribner, International, Maine, Spaulding, and Herring, and combinations of these rules. The Scribner and Doyle rules are most frequently used for purchasing sawtimber and sawlogs. The International rule is used almost exclusively for forest research purposes.

The volumes derived for the Doyle log rule come from the following formula, where D is diameter in inches at the small end of the log and L is log length in feet:

$$\text{Volume (board feet)} = \left(\frac{D-4}{4}\right)^2 \times L$$

In this rule, an arbitrary deduction is made for lumber processing losses from the volume of a cylinder.

A 10-inch log, 16 feet long would contain:

$$\left(\frac{10-4}{4}\right)^2 \times 16 = 36 \text{ bd. ft.}$$

The Doyle rule indicates less volume for the small-diametered logs than the other commonly used rules. The lumber overrun tends to be high for logs less than 28 inches but is excessive for logs under 16 inches.

The Scribner rule is preferred by forest agency people throughout the United States. It is derived by graphic means to estimate the amount of 1-inch lumber which can be sawn from logs of specific dimensions. An abbreviated version called Scribner Decimal C is popular because it rounds the exact board feet to the nearest 10, which facilitates computations. Many forest agencies, including the U.S. Forest Service, have adopted this rule for timber sale purposes. The Scribner rule gives a lumber overrun for large logs.

The International log rule, like the Doyle, is derived by a formula and is the only rule which adds volume for taper. It provides one of the highest estimates of volume of any of the log rules and closely approaches the actual quantity of lumber which can be cut from a tree or log without the normal provision for a slight lumber overrun. This rule is no longer used for making timber sales but is continuing to find use for forest survey and research purposes.

A tabular tree volume comparison of the Doyle, Scribner, and International log rules (Table 4-2) reveals the variation between the three.

TABLE 4-2

**BOARD FOOT TREE VOLUME COMPARISONS
BY LOG RULES USING A 78 FORM CLASS**

| Tree dbh | Doyle 2 16-ft. logs | Scribner 2 16-ft. logs | International 2 16-ft. logs |
|---|---|---|---|
| 10 | 20 | 44 | 59 |
| 16 | 116 | 159 | 180 |
| 22 | 295 | 338 | 368 |
| 28 | 551 | 578 | 572 |

The overrun and underrun of lumber output compared to tree and log volumes has received careful study by forest industries and agencies. Many timber growers feel that overrun, or producing more lumber than the log rule allows, is unfair. Timber buyers, on the other hand, say that overrun makes little difference since the price paid reflects its existence; that is, a higher overrun commands a higher price. This same economic logic occurs for variations in log rules in that the price paid for timber purchased by the Doyle rule commands a proportionally higher price than that bought by the Scribner rule. In addition, overrun provides a safeguard to compensate for hidden tree defects.

Table 4-3 reflects the overrun and underrun percentages for a study on southern pine sawlogs in five southern states.

## Defect

Once gross tree volume has been determined, some deduction in volume and quality must be made for the occurrence of certain defects in the tree. These defects include excessive knots, taper, and crook, or sweep; occurrence of fire and lightning scars and catfaces; incidence of stem and butt rots, beetle holes, and blue stain; and existence of heart shake, pitch seam, or split. These terms are defined in the glossary, but they refer to certain external or internal characteristics which reduce the amount of useable wood fiber in a tree. Pulp timber must be free of charred portions, nails, wire, and other metals. Unsplit tree crotches and very rough wood are usually unacceptable for pulpwood.

TABLE 4-3

**PINE LOG SCALE VARIATIONS
COMPARED WITH GREEN LUMBER CUT**

| Log Dia. (in.) | Log Rule | | |
|---|---|---|---|
| | Doyle | Scribner | International |
| | Per Cent Overrun or Underrun | | |
| 6 | +400 | +28 | −2 |
| 10 | +70 | +19 | −4 |
| 14 | +26 | +10 | −6 |
| 20 | 0 | −4 | −9 |

A defect in a tree may require a reduction in volume if the tree is infected with one of the rots or may result only in a loss in quality, as reflected by price, if the defect is excessive knots or blue stain infection. In the case of volume defect in individual trees, reduction may be made based upon an estimate of the extent of the affected portion of the tree. This may be just a few board feet or less than 5 per cent of the volume of one log in the tree, in the case of a lightning scar. On the other hand, it may involve 50 per cent or more of the volume of the first log in the tree in the case of a bad butt rot infection.

One way to determine the amount of defect in a forest stand is to visit mills that are utilizing timber from that area. From experience, mill operators will be able to provide a good estimate of the extent of defect. This will serve as a guide for volume and quality reduction of a cruised timber stand.

## Use of Tree Volume Tables

After the dbh, the merchantable or total height, and the form class are measured, the proper volume table should be selected by tree categories. Examples are given in Tables 4-4 and 4-5. Similar tables are readily available for northern conifers and western species from forestry agencies.

As trees are measured, they are tallied (marked) on a tally sheet by species, dbh, and height. If the timber cruise is made for a timber sale, trees that may be sold for high-value products such

### TABLE 4-4

#### GROSS VOLUME FOR SOUTHERN CONIFERS AND EASTERN HARDWOODS
#### SCRIBNER LOG RULE—FORM CLASS 78

| DBH (in.) | No. of 16-ft. Logs | | | | | |
|---|---|---|---|---|---|---|
| | 1 | 1½ | 2 | 2½ | 3 | 3½ |
| | | | (bd. ft.) | | | |
| 10 | 28 | 36 | 44 | | | |
| 12 | 47 | 61 | 75 | 85 | | |
| 14 | 69 | 92 | 114 | 130 | 146 | |
| 16 | 95 | 127 | 159 | 185 | 211 | 229 |
| 18 | 123 | 166 | 209 | 244 | 280 | 306 |
| 20 | 157 | 214 | 270 | 317 | 364 | 398 |

### TABLE 4-5

#### GROSS PULPWOOD VOLUME OF SOUTHERN CONIFERS AND EASTERN HARDWOODS

| DBH (in.) | Merchantable Length of Stem (ft.) | | | | | | |
|---|---|---|---|---|---|---|---|
| | 20 | 25 | 30 | 35 | 40 | 45 | 50 |
| | | | | (rough cords) | | | |
| 6 | .039 | .046 | .053 | .059 | .066 | | |
| 8 | .067 | .078 | .088 | .099 | .110 | .120 | .131 |
| 10 | .100 | .115 | .130 | .146 | .161 | .176 | .192 |
| 12 | .135 | .155 | .176 | .196 | .216 | .237 | .257 |
| 14 | .183 | .211 | .239 | .267 | .295 | .323 | .351 |

as veneer logs or poles and piling should be designated on the tally sheet. An estimate of the total volume of these products is necessary to determine buyer interest and their worth.

Following completion of the cruise, volumes are totaled by species, tree sizes, and products. If the cruise represents a sample of a forest stand, then the volumes derived by the cruise must be multiplied by the factor determined by the difference in size between the sampled area and the total area. If the cruise is a 100 per cent one, then the total volume is the actual volume.

## LOG MEASUREMENTS

In addition to determining the volume of standing trees, products such as logs or bolts harvested from them must be measured. This practice is referred to as scaling, as opposed to cruising for standing timber. Since it is possible to make absolute measurements and to determine readily the extent of defect, scaling tends to be a more accurate estimate of wood volume than does cruising.

Log measurements, especially weight, generally are used as a basis of payment for logging and hauling harvested timber and for inventorying the raw material at a wood-using plant. In some areas of the United States, timber is bought and sold on the basis of a scale rather than a cruise.

Scaling uses the same units of measurement—such as the board foot, cubic foot, cord, and piece—as does cruising. An increasing amount of sawlogs and pulpwood is bought at the mill on the basis of weight. The same general weight factors discussed for timber apply to logs and bolts.

Scaling practices, including the log rule used, vary by areas. Sometimes several different methods are used within a single state. For this reason, the specific method should be established prior to entering an agreement.

Automated log scaling devices have been developed and are used to determine and record log volumes electronically. Currently these are restricted to in-mill installations.

### Sawlogs

This material, generally measured by board feet, is used to manufacture lumber, plywood, flooring, veneer, baskets, boxes, crates, pallets, and a host of other building and shipping materials. A standard method for determining volume is to measure the log diameter inside the bark and the log length.

Diameter of a log is measured at the small end (inside bark) to the nearest inch. On symmetrical logs, it may be necessary to measure both ends to determine the small end diameter. If the log is not round, two or more measurements should be taken to obtain an average diameter. This is generally done by measuring, at a right angle, the narrowest and widest portions of the log. Diameters are rounded to the nearest inch; that is, a diameter of 9¼ inches would be considered 9, 9¾ would be considered 10, and 9½ should be called a 10-inch log one time and a 9-inch log a second time, and so on.

Diameters may be measured with a separate log scale stick or one combined with the tree scale stick. Any standard tape or measuring rule can also be used, but the log scale stick is more convenient when scaling large quantities of logs. Most sticks also contain log volume tables imprinted on the wide side.

Log lengths are measured to even 2-foot lengths, such as 12, 14, 16 feet, etc. If logs are accidentally cut to lengths between these categories, then the length is dropped back to the next nearest even 2-foot length. For example, a log measuring 15 feet 5 inches would be considered a 14-foot log rather than a 16-foot log. An extra length of at least 3 inches must be allowed for trimming the rough ends of logs or lumber. Some mills require a greater amount of trim, so minimum trim length should be determined prior to cutting and scaling logs. Tree-length logs are scaled as a series of short logs, say 16 feet in length, so that no board foot volume loss occurs as compared to conventional short log scaling.

Several log rules, as previously discussed, have been developed to estimate the board foot content of logs. These vary by the log volume indicated for individual logs. The scaling of sound logs or those free of defect is a comparatively simple matter. Deductions need to be made for defects similar to the process discussed for standing timber.

The two common log rules are the Doyle and Scribner log rules (Tables 4-6 and 4-7).

## Pulpwood

Pulpwood is the raw material from which paper, container

**TABLE 4-6**

**THE CONTENT OF LOGS, IN BOARD FEET,
BY THE SCRIBNER RULE**

| Dia., Small End, Inside Bark | Length of Log in Feet | | | |
|---|---|---|---|---|
| | 10 | 12 | 14 | 16 |
| 8 | 22 | 24 | 28 | 32 |
| 9 | 25 | 30 | 35 | 40 |
| 10 | 32 | 40 | 45 | 50 |
| 11 | 40 | 50 | 55 | 65 |
| 12 | 49 | 59 | 69 | 79 |
| 13 | 61 | 73 | 85 | 97 |
| 14 | 72 | 86 | 100 | 114 |
| 15 | 89 | 107 | 125 | 142 |

**TABLE 4-7**

**THE CONTENT OF LOGS, IN BOARD FEET,
BY THE DOYLE RULE**

| Dia., Small End, Inside Bark | Length of Log in Feet | | | |
|---|---|---|---|---|
| | 10 | 12 | 14 | 16 |
| 8 | 10 | 12 | 14 | 16 |
| 9 | 16 | 19 | 22 | 25 |
| 10 | 22 | 27 | 31 | 36 |
| 11 | 31 | 37 | 43 | 49 |
| 12 | 40 | 48 | 56 | 64 |
| 13 | 51 | 61 | 71 | 81 |
| 14 | 62 | 75 | 87 | 100 |
| 15 | 76 | 91 | 106 | 121 |

board, and many other paper products are made. Pulpwood is measured on the basis of cubic feet, cords, "units" or cunits, or by weight. The standard measurement is the cord.

Pulpwood may be stacked in dimensions different from those of the cord. The following formula may be used to determine the number of cords in stacked wood:

$$\text{No. of cords} = \frac{\text{length} \times \text{width} \times \text{height (all in feet)}}{128}$$

For example, a stack of wood 14 feet long by 8 feet wide by 6 feet high contains the following number of cords:

$$\frac{14 \times 8 \times 6}{128} = 5.25 \text{ cords}$$

## Poles and Piling

These forest products are measured and sold on the basis of linear feet, or the length in feet. This simply means that round timbers are sold for special purposes, the price depending upon their total length. Certain diameter limitations are also a part of the specifications for poles and piling, even though these products are bought and sold only by length. These limitations refer to minimum top diameter and minimum circumferences, 6 feet from the butt for poles and piling of a certain length. Mine timbers are also measured in terms of linear feet. Classes are established on the basis of these measurements. A recent purchase innovation is to buy these products as standing timber on a per MBF basis to compete with sawtimber.

## Railroad Ties, Posts, and Small Poles

These forest products are usually sold by the piece or number. Certain maximum and minimum specifications or sizes are usually given, and the sticks that come within these sizes are counted.

## LOG GRADES

In addition to size specifications, logs are purchased on the basis of grade. Generally the grade refers to the log dimensions and to quality as exhibited by closeness of grain, lack of knots, and freedom from defects. Logs are inspected for the number and character of standard defects which determine the grade. Large logs are generally more valuable than small ones of the same grade.

Specific grades have been developed for softwood and hardwood logs in all areas of the United States. Although some softwood such as Douglas fir is sold by grade, southern pine log grades have not generally been adopted. Hardwood logs are universally sold by grade, partly due to the great variation in price between species and grades within species.

### TIMBER CRUISING

The estimation of the volume of standing timber is called cruising. Cruising may be done as a 100 per cent cruise where all the trees are measured or as a partial cruise or sample where only a fraction of the trees are measured. The extent or per cent of the cruise is based upon the timber values and the size of the stand. Generally, higher-valued timber justifies a higher per cent cruise. In addition, small timber tracts necessitate a high per cent of cruise due to the possible increase in sampling error. This error, which must be within acceptable limits, depends on the variation in volume between sampling units or plots and on the intensity of the cruise. Timber may also be estimated by ocular or "eyeball guesses," by the average tree method, or by point-sampling.

### The 100 Per Cent or Total Cruise

This method involves measuring all trees in a timber stand. The cumulative volume for each tree is the volume estimate for the entire stand. It is the most accurate method of cruising, but its cost may be prohibitive on large timber tracts.

### The Partial Cruise

If the woodland tract is large or the available time is short, a partial timber cruise may be made (1) to measure a fraction of the trees in the stand, (2) to assume the remaining trees are similar to those measured, and (3) to increase the values obtained on the partial estimate to apply to the whole stand. If the partial cruise is not a good representation of the whole area, then an appropriate adjustment is necessary. This adjustment is a frequent practice of experienced timber cruisers.

For example, one-fifth of a 100-acre timber tract is considered as representing a fair sample of the whole tract. The trees on one-fifth of the total area are measured and tallied, and the volumes calculated for the individual trees. Then the volume for all measured trees is multiplied by five to get an estimate of the total timber volume of the entire tract.

When you make a partial cruise, you may notice that the trees on the sample area tend to be a little larger than those on the timber tract as a whole. Measure the trees on several additional small areas off the sample area to determine the extent of variation or, if you are sufficiently experienced, you may make an ocular estimate of the difference. Continuing our example, estimate that the volume for the sample is 5 per cent higher than the total area, and then deduct 5 per cent of the total volume to provide a more nearly correct estimate of the timber volume on the whole tract. If the sample trees tend to be smaller than the whole stand, add volume to the estimate.

In addition to the size of the woodland and value of the timber involved, the amount or per cent of cruise necessary to obtain acceptable accuracies is also dependent upon the topography of the tract, the extent of openings and uniformity of the tree stand, the number of species represented, and the intent of the owner. For these reasons, no two timber stands are cruised alike. The following per cent of cruise may be used as a rough guide for the size of timber stands indicated:

| Size of timber stand (acres) | 0-10 | 11-25 | 26-50 | 51-100 | 101+ |
|---|---|---|---|---|---|
| Per cent cruise | 100 | 50 | 25 | 20 | 10-5 |

There are a variety of methods of making a partial estimate. One of the simplest of these is to lay out, at regular intervals, circular sample plots containing a quarter of an acre (up to an acre) and to measure all the trees on these areas. If the timber stand contains 40 acres and forty ¼-acre plots are measured, then a total of 10 acres is sampled. One-fourth of the area will have received a partial cruise. The amount of timber found on these plots, with adjustment if necessary, would be multiplied by four to obtain the estimate of the total stand volume.

A 1-acre circular plot is 117.75 feet in radius while a ¼-acre circular plot is 58.88, or roughly 59 feet. In the ¼-acre line plot method of cruising, all the trees in a circle, 59 feet in radius, are measured. The plots or circles are located in checkerboard fashion at specific intervals along parallel compass lines which are regularly spaced over the timber stand. The lines within the stand are equidistant while those adjacent to boundaries are one-half that distance from the boundary. Sample plots along the lines within the stand also are equidistant, but those plots at either end of the line are one-half this distance. For ¼-acre plots, a location at intervals of 2½ chains (165 feet) is as close as should be attempted. Cruise lines should be run at right angles to drainages or other natural features to obtain representative samples. Aerial photos are effective to determine plot layout based upon forest types and to-pography or physical features.

As an example, a 40-acre square timber tract is to receive a 25 per cent cruise, using ¼-acre line plots. This will require 10 acres of ¼-acre plots, or a total of 40. Using minimum intervals of 2½ chains, the 40 plots will require 100 chains of compass line. Since the 40-acre tract is square or 20 chains on a side, the 25 per cent cruise will require five parallel compass lines through the timber stand. The five lines within the timber stand will be set at inter-vals of 4 chains (264 feet) with the two outside lines set at 2 chains (132 feet) from the boundary lines. The centers of the first and last plot on the lines will be located 1¼ chains from the boundary lines.

A modification of the line-plot method is the strip method. Instead of measuring trees at circular intervals along the line, all the timber within a strip of specific width, usually 66 feet or 1 chain, is measured. In this method, 1 acre is measured for each 10 chains (660 feet) of strip. As opposed to the checkerboard pattern of the line-plot method, the strip system gridirons the tract.

The distance between center lines of the strip determines the per cent of cruise. If this distance is only 66 feet (1 chain), make a 100 per cent cruise; 132 feet (2 chains) make a 50 per cent cruise; and 264 feet (4 chains) make a 25 per cent cruise. Figure 4-8 illustrates this method for a 25 per cent cruise on an irregular-shaped timber tract. The compass line layout for the line-plot method would be identical with circular plots placed at 2½-chain intervals along the center line.

### Average Tree Cruise

There are several ways that experienced timber cruisers can make "calculated" estimates of the volume of timber in a forest tract. As stated before, one of these is the "eyeball" method and another is the average tree cruise.

The average tree cruise is applicable to stands of uniform trees, generally small in terms of area where a rough estimate of volume will suffice. The trees are inspected, and a tree of average diameter, height, and quality is selected as representing the entire tract. All the trees in the stand are counted, and this number is multiplied by the volume of the average tree. This technique is subject to errors of 15 per cent or more. An adaption of it for larger

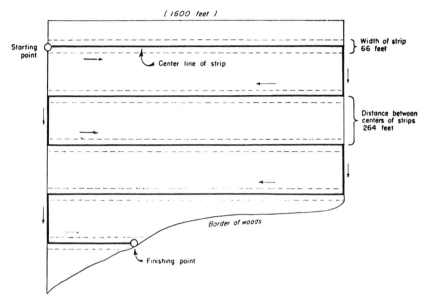

Fig. 4-8. The strip method used to make a 25 per cent cruise of a timber tract. The parallel compass lines would be identical for the line-plot method.

areas is to select an average acre, measure the trees on it, and multiply the volume calculated by the number of acres in the entire tract.

### Point-Sampling

Using this technique, the cruiser selects a series of sampling plots to fixed-size plots previously described. Following the description of wedge prism use in the basal area (ba) section, the stem count may be made by height classes. Average volumes per acre may be determined by an expansion of factors for each dbh class. The expansion factor may be calculated as follows with a 10 prism basal area factor (baf) and 14-inch dbh class.

$$\frac{\text{baf}}{\text{ba per tree}} = \frac{10}{1.069} = 9.35 \text{ trees per acre}$$

Timber volumes for each tree height by dbh class may be calculated by

$$\text{average volume per acre} = \frac{(\text{tree count}) \, (\text{expansion factor}) \, (\text{volume per tree})}{\text{number of sample points}}$$

For example, if ten 14-inch dbh and three 16-foot log trees on 20 sample points are counted, using the Doyle rule (78 form class) for southern pine, the average volume per acre for this height dbh class would be:

$$\frac{(10)\,(9.35)\,(93)}{20} = 435 \text{ board feet per acre}$$

Much of the computational work using point-sampling volume calculations is done in advance of the field tally. For this reason the principal advantage of this technique is a minimum of post-cruising calculations.

### The Ocular or "Eyeball" Cruise

Experienced cruisers are also able to make calculated guesses on the amount of timber in a stand based upon past knowledge of the volume of timber harvested from similar tracts. This is done merely by walking over the tract, in no specific pattern, to observe the species, size, amount, and quality of timber. The accuracy of this type of cruise may be low, varying up to 25 per cent or more. Generally a cruiser will "underestimate" the volume using this method, to provide a safeguard for the cruise. This method is effectively used for preliminary planning purposes to make more comprehensive cruises of large acreages.

For many years, forest survey information has been tediously recorded on paper tally sheets of one kind or another and the data transferred to punch cards for summarization and computation. This system is subject to human error, and key punching is expensive. Also, tally sheets are often exposed to moisture and dirt in the field. Increasingly, timber cruisers are using hand-held electronic data recorders in the field. Data from these compact machines can be easily transferred to data processing centers directly or by telephone, eliminating key punching costs and the source of errors inherent in the older methods of data collection and summarization.

### THE CRUISE REPORT

The data gathered by measurements of the forest stand should be used to develop a report which will find use for (1) developing overall plans for managing the timber tract, (2) making a sale of timber, (3) planning the logging of the stand, (4) establishing values for tax purposes, and (5) maintaining general records on the property, to name a few.

Tree volumes are calculated for the entire area in a 100 per cent cruise or for each plot or strip in a partial one by each tree species measured. In the latter case, the volumes are totaled for the sampled area and these multiplied by the factor represented by the difference in the area of the whole timbered tract and the sample. For purposes of a timber sale or logging plan, it is helpful, also, to calculate average-size trees by individual species.

A map of appropriate scale may be prepared showing (1) property boundaries; (2) physiographic features, such as drainages and ridges; (3) improvements, such as roads, bridges, fences, gates, buildings, etc.; and (4) the location of various types of species, such as softwood and hardwood. It should contain a legend defining the scale and general map features. In many instances, it is helpful to reference the property on the map to a known geographic feature, for example, the distance to a nearby community.

## GROWTH MEASUREMENTS

Changes in tree volume, height, and basal area, which are due to the rate of growth, can be calculated from the periodic measured changes in dbh or by increment borings. Diameter measurements of the same trees over a period of several years provide a sample of the diameter increase for the entire stand. On the other hand, borings or cores taken from trees at breast height provide an accurate measurement of past growth and a guide to future growth.

Growth determination provides an estimate of the periodic volume increase in a forest stand. This information is essential to determine if it is growing timber at the rate it is capable of producing and to determine the amount of timber which may be harvested from it. A favorable balance between timber growth and harvest (growth is equal to or exceeds harvest) is referred to as sustained yield timber growing. Growth determination also provides an estimate of the rate of return on the timber investment. A computerized form of growth estimates is known as continuous forest inventory.

The periodic rate of increase in volume of trees may be determined by measuring the number of annual rings in the last inch of tree growth. This can be done by the use of an increment borer, a hollow-tubed drill which cuts out a round core of wood. Figure 4-9 illustrates the use of the increment borer to estimate tree growth. The number of annual rings is correlated to the dbh of the tree, generally inside the bark. The diameter inside bark is determined by subtracting twice the bark thickness measured from the increment core.

Table 4-8 may be used as a short cut for determining growth per cent of individual trees. It is necessary to measure the dbh outside the bark, take an increment core at that point on the tree, count the number of annual rings in the last inch of radial growth, and measure the bark thickness.

Table 4-8 provides a rough estimate of the annual volume growth of a tree based upon the annual increase in basal area. If tree values are to be considered, changes in price must be accounted for along with increases in volume as reflected by the rate or per cent of growth.

Fig. 4-9. A forester employed by a wood-using industry uses an increment borer to measure tree growth. (Courtesy American Forest Institute)

**TABLE 4-8**

**PER CENT OF AVERAGE ANNUAL RECENT GROWTH BY THE TREE**

| dbh Inside Bark in Inches | Number of Annual Rings, Last Radial Inch of Growth | | | | | | |
|---|---|---|---|---|---|---|---|
| | 2 | 3 | 4 | 5 | 6 | 7 | 8 |
| 6 | 44.1 | 26.4 | 18.8 | 14.6 | 12.0 | 10.1 | 8.8 |
| 8 | 30.7 | 19.1 | 13.6 | 10.8 | 9.0 | 7.7 | 6.7 |
| 10 | 23.3 | 14.7 | 10.7 | 8.3 | 6.9 | 6.0 | 5.3 |
| 12 | 18.9 | 12.1 | 8.9 | 6.9 | 5.5 | 4.9 | 4.3 |
| 14 | 15.9 | 10.3 | 7.6 | 5.9 | 4.9 | 4.2 | 3.5 |
| 16 | 13.8 | 8.8 | 6.5 | 5.2 | 4.2 | 3.7 | 3.2 |
| 18 | 12.0 | 7.9 | 5.8 | 4.6 | 3.8 | 3.3 | 2.9 |
| 20 | 10.8 | 7.1 | 5.2 | 4.1 | 3.4 | 3.0 | 2.6 |

The per cent-of-growth rates of entire timber stands may be estimated during a timber cruise by measuring a portion of the trees on the sample plots or strips. On larger timber tracts, at least 100 trees per species should be measured. These should vary over the stand by size and location.

## USE OF COMPUTERS IN FORESTRY

In recent years computers, particularly the small electronic machines, or microcomputers, have made a major impact on how information relevant to forest investments, management, harvests, and product marketing decisions are developed and carried out. Microcomputers are being used increasingly in both the private and the public forestry sectors.

As in other sectors of the economy, some of the analyses of data needed in the management of forest resources are still done on centrally located large computers (mainframe computers); however, microcomputers are being used increasingly in the decentralization of management and operational activities. The move has been to field offices and into the forest itself. Microcomputers are particularly useful in the automation of routine office functions such as word processing, record keeping, data base management, and correspondence. In the forest, microcomputers are being used for inventory work, stand treatment decisions, location of harvesting sites, compartment mapping, and many other field forestry activities.

Public forest resource management agencies, such as the U.S.

Forest Service, the U.S. Soil Conservation Service, and many of the state forestry agencies, are rapidly expanding the use of microcomputers, not only to help in the making of forest management decisions but also to make possible the establishment of electronic networks which permit instant electronic communications between district and supervisory offices and provide for standardized electronic reporting and automation of office activities.

Forest industries and consulting foresters are also making increasing use of computers. The proliferation of computer programs (the set of electronic instructions which tells the computer how to carry out a particular job) is growing. Industry analysts can now do a better job—and faster—in such activities as evaluation of timber sale bids, budgeting and financial modeling, inventory and data base management, decision making of all kinds in the field, as well as automation of office routines and electronic communications.

Increasingly, people who work in forestry or in many other fields are finding it especially useful, if not absolutely necessary, to understand the application of computer technology to their work. Many universities and colleges are routinely urging, and sometimes requiring, forestry students to take courses in computer science as part of their forestry degree studies. Forestry students have increasing access to computers and computer programs and are encouraged to use them in their course work and for problem solving.

As the cost of small computers falls, more and more small woodland owners interested in managing their forests for timber and other forest values will turn to the use of personal computers. There are presently available a number of "user friendly," special application programs for forest landowners—developed by the forest industry, the U.S. Forest Service, the universities, and the Tennessee Valley Authority—which can help in the economic analyses of forest management decisions, timber inventory, and yield forecasting. Programs are also presently available to help in solving problems of integrated forest pest management and costs of pest control.

All indications point to further proliferation of software written specifically for forest management purposes. An organization of government resource agencies, universities, forest industry firms, consulting foresters, and forestry extension service agencies called the Forest Resources Systems Institute (FORS) currently evaluates and distributes forestry software and provides advice on computing hardware. The service provided by FORS can be secured from a state forestry agency, a university extension agent, or through a FORS membership available at nominal cost (FORS, Courtview Towers, Suite 24, 201 N. Pine St., Florence, Alabama 35630).

## BIBLIOGRAPHY

Avery, T. E. *Natural Resources Measurements*. New York, N.Y.: McGraw-Hill Book Company, Inc., 1975.

Beltz, R. C., and Keith, G. C. "Electronic Technology Speeds Forest Survey." Reprinted from *Southern Journal of Applied Forestry*. Volume 4:3, 1980.

Davis, R. E., Foote, F. S., and Kelly, J. W. *Surveying: Theory and Practice*. New York, N.Y.: McGraw-Hill Book Company, Inc., 1966.

Fiacco, J. B. "Personal Computers: A Primer for the Woodlot Owner." *American Forests*. Volume 91, pp. 18-23, 49-50, August, 1985.

Husch, B., Miller, C. L., and Beers, T. W. *Forest Mensuration*. New York, N.Y.: The Ronald Press Company, 1972.

"Landowner's Manual, Forest Management Shortcourse." Athens, Ga.: Forestry Department, Cooperative Extension Service, University of Georgia, Revised, 1970.

Society of American Foresters. *Forestry Handbook*. New York, N.Y.: The Ronald Press Company, 1961.

Vasievitch, J. M. "Computers and the Forestry Profession." *Journal of Forestry*. Volume 84, pp. 14-17, December, 1986.

"Volume Tables, Converting Factors and Other Information Applicable to Commercial Timber in the South." No. 7. Atlanta, Ga.: State and Private Forestry, U.S. Forest Service, 1959.

CHAPTER V

# The Forest and Its Environment

The tree in a forest is a good example of the interaction between its inherited (genetic) growth characteristics and its environment. A tiny pine seed should grow into a tall, majestic tree; however, in an unfavorable environment, the seed may not germinate and grow; or a small tree may be held back or suppressed by overtopping larger trees, shallow soil, exposure to harsh winds, and other environmental factors. The art of growing and reproducing a forest is called *silviculture*. Before silviculture can be effectively practiced, the relationship of individual species or trees within a species to environmental influences must be understood. This area of study lies within the scope of silvics, or forest ecology.

## THE TOTAL ENVIRONMENT

The total tree environment is a very complex interaction of a variety of biological and physical factors. The physical factors include (1) those of climate, such as temperature, light, air, and moisture, and (2) the soil, such as texture, structure and depth, moisture-holding capacity and drainage, nutrient content, and topographic position. The biological factors include the interaction between (1) plants, such as trees, shrubs, and herbs; (2) animals, such as deer, upland birds, and squirrels, which use the forest for food and cover; (3) small animal life, such as insects; (4) fungi to which trees are hosts; and (5) microorganisms in the soil, some of which are beneficial to trees.

The complexity of the total environment makes it impossible to measure all the factors and combinations of them. Certain broad combinations of silvical factors divided into physical and biological elements may be useful to characterize environmental conditions and provide a better understanding of silvicultural practices.

## PHYSICAL FACTORS

An environmental change can rarely be related to a single factor. Knowledge of the nature and interrelations of the major environmental factors may be helpful in understanding how plants behave and how they respond to environmental changes.

### Temperature

Temperature directly affects the daily growth processes of plants and their seasonal development. Chemical reactions, such as photosynthesis, tend to speed up with temperature increases from low to high, but slow down again when approaching maximum survival temperatures. The range within which optimum or best growth may occur varies by tree species.

In fact, each individual tree has a set of temperature ranges controlling its survival, growth, and development. These include minimum temperature for growth, maximum temperature limiting growth, and optimum temperature for best growth (Table 5-1).

**TABLE 5-1**

**TEMPERATURE RANGES FOR PLANT TYPES**

| Plant Types | Temperature Ranges | | |
| --- | --- | --- | --- |
| | Minimum | Maximum | Optimum |
| Alpine | 32° F. | 68° to 86° F. | 50° F. |
| Temperate | 40° F. | 105° F. | 77° to 86° F. |
| Tropical | 50° F. | 122° F. | 86° to 95° F. |

In a dormant condition, trees can withstand greater temperature extremes. Dormant softwoods may withstand winter temperatures of −60° F. or lower but suffer twig kill at temperatures just below freezing during the growing season. In the Temperate Zone, summer growth is often completed before maximum temperatures are reached. Early high maximum temperatures may result in a summer dormancy with a false annual ring being formed by the tree.

Trees also respond to daily or seasonal temperature variations; for example, loblolly pine seedlings grow best with a daytime temperature of 80° F. and nighttime temperature of 63° F. This may be due to different temperature relationships between photosynthesis and respiration or to a decrease in movement of photosynthate solutions in the tree with increases in temperature. Redwood, on the other hand, reflects its native western coastal climate and grows best with only slight or no day-night temperature differences.

## Light

The visible light portion of solar radiation is important as a source of energy in the process of photosynthesis. Radiant energy from the sun triggers the photochemical reaction in which chlorophyll and other light-absorbing pigments capture energy that is used to fix carbon dioxide and split water to produce carbohydrates and oxygen. Sunlight is also important in regulating tree growth processes including growth, leaf fall, fruiting, flowering, reproduction, and dormancy.

The quality, intensity, and duration of light affect the photosynthetic process. Trees growing in the understory (beneath the crown canopies of the tallest trees) are exposed to light quite different in color and intensity from the overstory, or upper canopy trees. Increases in the rate of photosynthesis of loblolly pine occur with increasing light intensity up to full sunlight. On the other hand, photosynthetic rates of associated species, such as oaks and dogwood, do not increase at light intensities of more than 30 per cent of full sunlight.

The length of daylight also affects tree growth. Many trees either cease or continue terminal growth, depending upon the duration of light within a day. In one research study, loblolly pine, Virginia pine, and Scotch pine seedlings grew continuously on 14-hour days and with repeated new growth on 16-hour days. Hardwood trees, such as elm, catalpa, maple, and birch, grew continuously with exposures to 16-hour days while others, such as sweet gum and horse chestnut, did not.

Day length, called *photoperiod*, also influences diameter growth of trees. Periods of long daylight (spring and early summer) result in the production of large-diametered, thin-walled springwood cells. A shortening of daylight results in the production of narrow-diametered, thick-walled summerwood cells. Length of daylight also affects the time of flushing, or new growth, in the spring and the onset of dormancy and defoliation in the fall. Moving a more northerly species to the South upsets the hardening-off process in the tree. Generally, these trees do not survive in the South. In this case, long daylight may promote growth until frost damages the tree. Light distribution can also affect tree form, resulting in greater development of the crown on the exposed side of the tree than on the shaded side.

### Air

Air is the principal source of carbon dioxide required for photosynthesis. Less than 1 per cent of carbon dioxide exists in the air. Oxygen is also taken from the air for respiration.

Air movement, or wind, is generally not an important environmental factor except under extreme conditions. An increase in wind velocity results in greater evaporation and transpiration, taking moisture which might otherwise find use for tree growth. Strong prevailing winds along sea coasts may also deform tree crowns and trunks. Hurricanes and tornadoes may cause uprooting of trees or breaking of tree stems. Silvicultural practices may be adapted to minimize the effects of windstorms.

Wind, combined with sleet and ice storms, may also cause considerable damage in timber stands, especially stands of conifers. Certain species are more resistant to ice damage than others and should be considered for planting purposes where ice storms are common.

Trees are planted in some regions of the United States as windbreaks, or shelterbreaks, to reduce the effects of wind. Generally planted in the Great Plains of the central United States, but not restricted to that area, windbreaks protect farmsteads and feed lots, reduce wind erosion of topsoil, and serve as snow barriers while providing a more pleasing landscape.

### Moisture

Moisture is the most limiting element of all the environmental factors on the growth of trees. There is a wide range of annual precipitation in the forested areas of the United States—from an average high of about 140 inches to an average low of about 15 inches and occurring from the "fog drip" redwood forests along the Pacific Coast in northern California to the dry, arid ponderosa pine forests of the Southwest.

Silvicultural measures, or management of the forest, which make more of the total moisture available to the tree crop, generally increase tree growth more than practices which alter any other factor. The moisture-holding properties of the soil are also important in making precipitation available to the tree.

Trees use great quantities of water in the transpiration and photosynthesis processes. On very warm days, a large tree may transpire as much as 100 gallons of water. When soil moisture is low, the tree automatically closes the small leaf openings (stomata) to reduce the transpiration. The permanent wilting point of a tree is that point at which a tree is no longer able to obtain water fast enough to prevent wilting without recovery unless water is added. Some trees can live in a dormant-like state and extract water from the soil below the conventionally determined permanent wilting point. These trees are able to survive temporary droughts which would cause the death of less drought-hardy trees.

Water is used for a variety of purposes in the tree, but perhaps the most important use of water in terms of tree growth is in the process of photosynthesis, or food manufacture.

## Soil

Soil directly affects the tree by anchoring it and by serving as a growth medium. In addition to being a reservoir for moisture, the soil provides all the essential elements for tree growth except oxygen and carbon from carbon dioxide supplied by the air. Soil characteristics such as organic matter content, texture, structure, chemical composition, depth, and position influence tree growth by affecting the supply of moisture and nutrients available to it. In many soils, the movement of water or nutrients or the exchange of gases is so restricted as to reduce tree growth.

Soils generally contain all the chemical elements essential for the growth of trees; however, some elements may not be present to sustain good growth. Deficiencies of potassium, phosphorus, and nitrogen have been observed in forest soils of the United States. On a limited scale, fertilizer applications have resulted in increased survival and growth, greater fruit production, and more desirable foliage color—an indication of general health.

There is a strong relationship between soil texture, structure and depth, and the soil's ability to supply water and nutrients. Coarse-textured soils, such as sands, are low in water-holding capacity and nutrient content. Fine-textured soils may be high in nutrient content and water-holding capacity. Aeration may be impeded in heavy clays and become so severe under wet conditions as to inhibit chemical processes requiring oxygen in the roots.

Silvicultural practices should be planned to prevent destruction of organic matter and compaction of the soil, thus providing better conditions of soil moisture and aeration to facilitate tree growth.

## BIOLOGICAL FACTORS

Tree growth is also affected by certain biological factors. These, in combination with the physical factors, make up the sum total of the forest environment. Biological factors may occur within trees (inherent or genetic considerations) or between trees.

### Reproduction

Reproduction is a vital process of every self-perpetuating tree species; however, the reproductive habits vary widely among trees. Seed formation depends upon the amount of reserve carbohydrates and nitrogenous materials in the tree. These, in turn, vary by species and certain climatic factors. In addition, certain pests will attack the fruit destroying all or part of the seed crop. Some trees may also reproduce by sprouting from the stump or roots.

Trees often produce seed in varying quantities from year to year. This gives rise to the term "good seed years" as applied to periods when abundant seed crops are produced for satisfactory reproduction. Softwoods generally do not reproduce by sprouting, but shortleaf pine is an example of a pine which does sprout from stumps or roots. Redwood trees in the Pacific Coast forests readily reproduce by sprouting as illustrated by Figure 5-1.

Hardwood trees reproduce either by seed or by stump and root sprouts. Trees produced from hardwood sprouts are used for producing paper with very high yields of fiber. For sawtimber purposes, hardwood sprouts tend to produce trees of lower quality than those grown from seed. Some forests in Europe, Japan, and in other places where trees are reproduced through sprouting, are called "coppice" forests. Hardwoods readily reproduce themselves by natural means from seed so they very infrequently require artificial reforestation. In many instances, it is necessary to plant softwood seedlings or establish them by direct seeding.

Fig. 5-1. This monarch of California's redwood forests, being measured by an industrial forester, sprouted from root systems of the parent stump in the background after Russian colonists logged the area in 1812. Young-growth redwoods, such as this one, have reached diameters of over 6 feet in about 150 years. (Courtesy American Forest Council)

## Tree Form

Timber trees normally direct a maximum of growth energy into the development of one main stem, or bole, and into the maintenance of it during its life cycle. Deviations from the typical tree form may cause it to take on the form of a bush or shrub. Many tree species assume the form of a tall, pipe-like bole in moist, fertile soils but become shrub-like on dry, windy sites. Variations in tree form occur when certain trees are overtopped by others in a forest stand. In such instances, tree crowns become flat-topped, or umbrella-like branches spread out laterally and height growth is arrested. Open-grown softwood takes on a triangular form with limbs extending to the ground, while open-grown hardwood becomes bulb-like in form.

## Tree Tolerance

A silvical factor related to tree form is its tolerance. This refers to the tree's ability to withstand competition, such as developing and growing in the shade of other trees and still maintaining its normal growth. Tolerance is affected by light competition and by root competition for moisture and soil nutrients.

Specific groupings have been developed for tolerances of individual tree species. Generally, the hardwood species are considered tolerant and the softwoods intolerant. However, such hardwood species as cottonwood, sweet gum, and paper birch are intolerant, while a greater degree of tolerance is exhibited by the Douglas fir, loblolly pine, and red pine than by the longleaf pine, jack pine, and western larch.

A knowledge of the tolerance relationships of various tree species is essential to the application of silvicultural practices in forest management. Tolerant species must be managed in mixed timber stands so that they will not suppress or hold back the intolerant trees. Suppression of intolerant species in mixed forest conditions will mean their gradual disappearance from the stand. The application of selective timber-cutting practices can make conditions more favorable for intolerant trees.

## Root Growth

The development of roots is related to inherited characteristics of the tree and varies considerably from species to species. In general, root systems are adaptive and tend to modify themselves to suit the environmental conditions in which they grow. Virtually all tree seedlings first develop a taproot, or long central root, which dominates the root system for the life of the tree.

Generally, root development increases as soil moisture increases up to the point of poor soil aeration. Certain trees, such as mesquite, tend to develop relatively huge root systems to compensate for arid tree growth conditions. Roots also show a decided tendency to seek rich soil and develop large systems in it. Most tree species require well-drained, well-aerated soils for good root development. Others, such as bald cypress, inhabit swamps and flooded lands. Trees vary in their ability to withstand flooded conditions. Some can tolerate long periods of flooding while others cannot.

The presence in the soil of certain fungi that form mycorrhizae in combination with tree roots is essential for the successful growth of many tree species. This is especially true where soil moisture and phosphorus are limiting factors. Certain strains of fungi that modify tree roots into mycorrhizal roots can be artificially introduced into soil media. This is usually done with containerized seedlings to obtain better growth and survival on harsh sites. Mycorrhizal roots enable trees to more fully utilize water, phosphorus, and nitrogen in soils where these are not present in adequate amounts. It is thought that the longer life of mycorrhizal root tissue, compared to root hairs, enables mycorrhizal roots to more effectively make use of soil nutrients and water.

### Tree Hardiness

Hardiness of tree species and individuals within species varies according to their ability to resist heat, cold, droughts, insect infestations, disease attacks, and other elements limiting survival and growth. Hardiness is important when considering the planting of a species in an area in which it normally does not grow or is not native. When any stand of trees is artificially established, care should be taken to obtain seed or planting stock from an area or climatic province similar to that where the material will be planted.

## TREE DEVELOPMENTAL STAGES

Timber stands, or any forested area, vary according to the species' composition, their density, and their age. A stand which varies little in the age of its trees is termed "even-aged." As a general rule, a difference of less than 15 years in the age of individual trees in plantations and second-growth stands and 25 years in virgin stands would qualify them to be called even-aged. Uneven-aged stands may be those of greater variation than that described for even-aged stands with individual trees varying from 1 to 100 years of age or more.

In uneven-aged stands, there are few or no recognizable stages of development in the entire stand. In even-aged stands, however, specific developmental stages are evident because only one general age category is present at a time. Developmental stages of even-aged stands are:

*Seedling stage*—from seed to 5 to 15 years; hence, when the stand begins to close.

*Sapling stage*—from the closing of the stand to the death of lower limbs and with crowns well above the ground.

*Pole stage*—from the sapling stage through limb clearing of most of the stem to the decline of the height growth. Figure 5-2 illustrates a pine stand in the pole stage, but similar development occurs with other softwoods such as Douglas fir, western larch, etc.

*Young timber stage*—from a decline of height growth to the attainment of full height.

*Mature timber stage*—from the stage of height growth completion to the start of the decline in quality and volume.

*Overmature timber stage*—from the start of deterioration in the stand to a decline in quality and volume.

In terms of size, individual trees may be classified as (1) seedlings—live trees less than 1 inch in diameter and up to 3 feet tall, (2) small saplings—1 to 3 inches in diameter and up to 10 feet in height, (3) large saplings—3 to 5 inches dbh, (4) small poles—5 to 8 inches dbh, (5) large poles—8 to 12 inches dbh, and (6) sawtimber—over 12 inches dbh.

## TREE CROWN CLASSIFICATION

Trees in a timber stand may also be classified by the position of the crown in the forest canopy or by the cover formed by the combined tree crown. Tree species, tree age, vigor, and competition are the most important factors in determining the position of tree

Fig. 5.2. This stand of second-growth southern pine illustrates the pole stage with natural pruning of most of the limbs on the tree stem. (Courtesy American Forest Council)

crowns. In an even-aged forest, the following crown classifications are commonly used:

*Dominant*—larger trees with crowns forming the upper level of the forest canopy and receiving sunlight from above and partly from the side.

*Codominant*—trees with medium-sized crowns forming the general level of the crown cover or canopy and receiving full sunlight from above, but little from the sides.

*Intermediate*—shorter, smaller-crowned trees just extending into the general canopy level and receiving little direct sunlight from above.

*Overtopped*—small trees with crowns below the general canopy level and receiving no direct sunlight. These may be further classified as oppressed when they will respond to release or removal of competing trees and suppressed when the trees are dying.

Another category for individual trees would be "isolated." It refers to trees growing in the open with little or no competition from adjoining trees. Especially limby specimens of isolated trees are frequently called "wolf trees" or "grouse ladders." Some trees which extend above the main canopy are termed "emergents."


## FOREST TYPES

A group of individual trees is also classified into a stand or forest type. A stand of trees consisting principally of a single species of silvicultural or economical importance is considered a "pure" stand. If two or more species are present, the stand is "mixed." One commercial stand classification considers a stand pure when 80 per cent or more of the overstory is one species and it forms nearly all of the commercial products. Conversely, if more than 20 per cent of the overstory is other species, the stand is mixed. Other similar classifications are used.

Different means are used for classifying forest types. These include permanent or climax plant types, temporary or developmental plant types, .physical or site productivity types, management or silvicultural types, and cover or forest composition types. The last is more commonly used for surveys of forest resources. It considers, in addition to forest composition, the relative percentage of important species, their volume differences, and their relative economic importance.

The following are some of the general forest types used for forest surveys by the U.S. Forest Service:

*White–red–jack pine*—forests in which these species, singly or in combination, comprise a plurality of stocking with common associates including hemlock, aspen, birch, and maple.

*Loblolly–shortleaf pine*—forests in which loblolly, shortleaf, or other southern pines, except longleaf or slash pine, singly or in combination, comprise a plurality of the stocking with common associates including oak, hickory, and gum.

Fig. 5-3. The oak-hickory forest type, found on uplands, is common in the East and serves as a source of timber for the hardwood-using industry from the Northeast to Texas. (Courtesy American Forest Council)

*Oak-hickory*—forests in which upland oaks or hickory, singly or in combination, comprise a plurality of the stocking, except where pines comprise 25 to 50 per cent, in which case the type would be oak-pine. Common associates include elm, maple, yellow poplar, and black walnut. Figure 5-3 illustrates the upland oak-hickory forest type.

*Douglas fir*—forests in which Douglas fir comprises a plurality of stocking with common associates including western hemlock, western red cedar, the true firs, redwood, ponderosa pine, and larch.

*Ponderosa pine*—forests in which ponderosa pine comprises a plurality of stocking with common associates Jeffrey pine, sugar pine, limber pine, Arizona pine, Apache pine, Chihuahua pine, Douglas fir, incense cedar, and white fir.

## FOREST STAND DENSITY

The density of forest stands relates to the number of trees in a particular area. It may refer to the closeness of the crowns, the boles, or volume on a per acre basis expressed as board feet, cubic feet, or basal area. Regardless of the criterion used, good stocking means the forest area is producing all of the timber it is capable of growing. The crown canopy is sufficiently tight to bring about early pruning of the lower tree limbs of the tree, and competition is adequate to force maximum height growth. Any stocking less than these conditions is considered inadequate and requires silvicultural treatment, such as planting, removing cull trees, and other practices.

On the other hand, timber stands require a commercial thinning or removal of a fraction of the total quantity when they become overstocked in terms of volume, number of trees, or close crowns. Frequently, natural stands of saplings (and some artificial ones) become overstocked so that tree growth is sharply reduced. In the absence of a natural thinning, a precommercial thinning may be necessary. For these reasons, proper density may be considered as maintaining a good balance between the productive capacity of the timber-growing site and the trees growing on it. The better the site, the more trees it can sustain in terms of numbers, volumes, and crown densities. The poorer the site, the fewer the trees by numbers, volumes, and crown densities.

Degrees of relative crown density may be expressed as follows:

*Closed*—when three-fourths or more of the ground is shaded by the tree crowns.

*Thin*—when one-half to three-fourths of the ground is shaded.

*Open*—when less than half of the ground is shaded.

Forest land is generally defined in the United States for survey purposes by the U.S. Forest Service in terms of stand density. For many years, this was land at least 10 per cent stocked by forest trees of any size, or formerly having such tree cover and not currently developed for non-forest use. Recent U.S. Forest Service surveys changed this definition to land at least 16.7 per cent (one-sixth) stocked by forest trees of any size.

## SITE INDEX OF FOREST LAND

Another term commonly used by foresters to classify forest land is "site." "Site quality" indicates the productive capacity of a specific area of forest land for a single species or group of species as classified by forest types. Although many species may grow on the same site, they may not grow equally well.

The accepted method in the United States for determining forest site quality is on the basis of average total height attained by dominant trees at certain ages. This is called site index. Total height is used because it is relatively easy to measure; there is little or no change if the stand is opened by thinning or injury, and it is little affected by stand density.

The specific index age for species is usually 50 years in the eastern United States and 100 years for the longer-lived West Coast species. In some instances, the 50- and 100-year age applies only to natural stands with as low as 25 years used for southern plantations. The numerical rating of the site index is expressed as the number of feet of average height of dominant trees; for example, land capable of growing dominant or codominant black oaks to an average total height of 80 feet in 50 years is classified as being a site index 80 for black oak. On the other hand, if this were a planted black oak plantation with an average codominant tree height of 50 feet in 25 years, the site index would be 50 for planted black oak.

Basal area or the cross-sectional area of trees in square feet per acre, at breast height, may be used as an indicator of stocking. One rule of thumb on desired stocking is that the basal area should correspond to the 50-year site index of the land; for example, a Douglas fir stand growing on timber lands with a site index of 80 should have a stocking of 80 square feet of basal area per acre.

Site index curves and tables must be developed for each commercial timber species. Table 5-2 applies to black oak stands on the basis of a 50-year site index.

The degree of timber stocking in managed forests may be controlled by periodic thinnings; however, it is impossible to maintain the proper amount of basal area, since stocking will increase as timber grows or decrease as it is cut. Generally, some timber will be allowed to grow until an excess of 15 to 25 square feet of basal area per acre has accumulated. By thinning, the stocking is usually reduced to about 10 square feet of basal area below the site index; for example, if the optimum stocking is 85 square feet of basal area per acre for yellow poplar on a site index 85, then it may be thinned down to 75 square feet of basal area. The original stocking, prior to thinning, may be 100 square feet of basal area per acre or more.

## TABLE 5-2

### DOMINANT AND CODOMINANT TREE TOTAL HEIGHT FOR BLACK OAK STANDS BY AGE AND SITE INDEX

| Age | 50-Year Site Index | | | |
|---|---|---|---|---|
|  | 70 | 80 | 90 | 100 |
| 10 | 17 | 20 | 26 | 28 |
| 20 | 35 | 39 | 48 | 54 |
| 30 | 47 | 54 | 64 | 71 |
| 40 | 59 | 67 | 77 | 87 |
| 50 | 66 | 77 | 86 | 96 |
| 60 | 75 | 87 | 95 | 105 |
| 70 | 80 | 93 | 103 | 112 |
| 80 | 84 | 97 | 106 | 116 |
| 90 | 87 | 102 | 108 | 121 |
| 100 | 90 | 105 | 110 | 125 |

(U.S. Forest Service Research Paper NC-62, 1971)

### *BIBLIOGRAPHY*

Forest Survey reports for individual states are available from the U.S. Forest Service, U.S.D.A., Washington, D.C.

Daniel, Theodore, Helms, John A., and Baker, Frederick S. *Principles of Silviculture.* Second Edition. New York, N.Y.: McGraw-Hill Book Company, Inc., 1979.

Marx, Donald H., and Beattie, Daniel J. "Mycorrhiza Promising Aid to Timber Growers." Reprint from *Forest Farmer.* Asheville, N.C.: Southeastern Forest Experiment Station, 1978.

Osting, H. J. *Studies of Plant Communities.* Second Edition. San Francisco and London: W. H. Freeman & Company, Publishers, 1956.

Saltonstall, Richard, Jr. *Your Environment and What You Can Do About It.* New York, N.Y.: Walker & Company, 1970.

Southern Forest Resource Analysis Committee. *The South's Third Forest.* Atlanta, Ga.: Forest Farmers Association, 1969.

Spurr, S. H., and Barnes, B. V. *Forest Ecology.* Third Edition. New York, N.Y.: John Wiley and Sons, Inc., 1980.

Toumey, J. W., and Korstian, C. F. *Foundations of Silviculture upon an Ecological Basis.* New York, N.Y.: John Wiley and Sons, Inc., 1947.

U.S. Forest Service. Preliminary RPA Review Draft. Washington, D.C., 1988.

U.S. Forest Service. *Proceedings: A Symposium on Principles of Maintaining Productivity on Prepared Sites.* New Orleans, La.: Southern Forest Experiment Station, 1978.

U.S. Forest Service. *Silvics of Forest Trees of the United States.* Agricultural Handbook 271. U.S.D.A. Washington, D.C.: Superintendent of Documents, U.S. Government Printing Office, 1965.

# CHAPTER VI

# Silvicultural Practices

Silviculture is the application of various treatments, principally cutting practices, to forest stands to increase their productivity. Silvicultural practices are based on knowledge of the ecology of forest ecosystems. These practices include tree planting, pruning, intermediate cuttings, and harvest cuttings. Planting is of such importance that it is dealt with separately in Chapter VII.

Forest managers must analyze each timber stand for the biological and economic factors that bear upon it and then devise the silvicultural practices which will best meet their management objectives. Management objectives may also include provision for wildlife habitat, protection of watershed values, or recreation opportunities, as well as production of timber. Fortunately, the many uses of the forest are compatible; however, in such cases, silvicultural procedures may differ from those used primarily to produce timber. For these reasons, no two forest stands are treated exactly the same. The practice of silviculture is tailored to each forest stand.

## *INTERMEDIATE CUTTINGS*

As the term implies, an "intermediate cutting" is the cutting of timber at any time from the reproduction stage to timber maturity or final harvest. It is applied during that long period in which the tree crop is growing and developing prior to the final harvest, when replacement of the stand by another crop takes place. This period is referred to as a rotation. The principal objectives of intermediate cuttings are (1) the improvement of the existing stand, (2) the regulation of tree and stand growth, (3) the opportunity for early financial returns, (4) the reduction of conditions favorable to forest pests such as insects and diseases, and (5) the creation of conditions favorable to reproduction.

## THINNINGS

A thinning is a form of intermediate cutting in immature or young trees which improves the yield of the stand as a whole. Competition between trees in a stand for such things as soil moisture, light, and nutrients may become so intense that growth rate is reduced, particularly in planted stands. The better trees are left so that the growth is concentrated on higher-valued stems. Trees attacked by forest pests should also be removed in thinnings. Thinnings may occur as early as 12 to 15 years in planted pine in the South to as late as 80 to 100 years in more longer-lived northern species.

The principal objectives of thinnings are (1) to regulate the distribution of growing space for the residual trees and (2) to utilize to the best financial advantage all the merchantable material produced by the stand during its rotation. In the latter case, an example under most pricing conditions is to remove some select trees as higher-valued poles, rather than allow them to grow larger than allowable pole specifications and be salable only as lower-valued sawlogs. Figure 6-1 illustrates thinning in a small pole timber-sized pine stand.

Due to increased mechanized logging, larger and larger timber harvests are being advocated. This has caused some opponents of thinning in timber stands to say it is no longer practical; however, clear cutting young timber stands occurs right at the time when the annual returns to the owner in terms of growth are at their highest. Stands composed of trees 8, 10, 12, and up to 14 inches dbh may be increasing in volume and value 25 per cent or more per year. In addition, the difference in price offered for clear-cut versus thinned timber may not offset the loss to the timber grower for not carrying part of the stand to larger trees and higher-value products. Possible price increases for timber resulting from changing utilization practices, such as occurred in manufacturing plywood from southern pine, may mean even greater future returns for landowners.

Various methods or techniques have been developed for thinning timber. Many of these date back a hundred years or more to early forest management efforts in Europe. Thinning methods include (1) low thinning, (2) crown thinning, (3) selection thinning, and (4) mechanical thinning. In practice, each of these may involve highly complex techniques and skills.

The low thinning technique is the oldest of the thinning methods. It is commonly called "thinning from below" or the "German" method because trees are removed from the lower crown classes. In a light thinning by this method, only overtopped trees would be cut. A modest thinning would remove the intermediate as well as the overtopped trees. A heavy thinning of this type would remove everything but the dominants and the best codominants.

Fig. 6-1. Thinnings in young timber allow timber growers to maintain high rates of growth and concentrate that growth on the better trees in the stand. Pulpwood and fence posts provide markets for small timber and early returns for tree farmers. (Courtesy Mississippi Cooperative Extension Service)

Crown thinning, sometimes called the "French" method, removes trees from the middle and upper levels of the range of crown and diameter classes rather than the lower, as in the case of low thinning. It is also called "thinning from above." Crown thinning opens up the canopy to concentrate growth on the most promising specimens of dominant and a few codominant trees.

Selection thinning is also commonly used in the United States. As opposed to the previous methods, selection thinning removes the dominant trees to concentrate growth on the lower crown classes. Trees favored in the low and crown thinning methods have limited value but selection thinning is often used as a form of high grading of timber stands because the best trees can be removed. In the latter instance, rather than selecting the trees to be left, the method degenerates into selecting all the best trees to be cut.

Mechanical thinning removes trees according to some predetermined pattern or spacing. There is little or no regard, however, for tree vigor, form, or position in the tree canopy. The method is based on a mathematical rather than a biological approach to thinning. Two general types of mechanical thinning are space thinning and row thinning. The former retains trees at fixed intervals while the latter removes all trees in lines or strips at fixed intervals throughout the stand.

A common rule of thumb for spacing is D + 6. It means that the average spacing in feet between trees should equal the average tree diameter in the stand (D) in inches plus the constant 6; for example, if the average tree dbh is 12 inches, then the spacing between residual trees would be 12 + 6 or 18 feet. In its strictest application, it takes no account for differences in trees and may provide poor results because the constant 6 will thin too heavy in young stands and not heavy enough in older ones.

Row thinning is becoming increasingly important as a silvicultural practice. Shortages of labor to log timber have forced the forest industry to use more machines. Row thinning by machine increases efficiency to suitable levels; for example, successful tree planting programs in the South during the 1950's resulted in over 6 million acres of plantations. Many of these plantations needed early thinnings to prevent stagnation of the stand. Row thinning by machines also increased the logging output to satisfy larger raw material requirements of the nation's growing pulp and paper industry.

It appears, therefore, that under present economic conditions a compromise in thinning young pine stands may be necessary. Such a compromise represented by limited row thinning can yield good returns to the owner, leave sufficient volume of the better trees for future growth, and still permit the logger to fully utilize modern machine harvesting equipment.

Row thinnings are performed in many different ways, from the removal of every other row, or two-row strips, to the removal of as few as every seventh row. In the latter case—that is, less than every third row—this system is coupled with another thinning technique, generally the low thinning method, to remove sufficient volumes of trees.

Row thinning in its strictest sense means the removal of every other row. In this system every residual tree is freed on two sides. Removal of about one-half of the volume occurs by this system. This heavy thinning may not be excessive in overstocked plantations; however, under normal conditions, the every-other-row thinning system removes too many trees.

The principal disadvantage of row thinning is that it arbitrarily selects trees to remain for future growth regardless of whether they are good ones or not. If there is substantial variation between trees in the stand, the unfavorable effects of removing good trees and leaving poor ones are critical. Like improper selective thinning, this method may also high-grade a stand. Variation in young stands in terms of tree form, vigor, and health is common. Variation can also be greater in naturally regenerated stands than in plantations. It increases with age and is often greater in stands of hardwoods than in stands of conifers.

Alternatives to strict row thinning are to increase row frequency to those greater than every other row and to combine this technique with low, crown, or selection thinning. Some of the modified row thinning methods designed to remove about one-third of the volume of young average-stocked stands would be to:

1. Remove every fourth row, and cut about one-eighth of the remaining volume by taking about one diseased, defective, and slow-growing tree out of every eight remaining. All trees to be harvested will be within at least one row of the logged row. During a second thinning, the entire middle row of the three may be cut.

2. Remove every fifth row, and cut about one-sixth of the remaining volume by taking about one of the poorer trees out of every six remaining. Again, all trees cut will be within at least one row of the logged row.

3. Remove every sixth row, and cut about one-fifth of the remaining volume by taking about one poor tree out of every five remaining. All trees cut will be within at least two rows of the logged row. A second thinning may allow the removal of the middle row of the remaining five.

Less frequent row thinnings may have some uses under certain stand conditions, but logging costs and damage to residual trees may be excessive. In stands of average variation, the sixth-row method provides the best means of maintaining quality of residual trees. Stands of less variation may be thinned best by either the five-row or the four-row method. For young stands which are too thick as a result of better-than-expected survival, the three-row or every-other-row method is generally best.

### Thinning Applications

A thinning schedule must be a systematic undertaking during the entire rotation of a timber stand. In addition to the method, the plan must include the timing of each thinning and an estimate of the amount of growing stock to be left.

Generally the stand needs thinning when its rate of growth as a result of crown and root competition begins to slow down. In some instances this may occur before the trees are large enough for harvest for traditional forest products. The land manager must decide whether to wait, even at reduced growth rates, until the trees are large enough for sale as pulpwood or fence posts, or consider some type of mechanical precommercial thinning. The latter has not received widespread use because of cost limitations; however, many timber growers have been able to precommercially thin their stands for small fence posts for use on their own farms or ranches, even though the trees were not generally large enough for commercial fence posts.

On the other hand, some natural and overplanted stands of precommercial size may stagnate and even deteriorate without treatment. Stagnation of height growth and failure to express dominance occur most commonly on poor sites and with species which can prolifically reproduce themselves on these sites. In these cases, some type of precommercial thinning is necessary.

It should be noted that tree species respond differently to thinnings. Furthermore, the longer trees stagnate, the longer the time they need to respond with accelerated growth after release.

## Time and Amount of Thinning

Many techniques are used to determine when timber stands need thinning. The one generally accepted as the best is the live crown ratio of the potential crop or residual trees. The satisfactory ratio between total height of the tree and its crown must be maintained for optimum growth and financial returns to the owner. In pine stands, sapling-size, or larger, trees should have live crown length of about one-third of their total height for a proper growth ratio. Overcrowding may cause the crown to recede to one-fourth or even less of the height. In this case, the stand needs thinning. Crowns will exceed one-third the height in understocked stands.

Taking an increment boring may also be an effective means of measuring the tree's growth rate. It provides a direct measure of diameter growth which generally is an indicator of growth in height and volume. Usually codominant trees are bored because they will reflect growth rate changes or competition sooner than dominant trees will. A reduction in the width of annual rings indicates a need for thinning.

Basal area provides an excellent indicator of the degree of stocking in a stand and the need and extent of thinning required. Generally, if the objective is to increase diameter growth without sacrificing cubic volume growth, the proper basal area level per acre is between 50 and 175 square feet. (The basal area per acre is determined by totalling the basal area for all trees in the stand and dividing this sum by the total area of the stand in acres.) In practice, the range may be from 60 square feet of basal area per acre for the least tolerant pines to about 125 square feet for the most tolerant; from 130 to 175 square feet basal area per acre for the spruces, hemlocks, and true firs; and finally, as low as 40 square feet basal area per acre for the most intolerant hardwood to 100 square feet for the most tolerant hardwoods such as beech. The frequency of thinning may run from 5 to 15 years.

The general tendency for forest managers is to thin timber stands too lightly. Stands that are properly marked to remove enough volume to accelerate tree growth appear to be overmarked to the inexperienced eye; however, a few years after the stand is cut, the remains of tops and stumps are the only evidence that the stand has been thinned. A check of the basal area in the unmarked trees, by use of the wedge prism during the marking operation, provides a ready measure of the extent of thinning to be done.

Thinning timber to a diameter limit reduces the future productivity of forest stands. If the limit is set to larger diameters, say 14 inches, it may high-grade the stand. Thinning by lower-diameter limits, say 8 inches, seriously affects the future potential timber growth of the stand. In virtually all cases, thinning on the basis of a diameter limit is designed solely to allow buyers to cut all the merchantable timber, which reduces optimum timber production. Small timber tracts may have to be sold by high-diameter limit because the cost of hiring expert help is prohibitive.

## CLEANINGS

Another type of operation in young stands not past the sapling stage is a cleaning. This method is used to free the best trees from undesirable individuals of the same age which overtop them or are likely to overtop them, and where the method of cutting and preparation of the site during regeneration tend to favor preferred and desirable species.

The main reason for a cleaning is to free the desired species from competition by regulating the composition of mixed stands. It is the first type of cutting or tree deadening generally used on new stands after establishment. In softwood stands, cleanings may be directed toward low-quality hardwoods, and in hardwood stands, toward inferior hardwoods.

### Prescription Burning

The use of fire under very carefully controlled conditions is the most economical tool which can be used in cleaning operations in young pine stands. Under ideal conditions, fire can be used for less than $3 per acre, but may run in excess of $10 per acre. The term "prescription" implies that the user will measure the relative humidity, temperature, wind velocity and direction, fuel moisture, and other factors to determine if fire can be safely and satisfactorily used. Prescription burning should be used only by persons trained and experienced in its use, which is often regulated by state laws. Regulations of the Environmental Protection Agency must also be followed.

Prescription burning is effective for controlling scrub hardwood up to 4 inches dbh on pine sites. The flames are intense but are kept at low levels. The flame levels must be controlled to keep them below the crowns of the young pine. Sufficient fuel in the form of pine straw or needles is essential. Hardwoods are susceptible to fire and are killed by girdling, whereas young pines are protected by their cork-like bark. Several burns at two- to four-year intervals are usually necessary for satisfactory hardwood control. Prescription burning may also be used for (1) fire hazard reduction, (2) seedbed preparation, (3) control of long-leaf pine brown spot needle blight, and (4) grazing and wildlife management improvement.

It should be noted that some closed-cone pines require fire of high temperatures to open them. These include jack, lodgepole, Monterey, Bishop, and sand pines. They reproduce better after severe fires such as broadcast burnings than from the gentler disturbance resulting from prescription burning. Broadcast burning, another form of prescription burning, is used in the West to dispose of logging slash to reduce fire hazards and to aid planting.

## Cutting

Earlier methods of cleaning involved cutting and felling small trees. Sprouting usually occurred, so chemicals were combined with the cutting to prevent sprouting. Ammonium sulfamate (Ammate®) was applied on stumps or in notches at the base of trees as one of the earliest non-toxic chemicals. Improved chemicals and labor costs have made this method less economical. Cutting has limited use in situations where so little cleaning is involved that using large-scale chemical spray apparatus is not feasible.

## Basal Spraying

Basal spraying is the application of herbicides, often esters of 2,4-D in a fuel oil solution, to all bark around the base of a tree. Herbicides, for controlling inferior hardwoods, tend to derange many of the physiological processes of the tree, causing plant tissue, in part, to starve itself to death. Water-soluble formulations of various herbicides are also available.

Basal spraying is a very selective and reliable method but an expensive one for cleaning. When this method is used, enough herbicides may be translocated (transferred through the plant tissue) through the xylem to kill the top of the tree. It is not recommended for trees larger than 4 inches dbh and is most effective on stems 2 inches or less. It can be used at any time of the year.

## *Foliage Spraying*

Spraying of hardwood foliage with herbicides is effective for broadcast control methods and is still widely used by timber growers. In this method, the herbicide is applied to the leaves, and it is translocated to the living tissue of the tree. It is generally applied by tractor-mounted or back-pack–type mist blowers that reduce the solution to fine droplets and blow it out into the tree canopies. Aerial application of herbicides is also used for foliage spraying but must be limited to areas where drift may not be a problem. Foliage spraying of herbicides by either mist blowers or aerial applications may be regulated by state laws. Environmental Protection Agency regulations must also be observed.

Two types of foliage spraying are used. High-volume spraying, generally applying low concentrations of herbicides, is done from the ground, with the spray in the form of coarse droplets. Low-volume sprays are applied from either the air or the ground, applying considerably less volume but a higher concentration. Foliage spraying is most successful in late spring and early summer. Foliage spraying is relatively expensive with costs varying up to $40 per acre.

## *Sterilants*

Water-soluble herbicides, in a dry form such as pellets or wettable powder, may be applied directly to the soil for cleaning operations. Rainfall moves the herbicide into the soil, to be taken up by the tree roots.

Soil sterilants have found increasing use for site treatment prior to planting. These chemicals generally persist in the soil for a year or more so planting may be delayed. They may have limited applications for precommercial thinning of overstocked softwood and hardwood stands.

## *LIBERATION CUTTINGS*

A liberation operation is one designed to free a young stand, up to sapling size, from the competition of older, overtopping individual trees. The principal difference between liberations and cleanings is that liberations generally require cutting or deadening larger trees. Control techniques generally differ, but some of the same methods may be used. Both softwood and hardwood stands may require liberation, but trees should not be removed unless they are actually overtopping desired species.

The overtopping trees are usually the ones left from a previous cutting. As a result of growing under excessive open conditions, they develop an undesirable or wolf-tree form. The best way to remove them is by cutting for a commercial harvest. Those trees for which no market exists must be deadened. There are several methods for controlling inferior trees.

## Girdling

Girdling involves cutting through the bark and cambium and into the sapwood with an axe or a mechanical tool. The cut or groove must sever the cambial tissue completely around the tree. It is more effective when combined with the use of herbicides. Increased cost of labor has limited its present-day use.

## Basal Sprays

Basal and stump spraying may also be used on larger stems. The basal spray is extended up the stem to about 24 inches for the larger-diametered trees. Aerial spraying is also effective but expensive for liberation purposes.

Large trees are most effectively controlled by techniques in which herbicides are applied or injected into incisions in the bark. The herbicide goes directly into the cambium, xylem, and phloem tissues. Making incisions completely encircling the stem is best, but making spaced incisions using a tree injector is more economical. This tool is a large, hollow pipe with a sharp chisel bit on the lower end. It is jabbed into the base of the tree near the ground line and releases a small quantity of herbicide which flows into the wound through the chisel bit. The use of liberation operations, with metered injectors filled with concentrated 2,4-D amine, is the most widespread technique used to control inferior trees. It is also effective on small-diametered trees and as a follow-up to other methods.

## Cost-Sharing

Timber growers may be eligible for financial assistance for liberation operations. This program is administered by the Agricultural Stabilization and Conservation Service in each state. The availability and extent of cost-sharing may be determined by contacting the local A.S.C.S. office.

## IMPROVEMENT CUTTINGS

An improvement cutting is another form of intermediate cutting applicable to stands larger than saplings. It is done to improve stand composition, quality, condition, or form by removing inferior trees. Improvement cuttings are generally used in older stands that have not had the benefit of cleanings or liberation cuttings. The principal purpose of this method is to remove crooked, forked, diseased, or undesirable trees. It should be noted that improvement cuttings may be simultaneously combined with thinnings and reproduction cuttings. Figure 6-2 illustrates an improvement cutting in a hardwood stand.

Improvement cuttings should precede a harvest cut by a sufficient number of years so that adequate benefits are obtained from release of the crop trees.

### Sanitation Cuttings

A sanitation cutting is used to remove trees infested with insects or attacked by diseases. In some instances, it may be used as a preventive measure in anticipation of an outbreak of forest pests with those trees which appear in danger of being removed. It will remove all injured, diseased, or vulnerable trees in a stand regardless of merchantability.

### Salvage Cuttings

A salvage cutting is used to remove trees that have been or may be killed or damaged by injurious agents such as insects, ice, windstorms, diseases, and other factors. It, like a sanitation cutting, is normally done during regular intermediate harvests unless some catastrophe occurs. During recent outbreaks of southern pine bark beetles, salvage cuttings were used to utilize merchantable trees. They may be recommended as a principal control technique for beetles and other insects because of the danger of destroying predatory insects by the use of insecticides.

Fig. 6-2. An improvement cutting was used on this stand of hardwood timber. The cutting has removed all of the defective and low-value trees, leaving ample room for the remaining higher-quality red gum trees to grow. (Courtesy American Forest Institute)

## Pruning

Pruning involves the removal of side branches from standing trees in order to produce knot-free lumber from logs of higher quality. Research has proven that pruning can improve lumber grades by 60 per cent or more; however, pruning has not received widespread use because of the cost involved. For this reason, it is not generally recommended by foresters. Future high sawtimber prices for better quality trees may improve the economic feasibility of pruning.

Under normal management, timber growers depend upon natural pruning of lower limbs during tree height and diameter growth to produce high-quality timber. Natural pruning may be supplemented by artificial pruning. A long-handled saw is used to remove branches from the first 17 feet (about the first 16-foot log) of the stem during the winter months. Only the best or crop trees are selected for this purpose, and not more than one-third of the live crown should be removed. Figure 6-3 shows a timber grower pruning small pines to improve their quality.

One of the criteria for selecting outstanding specimens for breeding better trees in improvement programs is a tree's self-pruning ability.

Fig. 6-3. Pruning involves the removal of side branches to produce higher-quality timber. Here a southern timber grower uses a long-handled pruning saw to remove the lower limbs from a small pine. (Courtesy American Forest Institute)

## HARVEST CUTTINGS

This silvicultural practice involves the (1) removal of the mature timber, (2) establishment of reproduction, and (3) supplementary treatments of the timber-growing site to develop favorable conditions for seedling growth. Harvest cuttings are the last ones in the timber rotation and logically follow intermediate cuttings.

Timber stands may be regenerated by a variety of cutting methods. Most of these involve reproducing stands from seed, but one, the coppice forest method, reproduces stands by vegetative regeneration. The latter may be used by itself or in combination with regeneration from seed.

Experimental efforts with coppice forestry have produced fantastic yields. Sycamore and other fast growing hardwoods are planted at close spacing on good sites and then fertilized and irrigated. Grown for from one to four years, the material is harvested by silage cutters, with anticipated yields of 10 tons or more per acre per year of dry matter. This is more than five times the normal yield from conventional timber production. This short rotation woody material can be used in the manufacture of paper products but also has potential for certain building boards and may ultimately have applications for energy and chemicals.

There are a variety of methods involved in harvest-cutting timber. These methods include (1) clear cutting, (2) seed tree, (3) shelterwood, and (4) selection. The first three methods are used to regenerate even-aged stands, and the last is used to regenerate uneven-aged stands.

### Clear Cutting

In this method, virtually all the trees in the stand, both large and small, are cut. Often, clear cutting is applied improperly by cutting all merchantable timber, leaving trees which cannot be profitably utilized. This is really a very crude kind of selection cutting. True clear cutting lays bare the area cut prior to the establishment of an even-aged stand. In recent years, it has become synonymous with the statement "clear-cut and plant." After cutting, regeneration may occur by planting or direct seeding, or from seed from adjacent trees or those felled in the cutting.

Clear cutting is applicable in stands where the trees are no longer worth keeping for further growth and value increase, as a source of seed, for the protection of the new reproduction, or for other silvicultural purposes. It is used in mature or overmature stands to remove less desirable species and to facilitate site treatment, including the planting of superior tree stock.

Tree improvement and genetic breeding programs have produced planting stock which will yield up to 20 per cent more wood fiber per acre; grow into good timber trees on 30 per cent less rainfall than normally required; and produce taller, straighter, and better-formed trees. As a result, many timber growers are clear cutting their lands and reforesting with superior trees.

Where natural reproduction from adjacent trees is the regeneration system desired, clear cuttings are made in strips or blocks. The width and length of the openings are limited by the ability of the wind-disseminated seed of desired species to travel out into the clearing. This ranges from one to five times the height of the adjacent desired trees. In pine and some hardwood stands, the size of the opening should not exceed twice the height of the adjoining trees. It should not be used for stands composed principally of heavy-seeded species such as oak. Douglas fir stands should not exceed five times the adjacent timber height. A modified form of clear cutting may be used in harvesting hardwoods by cutting openings of a minimum of $\frac{1}{5}$ acre in size.

The story of clear cutting would not be complete without a discussion of very short rotations, say 30 years of age. A controversy rages over this drastic departure from traditional rotations of 60 to 100 years. The latter are designed to produce the full range of forest products from pulpwood, to poles, to sawlogs. The former is considered strictly a pulpwood rotation, although fence posts and barn poles might be complementary products of the short rotation. In terms of the total economic contribution of the wood-using industry to the economy, sawlogs are essential to supply the raw material needs of the lumber, plywood, and veneer industries. On the other hand, rising interest rates turn loose the skyrocketing effect of compound interest on the costs of land ownerships. Compound interest increases in geometric ratios. For example, $25 per acre invested in planting at age 0 is worth $116.52 at age 20 at 8 per cent compound interest. At age 30, the $25 initial investment is worth $251.57 at 8 percent compound interest, but $5,465.15 at age 70 at the same interest rate. This reveals a serious question as to the length of time timber-growing costs can be carried under increased interest rates and still be economically feasible. Such a condition makes a strong case for shortening rotation length.

## Seed Tree Cutting

Seed tree cutting is a form of clear cutting, except that seed-bearing trees are left suitably dispersed throughout the harvest area to provide for reproduction. This method is used with species that bear seed frequently and abundantly so that scattered seed trees, usually 4 to 10 large dbh trees per acre, will regenerate the area with desired species in a reasonable period of time. The ground condition as it relates to competitive vegetation is important in the use of seed tree cuts. Heavy adverse competititon for moisture and light drastically interferes with reproduction.

## Shelterwood Cutting

Shelterwood cutting is a harvest cutting method whereby only a portion of the stand is removed at any one time. Its purpose is to obtain natural reproduction under the partial shelter of a large number of seed trees. Shelterwood cuttings are divided into two or even three stages of tree removal. In the former case, about one-half of the stand is cut, leaving the balance long enough to reseed the area. The remaining timber is then removed. In a three-stage method, a preparatory cutting is made first, then a seed cutting, and finally a final harvest.

## Selection Cutting

Selection cutting is a complex method of cutting and removing individual trees throughout the stand based upon maturity, growth rate, diameter, and vigor. The term "selection," however, is controversial among foresters because it has been associated in the past with high-grade timber cuts, that is, selecting only the best trees to be harvested. Generally, in selection cutting, the total volume removed each year or cutting period does not exceed the timber growth for that period. It is a form of sustained yield harvest. The trees may be selected throughout the forest each year; or in the case of large tracts, they may be divided into a series of cutting units for efficiency and convenience. In this case, an annual cutting may be confined to one unit. This system continues until all units are harvested; then the cutting returns to the first unit. When properly applied, the volume cut each year is at least replaced by growth in the intervals between the cutting of each unit. The selection method, when used in some areas, tends to control stand composition and hastens hardwood encroachment problems.

### BIBLIOGRAPHY

Barrett, J. W., editor. *Regional Silviculture of the United States*. New York, N.Y.: John Wiley and Sons, Inc., 1980.

Carvell, K. L. *Improvement Cuttings in Immature Hardwood Stands*. Bulletin 492. Morgantown, W. Va.: West Virginia Agricultural Experiment Station, 1964.

Cheyney, E. G. *American Silvics and Silviculture*. Minneapolis, Minn.: The University of Minnesota Press, 1942.

Daniel, Theodore W., Helms, John A., and Baker, Frederick S. *Principles of Silviculture*. Second Edition. New York, N.Y.: McGraw-Hill Book Company, Inc., 1979.

Odum, E. P. *Basic Ecology*. Philadelphia, Pa.: Saunders College Publishing, 1983.

Smith, David M. *The Practice of Silviculture*. New York, N.Y.: John Wiley and Sons, Inc., 1986.

Spurr, S. H., and Barnes, B. V. *Forest Ecology*. Third Edition. New York, N.Y.: The Ronald Press Company, 1980.

*Trends in Hardwood Management and Use*. Atlanta, Ga.: Southern Forest Institute, 1966.

U.S. Forest Service. *Management and Inventory of Southern Hardwoods*. Agricultural Handbook 181. U.S.D.A. Washington, D.C.: Superintendent of Documents, U.S. Government Printing Office, 1960.

U.S. Forest Service. *Proceedings: A Symposium on Principles of Maintaining Productivity on Prepared Sites*. Mississippi State, Miss.: Southern Experiment Station, Mississippi State University, 1978.

U.S. Forest Service. *Seeds of Woody Plants in the United States*. Agricultural Handbook 450. U.S.D.A. Washington, D.C.: Superintendent of Documents, U.S. Government Printing Office, 1974.

U.S. Forest Service. *Silvics of Forest Trees of the United States*. Agricultural Handbook 271. U.S.D.A. Washington, D.C.: Superintendent of Documents, U.S. Government Printing Office, 1965.

van Buijtenen, J. P., et al. *Introduction to Practical Forest Tree Improvement*. Circular 207. College Station, Tex.: Texas Forest Service, 1976.

CHAPTER VII

# Artificial Reforestation

The planting and seeding of forest trees, although substantial, has covered a relatively small part of the estimated 8 million acres harvested annually in the United States. Forest owners still rely primarily on natural regeneration to restore most stands after logging. In many parts of the country this is an effective and economical method of regenerating forest cover; however, considerable acreage in this nation will not become productive without artificial reforestation.

Nationwide, more than 70 million acres of land are in need of planting. Such acreage includes cutover mismanaged woodlands, areas that have been severely burned by wildfire, and abandoned or submarginal crop land. There are currently millions of acres of agricultural land which should be removed from row crop production and put into permanent cover to protect the nation's soil and water resources. Considering the difficulty of getting desirable natural reproduction established on such a huge area, the slowness with which nature would reforest it to desirable species, and the growing importance of wood to our expanding economy, it is essential that reforestation be undertaken. It is to the woodland owner's advantage to have the lands producing to their maximum capacity.

## METHODS OF REFORESTATION

There are five means by which forests may be reproduced: by planting wild seedlings, by direct seeding, by cuttings, by planting seedlings grown in a nursery, and by the use of containerized seedlings.

### Use of Wild Seedlings

Wild seedlings are those growing in the woods in a natural state. For all practical purposes, the digging up and transplanting of such seedlings for reforestation purposes should be avoided. Such practice is uneconomical and inefficient.

### Direct Seeding

The sowing of repellent-coated seed on an area where trees are desired is known as direct seeding.

In 1986, a total of 48,476 acres of land were direct seeded in the United States (Table 7-1). The West Coast states and the South were leaders in this practice. Such seeding has been accomplished mainly on public lands and large industrial holdings. A total of 28 states reported some direct seeding activity in the year 1986 (Table 7-1).

While research is still being conducted on direct seeding, especially of pine, this method can be effectively and successfully employed under proper conditions. Direct-seeded pines grow as well as planted pine of the same age.

Large areas can be seeded broadcast by hand, airplane, or cyclone seeder (Figure 7-1) or seeded by a grain drill (Figure 7-2). Usually the stand establishment cost is less than the cost of planting tree seedlings. When direct seeding is accomplished by aircraft, it is, by economics, limited to areas in excess of 500 acres. A fixed-wing plane can sow up to 1,500 acres per day while a helicopter can sow about 2,500 acres. Sowing by aircraft is a specialty job requiring technical skill. Several commercial companies are available for this type of direct seeding.

Some factors which affect the success or failure of direct seeding are vegetative cover, soil moisture, climatic conditions, and bird and rodent populations.

Vegetative cover which prevents seed from reaching mineral soil will often interfere with germination. Prescription burning of some planting areas is the normal method used to reduce the rough. This is usually done in the preceding spring. Sometimes an area is disced as a whole, in other instances grass roughs are disced at 8- to 10-foot intervals, and seeds are planted with a grain drill or a cyclone seeder. Mechanical preparation assures higher survival in a dry year and also increases growth.

Where excess hardwood brush or a large number of undesirable hardwood trees are present on a planting site, they must be controlled either before or soon after direct seeding. Pine, being intolerant of shade, will not persist under a heavy overstory for many years. Also, the established root systems of hardwood will use avail-

TABLE 7-1

ACRES OF LAND DIRECT-SEEDED, BY
TYPE OF OWNERSHIP, 1986

| State | Federal | Other Public | Private Lands | Total |
|-------|---------|--------------|---------------|-------|
| Alabama | — | — | 1,918 | 1,918 |
| Arkansas | 915 | — | 880 | 1,795 |
| California | 65 | — | 8 | 73 |
| Colorado | 205 | — | — | 205 |
| Connecticut | — | — | 40 | 40 |
| Florida | 10,881 | — | 3,258 | 14,139 |
| Georgia | 525 | — | 5,866 | 6,391 |
| Indiana | 32 | — | — | 32 |
| Iowa | — | — | 56 | 56 |
| Kansas | 2 | — | 80 | 82 |
| Kentucky | 10 | — | — | 10 |
| Louisiana | 1,021 | 200 | 1,702 | 2,923 |
| Michigan | 297 | 90 | — | 387 |
| Minnesota | 999 | 2,820 | 150 | 3,969 |
| Mississippi | 10 | — | 5,765 | 5,775 |
| Missouri | 427 | 178 | 415 | 1,020 |
| Montana | 148 | — | 1,100 | 1,248 |
| New Hampshire | — | — | 37 | 37 |
| North Carolina | 35 | — | 754 | 789 |
| Oklahoma | 139 | — | 771 | 910 |
| Oregon | 816 | 100 | — | 916 |
| Pennsylvania | — | — | 7 | 7 |
| Tennessee | — | — | 10 | 10 |
| Virginia | — | — | 766 | 766 |
| Washington | 125 | 748 | — | 873 |
| West Virginia | — | 1 | 3,584 | 3,585 |
| Wisconsin | 118 | — | 2 | 120 |
| Wyoming | 100 | 300 | — | 400 |
| Totals | 16,870 | 4,437 | 27,169 | 48,476 |

(Source: *1986 U.S. Forest Planting Report*, U.S. Forest Service)

able soil moisture during frequent summer droughts when the moisture supply becomes critical for pine seedlings.

For killing large undesirable trees, the tree injection method is commonly used. The injector is a hollow tool with a cutting edge near the base. A chemical herbicide, poured into the top of the tube, is injected into a tree at the base when the bit is thrust into the trunk. A metered injector using an approved herbicide is proving an efficient and effective means of control. Users should seek the advice

Fig. 7-1. Direct seeding a cutover eroded area with a cyclone seeder. (Courtesy Georgia Forestry Commission)

of their state forestry department as to the type of herbicide recommended for this purpose.

Dense understory stands of hardwood can be killed by a mist blower using a herbicide; however, extreme care must be used in its application to prevent its spread to adjoining lands. Prescribed fire, if it can be used, would be more desirable; however, state and federal regulations must be observed.

Soil moisture affects germination of seed and the growth of the seedlings. An insufficient amount following direct seeding will result in a high mortality. Seedling mortality is highest during the dry summer period. At this time seedling roots are too short to reach available moisture. Seedlings should be established when climatic conditions are conducive to soil moisture.

Fig. 7-2. A two-row seeder, modified from a corn planter, is used to direct seed cutover pine land in Louisiana. (Courtesy Southern Forest Experiment Station)

Birds and rodents are also important factors in direct seeding, each consuming the seed for food. It is for this reason that seed must be treated with a bird and rodent repellent before being broadcast. A spreader-sticker, or a latex sticker, is thus added before finally coating the seeds with aluminum flakes to aid movement through sowing equipment. Most seed dealers will apply repellents at a nominal cost or furnish the material already mixed.

Those engaged in direct-seeding studies have suggested that almost all seeds be stratified prior to planting if the germination tests indicate that this would improve the germination and speed of germination. Longleaf pine is an exception which does not require a cold treatment. It is essential to use clean seed with at least 80 per cent germination for direct-seeding purposes.

The major advantages cited for direct seeding are speed of operation, low initial cost and labor requirements, applicability in unplantable areas, and better seedling growth. Disadvantages to this method are poor survival during first-year droughts and high seedling density that may retard growth.

Some hardwoods are direct seeded on desired planting sites, and this method is preferable when it can be feasibly accomplished. Squirrel and rodent depredation can be expected. Some state forestry agencies sell black walnuts in stratified condition for direct planting.

In general, direct seeding of hardwoods has not proven to be as practical as for conifers for several reasons: (1) lack of seed protection from animals, (2) improper treatment of seed prior to sowing, (3) lack of adequate site preparation because moisture cannot be controlled, and (4) lack of intensive post-cultural treatments to control weeds and stand density.

### Cuttings

Some species of trees, such as willow and cottonwood, can be reproduced from cuttings. Cuttings are pieces of branches, usually 8 to 12 inches in length, cut from a tree.

In practice, the cuttings are usually taken from trees in the winter and planted shortly thereafter in holes dug by a metal rod or other special tool. Cuttings are inserted in the holes with buds upright and in such a position that only the top bud on the cutting is exposed above ground. The soil must be firmly packed around the cutting. Bud areas below the soil level will develop into roots.

The planting of special strains of cottonwood for the production of pulpwood is giving this method of reproduction added emphasis.

### Nursery Seedlings

While direct seeding (Table 7-1) is being done on a large scale, the planting of nursery grown seedlings (Figures 7-3 and 7-4) is still the most certain method of acquiring a good stand, particularly for a small forest landowner. The chief advantages of planting are close control of stocking, uniformity of resulting stands, and conservation of seed.

In 1986, over 1,767 million seedlings were produced in tree nurseries in the United States (Table 7-2). Leading states, in descending order, were Georgia, Alabama, Texas, Florida, Washington, Oregon, Arkansas, South Carolina, and Mississippi.

Fig. 7-3. Mulching of seedbeds in a forest tree nursery. (Courtesy Illinois Division of Forest Resources)

Under conditions where forests cannot be established by nature, direct seeding or planting of seedlings is necessary. Advantages to the planting of seedlings are:

1. Desired species can be established.
2. Species with certain genetic characteristics for a specific purpose can be planted, for example, pine seedlings with a high or low specific gravity or those which will produce more gum.

Fig. 7-4. Harvesting pine seedlings at the end of the first growing season. (Courtesy Texas Forest Service)

3. The years that would normally be required to reforest an area will be fewer.
4. Where erosion is a problem, it will effect control much sooner.
5. Undesirable volunteer trees are better controlled.
6. Trees of desired species can be established on an area.
7. Planted stands are evenly stocked.
8. Tree spacing can be controlled by the planter.
9. Plantations, being even-aged, are easier to manage.

The major disadvantages to tree planting are:

1. An owner's investment in seedling planting and protection costs cannot be liquidated until the trees are large enough for

TABLE 7-2

**PRODUCTION OF FOREST TREE SEEDLINGS, 1986**

| State | Federal Nurseries | State Nurseries | Other Public Nurseries | Industry Nurseries | Total All Nurseries |
|-------|------------------|-----------------|------------------------|--------------------|--------------------|
| | . . . . . . . . . . . . . . . . . . . . (thousand trees) . . . . . . . . . . . . . . . . . . . . | | | | |
| Alabama | — | 53,000 | — | 150,960 | 203,960 |
| Alaska | 170 | 420 | — | — | 590 |
| Arkansas | — | 16,451 | — | 92,000 | 108,451 |
| California | 15,783 | 3,216 | 150 | 13,030 | 32,179 |
| Colorado | — | 1,457 | — | 100 | 1,557 |
| Connecticut | — | 2,000 | — | — | 2,000 |
| Florida | — | 71,838 | — | 67,394 | 139,232 |
| Georgia | — | 120,802 | — | 157,489 | 278,291 |
| Hawaii | — | 397 | — | — | 397 |
| Idaho | 18,539 | 554 | — | — | 19,093 |
| Illinois | — | 2,375 | — | — | 2,375 |
| Indiana | — | 4,454 | — | — | 4,454 |
| Iowa | — | 2,815 | — | — | 2,815 |
| Kansas | — | 146 | — | — | 146 |
| Kentucky | — | 10,282 | — | 80 | 10,362 |
| Louisiana | — | 44,000 | — | 30,000 | 74,000 |
| Maine | — | 1,212 | — | 5,700 | 6,912 |
| Michigan | 7,573 | 3,810 | 4,000 | 7,900 | 23,283 |
| Minnesota | 4,004 | 18,643 | — | 2,198 | 24,845 |
| Mississippi | 22,498 | 67,651 | — | 13,000 | 103,149 |
| Missouri | — | 6,128 | — | 500 | 6,628 |
| Montana | — | 986 | — | 4,675 | 5,661 |
| Nebraska | 2,808 | — | — | 200 | 3,008 |
| Nevada | — | 153 | — | — | 153 |
| New Hampshire | — | 300 | — | — | 300 |
| New Jersey | — | 762 | — | 2,100 | 2,862 |
| New Mexico | 4,068 | — | — | — | 4,068 |
| New York | — | 6,045 | — | — | 6,045 |
| North Carolina | — | 40,815 | — | 57,000 | 97,815 |
| North Dakota | — | 1,268 | — | — | 1,268 |
| Ohio | — | 5,400 | — | 1,550 | 6,950 |
| Oklahoma | — | 3,883 | — | — | 3,883 |
| Oregon | 21,645 | 17,658 | — | 70,750 | 110,053 |
| Pennsylvania | — | 3,694 | — | — | 3,694 |
| South Carolina | — | 65,465 | — | 41,550 | 107,015 |
| South Dakota | — | 1,519 | — | — | 1,519 |
| Tennessee | — | 7,604 | — | — | 7,604 |
| Texas | — | 18,265 | — | 122,000 | 140,265 |
| Utah | — | 215 | — | — | 215 |
| Vermont | — | 500 | — | — | 500 |
| Virginia | — | 65,243 | — | 17,799 | 83,042 |

(Continued)

TABLE 7-2 (Continued)

| State | Federal Nurseries | State Nurseries | Other Public Nurseries | Industry Nurseries | Total All Nurseries |
|---|---|---|---|---|---|
| | . . . . . . . . . . . . . . . . . . . . . . . . . . . . . (thousand trees) . . . . . . . . . . . . . . . . . . . . . . | | | | |
| Washington | 22,898 | 12,100 | 966 | 75,720 | 111,684 |
| West Virginia | — | 15 | 22 | 1,430 | 1,467 |
| Wisconsin | 240 | 19,453 | — | 3,100 | 22,793 |
| State Totals | 120,226 | 702,994 | 5,138 | 938,225 | 1,766,583 |
| Puerto Rico | 15 | 533 | — | — | 548 |
| Guam | — | 44 | 2 | 10 | 56 |
| Grand Totals | 120,241 | 703,571 | 5,140 | 938,235 | 1,767,187 |

(Source: 1986 U.S. Forest Planting Report, U.S. Forest Service)

initial thinnings and sale. Depending upon the site, initial returns may not be forthcoming for a period of 10 to 20 years; however, this should be contrasted with that which could be expected by awaiting action by nature.

2. Insects, disease, fire, or other pests may kill planted seedlings. This will require replanting.
3. Because of the monetary investment, there is need to protect a plantation from fire and other destructive agencies. This may require an additional investment.

## Containerized Seedlings

The practice of using containerized seedlings for artificial regeneration is becoming increasingly accepted. By this method seeds are germinated in small pots of soil or other growing medium (Figure 7-5). After a period of from 8 to 32 weeks, the seedlings are planted with undisturbed roots.

Among the advantages cited for containerized seedlings by its proponents are the ability to (1) improve survival and growth of seedling, (2) produce difficult species more readily, (3) extend the planting season, (4) achieve greater production and planting efficiency, and (5) out-plant an intact seedling.

Several industrial firms and the United States and Canadian Forest Services are currently utilizing this technique for regeneration of a portion of their lands. In 1979, about one out of four seed-lings planted were grown in containers.

The Pacific Northwest has shown the greatest interest in this means of reforestation. Seedlings of hemlock, spruces, some true firs, and a few pines are grown in large numbers. In other parts of

Fig. 7-5. Loblolly pine seedlings growing in three types of containers used throughout the United States. Left, biodegradable; center, peat moss-vermiculite molded block; right, a plug as removed from a styro-block in which it grew. (Courtesy Southern Forest Experiment Station, Pineville, Louisiana)

the United States, planting of containerized seedlings by private landowners is not common. Where accomplished, pines are the most widely grown species. Much study in the South is being given to pine. Hardwoods, such as paper birch, yellow birch, and maple, are under study in the Northeast United States.

Despite advantages attributed to this method of planting, there are some drawbacks. Containerized seedlings will often cost at least twice as much as bare-rooted stock. Such seedlings are bulky and more difficult to handle and transport, and evidence tends to indicate that their planting might necessitate more complete site preparation, making for an added cost to a landowner. Producing containerized seedlings also requires a higher level of technical knowledge. Since they are grown under greenhouse conditions, the seedlings are conducive to diseases, nutritional imbalances, and other problems.

It has not, as yet, been conclusively established that the extra cost will be fully offset by reductions in planting costs or gains in survival or early growth.

While further research will continue on containerized seedlings, including the mechanics of planting, it can be reasonably assumed that such seedlings will be a supplement to, not a replacement of, the planting of bare-root stock, at least in the immediate future.

### SOURCE OF SEEDLINGS

Forest landowners interested in securing seedlings for reforestation, Christmas trees, or windbreaks should request an application from their state forestry agency (see Appendix III). Seedlings are not sold by these agencies for ornamental purposes.

In a few states, a limited number of seedlings are provided free to farmers by the state forestry agency. In some others, the forest industry either donates some seedlings or offsets the cost to small forest landowners. In most states, seedlings are sold at or below the cost of production. Prices from state tree nurseries range from about $13 to $60, or more, per thousand for regular nursery stock, depending upon species. Some pine species, such as white pine or Scotch pine, may be higher. As a general rule, hardwood species are more expensive than pine. A few, such as genetically improved black walnut, may sell for several hundred dollars per thousand. For pine with certain genetic characteristics, the price per thousand seedlings is about $7 per thousand more in cost over regular run nursery stock. Prices

Fig. 7-6. A cutover, burned area as it appeared originally (top) and as it appeared 20 years later (bottom), following planting and protection from grazing and fire. (Courtesy Texas Forest Service)

are given on application blanks available from state forestry agencies (Appendix III).

The planting season is quite variable over various regions of the country. Usually, nursery seedlings will have developed healthy tops and a good root system by the middle of November and be ready for a late winter to early spring planting.

Seedlings planted from late winter to early spring benefit from heavy winter rains and can become adjusted to the site before growth starts in the spring.

Seedlings obtained from northern tree nurseries will range from $30 to $75 and more per thousand for certain species. Western nursery stock is much higher, ranging from $75 to $500 per thousand. The reason for the higher price of northern and western seedlings is that they must be cared for in the nursery for two and sometimes three years before they are of sufficient size to send out to tree planters.

## TREE PLANTING GUIDELINES

### Estimating Needs

It is very important to order the proper species and number of seedlings required for the area to be reforested. The state forestry agency or extension forester will help in the selection of the best species for the site and in making other recommendations for a particular area. The importance of selection of the proper species cannot be overemphasized.

If an open area is to be reforested, the following guide gives the number of seedlings per acre, depending upon spacing used: 6 feet × 8 feet—908 seedlings, 6 feet × 10 feet—726 seedlings, 8 feet × 8 feet—680 seedlings, 8 feet × 10 feet—544 seedlings, and 10 feet × 10 feet—436 seedlings. For interplanting an area, judgment will have to be exercised as to needs. With respect to windbreaks, the recommendations of the forestry agency or extension forester should be followed.

Some states have a deadline for ordering seedlings. For this reason landowners should place their orders early.

### Areas in Need of Planting

The need for planting cleared or abandoned farmlands that are submarginal for agriculture is obvious. Planting of trees can also be made on non-restocking forest land where full stocking is desired, and on non-forest land for windbreaks or watershed protection.

*Cleared or abandoned farmlands.* While reproduction is generally found encroaching on such land, it may take many years for nature to completely reforest the area. Thus, planting will help make the land more productive at an earlier period. Also, natural reproduction which slowly takes over an area of this type is what is called "old field succession" in that the trees are usually far apart, have limbs low on the trunk, and produce wood of low quality. Planting areas of this type, which have little or no commercial value for agriculture, produce an income for a landowner and provide for the multiple benefits of cover, wildlife, and recreation, which only the forest can provide.

*Non-restocking forest lands.* Throughout the country there are many areas of forest land that are not restocking naturally. This may be due to an insufficient number of seed trees to reforest the area, to repeated fire, or to depredation of natural seedlings by farm animals. In such instances, planting, followed by protection from fire and livestock, is essential to get such lands productive (Figure 7-6).

*Openings in forest stands.* In some instances there are openings in forests in which there is little natural reproduction. This may be due to damaging fire, poor seed years, or damage from livestock. Planting will bring these areas back to immediate productivity.

Where seed trees are available, pines and some hardwoods will generally produce a fair crop of seed each year with heavier crops at three- to five-year intervals. While longleaf pine will produce some seed each year, it is not generally of good quality. Good seed years are at about seven- to nine-year intervals.

Birds and rodents are also factors in natural reforestation. During light seed years these animals consume much of the crop.

Foresters sometimes recommend a prescribed fire to eliminate the rough and prepare a seedbed prior to seed fall; however, such burning must be done by one who is competent to do so. The state forestry agency should be contacted for advice in this instance. There are state and federal regulations on burning.

*For watershed protection.* The planting of trees is desirable around the watersheds of lakes or streams to prevent erosion and the subsequent silting of these bodies of water. Trees will help prevent rapid runoff of water.

*Windbreaks.* In areas where strong winds and snow storms are common, the establishment of tree windbreaks is desirable. These can aid in reducing soil erosion, conserving energy, and controlling snow drifting. Windbreaks should be considered as an integral part of the farm operation. Unfortunately, in some areas of the country, especially the Midwest, agricultural landowners view windbreaks as being a detriment to row crop agricultural yields; however, research does not support their concern. Rather, overall yields appear to be increased. The only loss is in the land taken out of production for the windbreak.

A total of 39 states planted windbreaks in 1979 (Table 7-3). Leading states, in descending order of importance are North Dakota, Nebraska, Wisconsin, Colorado, Kansas, and Oklahoma.

*Selection of species.* What species should be grown on a specific area? The choice is largely governed by the trees growing naturally in the area and by specific planting site conditions.

It is important to consider where various kinds of trees normally grow; for example, planting a northern hardwood species in the South would not be successful since environmental factors such as temperature, sunlight, and soil moisture would be considerably different and would restrict survival. Generally species should be planted within or near their natural range.

Specific site conditions such as erosion, competition, drainage, and overall site quality must also be considered when choosing a species. Site requirements of candidate species are readily available from professional foresters and should be considered before selecting a species for planting.

Another factor to consider in species selection is the market potential at the time of harvest. It would not be economically attractive to plant a particular species which could be in oversupply at some time in the future. Again, professional foresters can be of assistance in this regard.

Some woodland owners may desire to plant trees for fence posts. Among the species with naturally durable heartwood are black locust, honey locust, catalpa, mulberry, sassafras, chinkapin, and bois d'arc.

From a silvicultural point of view it is often desirable to intermingle two species on the same area, such as loblolly and shortleaf pine. This would be a safeguard against some future catastrophe that might affect one species. Mixed stands are more difficult to manage but do provide safeguards for the landowner.

**TABLE 7-3**

### ACRES OF WINDBARRIER PLANTING ON ALL OWNERSHIPS OF LAND, 1979

| State | Federal | Other Public | Privately Owned | Total |
|-------|---------|--------------|-----------------|-------|
| Alabama | 15 | — | — | 15 |
| Alaska | — | — | 400 | 400 |
| Arizona | — | — | 193 | 193 |
| Arkansas | — | — | 162 | 162 |
| California | 3 | 19 | 1,455 | 1,477 |
| Colorado | 2 | — | 4,073 | 4,075 |
| Connecticut | — | — | — | — |
| Delaware | — | — | 10 | 10 |
| Florida | — | — | 513 | 513 |
| Georgia | 12 | — | 20 | 32 |
| Hawaii | — | 12 | 113 | 125 |
| Idaho | — | — | 66 | 66 |
| Illinois | 9 | 60 | 790 | 859 |
| Indiana | 3 | — | 3 | 6 |
| Iowa | 2 | — | 2,592 | 2,594 |
| Kansas | 4 | 70 | 3,969 | 4,043 |
| Kentucky | — | — | 2,026 | 2,026 |
| Louisiana | — | — | — | — |
| Maine | — | — | — | — |
| Maryland | — | 3 | 69 | 72 |
| Massachusetts | — | — | — | — |
| Michigan | 15 | 40 | 1,750 | 1,805 |
| Minnesota | — | 1,000 | 1,440 | 2,440 |
| Mississippi | — | — | 20 | 20 |
| Missouri | — | 30 | 1,348 | 1,378 |
| Montana | 41 | — | 445 | 486 |
| Nebraska | 61 | 590 | 11,221 | 11,872 |
| Nevada | — | — | — | — |
| New Hampshire | — | — | 32 | 32 |
| New Jersey | — | 33 | 39 | 72 |
| New Mexico | 6 | — | — | 6 |
| New York | — | — | — | — |
| North Carolina | — | 25 | — | 25 |
| North Dakota | 170 | — | 12,230 | 12,400 |
| Ohio | 80 | 18 | 678 | 776 |
| Oklahoma | 4 | — | 3,874 | 3,878 |
| Oregon | 1 | — | — | 1 |
| Pennsylvania | — | — | 200 | 200 |
| Rhode Island | — | — | — | — |
| South Carolina | 1 | — | — | 1 |
| South Dakota | 36 | — | 3 | 39 |
| Tennessee | — | — | — | — |

(Continued)

**TABLE 7-3 (Continued)**

| State | Federal | Other Public | Privately Owned | Total |
|-------|---------|--------------|-----------------|-------|
| Texas | — | 250 | 1,972 | 2,222 |
| Utah | — | — | 100 | 100 |
| Vermont | — | — | — | — |
| Virginia | 1 | 90 | — | 91 |
| Washington | — | — | — | — |
| West Virginia | — | — | 217 | 217 |
| Wisconsin | — | — | 7,653 | 7,653 |
| Wyoming | — | — | — | — |
| Totals | 466 | 2,240 | 59,676 | 62,382 |

(Source: U.S. Forest Service, 1986)

## Care of Seedlings upon Receipt from Nursery

It is important that seedlings be planted as soon as possible upon their receipt from the nursery. If the planting must be delayed because of inclement weather, the seedling bales should be opened and the trees heeled-in at the planting site (Figure 7-7). It is important to stress, however, that the bales should not be opened until the temperature is above freezing, otherwise the roots may freeze and die.

When seedlings are removed from the bundle to the heel-in bed, roots should not be exposed to the air any longer than required. This action will prevent the roots from drying out.

Seedlings should be placed in a V-shaped heel-in trench in an upright position with roots fully extended to the bottom of the hole and about one-half of the top extending above the ground line. Seedlings with curled roots are difficult to plant correctly since the roots must be straightened before they will extend down into the planting hole.

Seedlings may be stacked 8 to 10 deep, one on the other, without any adverse effect on them.

After the seedlings are placed correctly in the trench, it should be three-fourths filled with soil. The soil should be packed around the roots and given a thorough watering to further compact the soil around the roots. The trench is then filled with soil and compacted once again. Again the soil is watered, with any depressions noted filled with soil.

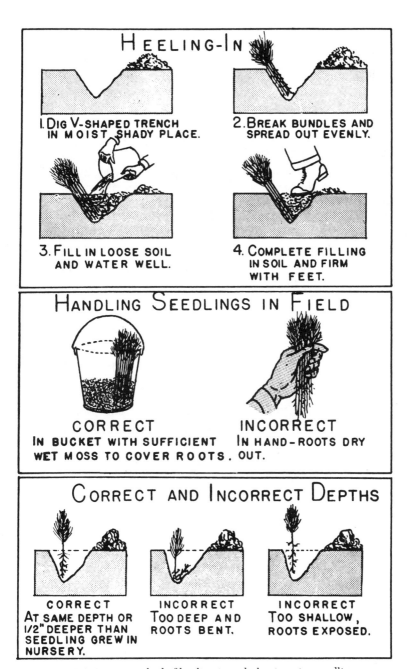

Fig. 7-7. Proper method of heeling-in and planting pine seedlings.

Subsequent watering of heeled-in seedlings is done only when the soil is dry and when there is no danger from a freeze.

If the trees are to be left heeled-in for any length of time, the soil should be covered with leaves to conserve soil moisture.

## Preparation of Site for Planting

Prior to planting, attention should be directed toward the preparation of the site. In old fields there may be a heavy stand of grass with such density as to seriously compete with young seedlings for moisture. In such cases the area should be prescribe-burned at least a month before planting, but preferably in the preceding summer. Such burning should be done safely so that the fire is confined solely to the area to be planted. A dry day, with a steady wind, should be selected. Firebreaks should be established around the area to be burned. A backfire, one that burns into the wind, should be used. This will consume more of the rough than a running head fire which is also difficult to control. Such burning also lessens the potential fire damage to the young stand. Most states require a burning permit, and strict adherence to state and federal regulations must be followed. The local representative of the forestry agency should be notified of the intent to burn in order to advise the landowner concerning locally required permits and state and federal regulations and to offer safety recommendations for getting the job done safely.

In cases where it is undesirable to burn, a shallow furrow should be made with a plow in which to plant. This is especially effective for pine species except for longleaf pine. Longleaf should not be planted in this manner since dirt from the shoulders may cover the longleaf buds and kill the seedlings.

Converting brush land to pine necessitates control of the undesirable hardwoods prior to planting. Pine is intolerant of shade, requiring full sunshine for good growth and survival. In instances where brush is heavy, prescription burning will temporarily eliminate competition so that pine can be established. Removal of brush overtopping pine may be necessary after the first year or two. Pine, if given a chance, will eventually outgrow the hardwood.

Sites with much shrub growth may need further site preparation. Cost sharing for the added work may be available under the Federal Incentives Program (FIP) created by Congress in 1973. It provides partial financial assistance for planting seedlings, preparing the site, and direct seeding. The various state forestry agencies can provide technical information on the program to landowners. The program is sponsored by the Agricultural Conservation Program. The local A.C.P. office manager, county agent, or district forester can be contacted concerning details.

Hardwood seedlings grow exceedingly well on cleared sites. Two cultivations per year for the first two years will promote good survival and early rapid growth. It cannot be overemphasized that good hardwood production demands carefully selecting and preparing the site and matching species to the site.

The extent of site preparation for natural regeneration, by states, is reflected in Table 7-4.

### Spacing of Trees

The choice of spacing of pine trees is dependent upon the owner's objective. A spacing of 6 × 8 feet or 8 × 8 feet favors maximum cubic foot volume growth. A few landowners prefer a spacing of 12 feet between rows, such as 8 × 12 feet, to permit the passage of trucks and other equipment and to reduce cost where trees are planted by machine.

Generally an 8- × 8-foot spacing, wherein the seedlings are planted 8 feet apart with rows 8 feet apart, is recommended over wider spacing. This is about 680 trees per acre. As the trees grow, they begin to compete with one another, causing the lower limbs to die and drop from the trees. This leaves clearer trunks, producing wood of better grades.

Wide spacings, such as 10 × 10 or 12 × 12 feet, may be used when trees of large diameters are desired in a relatively short time.

In field planting, an attempt should be made to keep rows relatively straight. While a curve in a row is acceptable, sharp curves should be avoided. Through the use of flags set at the end of the rows the chief of a hand-planting crew can be guided in keeping rows relatively straight. Hardwood species are generally planted at wider spacings than pine but still sufficiently dense to allow some selection of final crop trees.

### Planting Procedure

As a general rule, about 75 to 80 per cent of all properly planted seedlings will survive. Therefore, the more care one uses in planting seedlings, the greater the success. If survival is less than 400 trees

## TABLE 7-4

### ACRES OF SITE PREPARATION FOR NATURAL REGENERATION, BY STATES, 1979

| State | Non-industrial Private | Forest and Other Industry | Non-federal Public | Total |
|---|---|---|---|---|
| Alabama | 48,385 | 52,968 | — | 101,353 |
| Alaska | — | — | — | — |
| Arizona | 6 | — | — | 6 |
| Arkansas | 20,679 | 75,360 | 660 | 96,699 |
| California | 15,678 | 111,783 | 359 | 127,820 |
| Colorado | 2,000 | — | — | 2,000 |
| Connecticut | 131 | — | — | 131 |
| Delaware | 750 | 6,000 | 100 | 6,850 |
| Florida | 39,348 | — | 6,476 | 45,824 |
| Georgia | 148,088 | 156,010 | 2,694 | 306,792 |
| Hawaii | 3,174 | 50 | 1,002 | 4,226 |
| Idaho | 70 | 7,424 | — | 7,494 |
| Illinois | — | — | — | — |
| Indiana | 72 | — | 4 | 76 |
| Iowa | 1,760 | — | — | 1,760 |
| Kansas | 3,771 | — | 60 | 3,831 |
| Kentucky | 1,875 | 1,800 | — | 3,675 |
| Louisiana | 72,523 | 93,200 | 3,490 | 169,213 |
| Maine | 493 | 1,512 | — | 2,005 |
| Maryland | 2,545 | 1,236 | 208 | 3,989 |
| Massachusetts | 11 | — | — | 11 |
| Michigan | 279 | 200 | 3,100 | 3,579 |
| Minnesota | 4,878 | 6,245 | 3,390 | 14,513 |
| Mississippi | 112,580 | 107,723 | 4,119 | 224,422 |
| Missouri | 3,400 | — | 687 | 4,087 |
| Montana | 58 | 12,895 | 2,951 | 15,904 |
| Nebraska | 6,508 | — | 487 | 6,995 |
| Nevada | 21 | — | — | 21 |
| New Hampshire | 308 | — | — | 308 |
| New Jersey | 9,097 | — | 3,925 | 13,022 |
| New Mexico | 40 | — | — | 40 |
| New York | 204 | — | — | 204 |
| North Carolina | 71,607 | — | — | 71,607 |
| North Dakota | 31 | — | — | 31 |
| Ohio | 491 | — | 231 | 722 |
| Oklahoma | 1,953 | 38,222 | — | 40.175 |
| Oregon | 21,777 | 30,672 | 6,132 | 58,581 |
| Pennsylvania | 109 | — | — | 109 |
| Rhode Island | 71 | — | — | 71 |
| South Carolina | 55,660 | 60,134 | 675 | 116,469 |
| South Dakota | — | — | — | — |

(Continued)

**TABLE 7-4 (Continued)**

| State | Non-industrial Private | Forest and Other Industry | Non-federal Public | Total |
|-------|-----------------------|---------------------------|--------------------|-------|
| Tennessee | 2,228 | — | 199 | 2,427 |
| Texas | 15,761 | 100,000 | 538 | 116,299 |
| Utah | 54 | — | — | 54 |
| Vermont | — | — | — | — |
| Virginia | 57,944 | 43,516 | 783 | 102,243 |
| Washington | 6,320 | 21,895 | 6,650 | 34,865 |
| West Virginia | 405 | 1,144 | — | 1,549 |
| Wisconsin | 2,154 | 3,500 | 1,200 | 6,854 |
| Wyoming | — | 20 | 600 | 620 |
| Totals | 735,297 | 933,509 | 50,720 | 1,719,526 |

(Source: U.S. Forest Service. 1980)

per acre or if large openings exist, it may be desirable to replant the area the following year. See Figure 7-8.

*Hand planting.* Either one person or a two-person crew can successfully plant seedlings. If planting is done by one individual, that person carries the trees, operates the planting tool, and plants the trees properly. If done by a two-person crew, one person carries the planting tray containing the seedlings, keeps them from drying out, places each seedling in the planting hole at the proper depth, shakes it to see that the taproot is straight, and holds it in place while the second person closes the hole with a planting tool.

The second individual in the crew is responsible for opening and closing the hole and for the proper spacing of the trees.

Planting with a two-person crew is much easier, since the individuals can alternate positions, making the job less tiring.

Seedlings distributed by forest tree nurseries are bare-rooted. That is, the seedlings do not come balled in dirt. While this may account for some mortality, the loss is offset by the ease of transportation, handling, and planting. Cost is also a factor, since bare-rooted stock can be sold much more cheaply.

*Planting bar.* The planting bar, known otherwise as a dibble, is one of the best tools for planting seedlings. It is inexpensive, allows for speed in planting, and can be effectively used to compact soil around the roots; however, if used carelessly, poor survival can be expected.

The planting bar has four parts: handle, shaft, foot step, and

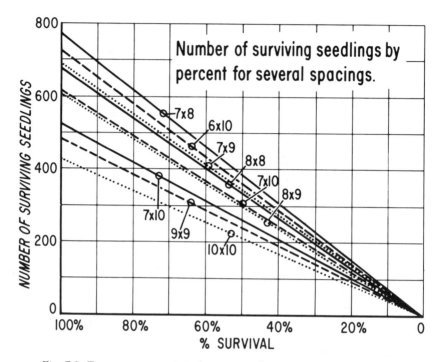

Fig. 7-8. Trees per acre at initial spacing and varying percentages of survival. (Courtesy U.S. Forest Service)

blade (Figures 7-9 and 7-10). The handle of ⅞-inch round pipe is welded to the top of the shaft of similar-sized pipe. The wedge-shaped steel blade is usually 8 to 10 inches long and about 3 inches wide, tapering to a sharp edge at the base. A foot step extends horizontally 4 inches from the top of the blade.

A sharpshooter, a long, narrow-bladed shovel, may be effectively used to plant seedlings. In some parts of the country a matlock is also used; in others, a mechanical auger is employed.

*Machine planting.* Machine planting with a mechanical tree planter (Figures 7-11 and 7-12) is much faster than hand planting. A tractor, a mechanical planter, and a two-person crew can set out 7,000 to 10,000 seedlings a day on suitable sites. Some mechanical planters utilize three workers, two of whom are planters.

Mechanical tree planters vary in design and operation. They can be divided into two groups. In one, the mechanical unit is hitched firmly to a tractor and is raised and lowered by a hydraulic unit. In

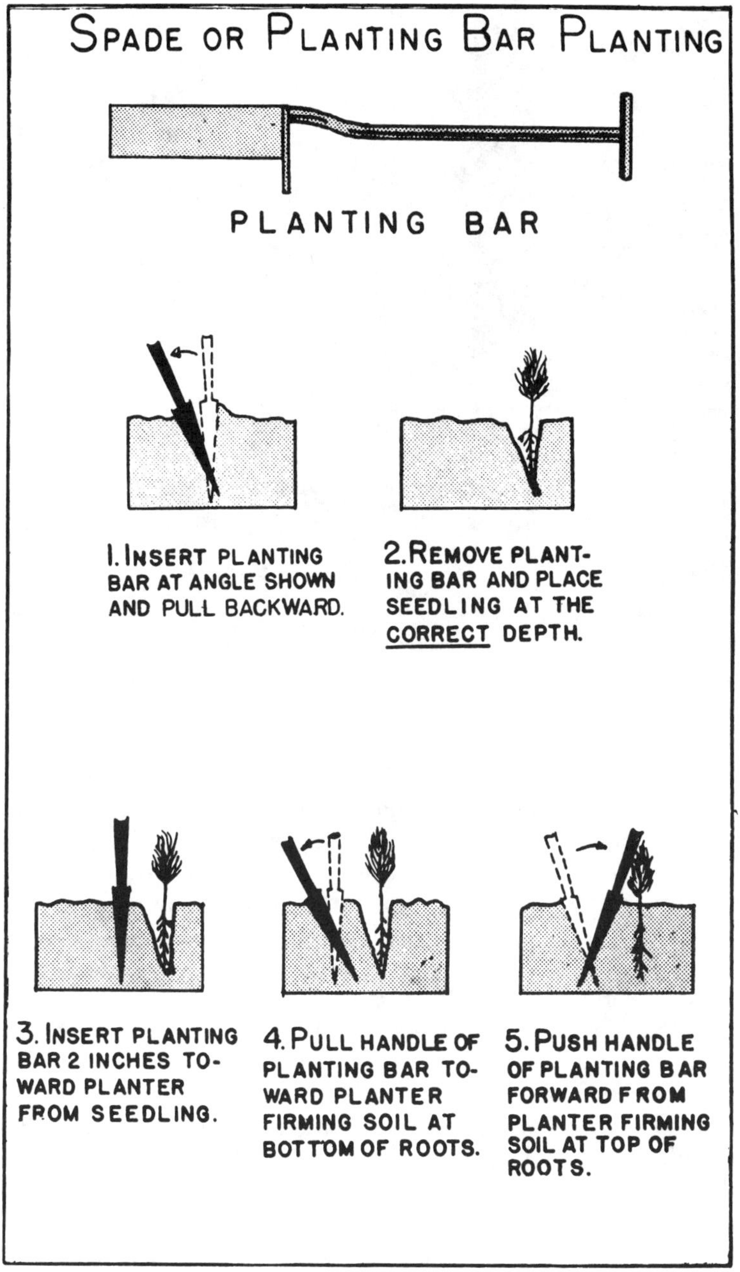


Fig. 7-9. Proper planting with planting bar or dibble.

Fig. 7-10. Planting crew using planting bars or dibbles to establish seedlings on a non-productive area. (Courtesy Kentucky Division of Forestry)

the other, the planting machine operates independently of the tractor, which merely serves as the power source.

Tractor power for a tree-planting machine can be a small- or medium-sized crawler tractor or a farm-type wheel tractor.

In operation, a planting machine has a furrow opener which opens a trench in the soil in which the seedlings are placed. Behind the furrow opener are two packing wheels which close the hole and firm the soil around the roots (Figure 7-13). Generally a coulter is in front of the furrow opener which cuts roots and the soil to a shallow depth.

Two persons are used in planting trees with a mechanical tree planter. One drives the tractor while the other operates the planter. These planting machines are equipped with a container to carry seedlings, seats, and foot rests.

As the furrow is opened, the person in the tree planter places seedlings in the opening at the proper spacing, setting them properly in the hole and holding the seedling until it is gripped by the soil.

Fig. 7-11. Planting of seedlings with a machine planter. (Courtesy Illinois Division of Forest Resources)

In some areas, planting machines can be rented at a nominal cost from a state forestry agency or Soil Conservation District. There are also private contractors that will plant for a landowner for a fee. Prices vary as to the condition of the planting site, number of trees to be planted, and travel distance. Costs may range from $30 to $100 or more per thousand trees planted, including labor and seedlings.

Whether planting pine seedlings with a machine or by hand, there are certain procedures that must be followed:

1.  Plant a seedling slightly lower, never higher, than it grew in the nursery.
2.  Plant seedlings in an upright position with the roots straight down. Do not double up roots. Trees whose roots were doubled up may survive for a period but will grow slowly and be subject to windfall.
3.  Always pack soil firmly around the roots to hold trees in an upright position.
4.  Plant only one tree in a given spot.

Fig. 7-12. Worker riding behind planter placing seedlings in furrow. (Courtesy Illinois Division of Forest Resources)

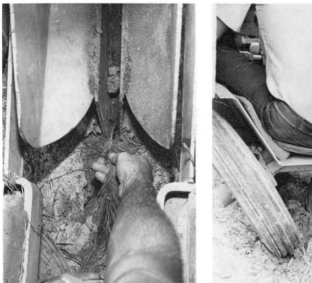

Fig. 7-13. Left, seedling being placed in trench made by furrow opener. Right, seedling being packed in by packing wheels. (Courtesy Texas Forest Service)

## TREE FERTILIZATION

While tree fertilization (Figure 7-14) has been found to be of some benefit, there is still an uncertainty about physical gains that might be realized, considering the cost. There is also the question of environmental impacts.

The forest industries are leaders in investigative work on tree fertilization. Thousands of acres, mainly of Douglas fir, have been fertilized on the Pacific Coast. Good response has been reported in the South from the addition of nitrogen in older stands and phosphorus in poorly drained pine flatwoods of the Gulf and Atlantic coastal plain.

The use of fertilizer by a small woodland owner is not recommended at this time. Cost benefits have not been adequately demonstrated.

Fig. 7-14. Flying over a luxuriant young forest, part of which was recently a clear cut Douglas fir stand, a pilot triggers a streamer of fertilizer from the hanging spreader over Georgia-Pacific Corporation lands in Oregon. (Courtesy Georgia-Pacific Corporation)

## *PROTECTING PLANTATION INVESTMENT*

Regardless of how seedlings were established, the plantings have a high potential value (Figure 7-15) and must be protected from wildfire, animals, insects, and diseases. Older plantings are less susceptible to damage from grazing animals and most insects but fire and disease are continued threats to survival and growth.

Fig. 7-15. A plantation with a high potential value. (Courtesy Georgia Forestry Commission)

### *Fire*

To help insure protection from wildfire, an 8- to 12- foot firebreak should be established around a plantation. Additional firebreaks should be established to divide a large planting into 20- to 40-acre blocks. Firebreaks should be maintained.

Discing and maintaining 30-foot strips around and through a

plantation will serve equally well as a good fire barrier. When seedlings are old enough that they are not subject to damage by cattle, these strips could be fertilized and sown to grass for grazing. Cattle would then help maintain the fire barrier.

## Insects

Insects are very important in the forest environment. They have many useful roles in the forest ecosystem including decomposition and serve as predators or parasites of many more destructive insects; however, we often focus on the potentially destructive role of forest insects because of the possible economic impact to the forest landowner.

Harmful forest insects are those that are primarily responsible for economic loss. Trees can be economically damaged by insects in a variety of ways, including insects which damage flowers or seeds of trees, species that are particularly damaging to nursery stock, species that eat foliage (defoliaters), and species that bore into the bark and wood or develop tunnels under the bark.

Many of our forest insects are native to the country and are active within their natural ranges. These native insects generally cause little damage at normal population levels but can be damaging when populations get out of balance. Some of the most destructive insects are introduced from other countries and can cause considerable problems; for example the gypsy moth, the European pine shoot moth, the balsam woolly aphid, and the European pine sawfly.

The causes of insect outbreaks are not well understood by researchers; however, there are some general forest stand conditions which favor insect outbreaks. Outbreaks generally occur in pure stands rather than in stands with a high species diversity. Plantations which offer many other management advantages are a high risk in terms of potential insect problems. Older, overmature stands are also a high risk as is any stand which has suffered significant damage from wind, fire, disease, logging damage, or drought.

Forest insect outbreaks are considerably variable and generally unpredictable in terms of frequency, extent, and duration. Fortunately, most outbreaks are generally small in size and last only a short time. Landowners should carefully examine their stands each year for problems and initiate adequate control measures to prevent potential major outbreaks.

### Diseases

Disease problems of forest stands are frequently closely associated with insect outbreaks or damage. They are primarily caused by various species of fungi. Some disease organisms, such as those causing Dutch elm disease and chestnut blight, attack living, healthy trees and result in quick death. Other diseases, such as heartrot, occur in living but injured or weakened trees.

Fungal diseases are often transmitted by insects through the direct transfer of disease spores from infested to healthy trees. The insects as they move from a diseased host to a healthy tree carry the disease spores along with them and introduce the spore to the healthy individual. Physical damage by insects creating wounds also allows for the entry of airborne or rainborne disease spores.

Fig. 7-16. Stand of pine trees severely damaged by an ice storm. Damaged trees should be sold for pulpwood as soon as possible. Present condition encourages the presence of insects and disease. (Courtesy Texas Forest Service)

## Other Hazards

Young seedlings can be heavily damaged by trampling or grazing of livestock. Sheep and goats will eat seedlings. Grazing or browsing animals will eat the terminal buds. Rabbits may girdle the trunks of seedlings. Deer browse can be a particular problem with high value species such as Christmas trees.

Mice, squirrels, and birds consume most of the seed produced in years when the seed crop is poor.

Young trees may be uprooted and branches may break when ice accumulates (Figure 7-16). This may also occur during high winds, especially on saturated soils. Such trees can be cut or sold.

Rodents can be harmful to small seedlings. Gophers eat lateral roots and taproots and usually sever trees below the ground line. Poisioned bait placed in their tunnels will effectively control them.

## Periodic Inspections

Landowners should make frequent inspections of their forest lands to determine if damage is occurring from whatever cause. Prompt remedial measures should be taken, based on their findings.

### BIBLIOGRAPHY

*Action Needed to Discourage Removal of Trees That Shelter Cropland in the Great Plains*. Publication RED-75-375. Washington, D.C.: Report to Congress, Comptroller General of the United States, 1972.

Balmer, William E., and Williston, Hamlin L. *Guide for Planting Southern Pines*. Atlanta, Ga.: U.S. Forest Service, 1974.

Barnett, James P. *Advances in Container Production of Planting Stock*. Proceedings of Fifth North American Forest Biology Workshop. Gainesville, Fla.: School of Forest Resources and Conservation, University of Florida, and Southeast Forest Experiment Station, in cooperation with the Society of American Foresters, 1978.

Barnett, James P. "Forest Planting and Seeding." *McGraw-Hill Yearbook of Science and Technology: 1978*. New York, N.Y.: McGraw-Hill Book Company, Inc., 1978.

Clark, F. Bryan. *Planting Black Walnut for Timber*. U.S.D.A. Leaflet 487. Washington, D.C.: U.S. Forest Service, 1971.

Davenport, O. M., and Walters, Russell S. *Christmas Tree Culture in Kentucky*. Lexington, Ky.: Kentucky Experiment Station, 1970.

Derr, Harold J., and Mann, William F., Jr. *Direct-Seeding Pines in the South*. Agricultural Handbook 391. Washington, D.C.: U.S. Forest Service, 1973.

Gill, C. E. *Growing Christmas Trees in Virginia*. Publication 507. Blacksburg, Va: Virginia Polytechnic Institute and State University, Extension Division, 1973.

Graber, Raymond. *Summer Planting of Container-Grown Northern Hardwoods.* Research Note NE-263. Broomall, Pa.: Northeastern Forest Experiment Station, 1978.

*Growing Walnut for Profit and Pleasure.* Chicago, Ill.: American Walnut Manufacturers Association, 1969.

Little, S. *Local Seed Sources Recommended for Loblolly Pine in Maryland and Shortleaf Pine in New Jersey and Pennsylvania.* Research Paper NE-l34. Upper Darby, Pa.: Northeast Forest Experiment Station, 1969.

Lohrey, R. E. *Precommercial Thinning of Direct-Seeded Loblolly Pine.* Publication SO-139. New Orleans, La.: Southern Forest Experiment Station, 1973.

Mann, W. F., Jr. *Direct-Seeding Longleaf Pine.* Publication SO-57. New Orleans, La.: Southern Forest Experiment Station, 1970.

Mann, W. F., Jr., and Derr, H. J. *Direct-Seeding Loblolly Pine.* Occasional Paper 188. New Orleans, La.: Southern Forest Experiment Station, 1966.

Marx, Donald H., and Beattie, Daniel J. *Mycorrhizae-Promising Aid to Timber Growers.* Asheville, N.C.: Southeastern Forest Experiment Station, 1978.

Mignery, Arnold L. *Direct Seeding Oaks on the Cumberland Plateau in Tennessee.* Publication SO-107. New Orleans, La.: Southern Forest Experiment Station, 1975.

*Planting California Forest Land.* Leaflet 2925. Berkeley, Calif.: Division of Agricultural Sciences, University of California, 1978.

*Proceedings: Second Symposium on Southeastern Hardwoods.* Dothan, Ala.: Southeastern Area, State and Private Forestry, Southern and Southeastern Forest Experiment Stations, and Alabama Forestry Commission, 1977.

Read, Ralph A. *Windbreaks for the Central Great Plains. How to Use Trees to Protect Land and Crops.* Leaflet 1. Lincoln, Neb.: Rocky Mountain Forest and Range Experiment Station, 1965.

*Seeds of Woody Plants in the United States.* Agricultural Handbook 450. Washington, D.C.: U.S. Forest Service, 1974.

Tinus, Richard W., and McDonald, Stephen E. *How to Grow Tree Seedlings in Containers in Greenhouses.* General Technical Report RM-60. Fort Collins, Colo.: State and Private Forestry, Rocky Mountain Region and Rocky Mountain Forest and Range Experiment Station, 1979.

*Tree Planting Pays Well.* Publication 67. Charlottesville, Va.: Department of Conservation of Development, Virginia Forest Service, 1970.

U.S. Forest Service. *Insects of Eastern Forests.* Miscellaneous Publication 1426. Washington, D.C., 1985.

U.S. Forest Service. *A Report of the U.S. Forest Service on Planting, Seeding and Silvical Treatments in the United States.* Publication FS-368. Washington, D.C., 1980.

van Buijtenen, J. P., *et al. Introduction to Practical Forest Tree Improvement.* Circular 207. College Station, Tex.: Texas Forest Service, 1976.

Williston, Hamlin L., and Balmer, W. E. *Direct Seeding of Southern Pines: A Regeneration Alternative.* Forest Management Bulletin. Atlanta, Ga.: Southeastern Area, State and Private Forestry, 1977.

CHAPTER VIII

# The Economics of Forest
# Resources Management

Forest resources are managed for both economic and social values.
They have economic value when they yield an income. Timber,
grazing, recreation, water, minerals, fish, and wildlife are
income-producing values. These same resources have certain social values which may not be income producing but still have
worth in terms of the public good or interest.

Social values are generally those related to aesthetic considerations such as the scenic qualities of the forest area. Others are
concerned with biological aspects such as the uniqueness of the
plants and animals found in a forest locale. Timbered areas with
suitable topography for water reservoirs are being inundated for
water storage. Forests with high social values are being set aside
to preserve them for the future in the form of public and private
parks and monuments. Some of these areas may have concurrent
uses for other purposes, such as recreation, as well as being established as "biological preserves."

Obviously, conflicts arise between economic and social values or
uses for forest land. Areas flooded for water reservoirs or set aside in
preserves can no longer supply timber as raw material for wood-
using industries. On the other hand, small areas of virgin trees may
be saved from cutting to serve as examples of the "original" forest.
Many timber growers in all parts of the nation are setting aside forest
areas of unique social worth.

More and more attention is being given to social needs as they
relate to the forest resources of the United States. Many areas are set
aside in preserves without regard to the scientific management of the
land and the animals and plants found on it. Such preserves prohibit
many needed cultural practices to maintain the overall health of the
forest; for example, on most preserves, no cutting of timber is

allowed. Yet a salvage cutting is necessary when trees are attacked by insects and diseases. The removal of sick trees in many instances is the principal means of preventing outbreaks from destroying whole forests.

In addition to social values, the biology of trees should also be understood. In understanding the tree's biology, one must know *how* the tree grows and *what* must be done to accelerate forest growth. On the other hand, the economics of forestry emphasizes *why* the tree must be grown and *how* the forest's resources can be apportioned to produce the greatest good.

## THE ECONOMIC IMPORTANCE OF THE FOREST RESOURCE

Forests are important the world over. Table 8-1 shows estimated softwood, hardwood, and total cubic volumes of the world's forests. The Soviet Union and North America possess most of the world's softwood volume. About one-half of the world's hardwood volume is found in the tropical forests of Latin America with much of the remainder located in the forests of Africa and Asia.

TABLE 8-1

**FOREST GROWING STOCK IN THE WORLD, BY AREA AND SPECIES GROUP, 1973**

| Region or Country | Closed forests[1] and open woodlands | | | |
|---|---|---|---|---|
| | All Species | Softwoods | Hardwoods Temperate | Tropical |
| | . . . . . . . . . . . . . (billion cubic feet) . . . . . . . . . . . . . | | | |
| North America | 1,288 | 953 | 335 | —[3] |
| Latin America | 3,260 | 92 | 166 | 3,002 |
| Europe | 526 | 335 | 191 | —[3] |
| Africa[2] | 2,134 | 4 | 11 | 2,119 |
| Asia-Pacific (except Japan) | 1,330 | 201 | 176 | 953 |
| Japan | 71 | 39 | 32 | —[3] |
| U.S.S.R. | 2,790 | 2,366 | 424 | —[3] |
| Total | 11,399 | 3,990 | 1,335 | 6,074 |

[1]Forest land with 20 per cent or more tree crown cover.
[2]Includes the Near East.
[3]Not represented in the region.

(Source: *An Analysis of the Timber Situation in the United States, 1952-2030*, adapted from Table 4-11, p. 187, U.S. Forest Service Review Draft, 1980)

From reproducing a forest to the sale of finished wood products, considerable value is pumped into the nation's economy. Values are added at each step in the growing, harvesting, manufacturing, constructing, transporting, and marketing processes. The sum total of all kinds of timber-based economic activities amounted to over $40 billion in 1977, the last year for which statistics are available. This was 1.7 per cent of the total gross domestic product (GDP). About 1.4 million people were employed in various forest-based activities, accounting for 1.7 per cent of the nation's total full-time work force. (Present values are currently estimated to be considerably more than the 1977 figures.)

Grazing of forest ranges by livestock is a multimillion dollar industry in the United States. In addition to the value for livestock, considerable forage and food is made available to wildlife. Its value is appropriately combined with that of recreation.

Outdoor recreation, much of which occurs on forest land, is of increasing importance and will become a major economic factor in the future use of forest land. The total recreation industry is a multibillion dollar business in the United States. The annual leasing of these lands for hunting and fishing in the South alone is estimated at about $60 billion and has a potential of over five times as much.

Although no value estimates are available, considerable economic contribution is made through the production of minerals and the yield of water on forest lands. Minerals would include oil and gas production, gravel and stone, to name a few. Coal production is again becoming economically significant, and the value of water is increasing sharply with the increases in population and the construction of huge reservoirs to make more efficient use of existing water supplies.

## ECONOMIC FACTORS OF FORESTRY

Certain economic factors affect the cost of producing timber. These include the cost of forest land, timber-growing practices, taxes, forest credit, logging costs, timber supply and demand, and return on investments.

### Forest Land Costs

The price of land capable of and available for producing timber has risen sharply in the United States in the last three decades. Increased returns from growing timber, pressure from other uses, and inflation are some of the reasons. Forest land prices have increased steadily since the 1930's when cutover land in many parts of the United States was practically worthless. Much of this land was purchased for $1 per acre or less. Current land prices (land less timber, improvements, etc.) are $400 to $1,500 or more per acre when it is located near metropolitan centers or development areas.

It is difficult to determine exactly how much forest land is worth because of the difference in productivity between growing sites and the variation in timber values, in terms of both ease of logging and variation in future prices. The average value of land alone currently ranges from $400 to $600 per acre, and the value of land with timber ready for harvest ranges from $400 to $1,600 per acre.

## COSTS OF TIMBER-GROWING PRACTICES

The costs of growing timber have also risen sharply in recent years. Recent studies show that almost all timber-growing costs in the South have more than tripled since 1967 (Table 8-2).

Unfortunately, many forest lands receive little or no expenditures for improved management.

Despite the fact that much of the nation's forest land is not now managed to anywhere near its biological or economic potential, apparently opportunities exist for cost effective management which, if

TABLE 8-2

PER ACRE COSTS OF TIMBER GROWING IN THE SOUTH,
1961, 1967, 1974, 1976, AND 1980

| Practice | 1961 | 1967 | 1974 | 1976 | 1980 |
|---|---|---|---|---|---|
| Prescription burning | $ 0.68 | $ 1.60 | $ 2.51 | $ 3.65 | $ 2.95 |
| Site preparation | 14.09 | 23.52 | 48.01 | 73.36 | 93.09 |
| Hand planting | 14.67 | 20.52 | 48.06 | 48.06 | 46.60 |
| Machine planting | 10.80 | 14.31 | 29.70 | 34.56 | 40.90 |
| Poisoning | 7.93 | 10.17 | 22.86 | 23.41 | — |
| Girdling | 4.93 | 8.08 | — | — | — |
| Estimating (cruising) | 0.41 | 0.74 | 1.03 | 1.18 | 1.77 |
| Marking | 2.10 | 3.09 | 4.96 | 8.05 | 7.14 |
| Precommercial thinning | — | — | — | 25.97 | — |

exploited, would significantly increase future timber supplies. According to a recent U.S. Forest Service study, there is a potential for intensifying management on 168 million areas of forest land. The economic return from the needed investment would be 4 per cent or more. With more extensive management, net annual growth could be increased by 12.9 billion cubic feet—an additional yield amounting to over 70 per cent of the entire volume of timber harvested in 1976. It would take several decades to achieve these results and would require an estimated $15.2 billion investment. Table 8-3 summarizes the results of the study by region.

**TABLE 8-3**

**ECONOMIC OPPORTUNITIES FOR INCREASING TIMBER SUPPLIES[1]**

| Region | Area Treated Thousand Acres | Total Cost Million Dollars | Average Cost/Acre Dollars | Net Annual Growth Increment Million Cubic Feet |
|---|---|---|---|---|
| Northeast | 16,340 | 725.3 | 22.5 | 414.9 |
| North Central | 18,527 | 1,743.7 | 94 | 1,127.3 |
| Southeast | 53,155 | 4,917.7 | 94 | 4,486.9 |
| South Central | 63,604 | 5,133.4 | 81 | 4,605.9 |
| Rocky Mountains | 222 | 25.8 | 116 | 8.2 |
| Pacific Northwest | 8,830 | 1,833.1 | 208 | 1,481.3 |
| Pacific Southwest | 7,668 | 784.1 | 102 | 760.5 |
| Totals | 168,346 | 15,163.1 | | |

[1]Includes those opportunities which would yield 4 per cent or more on the investment measured in constant dollars, i.e., net of inflation or deflation. Most of the proposed opportunities involve establishing and maintaining softwood species in the East primarily on private, non-industrial forest lands.

(Source: *An Analysis of the Timber Situation in the United States, 1952-2030*, Tables 9-12 and 9-17, U.S. Forest Service Review Draft, 1980)

## State and Local Taxes

Property or *ad valorem* taxes have generally risen faster than the costs of timber-growing practices. In some instances, state and local taxes have increased five times or more in the last two decades. Annual per-acre *ad valorem* taxes on timberlands may vary from a low of 50 cents to $20 or more. Excessive taxes are a threat to timber growers whose income may be delayed for several decades. Without current income, taxes, plus the interest they accrue, must be paid out of future income. A tax of $1 per acre per year at

8 per cent compound interest adds up to $45.76 after 20 years and to nearly $575 after 50 years.

The system of taxation varies considerably among states. Timberlands are generally assessed as real property on the same basis as other real estate. Land and timber values are usually combined for assessment. In some states, for example, Kentucky, Tennessee, and West Virginia, there is no tax on timber. Many states have a severance or cutting tax based upon the volume of timber products removed. In Alabama, Florida, and Louisiana the severance tax is a yield tax in place of the *ad valorem* tax. In Arkansas, Oregon, and Virginia, for example, the severance tax is an excise tax for general or special revenue purposes and is in addition to local *ad valorem* taxes.

### Federal Income Taxes

The federal income tax is one applied to timber after it is cut. Timber is considered a capital asset. Before the recent revision in the federal income tax, income from the cutting of timber held the length of time required by the Internal Revenue Code was considered capital gain and taxed at a rate substantially lower than that required for ordinary income. Capital gain income status can still be important under the new income tax code even though net capital gain will be taxed at the same rates as ordinary income. The benefits accrue from the treatment of losses and the fact that long-term capital gains are not taxable for social security reasons. Under the new law, capital losses can be used to offset only $3,000 of ordinary income per year; however, there is no limit on using capital losses to offset capital gains. Thus, timber owners who incur large capital losses from any source can use a greater proportion of those losses in any year they have capital gain income. Timber growers should consult a tax preparer or an attorney for compliance with the new regulations. Also, the cooperative extension service continues to be a source on tax matters.

In addition to capital gains, owners are allowed deductions for their depletable basis in timber. This is frequently referred to as the timber depletion unit. This unit (value) is established at purchase time for each timber product by species and inserted in a timber account. After each sale, the depletion unit for each product may be deducted and federal income tax paid only on the remaining income.

## Forest Credit

In the past it has been difficult, if not impossible, to use timber as collateral for loan purposes. As a result, many timber growers have had to liquidate their timber to meet financial obligations. Suitable sources of credit have been a major handicap to improving levels of management on timberlands.

In recent years forest credit has become more readily available, although loans are still made on a very selective basis. Principal sources are the Federal Land Bank system, Farmers Home Administration, some nationally chartered savings banks, and several insurance companies. The rate of interest, method of payment, length of loan, and size of the loan based upon a percentage of the appraised value vary, depending upon the market for money and the lending institution.

## Timber Value

The value of stumpage, or the price received for trees where they stand in the woods, varies according to the individual stand. No two timber stands have identical value. Some of the more important reasons include (1) timber quality, including tree size; (2) timber quantity on a per acre and total basis offered for sale; (3) nearness to a mill; (4) ease of logging; and (5) condition of the haul roads, to name a few. Most important are the products the timber will yield and their values and the extent of competition for them in the area where the timber is growing.

Determining the value of timber is called "stumpage appraisal." Stumpage usually represents a residual value after the costs of harvesting, transportation, processing, and some margin for operator profit have been subtracted from the value of the product made from the timber. Placing a value on timber from which a number of products can be made is more difficult. However, a method called "appraisal by comparison" where the price set for a stand of timber is compared to average prices established in previous transactions can be used.

## Logging Costs

The cost of removing timber from forest land has increased dramatically in the past two decades. Rising labor costs, increases in equipment investments, reductions in the availability of large-sized timber, and large-volume sales are just a few of the factors. The trend is to cut long logs, cut tree lengths, and to scale by weight. Large tree harvesters have been developed for logging large tracts. Small crews and trucks are still used on smaller tracts.

Accessibility of timber for cutting is an important factor in logging costs. It is generally good in most of the South and parts of the North and West where the terrain may be flat or gently rolling. Steep or mountainous terrain and wet or swampy ground are the biggest handicaps. Many wet areas are accessible for only a few months of the year.

The logging of small tracts under 40 acres creates problems for mechanized logging. Small, poorly stocked tracts may be suitable for small crews with bobtail trucks but may have to be passed up by large tree harvesters.

Logging costs generally run about 50 per cent of the cost of sawtimber and poletimber delivered to a mill. In terms of pulpwood, the logging cost is about three-fourths of the delivered price.

### Timber Supply and Demand

Generally, there is no current shortage of softwood timber in the United States. Certain specific product shortages may occur—for example, plywood timber or poles—but the present overall picture is good. The story for hardwood timber nationwide is not nearly so good. Critical shortages occur for many species, especially for the more desirable woods such as black walnut. The U.S. timber demand is expected to increase from a little over 13 billion cubic feet in 1977 to almost 23 billion cubic feet in 2030.

The softwood timber resources of the United States are in only fair condition. Statistics for 1986 reveal that the annual softwood timber growth exceeded its harvest by about 7 per cent. The situation is more favorable in the North and South than it is in the West due to old-growth timber harvests. Hardwood timber resources as of 1986 showed a favorable growth-cut ratio which was much larger than that for softwood timber. Annual U.S. hardwood growth greatly exceeded cut by 70 per cent, but much of this growth occurred on the undesirable species or cull trees.

There will continue to be removals of both hardwood and softwood timberland by changes in land use such as clearing for cropland, highways, housing developments, reservoirs, and with-drawals of forest lands for parks or other non-timber uses. The U.S. Forest Service estimates that 27 million acres of forest land were lost between 1962 and 1977, a 5 per cent drop from 509 million acres to 482 million. The decline has occurred in all regions but was greatest in the South. By 2030, a further decline to 446 million acres is projected. Nevertheless, softwood timber supply in the South is expected to increase from 4.2 billion cubic feet in 1976 to 7.5 billion cubic feet in 2030. Substantial increases are expected in the North and in the Rocky Mountains, but these will still be minor additions to national softwood timber supply. Softwood timber supply is expected to drop in the Pacific Coast region from 4 billion cubic feet in 1976 to 3.7 billion cubic feet in 2030. Hardwood timber supply is projected to double between 1976 and 2030, rising from 3.3 to 7.7 billion cubic feet. The South is expected to account for almost 60 per cent of the increase.

Not all timber volume is available to a mill or is placed on the open market. Much timber is captive in the sense that it is owned by a wood-using industry or obligated to it through a contractual arrangement. Some timber is owned by persons who feel no economic compunction to sell and are not motivated by price. Additional volumes of timber are held entirely for aesthetic purposes and may never be cut. Time may alter these conditions so that most timber growth over the long run may be available for some utilization.

Timber demand, or the quantity required from the open market, generally establishes its price. Demand for timber, however, is a product of the demand for finished wood items such as paper, building boards, lumber, poles, and piling. Therefore, the price paid for timber is really a product of the price paid for the finished materials. Inventories of timber at mills will alter this relationship in the short run.

Prior to 1958, timber demand in the United States was strong. Timber growers had little problem in finding suitable markets for their timber. Since that time, with the increase in available timber supplies, growers have experienced some short-term periods of slow, or in a few cases, even non-existent, demand. Recent sharp demand increases in the 1970's and 1980's have led to much higher prices.

Demand varies between (1) softwoods and hardwoods, (2) individual species, (3) products to be harvested, and (4) the location of the timber. The demand for softwood generally exceeds that for hardwood. The latter is increasing, however, and closing the gap between it and softwood. Demand for timber also varies between states; for example, the demand for pulpwood in the Southeast may be stronger than elsewhere in the nation.

Variable timber demand, however, places a greater burden upon timber growers to produce higher qualities and quantities of raw material required by plants within hauling distance of their lands. It also requires that they become more observant of timber markets and that they apply good selling practices.

### Forest Investment Returns

In most instances, returns on forest investments are less than the 10 per cent expected by industry for investments in manufacturing. Exceptions to this rule are returns received from timber stand improvement efforts on most sites, timber production on the very best sites, and short periods of unusually high demand causing record (or near record) prices. Recent emphasis on shortening the length of rotations, say to something less than 50 years, also

Fig. 8-1. Small-diameter logs in a pulpwood storage yard. Pulpwood provides the raw material for the multibillion-dollar southern pulp and paper industry. (Courtesy Department of Forestry, University of Illinois)

increases the potential for improvement in returns. The average annual per cent of growth, sometimes called increment, is greater for stands from 0 to age 30 than from 0 to age 60. The effect of interest upon costs invested in improved management practices is greatly lessened by harvesting the stand at age 30 than by holding it, along with costs at interest, until age 60 or more. Returns from average and good sites generally compare favorably with those from bank accounts and stocks and bonds. Some risk is involved, but it is not unusually great after stands are well established. Salvage value of damaged stands may closely approach original value. Long-term returns compare favorably with those from other conservative investments.

Historical appreciation has generally increased both land and timber values. Studies in the South have shown long-term average annual land values have increased by about 5 per cent and short-term averages have increased by as high as 15 per cent. In the most recent decade, some softwood timber prices have fallen; hardwood prices have increased or remained the same.

Timber growers with bare or poorly stocked stands should invest in planting, timber stand improvement, or other management practices to increase land and timber values many times over. The many small timber growers who feel no obligation to improve the productivity of their stands are costing the United States billions of dollars a year in economic loss.

## MARKETING TIMBER

Making a profitable timber sale is the best incentive to improved management of timberlands. Poor sales will likely lead to improper cutting practices, reduced timber income, and loss of interest in growing timber as a crop; however, most timber growers do an inadequate job of marketing timber.

Timber may be sold in several ways. These include (1) lump sum, (2) individual tree, (3) tree scale, (4) load scale, and (5) weight. Lump sum refers to the payment made at one time for a total price for all products or trees to be sold. Individual tree sales may be made on the basis of so much per tree for high-value products like veneer bolts and poles and piling. Tree scale would be on the basis of so much per thousand board feet or cords. Load scale refers to measurement of the log or bolt load at the mill or concentration point (usually traditional dimensional measurement techniques). Finally, weight involves the sale of timber for a set price per ton weight of wood fiber.

The business of selling timber for the highest returns involves following certain timber-marketing practices. These steps include (1) marking and estimating timber by the products to be sold, (2) selling the timber for the highest-value products first, (3) offering the timber to several buyers on a bid basis, and (4) selling the timber by the use of a written contract (Appendix XII). It should be noted that the contract serves only as a guide and may be used by a lawyer competent in timber harvesting to develop one for each individual timber sale.

In step one, timber should be marked and its volume estimated by the volume it will bring so that only trees that should be cut will be removed, and enough timber will be left for good rates of future growth or natural regeneration. Due to the variability in values for timber products, it is necessary that the owners know what they have to sell. The only way this can be done is to have a timber cruise made by a competent person, preferably a professional forester. Generally, consultants are available for hire to represent timber growers.

For example, pulpwood prices may vary as much as $10 per cord, sawtimber as much as $100 per thousand board feet, poles and piling as much as $100 per piece, and hardwood veneer bolts as much as $500 or more per thousand board feet. There is no way to determine timber values except by a timber cruise.

The second step is to sell the timber by its highest-value product first. In the case of softwood, this would be poles and piling, then sawtimber, followed by fence posts and pulpwood in that order of value. In the case of hardwood, it would be veneer logs, sawtimber, cross-ties, and then pulpwood.

For example, the difference in value might be emphasized by looking at one individual tall, straight, high-quality pine tree about 14 inches in diameter at a point about 4½ feet above the ground. This individual tree could be sold for poles, sawtimber, or pulpwood. Using current prices, it would have a value of about $3.50 for pulpwood, about $15 for sawtimber, or about $20 for poles. These varied prices occur for the same identical high-quality tree. For this reason, the owner would want to sell the poles prior to allowing the sawtimber and pulpwood cutters to enter the stand because they might remove potential pole trees for products of lesser value. This is the case for pine and other softwoods, but even greater variations exist for quality hardwood timber.

One word of caution is that it requires enough volume of the individual products to interest a buyer. Pole buyers are unable to come into a stand for just a few trees. It takes a good many of them before they can economically move their equipment to a site to harvest poles; however, if an owner has just a few poles they might be combined with a sale of poles from the forest lands of a nearby neighbor in order to provide enough volume to interest a buyer and take advantage of even better prices. This may not only be true for poles but also for all other timber products as well.

It should be emphasized that only a few trees in an ordinary stand of timber are suitable for the higher classes of poles—perhaps less than 5 per cent of the trees. This is one reason that poles command a very high value.

The third step is to offer the timber to several buyers. This step is important if the owner wants to be assured of the best price, because it helps introduce competition into the bid. It's the only way the owner can be sure of a fair price because each stand of timber has its own unique value. Since timber values are based on a variety of factors, timber growers are unable to use prices paid for other stands of timber as an absolute guide, because these factors will vary between two stands.

When offering timber for sale on a bid basis, an owner should ask each buyer to bid on the timber. This may be done in writing. However, the top price may not be the only consideration. Many tree farmers wisely sell their timber for less than the top bid price because they prefer to sell to a reputable timber buyer who has done a good job in harvesting timber from their lands or their neighbor's lands in the past.

Finally, a written contract should be used to protect the interests of the timber grower as well as those of the timber buyer. A written contract should be simple but should include all items agreed upon. Its use may save costly court litigation.

A suitable contract may include some of the following points:

1. The names of the buyer and seller and a description of the property and its location.
2. The price and method of payment on the basis of species, products, and units of measurement.
3. The understanding that trees to be cut will receive two paint marks of a specified color, one at the ground line and one at eye level.

4. Trees to be utilized to the lowest top diameter of a specified product.
5. The guarantee that the timber stand, other improvements, and the land will be protected from fire and excessive logging damage.
6. A specific termination date.
7. The title to the timber guaranteed by the seller.
8. Prohibition of the buyer's reassigning the contract without the written consent of the seller.

## FOREST MANAGEMENT PLANS

An integral part of making the most economical use of forest resources is the development of suitable forest management plans. Forest management plans have been developed for many years for public forest lands, such as national forests and state forests, and for industrial forest holdings and many large individual timber ownerships. Relatively few small private ownerships have utilized them.

These plans are the basis on which management decisions are made. They enable timber growers to allocate their time and financial resources most economically to obtain maximum timber production and return from their forest lands. Forest management plans are required for participation in the Forest Incentives Program, a financial assistance program available to small forest landowners through county A.S.C.S. offices.

Many timber growers operating their holdings without forest management plans make mistakes in handling their woodlands. Timber is harvested prematurely or is overdue for cutting, depending upon the financial needs of the individual. Undertaking management practices such as planting, thinning or other intermediate cuts, hardwood control, fire and pest protection, and others may be initiated or delayed, based upon a hasty decision. Spur-of-the-moment forestry decisions are not conducive to maximizing timber output and returns. In some cases, these efforts may result in a waste of time and money.

Timber growing is an extensive form of land use with minimal returns. Expenditures or investments must be made with care because of the delay in replacing these expenditures with income. This delay may be up to 20 years or more during which time interest is accruing. As a result, timber growers cannot afford to undertake forest management activities without careful planning by competent persons.

In addition to management costs, the current investment in land and timber also necessitates determined efforts to plan management practices to assure maximum returns. Land and timber prices in recent times have reached all-time highs. A 100-acre timber tract may be valued as high as $50,000 to $60,000 and a 1,000-acre forest may be valued for as much as $400,000 to $800,000. Investments of this type require professional management.

Properly designed forest management plans will help timber growers to maximize net returns; that is, gross income less all costs including reasonable interest on the investment. This must be done on a sustained or long-term basis, especially as a result of increasing costs due to rising labor rates and land taxes.

A management plan serves as a guide to enable timber growers to make decisions based on factual information developed from and for their forest land. Basic data on the forest resources are assembled from an on-the-ground inventory, including a cruise of the timberland, and then recorded and analyzed on the basis of the timber grower's intent of ownership, management practice needs, and timber markets. These considerations are used to prepare a workable management plan to cover specific periods of time—say 5, 10, or more years in the future.

Plans for improved management of timber may be simple or elaborate, depending upon the value of the stand and the owner's needs. Basic information in management plans generally includes:

1. A cruise or inventory of the timber stand by species, size, distribution, and volume by products.
2. A map showing boundaries, streams, roads, other improvements, and timber types by species, size, condition, and acreage.
3. An estimate of growth rates by species.
4. An evaluation of site index or timber capability.
5. An estimate or evaluation of income and its potential.
6. A description of stand condition by timber types.
7. Recommendations regarding needed management practices such as protection, planting, and hardwood control, with cost estimates including cutting along with estimates of returns.

Management plans are best prepared by professional foresters who are equipped by training and experience to make the most effective use of the timber and other forest resources.

## FOREST MANAGEMENT ASSISTANCE

Timber growers may receive professional forestry assistance (Figure 8-2) from a variety of private and public sources. Public sources include the state forestry agencies, the agricultural extension services, the Soil Conservation Service, and on a very limited basis the U.S. Forest Service.

Fig. 8-2. An extension forester collecting tree growth data. Forest management assistance is available to timber growers from public agencies, wood-using industries, and consulting foresters. (Courtesy Department of Forestry, University of Illinois)

Private sources include wood-using industries and consulting foresters. Industrial foresters may assist owners on timber marking and estimating and general management practices, but their assistance of necessity is limited. In some instances, industries sponsor "tree farm family" programs, and they will provide fairly comprehensive plans for participating timber growers. Consulting foresters are professional persons available for hire to provide indepth assistance to timber growers. They are especially effective in making the most profitable timber sale for an owner.

Offices of the state forestry agencies and county agricultural agents have lists of professional consulting foresters. These offices will also be able to furnish timber growers with information on other services available.

### BIBLIOGRAPHY

*An Assessment of the Forest and Range Land Situation in the United States.* Review Draft. Washington, D.C.: U.S. Forest Service, 1979.

Condrell, W. K., Tierny, J. E., and Siegel, W. C. "Timber and Tax Reform: An Overview of Recent Changes." Reprinted from *Taxes—The Tax Magazine,* 65 (7): 411-433, 1987.

Congress of the United States. Office of Technology Assessment. *Wood Use: U.S. Competitiveness and Technology,* 1983.

Crothers, C. M. *Midsouth Pulpwood Prices–1977.* Volume 42:2. New Orleans, La.: Southern Pulp and Paper Manufacturer, 1979.

*The Demand and Price Situation for Forest Products, 1976-77.* Miscellaneous Publication 1357. Washington, D.C.: U.S. Forest Service, 1977.

Duerr, W. A. *Fundamentals of Forestry Economics.* New York, N.Y.: McGraw-Hill Book Company, Inc., 1960.

*Forest Farmers, Manual Edition.* Atlanta, Ga.: Forest Farmers Association, 1975.

Gregory, G. R. *Forest Resource Economics.* New York, N.Y.: The Ronald Press Company, 1972.

"Landowner's Manual, Forest Management Shortcourse." Forestry Department, Cooperative Extension Service, University of Georgia, Revised 1970.

*Louisiana Forest Products Quarterly Market Report.* Volume XXV:3. Baton Rouge, La.: Louisiana Department of Agriculture, November, 1979.

*A Method for Appraising Multiple-Product Sales of Southern Pine Stumpage.* F.S. Research Paper SO-126. New Orleans, La.: Southern Forest Experiment Service, U.S. Forest Service, 1976.

Moak, J. E., Kucera, J. M., and Watson, W. F. "Current Costs and Cost Trends for Forestry Practices in the South," *Forest Farmer,* March, 1977.

*Publications for the Forest Land Manager and Users of Forest Resources in the South.* Atlanta, Ga.: Southeastern Area, State and Private Forestry, U.S. Forest Service, 1978.

U.S. Forest Service. *An Analysis of the Timber Situation in the U.S. 1952-2030.* Review Draft, 1980.

U.S. Forest Service. *The Economic Importance of Timber in the United States.* Miscellaneous Publication 941. U.S.D.A. Washington, D.C.: Superintendent of Documents, U.S. Government Printing Office, 1963.

Worrell, A.C. *Economics of American Forestry.* New York, N.Y.: John Wiley and Sons, Inc., 1959.

# CHAPTER IX

# Management of Forest Range

Range management is the science and art of planning and directing range use so as to obtain the maximum in livestock production consistent with the wise use of the range resources. Range is land that is capable of providing forage for grazing or browsing animals. As such, it includes grasslands, shrublands, and forested lands which support an understory of herbaceous vegetation that can be utilized by grazing or browsing animals. Improved pasture lands, cropland pasture, and grazed cropland are not usually classed as range lands because they are often cultivated, seeded, fertilized, or irrigated.

It is estimated that there are 727 million acres of forest land and 770 million acres of range land distributed geographically as follows:

| Region | Forest Land[1] | | Range Land[2] | |
|---|---|---|---|---|
| | Million Acres | Per Cent | Million Acres | Per Cent |
| Pacific Coast | 101 | 14 | 68 | 9 |
| Rocky Mountains & Great Plains | 143 | 20 | 413 | 54 |
| South | 199 | 27 | 116 | 15 |
| North | 165 | 23 | —[3] | —[3] |
| Alaska | 119 | 16 | 173 | 22 |
| Total | 727 | 100 | 770 | 100 |

[1]Forest land includes land that is at least 10 per cent stocked by forest trees of any size. Timberland is forest land capable of producing wood in excess of 20 cubic feet/acre.

[2]Range land is land on which the native vegetation is predominantly grasses, grass-like plants, forbs, or shrubs.

[3]Less than 1 per cent.

(Source: U.S. Forest Service. *An Analysis of the Range Forage Situation in the United States: 1989-2040.* A Technical Document Supporting the 1989 RPA Assessment. Table 1.9, p. 1-20a. Draft, 1988.)

In terms of total livestock grazing, the western states, which include the Great Plains, the Rocky Mountains, and Alaska accounted for 85 per cent of the range lands and 50 per cent of the forest lands in the United States. Although the range lands of the West, and especially the Great Plains, produce the bulk of the national forage and browse, forested areas can also be important sources of forage, particularly for cattle. Thus, while most forest lands of the United States provide some range grazing, it is the western forests, and especially the southern forests in the eastern half of the country, that are of the greatest economic importance (Table 9-1). In a national 1974 report, the South provided about 54 million animal-unit months of grazing compared to about 11 million on the western forest ranges. An animal-unit month is the amount of forage required by a 1,000-pound cow or equivalent in one month.

Private and other non-federal owners have control over three-quarters of the forest lands and 57 per cent of the range lands in the United States. Except for local ordinances and laws, private owners are not restrained concerning use of their lands. They are essentially free to use any system of grazing they wish; however, range management on federal lands is directly controlled by laws and regulations

TABLE 9-1

**PRINCIPAL FOREST RANGE LANDS OF THE UNITED STATES**

| Forest Type | Acres (millions) | Per Cent of Area, U.S. (48 contiguous states) | Million Animal Unit Months of Grazing | Estimated AUM Attainable Goal with Efficient Use of Range by Year 2000 |
|---|---|---|---|---|
| *Western Forests* | | | | |
| Pinyon-juniper woodland | 42.7 | 2.2 | | |
| Ponderosa pine | 37.6 | 2.0 | | |
| Fir-spruce | 24.4 | 1.3 | | |
| Lodgepole pine | 19.1 | 1.0 | | |
| Hardwood (oak and aspen) | 23.4 | 1.2 | | |
| Total | 147.2 | 7.7 | 10.7 | 13.6 |
| *Eastern Forests* (Open forests—South primarily) | | | | |
| Longleaf-slash pine | 20.9 | 1.1 | | |
| Loblolly-shortleaf pine | 55.1 | 2.9 | | |
| Oak-hickory | 125.1 | 6.6 | | |
| Oak-pine | 34.5 | 1.8 | | |
| Oak-gum-cypress | 34.1 | 1.8 | | |
| Total | 269.7 | 14.2 | 53.5 | 132.1 |

(Adapted from U.S.D.A. Interagency Work Group on Range Production Report, June, 1974)

concerning how these lands can be used. The two major federal land managing agencies, the Bureau of Land Management and the U.S. Forest Service, are required to manage public lands under their control in accordance with multiple-use principles and to maintain the productivity of these lands. Livestock grazing is considered one of the multiple uses. Lands such as national parks, wildlife refuges, and military reserves administered by other federal agencies are not necessarily managed for multiple use, and grazing by livestock is often limited or prohibited.

The major difficulty in the management of privately held forest ranges in the South and elsewhere is the integration of grazing and forest management in such a manner that the forest resource can be used without damage to desirable trees and other forest values. Proper control of animal numbers, animal distribution, and grazing seasons must be exercised if tree damage is to be minimized. While private forest lands in the nation will continue to provide native forage for livestock, it should be pointed out that a landowner cannot practice intensive forest management and intensive range management on the same land at the same time. In 1987, it was estimated that almost 85 per cent of the range lands in the South were in poor to fair condition, and forest range was still being exploitively grazed to the detriment of the forest resources. This compares with about 65 per cent in the North, 10 per cent in California, and 65 per cent in the Pacific Northwest.

There is sufficient research information to show that most eastern forest lands, and especially southern forest lands, are much more valuable for timber production than for native forage. This is especially so where there are stands of desirable trees. Forest management should be given first consideration in these areas, with livestock management being a secondary consideration.

Total volume of sawlogs, pulpwood, veneer logs, fuelwood, and other industrial wood produced in the United States in 1986 was almost 18 billion cubic feet. Of this total, about 44 per cent was produced in the South, 33 per cent in the West and 11 per cent in the Northeast. The importance of timber production in the South is obvious, and its importance as the major timber producing region will likely increase. As noted above, the production of forage in the South in forested areas was almost four times greater than in the forests of the West. If the South is to maintain its position as both a wood and a forage producing region, private woodland owners will need to do a much better job of managing their lands for both products without continued destruction of the basic forest resource and probably with the conversion of marginal forest land to improved pasture.

## PAST RANGE USE

From the colonial period until about 1950, forest clearings and cutover forests (Figure 9-1) provided free-range grazing in most areas of the South. It was on this area that an important livestock industry developed. At first the area had unmanaged grazing with poor-quality livestock; subsequently it had better management and improved stock.

The southern forest range livestock industry was based on a minimum investment in labor and capital. Free grazing and a mild climate favored this practice. Livestock were left to forage for themselves. While the return per animal was low, the investment was lower, and a small margin of profit was realized.

Until about 1950 many areas were open range. Some localized areas still remain today, but expansive areas no longer exist since

Fig. 9-1. Scene of a typical longleaf pine open range in the early 1900's. Such areas do not exist today. They have been reseeded or planted and are under fire protection. (Courtesy Texas Forest Service)

landowners have exerted ownership over such land through fencing. What was formerly open range has been primarily converted to the growth of trees.

There is no doubt that beef cattle production has increased in the South. Cattle numbers increased from 28 million in 1950 to 49 million in 1975, 38 million in 1980, and 37 million in 1986. While forest grazing accompanied the increase, improved pastures were the primary source of forage. Fertilizer, plus high yielding species or strains of grasses and legumes, among them coastal bermuda, permitted this increase in beef cattle production. Today there are over 28½ million acres of improved pasture southwide, many acres of which are used to supplement seasonal grazing of native range.

## FORAGE VALUE IN SOUTHERN RANGES

Progressive landowners and stockproducers realize today that one cannot manage improved cattle on forest range alone. The forage is usually deficient in amounts of nutrients required for good animal growth (Figure 9-2). Range management specialists report that lactating cattle generally require a minimum of 7 to 8 per cent crude protein, 0.18 per cent phosphorus, and 0.24 per cent calcium in their diets to maintain reproductive capacity and health. It is obvious from Figure 9-2 that animals will lose vigor and weight if dependence is placed solely on native forage.

While native range forage is inexpensive, it is valuable only when used wisely. Native grasses provide what can be called good forage for three months in the spring and a few weeks in the early fall. During the remaining part of the year the range provides only roughage. To carry the herd during the balance of the year, one must resort to cultivated pastures, concentrated feeds, minerals, and harvested forage.

In Appendix XI, characteristics of the common range grasses of the South are given.

### Grazing in Forest Areas

Grazing, when properly conducted so as not to damage forest values, can be beneficial. It can furnish income to a landowner while a young stand of pines is growing to merchantable size. It also makes use of a resource that would otherwise be wasted.

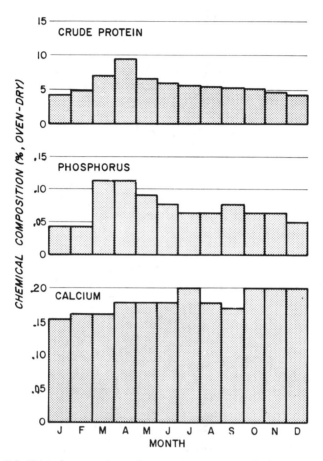

Fig. 9-2. Typical seasonal trends in major nutrients of southern pine native forage. (Courtesy State and Private Forestry, Southeastern Area, U.S. Forest Service)

Grazing also has value in reducing forest fire hazard, which is important to a woodland owner.

In some areas of the South, firebreaks are established around and through plantations and other forest areas as a fire prevention measure. In many instances these firebreaks are disced, fertilized, and seeded to introduce forage species to induce preferential grazing (Figure 9-3). Such practice serves a dual purpose in that it provides improved grazing and a forest fire barrier.

Fig. 9-3. Firebreaks around forest stands which have been fertilized and seeded to introduce forage species induce preferential grazing. Such grazing makes a fire barrier. (Courtesy Texas Forest Service)

To a landowner, grazing provides some monetary return that would not otherwise be realized.

In general, the forage in a forested area is better than in open areas in that a greater variety of plants is present.

Range scientists report that the most ideal native grazing is where open areas, young trees, and mature timber are found together.

## FOREST RANGE TYPES IN THE SOUTH

Forest range types in the South are associated with the various forest types (Figure 1-2). The principal forest range types, as recognized by range specialists, are shown in Figure 9-4.

In general, the amount and value of native forage is inversely proportional to the density of the trees in the forest types (Figure 9-5).

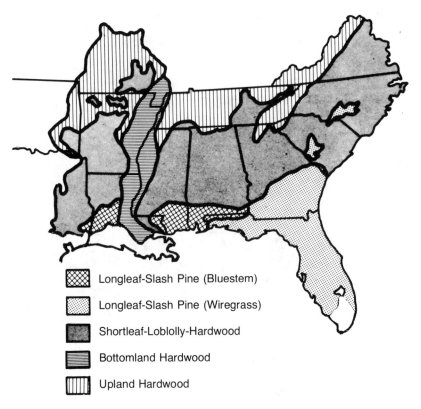

Longleaf-Slash Pine (Bluestem)

Longleaf-Slash Pine (Wiregrass)

Shortleaf-Loblolly-Hardwood

Bottomland Hardwood

Upland Hardwood

Fig. 9-4. Principal forest range types in the South. (Adapted from Forest Management Bulletin, Southeastern Area, State and Private Forestry, U.S. Forest Service)

### Longleaf-Slash Pine Type

Of the approximately 185 million acres of forest land in the southern states, 29 million acres are covered by the longleaf-slash pine forest type, extending from Texas to the Carolinas. The amount of forage in this area is abundant (Figure 9-6). Essentially, the region is a low to rolling plain of sandy loam soils, with slow drainage, and relatively open forests.

Within this forest type two subtypes of herbaceous vegetation are recognized; namely, wiregrass and bluestem. The wiregrass subtype is confined primarily to an area from South Carolina, south to Florida, thence west to Alabama. Forage plants common

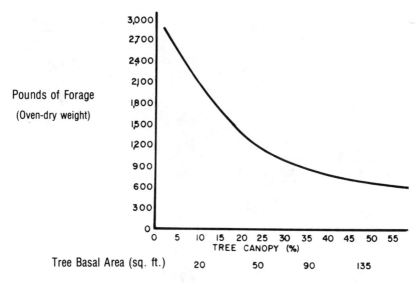

Fig. 9-5. Effect of tree shading on forage yields. (Courtesy U.S. Forest Service)

to this area include Curtis dropseed, yellowsedge bluestem, pine-land three-awn, slender bluestem, carpetgrass, panicums, other grasses, and shrubs. Range scientists report that the forage provides good grazing only from about mid-March through mid-July. Carrying capacity is rated as ranging from about 8 to 30 acres per cow for the available grazing period.

In the bluestem subtype, found principally in the longleaf belt from Mississippi to East Texas, slender bluestem and sandhill bluestem are the predominant species. Associated therewith are panic grasses, wiregrass, paspalums, big and little bluestem, and Indian grass. Average carrying capacity on this range is about 6 to 22 acres per cow for the period of desirable grazing.

The plant composition of cattle diets collected monthly from two esophageally fistulated animals on the bluestem subtype is shown in Table 9-2.

## Shortleaf-Loblolly-Hardwood Type

Of next importance are the shortleaf-loblolly-hardwood forests occupying about 55 million acres. These are sometimes referred to as the pine-hardwood type. Forage is less abundant than in the

Fig. 9-6. Forest grazing in the longleaf-slash pine type. The more openness provides more forage for livestock. Contrast this to Figure 9-7. (Courtesy U.S. Forest Service)

longleaf-slash pine type due to the denseness of trees (Figure 9-7). It comprises the same forage species but in lower density due to the shading of trees and shrubs and the accompanying litter from overhead plants. In this type, the stocking rate is about one cow per 15 to 40 acres for the grazing period.

### Bottomland-Hardwood Type

The bottomland-hardwood forests which occupy river valleys, and especially the broad Mississippi Valley, occupy approximately

**TABLE 9-2**

**PLANT COMPOSITION OF CATTLE DIETS COLLECTED MONTHLY
FROM TWO ESOPHAGEALLY FISTULATED ANIMALS
ON A LONGLEAF PINE-BLUESTEM RANGE**

| | | | Botanical Composition | | | | |
|---|---|---|---|---|---|---|---|
| Date | Grasses | Grass-like Plants | Forbs | Browse | Green Pine Needles | Pine Needle Cast | Seeds |
| | | | | *(percent)* | | | |
| Apr 20 | 70 | 0 | 27 | 1 | 0 | 1 | 1 |
| May 21 | 80 | T[1] | 13 | 3 | T | 2 | 1 |
| Jun 27 | 80 | T | 18 | 1 | 0 | 1 | T |
| Jul 27 | 85 | T | 14 | T | 0 | 2 | T |
| Aug 29 | 85 | 0 | 12 | T | 0 | 3 | T |
| Sep 28 | 70 | T | 21 | 2 | 0 | 4 | 2 |
| Nov 3 | 60 | 0 | 26 | 4 | 0 | 6 | 4 |
| Dec 12 | 53 | 1 | 7 | 22 | 2 | 16 | T |
| Jan 27 | 52 | 0 | 21 | 13 | 2 | 12 | 1 |
| Feb 27 | 53 | T | 23 | 8 | 1 | 15 | T |
| Yearly average | 69 | T | 18 | 5 | 1 | 6 | 1 |

[1]T = Trace.

(Adapted from Southern Forest Experiment Station Research Note SO-216)

30 million acres. Browse is the principal forage in this area. Not too much grass grows under the dense hardwoods. Forage density is low except in openings. The most prominent forage plants include bluestems, carpetgrass, sedges, switch cane, green briar, and hardwood sprouts. Cattle browse extensively during the winter months on such species as green briar, sweetleaf, ti-ti, ash, magnolia, and maple. Switch cane provides excellent winter grazing where it has not been destroyed by overgrazing.

In this forest type care must be taken to protect valuable hardwood reproduction from excessive grazing. Grazing should be deferred until desirable tree species grow to such a height that they cannot be browsed.

## Upland-Hardwood Type

The upland-hardwood forests of the upper Coastal Plain, from the Ozark Mountains to the Southern Appalachians, occupy about 46 million acres. Forage plants are the same species found in the

Fig. 9-7. Forest grazing in a typical shortleaf-loblolly-hardwood–type forest. (Courtesy Texas Forest Service)

bluestem regions. Carrying capacity is low. It has been estimated that 20 to 60 acres are required to graze a cow for six months.

## PROBLEMS AND BENEFITS IN GRAZING SOUTHERN FOREST RANGES

While the practice of year-long grazing on forest ranges alone is in the descendancy, it is still practiced in some portions of the South. The results are a severe weight loss in winter, low calf crops, high death losses, and poor calves.

The answer is proper seasonal use of the range, coupled with supplemental feeding, more improved pastures, a better grade of stock, and year-long proper range management. The need is for adequate nutrition for animals when the native forage is poor (Figure 9-8).

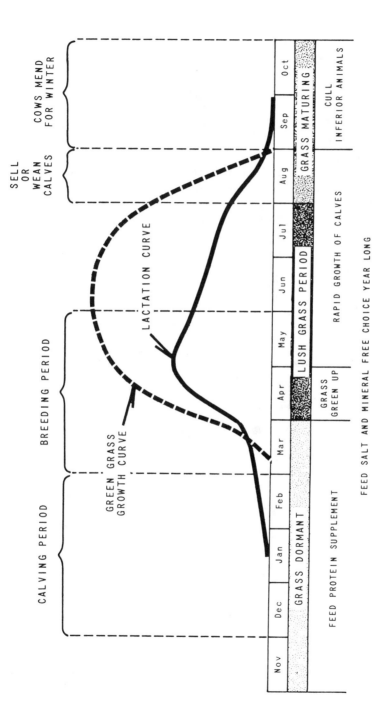

Fig. 9-8. The manner of relating livestock management into a woodland program for the greatest net return per acre. (Adapted from *Forest and Grazing*, U.S. Forest Service, S. & P. Forestry, Southeastern Area)

Fortunately, today most livestock owners in the South are aware of the nutritional needs of stock and are using forest ranges only in the spring and early fall when native grasses provide good forage.

The major problem on forest ranges is to integrate grazing and forest management in such a manner that the forage resource can be utilized without damage to desirable trees. Proper control of animal numbers, animal distribution, and grazing seasons must be exercised if tree damage is to be minimized. If properly coordinated, financial returns will be higher.

Readers interested in obtaining specific information on forest range grazing for their particular area of the South are directed to Appendix VII. Therein are shown agencies having responsibility in both range and wildlife programs.

## BIBLIOGRAPHY

Byrd, Nathan A. "Forest Grazing Opportunities," *Forest Farmer*, May, 1976.
Byrd, Nathan A., and Lewis, Clifford E. *Managing Southern Pine Forests to Produce Forage for Beef Cattle*. Forest Management Bulletin. Atlanta, Ga.: Southeastern Area, State and Private Forestry, U.S. Forest Service, 1976.
Crawford, H. S., Kucera, Clair L., and Ehrenreich, John H. *Ozark Range and Wildlife Plants*. Handbook No. 356. Washington, D.C.: U.S.D.A. 1969.
Duran, Gilbert, and Kaiser, H. F. *Range Management Practices: Investment Costs, 1970*. Agricultural Handbook No. 435. Washington, D.C.: U.S. Forest Service, 1972.
Duvall, Vinson L., Johnson, A. W., and Yarlett, L. L. *Selected Bibliography on Southern Range Management*. Research Paper SO-38. New Orleans, La.: Southern Forest Experiment Station, U.S. Forest Service, 1968.
*The Forest and Rangeland Renewable Resources Planning Act of 1974*. Washington, D.C.: U.S. Forest Service, 1975.
*Grass: The 1948 Yearbook of Agriculture*. Washington, D.C.: U.S.D.A.
Grelen, Harold E. "Forest Grazing in the South," *Journal of Range Management*, Volume 31:1, July, 1978.
Grelen, Harold E., and Duvall, Vinson L. *Common Plants of Longleaf Pine— Bluestem Range*. Research Paper SO-23. New Orleans, La.: Southern Forest Experiment Station, U.S. Forest Service, 1972.
Halls, L. K., and Alcaniz, R. *Growth Patterns of Deer-Browse Plants in Southern Forests*. Research Paper SO-75. New Orleans, La.: Southern Forest Experiment Station U.S. Forest Service, 1972.
Heady, Harold F. *Rangeland Management*. New York, N.Y.: McGraw-Hill Book Company, Inc., 1975.
*Inter-Agency Work Group on Range Production Opportunities to Increase Red Meat Production from Ranges in the United States*. Washington, D.C.: U.S.D.A., 1974.

Lewis, Clifford E. *Principles and Status of Integrated Management from the Range Standpoint.* Resources Report 4. Gainesville, Fla.: University of Florida, 1977.

Lewis, Clifford E., *et al. Range Resources of the South.* Bulletin NS-9. Tifton, Ga.: Georgia Coastal Plain Experiment Station, 1974.

Lewis, Clifford E., *et al.* "Seasonal Trends in Nutrients and Cattle Digestibility of Forage on Pine-Wiregrass Range," *Journal of Animal Science,* Volume 41:1, 1975.

Nickerson, Mona F., Brink, Glen E., and Feddema, Charles. *Principal Range Plants of the Central and Southern Rocky Mountains.* General Technical Report RM-20. Fort Collins, Colo.: Rocky Mountain Forest and Range Experiment Station, 1976.

Pearson, H. A. *Botancial Composition of Cattle Diets on a Southern Pine-Bluestem Range.* Research Note SO-216. New Orleans, La.: Southern Forest Experiment Station, 1976.

Pearson, H. A., and Whitaker, L. B. "Returns from Southern Forest Grazing," *Journal of Range Management,* 26:85-87, 1972.

*Range Resources of the South.* Bulletin N.S. 9. Tifton, Ga.: University of Georgia, Coastal Plain Experiment Station, 1979.

Rummell, Robert S. *The Nation's Range Resources.* Forest Resource Report No. 19. Washington, D.C.: U.S. Forest Service, 1972.

Southwell, B. L., and Hughes, R. H. *Beef Cattle Management Practices for Wiregrass Pine Ranges of Georgia.* Georgia Agricultural Experiment Station Bulletin No. 129, 1965.

Stoddard, Laurence A., Smith, Arthur D., and Box, Thadis W. *Range Management.* New York, N.Y.: McGraw-Hill Book Company, Inc., 1975.

Stoin, Harlan R. *A Review of the Southern Pine Forest-Range Ecosystem.* Special Report 73. Fayette, Ark.: Agricultural Experiment Station, 1979.

U.S. Forest Service. *An Analysis of the Range Forest Situation in the United States: 1989-2040.* A Technical Document Supporting the 1989 R.P.A. Assessment. Draft, 1989.

U.S. Forest Service. *An Assessment of the Forest and Range Land Situation in the United States.* FS-345, U.S.D.A., 1980.

U.S. Forest Service. *The Nation's Range Resources—A Forest Range Experimental Study.* Forest Resource No. 19. Washington, D.C.: U.S.D.A., 1972.

# CHAPTER X

# Wood Characteristics, Identification, and Uses

A well-known dictionary defines wood as the hard, fibrous substance which makes up the greater part of the stems and branches of trees. To the botanist and wood technologist, wood is a complex plant tissue comprising the xylem part of vascular bundles and consisting mainly of parenchyma, fibers, tracheids, and vessels. To a chemist, wood is a product that is chiefly cellulose and lignin, with related materials. Foresters think of wood in terms of use and service. Wood is an indispensable product of every person's everyday life. From trees, many products are derived (Figure 10-1).

Every forest landowner should have as an objective the growing of successive crops of wood that in quality, quantity, and value will be of the highest use. Since the properties of wood determine use, a general knowledge of such on the part of a forest landowner is desirable. In this chapter, only pertinent features of wood characteristics, identification, and use will be given.

## WOOD CHARACTERISTICS

### Chemical Properties

Wood is made up of about 50 per cent cellulose, 28 per cent lignin, and minor quantities of other materials. Less lignin occurs in hardwoods than in softwoods. Cellulose forms the framework of the cell wall and is the product used in the manufacture of paper. Lignin is the cementing material that binds the cells together and is also found mixed with cellulose in the cell walls. When the lignin is dissolved with chemicals, the cells may be separated for paper making. Cellulose and lignin are responsible for some differences in the properties of wood, such as ability to absorb mois-

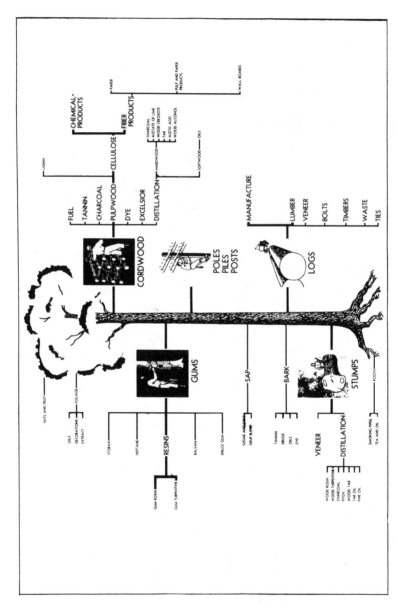

Fig. 10-1. Forest products derived from commercial tree species. (Adapted from U.S. Forest Service poster, "What We Get from Trees")

ture and resistance to corrosion by salt water. Characteristics such as color, odor, and natural resistance to decay cannot be attributed to cellulose or lignin, but rather to other materials in the wood.

## PHYSICAL CHARACTERISTICS

### Porous and Non-porous Woods

The wood of trees can be divided into two major groups; namely, those without pores and those with pores. The former are referred to as non-porous, while the latter are called porous. The porous are further divided into ring-porous and diffuse-porous. Examples of each of the three groupings are:

| Non-porous | Diffuse-porous | Ring-porous |
|---|---|---|
| Cedar | Basswoods | Ash |
| Fir | Beeches | White oaks |
| Spruce | Maples | Hickories |
| Pine | Birches | Elms |
| Larch | Black walnut | Red oaks |

In ring-porous woods larger pores are found in the springwood and smaller pores in the summerwood. In diffuse-porous woods, the pores are rather small and evenly scattered throughout the summerwood and springwood. See Figure 10-2.

### Weight and Strength

The weight of wood is usually expressed in terms of its specific gravity, or weight per cubic or thousand board feet (Appendix VIII). If the specific gravity of a wood is expressed as 0.56, it means that a given volume of this wood weighs 0.56 times as much as an equal volume of water. Since a cubic foot of water weighs 62.5 pounds, a cubic foot of wood of the species with a specific gravity of 0.56 would weigh 0.56 × 62.5, or 35 pounds. Specific gravity of wood is influenced to a large degree by the amount of gum, resins, and other extractives, size of cell cavities, and thickness of cell walls. Specific gravity of a few commercial species is:

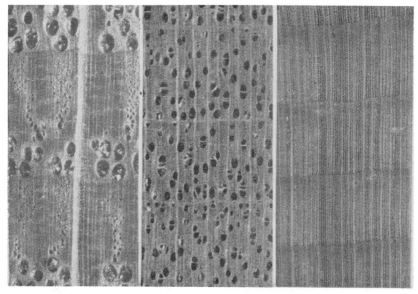

Fig. 10-2. Porous and non-porous woods. Left to right, ring-porous (white oak), diffuse-porous (yellow birch), non-porous (Engelmann spruce).

| Species | Specific Gravity | |
|---|---|---|
| | Green | Air-Dry |
| Red maple | .49 | .54 |
| Southern red oak | .52 | .59 |
| White oak | .59 | .67 |
| Loblolly pine | .47 | .51 |
| Longleaf pine | .54 | .59 |
| Shortleaf pine | .47 | .51 |
| Black locust | .66 | .69 |
| Eastern hemlock | .38 | .40 |
| Western hemlock | .42 | .45 |
| Redwood (young growth) | .34 | .35 |
| Tamarack | .49 | .53 |
| Sitka spruce | .37 | .40 |
| Ponderosa pine | .38 | .40 |
| Eastern white pine | .34 | .35 |

## Bending

For certain uses, such as in manufacturing furniture, it is necessary to bend wood. Some hardwoods are more readily softened by heat and moisture for this purpose than are others. Elms, ashes, and pecan hickories are preferred where extreme bending is required. Oaks, birches, beeches, red gum, and maples are also used for bent parts where moderate bending is required. Southern pine can be used for minimum bends only.

A variety of chemicals are used to aid in the bending of wood. Among them are urea, dimethyl sulfoxide, and liquid ammonia.

### Other Features

Resin canals are found in pine. These are intercellular passages surrounded by secreting cells and are often filled with resin.

Properties such as color, lustre, taste, hardness, odor, and texture are important considerations in wood identification. To the wood user, weight, strength, stiffness, bending and woodworking qualities, hardness, toughness, ability to be stained, and shrinkage are among the most important (Table 10-1).

Sassafras and cedar have such characteristic odors and tastes. Other species, such as cypress and sweetgum, have colors that are characteristic to these species. In black locust the deposition of material in the heartwood increases its weight and certain strength properties.

In hardwoods the hardwood fibers are about $1/25$ of an inch in length. In contrast, softwood fibers range from about $1/8$ to $1/3$ of an inch. Length of fibers has no direct effect on the strength of wood. Most important are the thickness and structure of the fiber walls.

There is no consistent difference, either in the weight when dry, or in the strength, of sapwood and heartwood of hardwoods.

The width of annual rings does affect the weight and strength of wood in species that are ring-porous. Normally, increased growth increases the strength of the wood. As such, second-growth ring-porous trees are somewhat stronger than virgin-growth hardwoods.

Southern pine wood decreases in strength with an increase in growth rate. Trees with wide annual rings are weaker, and for this reason a forest landowner should strive for uniform growth of trees to produce the best lumber.

## HARDWOODS AND SOFTWOODS

Trees are divided into two classes: hardwoods, which have

TABLE 10-1

**PROPERTIES OF SOME COMMON WOODS**

| Species | Working and Behavior Characteristics | | | | | | Strength Properties | | | |
|---|---|---|---|---|---|---|---|---|---|---|
| | Hardness | Ease of working | Paint holding | Nail holding | Decay resistance of heartwood | Freedom from odor and taste (dry) | Bending strength | Stiffness | Strength as post | Toughness |
| Ash: White .......... | A | C | — | A | C | A | A | A | A | A |
| Bald cypress ........ | B | B | A | B | A | B | B | B | B | B |
| Basswood .......... | C | A | — | C | C | A | C | B | C | C |
| Beech ............. | A | C | — | A | C | A | A | A | B | A |
| Birch, yellow ....... | A | C | — | A | C | A | A | A | B | A |
| Cherry ............. | A | C | — | — | — | B | A | A | A | B |
| Cottonwood ........ | C | B | — | C | C | B | C | B | C | B |
| Cypress ............ | B | B | A | B | A | B | B | B | B | B |
| Douglas fir ......... | B | C | C | B | B | C | A | A | A | B |
| Elm: Rock ......... | A | C | — | — | B | A | A | A | B | A |
| Elm: Soft .......... | A | C | — | A | B | A | B | B | B | A |
| Fir: Balsam ........ | C | B | B | — | C | A | C | C | C | C |
| Fir: White ......... | C | B | B | C | C | A | B | B | B | C |
| Hackberry ......... | A | C | — | — | — | A | B | C | C | A |
| Hemlock: | | | | | | | | | | |
|   Eastern .......... | B | B | B | B | C | A | B | B | B | B |
|   Western ......... | B | B | B | B | C | A | B | A | B | B |
| Hickory: Pecan ...... | A | C | — | — | C | — | A | A | A | A |
| Hickory: True ....... | A | C | — | A | C | — | A | A | A | A |
| Junipers ........... | C | A | A | C | A | C | C | C | C | C |
| Larch, western ...... | A | C | C | A | B | C | A | A | A | B |
| Locust, black ........ | A | C | — | A | A | B | A | A | A | A |
| Magnolia .......... | B | A | A | A | — | C | B | B | C | C |
| Maple: Hard ........ | A | C | — | A | C | A | A | A | A | A |
| Maple: Soft ......... | A | C | — | A | C | A | C | C | C | C |
| Mesquite .......... | A | — | — | — | A | — | — | — | — | — |
| Oak: Red .......... | A | C | — | A | C | — | A | A | B | A |
| Oak: White ........ | A | C | — | A | A | — | A | A | B | A |
| Pine: | | | | | | | | | | |
|   Eastern white ..... | C | A | A | B | — | C | C | C | C | C |
|   Ponderosa ........ | C | A | B | B | — | C | C | C | C | C |
|   Southern yellow ... | A | C | C | A | B | C | A | A | A | B |
|   Sugar ............ | C | A | A | — | — | C | C | C | C | C |
|   Western white .... | C | A | A | B | — | C | B | B | B | B |
| Red cedar: | | | | | | | | | | |
|   Eastern .......... | A | B | — | — | A | C | B | C | A | B |
|   Western .......... | C | A | A | C | A | C | C | C | B | C |

(Continued)

**TABLE 10-1 (Continued)**

| Species | Working and Behavior Characteristics | | | | | | Strength Properties | | | |
|---|---|---|---|---|---|---|---|---|---|---|
| | Hardness | Ease of working | Paint holding | Nail holding | Decay resistance of heartwood | Freedom from odor and taste (dry) | Bending strength | Stiffness | Strength as post | Toughness |
| Red gum ............ | B | B | — | B | B | B | B | B | B | B |
| Redwood ........... | B | B | A | B | A | — | B | B | A | B |
| Spruce: (East.) ...... | C | B | B | B | C | A | B | B | B | B |
| Sweet gum ......... | B | B | — | B | B | B | B | B | B | B |
| Sycamore .......... | A | C | — | A | C | — | B | B | B | B |
| Tupelo ............ | A | C | — | A | C | A | B | B | B | B |
| Walnut ............ | A | B | — | — | A | — | A | A | A | A |
| Willow ............ | C | A | — | — | C | C | C | C | C | C |
| Yellow poplar ....... | C | A | — | B | C | A | B | B | C | C |

A: Relative high value in the particular property listed; B: medium value in the particular property listed; C: relative low value in the particular property listed.

(Courtesy United States Forest Products Laboratory)

broad leaves, and softwoods or conifers, which have needlelike leaves or scale leaves.

No degree of hardness divides the hardwoods from the softwoods. Some softwoods are hard while some hardwoods are soft.

The term "softwood" had its origin in New England. The loggers applied it to the light wood of white pine, a conifer. It was subsequently applied to all conifers irrespective of density of wood. "Hardwood" was given to hard maple, a dense wood, and thereafter to all deciduous species.

## WOOD IDENTIFICATION

Only through familiarity with wood can a forest landowner identify wood from general appearances. Some woods, as black walnut, have a distinctive color. Cypress, sassafras, and cedar can be distinguished by their odor. Some woods have a pronounced difference in color between the heartwood and sapwood while in others there is no difference. Pitch is found in pine wood. Pores in wood are an important means to aid in wood identification as related earlier in this chapter.

Wood can readily be identified as a "hardwood" or "softwood" by the presence or absence of vessels (commonly called "pores") when viewed in a transverse section (Figures 10-2, 10-3, and 10-4). If pores are not present, it is a softwood. Pines show small, fairly evenly distributed openings called *resin ducts* on a transverse surface. They appear as small, light areas in the dark rings of summerwood in southern yellow pine. Resin ducts should not be confused with the pores noted in hardwoods, since the pores in hardwood are closer together than are resin ducts.

A conifer is represented in Figure 10-3. When it is viewed from the top, in transverse section, *tracheids*, or water carriers (TR), form the bulk of the wood surface. Between the various cells is a cementing substance called the *middle lamella* (ML). Springwood cells (S) are distinguishable by their larger size, in contrast to the summerwood cells (SM). Together the springwood and summerwood cells make up the annual ring (AR). One such ring is added annually to the outside of a tree.

When the wood is viewed in a vertical plane, *medullary rays* (MR) will be noted. The function of the rays is to store and distribute food material of the tree horizontally. The rays are of two types, fusiform medullary rays (FMR) and rays with horizontal resin ducts (HRD).

The large hole as viewed in the top surface is a vertical resin duct.

The surface of the wood represented by (RR) is commonly called "edge grain" in softwoods and "quarter sawn" in hardwoods. It is not so distinctive in softwoods however as it is in most hardwoods. In some hardwood species, the "quartered" surface, with its lustrous flakes formed by the medullary rays entering and leaving the plane in which it was cut, is sought after by furniture manufacturers because of its attractive figure.

Simple pits (SP) are unthickened portions of cell walls through which sap passes from ray cells to fibers or vice versa. Bordered pits (BP) on the surface (TG) have their margins overhung by the surrounding cell walls. The surface (TG) at right angles to the radial or quarter-sawn surface corresponds to the flat grain or plain-sawn surface of lumber.

The cell structure of hardwood is represented by Figure 10-4. The horizontal plane (TT) corresponds to the end surface of a log.

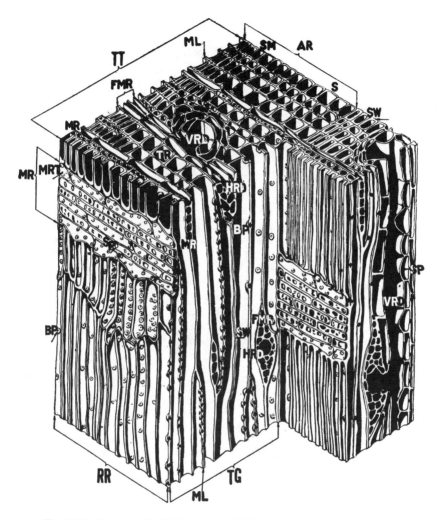

Fig. 10-3. Drawing of a highly magnified block of white pine (a softwood) about 1/32 inch in length.

The vertical plane (RR) corresponds to a surface cut parallel to the radius, while the vertical (TG) represents a surface cut at right angles to the radius. Hardwoods may be cut at a sawmill in these three planes and are known, respectively, as end grain, quarter sawn, and plain sawn surfaces.

Hardwoods have specialized vessels or pores (P) for conduct-

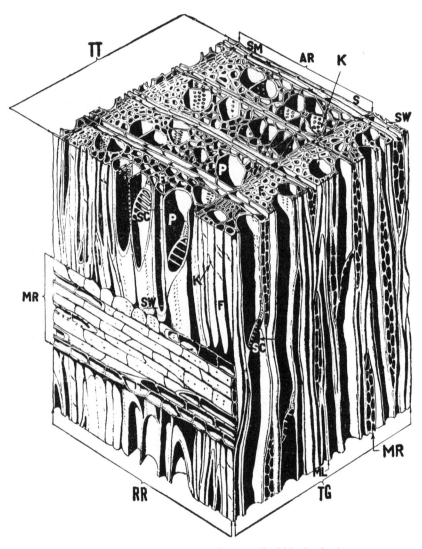

Fig. 10-4. Drawing of a highly magnified block of oak.

ing sap. In softwoods, fibers are used to transfer sap. Hardwood
vessels are relatively large cells with open ends, one above the
other, and continuing as open passages for long distances. In the
heartwood and sapwood of some species, the pores are filled with
tyloses.

Pores of hardwoods vary in size. In some they are visible to the naked eye. In most of the hardwoods the ends of the individual cells of the pores are open, while in others they may be separated by a grating (SC).

The strength-giving elements of hardwood are wood fibers (F). Usually they have small cavities and thick walls. In the fiber walls are found pits (K) by which sap passes from one cavity to another. Medullary rays (MR) are short horizontal cells which extend in a radial direction and serve to store food and distribute it horizontally. In the illustrated surface (TG) cells are shown as being two cells wide. However, in some hardwood species the width may vary, some having over 50 cells.

In temperate climate the annual ring (AR) is usually sharply defined. Generally, wood formed in the spring, or springwood (S), is more porous than the summerwood (SM).

All wood cells, including pores, fibers, ray cells, etc., are cemented together by what is called, technically, the middle lamella (ML). By the use of certain chemicals, this layer can be dissolved, permitting the fibers to be separated. This process is used in paper making.

A non-technical guide to the identification of some of the major tree species is presented in Figure 10-5.

For those interested in the study of wood identification in depth, a wood technology text should be consulted.

## COMMERCIAL TREES OF THE SOUTH
## AND THEIR USES

Wood, a renewable resource, is the most widely used construction material in the nation. Lumber, plywood, and pulp are the principal products derived from wood; however, many other products are derived from trees (Figure 10-1). Some uses will be given in the descriptions which follow and in other chapters.

### Major Species

*Southern pine.* The term "southern pine" is applied in the lumber trade to include shortleaf *(Pinus echinata)*, loblolly *(Pinus taeda)*, slash *(Pinus alliottii)*, and longleaf pine *(Pinus palustris)*. Equally common is the term "yellow pine" as it applied to these species, being derived from the yellowish color of the wood.

| Porous Woods (broad-leaved trees) | Diffuse porous | Pores indistinct to naked eye, wood moderately hard, medium weight. | | Growth rings conspicuous and delineated by a whitish line of terminal parenchyma (connective tissue); rays distinct to naked eye. | MAGNOLIA |
|---|---|---|---|---|---|
| | | | | Growth rings inconspicuous, parenchyma invisible, rays indistinct to naked eye. | RED GUM |
| | | Some pores distinct to naked eye; wood soft, light weight. | | Heartwood grayish-white to light grayish-brown. | COTTONWOOD |
| | | | | Heartwood brown to reddish-brown. | WILLOW |
| | Ring-porous | Without broad rays | Summerwood without wavy bands of pores | Wood used mostly sapwood; nearly white; heartwood yellow to brown. — Lines of parenchyma, usually indistinct; if distinct can be seen connecting pores. | ASH |
| | | | | Wood used mostly sapwood; nearly white; heartwood yellow to brown. — With fine parallel lines of parenchyma, not connecting pores. | HICKORY and PECAN |
| | | | | Wood used mostly heartwood, reddish-brown to yellow-brown. | MESQUITE |
| | | | Summerwood figured with wavy bands of pores. | | ELM and HACKBERRY |
| | | With broad rays | Heartwood light to dark brown without reddish-cast; springwood pores usually clogged. | | WHITE OAK GROUP |
| | | | Heartwood usually pinkish to reddish-brown; springwood pores usually open. | | RED OAK GROUP |
| Non-porous woods (needle-leaved trees) | Without resin canals; little contrast between springwood and summerwood. | Fine-textured heartwood purplish-red to purplish-brown, fragrant. | | | CEDAR |
| | | Coarse-textured heartwood yellowish to dark brown or reddish-brown, not fragrant. | | | CYPRESS |
| | With resin canals; distinct contrast between springwood and summerwood. | | | | SOUTHERN PINES |

Fig. 10-5. A key to some common woods. Read left to right.

The commercial practice in the South is to class all southern pines as either "longleaf" or "shortleaf." Species of longleaf and slash pine with certain dense classifications are classed as "longleaf" by the trade.

Except for the fact that pith is often a distinguishing characteristic of longleaf pine in contrast to other southern pine species, each species cannot be positively distinguished from the other by the wood alone.

Longleaf derived its name from the needles which are longer than other pine species. Its wood is one of strength, toughness, durability, and resiliency. Originally extending in a broad coastal belt about 150 miles in width along the Gulf Coast from Virginia to East Texas it is largely cutover and its range diminished.

Slash pine grows naturally east of the Mississippi River along the Gulf Coast and South Atlantic regions. It, like longleaf pine, has the ability to produce turpentine and resin. A tree of the coastal area, it has spread over much of the land formerly dominated by longleaf pine.

Shortleaf and loblolly pine grow throughout the southern pine region and have a wider range than either longleaf or shortleaf pine.

Shortleaf pine has a long taproot which enables a tree to obtain water at considerable depth below the surface of the ground.

Loblolly pine is frequently referred to as "old field pine" since it is commonly found in abandoned fields. It grows faster than either longleaf or shortleaf pine, but not so fast as slash pine, during the first 20 years. Beyond this age loblolly shows the greatest growth. Wood produced from shortleaf and loblolly pine ranges from dense to soft texture, making it suitable for many uses. Lumber produced from shortleaf pine stands in the Ozark Mountains is soft and of uniform texture and is known as Arkansas soft pine.

Southern pine lumber is used for a wide range of purposes, as in heavy structural and light framing, interior finish, flooring, sheathing, crates, boxes, railroad cars, and for many more industrial purposes. About 15 per cent of the annual production goes into structural timbers. The balance goes into dimension material and other items sold by retail lumber yards.

The wood of southern pine takes preservative treatment readily and is used extensively for poles, piling, fence posts, cross ties, treated foundation timbers, and other construction materials.

Southern yellow pine supplies much of the raw material for the plywood, lumber, and pulpwood industries in the South and will continue to serve this purpose.

There are a few minor southern pine species that are marketed to some extent. These include pond pine *(Pinus rigida serotina),* spruce pine *(Pinus glabra),* sand pine *(Pinus clausa),* and Virginia pine *(Pinus virginiana).* Table 10-2 shows the volumes of the principal softwood timber species in the eastern United States.

TABLE 10-2

**NET VOLUME OF SOFTWOOD SAWTIMBER ON TIMBERLAND
IN THE EASTERN UNITED STATES, 1987**

| Species | Volume |
|---|---|
| | *(million board feet)* |
| Longleaf and slash pine | 54,253 |
| Loblolly and shortleaf pine | 271,104 |
| Other yellow pines | 28,465 |
| White and red pines | 48,024 |
| Jack pine | 3,795 |
| Spruce and balsam fir | 37,432 |
| Eastern hemlock | 22,761 |
| Cypress | 22,112 |
| Other softwoods | 23,535 |
| Total | 511,481 |

(Source: U.S. Forest Service, Preliminary RPA Review Draft, 1988)

The status of hardwood volume on the commercial forest land in the eastern United States is shown in Table 10-3 by major hardwood groupings.

*Ash.* Of the seven commercially valuable species of ash, six are sold under the name of white ash. Two of these species, white ash *(Fraxinus americana)* and green ash *(Fraxinus pennsylvanica),* together make up over three-fourths of the annual cut. Ash is found in mixed hardwood stands on rich soil where moisture is abundant. The wood is slightly lighter in color than oak, straight grained, and in appearance similar to plain sawn oak, with the exception of having no visible medullary rays. The sapwood is nearly white; the heartwood is pale brown. The wood possesses high-strength properties for its weight. In the area of sports, ash is indispensable. Baseball bats, polo and hockey sticks, playground equipment, skis, and tennis rackets are but a few of the many items made. Ash is also recognized as the best wood for handles for such things as shovels and rakes. It has many other uses, such

TABLE 10-3

NET VOLUME OF HARDWOOD SAWTIMBER ON TIMBERLAND
IN THE EASTERN UNITED STATES, 1987

| Species | Volume |
|---------|--------|
| | (million board feet) |
| Select white oak | 71,274 |
| Select red oak | 62,732 |
| Other oak | 155,852 |
| Yellow birch and hard maple | 48,297 |
| Soft maple and beech | 68,016 |
| Sweet gum | 39,341 |
| Tupelo and black gum | 30,891 |
| Hickory | 40,536 |
| Yellow poplar | 52,949 |
| Ash, basswood, and walnut | 40,720 |
| Cottonwood and aspen | 32,055 |
| Other | 66,034 |
| Total | 708,697 |

(Source: U.S. Forest Service, Preliminary RPA Review Draft, 1988)

as in trim, doors, and other woodwork. It has extensive use in bent wood parts, as it responds to steam bending.

*Beech.* One characteristic of beech *(Fagus grandifolia)* is its slow growth. It is found, in varying amounts, in all southern states and only on sites that are well drained. It is not found in swamps or on lands that are inundated. The wood of beech is hard, dense, and light in color. It has a diffuse-porous structure and numerous pith or medullary rays. The sapwood is pale flesh while the heartwood is a reddish color. Flooring is the most important product made from beech. Beech is also used extensively by the furniture and brush industries. Other major uses include truck body parts, toys, woodenware, and novelties.

*Cottonwood.* The bulk of cottonwood lumber in the South is produced from the species known as eastern cottonwood *(Populus deltoides)*. Some production is from the swamp cottonwood *(Populus heterophylla)*. Cottonwood is a rapid-growing tree which thrives in rich bottomlands and flood plains. As a general rule it is found in mixture with other hardwoods but does grow in the delta region in pure stands. Its commercial region is restricted to the South. The wood of cottonwood is soft-textured and light in weight. It has an especially long fiber which makes it strong and tough for its weight. Cottonwood sapwood is generally very white, but wood from the Southeast tends to be darker in color. Principal uses include shipping containers, paper production, furniture, agricultural implements, and veneer. It is used also for excelsior and in the manufacture of matches. Louisiana, Arkansas, and Mississippi are the most important states in production. Other important producing states are Tennessee, Alabama, Texas, and South Carolina.

*Cypress.* From a botanical standpoint, cypress *(Taxodium distichum)* is a softwood. Since it is usually manufactured with other hardwoods, with which it grows, it is considered as one of them. Cypress is known throughout the South under a number of different names. These are Louisiana red cypress, yellow cypress, gulf cypress, tidewater red cypress, and white cypress. Cypress is found in the Gulf States in swamps, river bottoms, and sloughs— wherever the tree roots have access to water. Cypress is the only deciduous softwood in the South. Its wood is soft in texture. In old growth timber the grain is very fine, yielding the highly prized reddish heartwood. Cypress does not warp or check and may be depended upon to stay in place. It holds paint very well. It is one of the few native woods in which the heartwood of old growth trees is naturally resistant to termites. In certain logs, "pecks" or elongated cavities are found, being made into "pecky cypress" lumber. The "pecks" are the result of a fungus about which little is known. Cypress is in demand for interior and exterior trim, paneling, sash, and doors. Manufacturers of factory equipment such as food processing containers, refrigerating equipment, and laundry machines all use the wood. Lower grades of cypress are favored for fencing boards. Florida is reported to have the greatest remaining volume in board feet. Other leading states are Louisiana, Georgia, and Mississippi, in the order named.

*Elm.* There are five elms of commercial importance in the South. These are: American elm *(Ulmus americana)*, slippery elm *(Ulmus rubra)*, cedar elm *(Ulmus crassifolia)*, winged elm *(Ulmus alata)*, and September elm *(Ulmus serotina)*. The American and slippery elm account for 73 per cent of the annual volume cut. The elms are divided into two groups, one known as soft elm, the other as rock elm. Soft elm, as the name implies, is soft in texture. Most of the southern production is soft elm (American elm). Rock elm *(Ulmus thomesii),* found in the North, produces the major quantity of "hard" elm. There are, however, two species that compare favorably in density to these species. These are cedar elm and winged elm. Winged elm is found throughout the South. The range of the cedar elm is limited to western Mississippi, southern Arkansas, Louisiana, and eastern Texas. Soft elm heartwood is light brown while the sapwood is almost white. It is ring-porous. In the summerwood will be found many narrow wavy lines of fine pores. This elm is an excellent bending wood. As such, it is used extensively for boats and bent parts. It is also used in truck body parts and furniture. Its wood is difficult to split. The Mississippi delta contains the largest remaining volume in the United States.

*Sweet gum.* Sweet gum is second to oak in hardwood production in the United States. It is also our most important southern hardwood. Both sap gum and red gum lumber come from the same species of tree *(Liquidambar styraciflua).* Sap gum comes from the sapwood and red gum from the heartwood, the latter bringing a more favorable market price. Sweet gum—or, as it is sometimes called, red gum—has a uniform texture prized by cabinet makers. In turning properties it has a top rating. The quarter wood has a lustrous satin, reddish-brown cast. Many industries use sap gum entirely, finding its smooth surface adaptable to many types of stain and suitable for paint and enamel finish. The furniture industry in particular uses a large quantity of this wood. It is also used in cabinets, containers, and general millwork. Louisiana is reported to have a larger volume of sawtimber than any other state.

*Tupelo.* There are four common species of tupelo found in the South, but only two are of major economic importance. These are water tupelo *(Nyssa aquatica)* and black tupelo *(Nyssa sylvatica).* Water tupelo is the most water-loving species in the United States. Black tupelo, though water loving, is not a deep-swamp species. All tupelos grow slowly. The wood of the different species is similar in appearance and can be distinguished only by microscopic examination. The heartwood is light brownish-grey, while the sapwood is a creamy white. Tupelo wood has a uniform appearance, indistinct annual rings, and an interlocking grain. It is a tough wood, most difficult to split.

*Hackberry.* Two species comprise the hackberry lumber of commerce. The southern hackberry, more properly known as sugarberry *(Celtis laevigata)*, makes up 90 per cent of the production, with the balance being the tree more commonly known as hackberry *(Celtis occidentalis)*. Both of these species are found in all southern states. Sugarberry reaches its greatest development in the Gulf States and in the Mississippi delta. Both species are sold as one. The wood is creamy white, ring-porous, and uniform in texture. It has a high rating with respect to resistance to warping and shrinkage. For machining purpose it has good turning properties. The wood is used extensively in the furniture industry and in veneer. Lower grades are used in shipping containers.

*Hickory.* While there are over 45 recognized species and varieties of hickory in the United States, only 8 are commercially valuable. Of these eight, half are known as "true hickories," while the other half are called "pecan hickories." Comprising the "true hickories" are: shagbark hickory *(Carya ovata)*, bigleaf shagbark hickory *(Carya laciniosa)*, mockernut hickory *(Carya tomentosa)*, and pignut hickory *(Carya glabra)*. The lumber from these species is about identical, and in the trade one species is not distinguished from the other. Hickory thrives in company with other hardwoods, particularly the oak. It is not found in pure stands and is a slow grower. No wood compares to hickory for strength, toughness, and elasticity. Its sapwood is whitish, while the heartwood is reddish-brown. The tool industry is the major consumer of hickory. Domestic skis are also made from the wood, with a large quantity of ski blanks shipped to Europe. It is the chosen material for rungs on ladders and for other specialty uses. Veneer is also made from the wood.

*Pecan.* The four "pecan hickories" of commercial value are: pecan *(Carya illinoensis)*, water hickory *(Carya aquatica)*, bitternut hickory *(Carya cordiformis)*, and nutmeg hickory *(Carya myristiciformis)*. All woods within this group are about identical and are marketed as pecan. Pecan has widespread popularity as a premium cabinet wood. It is found throughout the South but reaches its greatest development in eastern Texas, Louisiana, Mississippi, and Arkansas. Pecan heartwood is reddish-brown in color. The sapwood is white. The wood has a pleasing grain pattern and is not so hard as the "true hickories." The furniture industry is the largest market for pecan. It makes excellent flooring. Other uses include decking in railroad cars, trailer parts, and expensive cabinets. The annual cut is estimated at 90 million board feet per year. Louisiana is the largest pecan-producing state.

*Magnolia.* There are a number of magnolia species in the South. Those of greatest economic importance are southern magnolia *(Magnolia grandiflora)* and swamp magnolia, commonly referred to as sweet bay *(Magnolia virginiana).* The wood of each is sold as magnolia lumber. Southern magnolia is most common. Both species are found throughout the South in the same range. In the deep South sweet bay is evergreen, while in the extreme northern portion of its range the leaves drop from the tree annually. The wood of magnolia is soft, fine-textured, and straight-grained. It is easy to work. The heartwood is yellowish-brown in color, while the sapwood is a creamy white. The wood is excellent for interior trim, paneling, and doors. Most of the wood milled goes into furniture. It is also used in veneer.

*Maple.* Commercial production of maple in the South is restricted to three species, all of which are soft maples. Sugar maple, found in the North, is a hard maple, being more dense. Soft maples are: box elder *(Acer negundo),* silver maple *(Acer saccharinum),* and red maple *(Acer rubra).* Commercial production of box elder is limited primarily to the Mississippi delta region. The greatest production of red maple is from mills in the area from southern Virginia through the Carolinas. The sapwood of the maples is whitish. The heartwood is an off-tan, being slightly darker in red maple. Soft maple is in big demand by furniture manufacturers. It can be steam-bent without difficulty. Other products made from the wood are paneling, toys, shipping containers, and specialty kitchen cabinets. North and South Carolina and Georgia are reported to have the largest commercial volume in soft maple.

*Oak.* No hardwood is more widely known or used than the oak. Its use goes back to early civilization. Many species and varieties of oak are known. However, in the lumber industry, two groups are recognized: white oak and red oak. Some place live oak, generally classed as a white oak, in a separate category or group known as live oak because of certain botanical characteristics. A few distinguishing characteristics of the white oak group are: leaf lobes are rounded, heartwood is brownish or tan, vessels in heartwood contain tyloses, newly cut wood does not have unpleasant odor, and pores in summerwood are numerous and small, making counting difficult. In contrast, the red oak group have bristle-tipped leaves, heartwood is reddish, there are few tyloses in heartwood, freshly cut wood has an unpleasant odor, and pores in summerwood are few and can be counted more easily. Among commercial species in the red oak group are southern red oak *(Quercus falcata),* water oak *(Quercus nigra),* and willow oak *(Quercus phellos).* Some species in the white oak group are overcup oak *(Quercus lyrata),* post oak *(Quercus stellata),* and chestnut oak *(Quercus prinus).* Oak wood is well adapted to any finishing treatment. It has strength for structure. Oak is a universal wood, used for many purposes. It has no equal for flooring. It makes the best railroad ties. The wood of white oak is used for tight cooperage for liquids. Uses for oak also include decking for railroad cars, furniture, millwork, and novelties. The red oak group leads in production because it is found in greater abundance.

*Sycamore.* This species is found in all states of the South, particularly in the rich soil along the borders of creeks and streams. In some areas it is variously known as buttonwood, button ball or plane tree but is the same species *(Platanus occidentalis).* The wood of sycamore is fairly hard, stiff, and strong. The sapwood is pink in color, with the heartwood slightly darker. The important market for the wood is in furniture and furniture parts. Other uses include millwork and novelties.

*Yellow poplar.* This species *(Lirodendron tulipifera)* is found in all southern states except Texas. It is most intolerant to light and prefers a rich, moist soil. The wood is light and soft and is easily worked. It is known for its ability to resist warping and take a smooth, lasting paint or enamel finish. The greatest consumer of the wood is the furniture industry. Yellow poplar is used as core stock in veneer and for wood boxes, exterior trim, piano parts, fixtures, toys, and novelties.

*Black willow.* While there are a number of willow species found in the South, only one reaches commercial size. This is black willow *(Salix nigra).* The wood of willow is one of the lightest and softest in North America, yet it is a strong wood. The sapwood ranges in color from white to tan. The heartwood is found in a number of colors from reddish to gray. The range in colors of the wood makes it adaptable to paneling. Willow grows in pure stands or in mixture with other hardwoods, as cottonwood. Uses include furniture, caskets, shipping containers, interior trim, veneer, toys, and miscellaneous wood products. Black willow is found in all southern states. States having the greatest standing volume are Arkansas, Louisiana, and Mississippi.

### Species of Localized Importance

*Honey locust.* A tree with thorny bark, honey locust *(Gleditsia triacanthos)* is used in the manufacture of furniture, pallets, and skis. Its heartwood is heavy, of coarse grain, and light red in color while the sapwood is white. The principal commercial region is the Mississippi Valley. It is, however, found in all southern states.

*Sassafras.* This species *(Sassafras varifolium)* grows throughout the South but is found in greater commercial quantities in the lower part of the Mississippi Valley. The wood is used in boat construction, oars, exterior trim, and general millwork.

*Red cedar.* Common to all southern states, red cedar *(Juniperus virginiana)* is a species always in demand. Its durability as a fence post is well known. The heartwood is red and fragrant. The sapwood is white. It is most commonly used in cedar chests and in the lining of closets.

*Southern white cedar.* This species *(Chamaecyparis thyoides)* is common to the Southeast and is found particularly in Virginia, North Carolina, Alabama, and Florida in swamp areas. Fires will readily kill the tree. The wood is used for boat planks, tank stock, shingles, millwork, and lumber for crating. It is soft, light, and straight-grained. This species is also called "juniper."

*Red mulberry.* While found growing throughout the South, red mulberry *(Morus rubra)* is not commonly found on the hardwood market in large quantities. Its commercial range is the Southeast. It is a hard, ring-porous wood, with its lumber being used primarily in the manufacture of caskets.

*Red bay.* A species *(Persia borbonia)* of swampy areas, red bay ranges throughout the South but is produced only in small quantities. The leaves are aromatic. The wood is diffuse-porous and has a fine texture. At one time it was in demand for use in ship building.

*Black walnut.* This species *(Juglans nigra)*, known also by the name American walnut, grows in all southern states. It reaches its greatest growth, however, in the Mississippi Valley area. The wood is a walnut color. Few woods are in greater demand for furniture manufacture than this species.

*Holly.* This species *(Ilex opaca)* is a typical southern species. It reaches its greatest size in eastern Texas, Louisiana, southern Arkansas, and Alabama. Its wood is the whitest of all woods; it is sometimes dyed and used for making piano keys. It is also used in cabinets, veneer, and fancy inlays.

*Catalpa.* Commonly called "catawba," catalpa *(Catalpa bignonioides)* is found in all states. It is an excellent fence post species. The wood is coarse-grained. Since it is a slow-growing tree, its rings are close together. The tree is rarely found in sawlog size. The west coast of Florida is where trees of more commercial size are found.

*Black cherry.* This tree *(Prunus serotina)* is one of several species of cherry found in the South. It is the only one that reaches merchantable size. Its wood is dark-colored and in demand for quality furniture. Other uses include interior trim, paneling, and cabinet making.

*Persimmon.* The common persimmon *(Diospyros virginiana)* is a native to all southern states. Rarely is it found as a large tree. The wood is hard and strong and is in demand for golf club heads and shuttle blocks. About 5 million board feet is cut annually. Only the sapwood is favored by manufacturers for products. The heartwood has limited value.

*Basswood.* There are many species of basswood *(Tilia* sp.*)* in the South that are marketed as basswood. The greatest volume, however, is cut from the species known scientifically as *Tilia americana.* The wood of basswood is very light. It is soft-textured and does not warp to any degree. This species grows rapidly on rich, well-drained sites. Common uses are molding, venetian blinds, core stock for veneer paneling, excelsior, food containers, and pulpwood, to name but a few.

## COMMERCIAL TREES OF OTHER FOREST REGIONS

Throughout the nation, many coniferous and hardwood species are used for commercial purposes. The size of the trees and the quantity of trees are the principal factors relating to the utilization of a given species.

In the northeastern part of the United States, white pine, red spruce, hemlock, oak, beech, birch, and maple are among the principal species used for commercial purposes.

The forests of the western part of the United States, excluding the coast forests, are primarily open forests. The volume of saw-timber per acre is light due to limited rainfall. Among the major species used commercially are ponderosa pine, Idaho white pine, and sugar pine, and to a lesser extent, Douglas fir, white pine, Engelmann spruce, lodgepole pine, incense cedar, red cedar, cottonwood, and aspen.

Forests of the West Coast, located on the slopes of the Cascade Mountains in Washington and Oregon and in the coast range of northern California, contain the largest trees and the heaviest forest stands in the world. Along with the South, this is one of the country's greatest timber storehouses. Among the major species utilized commercially are Douglas fir, redwood, hemlock, western red cedar, Sitka spruce, Port Orford cedar, and several species of true fir.

A comprehensive listing of forest trees of the United States and the region in which they are located is found in Appendix VI.

A description of some of the commercial forest trees follows. Refer also to Figures 3-13 to 3-18.

*Red alder.* This species *(Alnus rubra)* grows along the Pacific Coast. Its wood varies from white to pinkish-brown and has low shrinkage. It is difficult to distinguish between heartwood and sapwood. The wood is light in weight and is used principally for furniture. Other uses include doors, sash, panel stock, and mill-work.

*Aspen.* This is the name applied to bigtooth aspen *(Populus grandidentata)* and quaking aspen *(Populus tremuloides)*. Lumber is produced from these species principally in the Northeastern and Lake States. There is some production in the Rocky Mountain States. The heartwood is grayish-white; the sapwood is lighter colored. The wood is straight-grained and easily worked. Produced from the wood are lumber, pulpwood, veneer, excelsior, matches, pallets, boxes, crating, and particleboard.

*Birch.* The principal birches are yellow birch *(Betula alleghaniensis)*, sweet birch *(Betula lenta)*, and paper birch *(Betula papyrifera)*. The sapwood of each is light-colored. The heartwood is brownish. The wood of yellow and sweet birch is heavy and strong and uniform in texture. Paper birch weighs less, is softer, and is weaker than yellow and sweet birch. The wood is used for turned products. Yellow and sweet birch are made principally into furniture, crates, cooperage, interior finish, baskets, and wooden-ware.

*Alaska cedar.* This species *(Chamaecyparis nootkatensis)* is common to Washington and Oregon. The heartwood is yellowish. The sapwood is hard to distinguish from the heartwood. The wood is fine-textured and straight-grained. It is moderately heavy. The heartwood is very resistant to decay. Principal products made from the wood include furniture, small boats, and novelties.

*Balsam fir.* This species *(Abies balsamea)* grows in the north-eastern states. The yellowish sapwood is difficult to distinguish from the heartwood. The wood is considered light in weight and is used primarily for pulpwood.

*Western firs.* Six commercial species include subalpine fir *(Abies lasiocarpa)*, California red fir *(Abies magnifica)*, grand fir *(Abies grandis)*, noble fir *(Abies procera)*, Pacific silver fir *(Abies amabilis)*, and white fir *(Abies concolor)*. The wood of these firs is light in weight but strong. All firs are marketed as white fir. The wood is used principally for lumber and general millwork.

*Eastern hemlock.* This species *(Tsuga canadensis)* grows in the northeastern part of the United States. The heartwood is pale brown while the sapwood is slightly lighter in color. The wood is coarse, light in weight, and low in strength. Hemlock is used principally for lumber, pulpwood, and in the manufacture of boxes and crates.

*Western hemlock. (Tsuga heterophylla)* grows along the Pacific Coast of Oregon and Washington and in the northern Rocky Mountains. The heartwood and sapwood are almost white with a purple tinge. Hemlock is moderately light in weight and moderate in strength. The wood is used principally for pulpwood, lumber, and plywood. Large quantities are used in the manufacture of boxes, crates, flooring, and pallets.

*Incense cedar.* Incense cedar *(Libocedrus decurrens)* grows in California, Oregon, and Nevada. The sapwood is white or cream-colored. The heartwood is light brown. The wood is fine-textured and has a spicy odor. It is light in weight and moderately low in strength. The wood is used principally for lumber and fence posts.

*Eastern white pine.* This white pine *(Pinus strobus)* grows in the northeastern portion of the United States. The wood is very uniform in texture and straight-grained. It is light in weight and moderately soft. The wood is converted mainly to lumber from which many secondary products are made.

*Ponderosa pine.* Ponderosa pine *(Pinus ponderosa)* has a wide range in the Pacific Northwest. The heartwood is a reddish-brown and the wide sapwood is nearly white to yellowish. The wood is used mainly for lumber and to a lesser extent for poles, posts, veneer, ties, and piles.

*Sugar pine.* This species *(Pinus lambertiana)* is common to California and Oregon. The heartwood is light brown while the sapwood is creamy white. The wood is straight-grained, uniform in texture, and easy to work with tools. Sugar pine is used almost entirely for lumber products.

*Western white pine.* This tree *(Pinus monticola)* is better known as Idaho white pine since Idaho is the main producing area. It does grow in Washington, Montana, and Oregon as well. Its heartwood is creamy white which darkens on exposure. The sapwood is yellowish-white. The wood is light in weight and moderately low in strength. Practically all western white pine is sawed into lumber and used in building construction.

*Redwood.* Known also as sequoia, this species *(Sequoia sempervirens)* grows in a limited area in the Sierra Nevadas of California. The heartwood of the tree ranges from a light cherry to a dark mahogany. The narrow sapwood is almost white. The wood is straight-grained and is easy to work. The heartwood has high decay resistance. Most redwood is used for building purposes. Because of its durability, it is used in cooling towers and tanks.

*Eastern spruce.* The term "eastern spruce" includes red spruce *(Picea rubens)*, white spruce *(Picea glauca)*, and black spruce *(Picea mariana)*. The latter two grow principally in the Lake States and New England while red spruce grows in New England and the Appalachian Mountains. No distinction is made in commerce between these species. The wood is light in color, with little distinction between sapwood and heartwood. The wood is moderately light in weight and easily worked. The greatest use of the wood is for pulpwood.

*Sitka spruce.* This tree *(Picea sitchensis)* grows in an area from California to Alaska. The heartwood is light brown. The sapwood is creamy white. The wood has uniform texture and straight grain. It is used primarily for lumber, pulpwood, and cooperage. Other important uses include furniture, millwork, and boats.

Table 10-4 shows the volumes of the principal softwood and hardwood species found in the western United States.

### TABLE 10-4

### NET VOLUME OF SAWTIMBER ON TIMBERLAND IN THE WESTERN UNITED STATES, 1987

| Species | Volume |
|---|---|
| | *(million board feet)* |
| Douglas fir | 505,926 |
| Ponderosa and Jeffrey pines | 188,227 |
| True fir | 208,557 |
| Western hemlock | 195,118 |
| Sugar pine | 23,972 |
| Western white pine | 14,329 |
| Redwood | 30,495 |
| Sitka spruce | 65,148 |
| Englemann and other spruces | 93,489 |
| Western larch | 34,388 |
| Incense cedar | 24,167 |
| Lodgepole pine | 76,279 |
| Other western softwoods | 53,218 |
| Total softwoods | 1,513,313 |
| Cottonwood-aspen | 17,748 |
| Red alder | 26,261 |
| Oak | 17,575 |
| Other western hardwoods | 17,130 |
| Total hardwoods | 78,714 |
| Total all species | 1,592,027 |

(Source: U.S. Forest Service, Preliminary RPA Review Draft, 1988)

### *BIBLIOGRAPHY*

Anderson, LeRoy O. *Selection and Use of Wood Products for Home and Farm Buildings.* Agriculture Information Bulletin No. 311. Madison, Wis.: U.S. Forest Products Laboratory, 1972.

Gurfinkel, German. *Wood Engineering.* New Orleans, La.: Southern Forest Products Association. Upton Printing Company, 1973.

Hedlund, Arnold, and Knight, Herbert A. *Hardwood Distribution Maps for the South.* Resource Bulletin SO-19. New Orleans, La.: Southern Forest Experiment Station, 1969.

Hoyle, Robert J. *Wood Technology in the Design of Structures.* Missoula, Mont.: Mountain Press Publishing Company, 1973.

Knight, Herbert A., and Hilmon, J. B. *The Hardwood Timber Supply Situation in the Eastern United States.* Asheville, N.C.: U.S. Forest Service, 1978.

Koch, Peter. *Utilization of the Southern Pines.* 4 Vols. Agricultural Handbook 420. Washington, D.C.: U.S. Forest Service, 1972.

Lewey, Helen J. *Trees of the North Central States—Their Distribution and Use.* General Technical Report NC-12. St. Paul, Minn.: North Central Forest Experiment Station, 1975.

Miller, William D. *An Annotated Bibliography of Southern Hardwoods.* Technical Bulletin No. 176. Raleigh, N.C.: North Carolina Experiment Station, 1967.

*Proceedings-Second Symposium on Southeastern Hardwoods.* Atlanta, Ga.: U.S. Forest Service, 1977.

*The Southern Hardwoods.* Memphis, Tenn.: Southern Hardwood Lumber Manufacturers Association, 1977.

U.S. Forest Products Laboratory. *Dividends from Wood Research.* Madison, Wis.: U.S. Forest Service, 1974.

U.S. Forest Products Laboratory. *Wood Handbook.* Agricultural Handbook 72. Madison, Wis.: U.S. Forest Service, 1987.

*Veneer Species That Grow in the United States.* Research Paper FPL 167. Washington, D.C.: U.S. Forest Service, 1972.

Wahlgren, H. E., and Schumann, D. R. *Properties of Major Southern Pines.* Research Paper FPL 176-177. Madison, Wis.: U.S. Forest Products Laboratory, 1972.

*What You Should Know About Lumber.* Washington, D.C.: National Lumber Manufacturers Association, Undated.

*Woodland Handbook for the Pacific Northwest.* Corvallis, Ore.: Cooperative Extension Service, Oregon State University, 1969.

# CHAPTER XI

# Harvesting and Manufacturing Forest Products

Over 10,000 different products are manufactured using wood as the raw material—from lumber to plastics, from paper to fabrics. The principal uses of timber are for lumber, paper, building boards—including plywood and veneer—poles, piling, and fuelwood. Table 11-1 shows the volume of timber harvested in the United States by major primary product and region of harvest in 1986, the latest year for which statistics are available.

Since 1952 sharp increases have occurred in the production of pulpwood and plywood logs. Pulpwood has risen from 1.8 billion cubic feet in 1952 to 4.3 billion cubic feet in 1986, with most of the increase occurring in the South. Veneer and plywood log production has risen rapidly in the last decades due to rising use of softwood plywood, much of it as a result of the spectacular expanding southern softwood plywood industry. Starting production in 1963, pine plywood now accounts for over 90 per cent of the nation's output of soft plywood.

Each timber product is important in the total picture of timber management; that is, each product allows the grower to remove timber, receive payment for it, and improve the productivity of the stand. One of the best examples is pulpwood, the raw material for the myriad of paper products. It is an important product for making timber stands very productive. In the case of a pine plantation, for example, about 700 trees per acre are commonly set out, but in the final harvest only about 60 trees per acre are cut. In the interim period, some of the trees are lost from natural mortality. Most of the trees, however, should be removed for pulpwood, with some harvested for fence posts, poles, and sawlogs. These intermediate cuts are the prime cash crops for timber growers.

**TABLE 11-1**

**VOLUME OF TIMBER HARVESTED
IN THE UNITED STATES, 1986**

| Region | Softwoods | Hardwoods | Total | Per Cent |
|---|---|---|---|---|
| | . . . . . . . . . . . . *(thousand cubic feet)*. . . . . . . . . . . | | | |
| *Northeast* | | | | |
| Sawlogs | 297,552 | 324,019 | 621,571 | 28 |
| Pulpwood | 264,078 | 246,037 | 510,115 | 23 |
| Veneer logs | 8,702 | 19,087 | 27,789 | 1 |
| Fuelwood | 86,335 | 890,561 | 976,896 | 46 |
| Other industrial[1] | 21,143 | 31,948 | 53,091 | 2 |
| Total | 677,810 | 1,511,652 | 2,189,462 | |
| Per Cent | 31 | 69 | | 100 |
| *North Central* | | | | |
| Sawlogs | 45,937 | 401,723 | 447,660 | 24 |
| Pulpwood | 113,923 | 351,980 | 465,903 | 25 |
| Veneer logs | 871 | 14,286 | 15,157 | 1 |
| Fuelwood | 38,706 | 749,767 | 788,473 | 41 |
| Other industrial[1] | 23,382 | 148,834 | 172,216 | 9 |
| Total | 222,819 | 1,666,590 | 1,889,409 | |
| Per Cent | 12 | 88 | | 100 |
| *Great Plains*[2] | | | | |
| Sawlogs | 22,571 | 8,626 | 31,197 | 34 |
| Pulpwood | 223 | — | 223 | — |
| Veneer logs | — | 193 | 193 | — |
| Fuelwood | 2,635 | 55,925 | 58,560 | 64 |
| Other industrial[1] | 971 | 357 | 1,328 | 2 |
| Total | 26,400 | 65,101 | 91,501 | |
| Per Cent | 29 | 71 | | 100 |
| *Southeast* | | | | |
| Sawlogs | 1,064,779 | 344,021 | 1,408,800 | 38 |
| Pulpwood | 1,149,361 | 433,990 | 1,583,351 | 42 |
| Veneer logs | 220,816 | 49,391 | 270,207 | 7 |
| Fuelwood | 43,389 | 358,091 | 401,480 | 11 |
| Other industrial[1] | 47,630 | 14,926 | 62,556 | 2 |
| Total | 2,525,975 | 1,200,419 | 3,726,394 | |
| Per Cent | 68 | 32 | | 100 |

(Continued)

**TABLE 11-1 (Continued)**

| Region | Softwoods | Hardwoods | Total | Per Cent |
|---|---|---|---|---|
| | . . . . . . . . . . . . *(thousand cubic feet)*. . . . . . . . . . . | | | |
| *South Central* | | | | |
| Sawlogs | 1,108,212 | 557,649 | 1,665,861 | 38 |
| Pulpwood | 1,058,619 | 642,166 | 1,700,785 | 39 |
| Veneer logs | 515,643 | 21,766 | 537,409 | 12 |
| Fuelwood | 9,836 | 335,382 | 345,218 | 8 |
| Other industrial[1] | 84,058 | 19,660 | 103,718 | 3 |
| Total | 2,776,368 | 1,576,623 | 4,352,991 | |
| Per Cent | 64 | 36 | | 100 |
| *Douglas Fir Subregion* | | | | |
| Sawlogs | 1,273,003 | 80,279 | 1,353,282 | 44 |
| Pulpwood | 99,806 | 34,719 | 134,525 | 4 |
| Veneer logs | 572,531 | 12,920 | 585,451 | 19 |
| Fuelwood | 139,522 | 87,832 | 227,354 | 7 |
| Other industrial[1] | 770,000 | 1,287 | 771,287 | 26 |
| Total | 2,854,862 | 217,037 | 3,071,899 | |
| Per Cent | 93 | 7 | | 100 |
| *Ponderosa Pine Subregion* | | | | |
| Sawlogs | 619,916 | — | 619,916 | 78 |
| Pulpwood | 94 | — | 94 | — |
| Veneer logs | 123,728 | — | 123,728 | 16 |
| Fuelwood | 51,103 | — | 51,103 | 6 |
| Other industrial[1] | 1,154 | — | 1,154 | — |
| Total | 795,995 | — | 795,995 | |
| Per Cent | 100 | — | | 100 |
| *Alaska* | | | | |
| Sawlogs | 36,839 | 77 | 36,916 | 35 |
| Pulpwood | 20,376 | — | 20,376 | 19 |
| Veneer logs | — | — | — | — |
| Fuelwood | 7,681 | 6,063 | 13,744 | 13 |
| Other industrial[1] | 33,931 | 12 | 33,943 | 33 |
| Total | 98,827 | 6,152 | 104,979 | |
| Per Cent | 94 | 6 | | 100 |

(Continued)

TABLE 11-1 (Continued)

| Region | Softwoods | Hardwoods | Total | Per Cent |
|---|---|---|---|---|
| | . . . . . . . . . . . . *(thousand cubic feet)* . . . . . . . . . . . | | | |
| *Pacific Northwest Total*[3] | | | | |
| Sawlogs | 1,929,758 | 80,356 | 2,010,114 | 51 |
| Pulpwood | 120,276 | 34,719 | 154,995 | 4 |
| Veneer logs | 696,259 | 12,920 | 709,179 | 18 |
| Fuelwood | 198,306 | 93,895 | 292,201 | 7 |
| Other industrial[1] | 805,085 | 1,299 | 806,384 | 20 |
| Total | 3,749,684 | 223,189 | 3,972,873 | |
| Per Cent | 94 | 6 | | 100 |
| *Pacific Southwest* | | | | |
| Sawlogs | 669,527 | 1,701 | 671,228 | 77 |
| Pulpwood | 4,166 | 7,904 | 12,070 | 1 |
| Veneer logs | 34,761 | — | 34,761 | 4 |
| Fuelwood | 84,119 | 60,937 | 145,056 | 16 |
| Other industrial[1] | 16,824 | — | 16,824 | 2 |
| Total | 809,397 | 70,542 | 879,939 | |
| Per Cent | 92 | 8 | | 100 |
| *Rocky Mountains* | | | | |
| Sawlogs | 584,822 | 3,115 | 587,937 | 69 |
| Pulpwood | 38,948 | 150 | 39,098 | 5 |
| Veneer logs | 77,695 | — | 77,695 | 9 |
| Fuelwood | 82,009 | 23,841 | 105,850 | 12 |
| Other industrial[1] | 42,631 | 3,135 | 45,766 | 5 |
| Total | 826,105 | 30,241 | 856,346 | |
| Per Cent | 96 | 4 | | 100 |
| *United States* | | | | |
| Sawlogs | 5,723,158 | 1,721,210 | 7,444,368 | 41 |
| Pulpwood | 2,749,594 | 1,716,946 | 4,466,540 | 25 |
| Veneer logs | 1,554,747 | 117,643 | 1,672,390 | 10 |
| Fuelwood | 545,335 | 2,568,399 | 3,113,734 | 17 |
| Other industrial[1] | 1,041,724 | 220,159 | 1,261,883 | 7 |
| Grand Total[4] | 11,614,558 | 6,344,357 | 17,958,915 | |
| Per Cent | 65 | 35 | | 100 |

[1]Includes roundwood used for cooperage, pilings, poles, posts, shakes, shingle, board mills, charcoal, export logs, etc.
[2]Includes Kansas, Nebraska, North Dakota, and east and west South Dakota.
[3]Includes Douglas Fir Subregion, Ponderosa Pine Subregion, and Alaska.
[4]Excludes figures for the Pacific Northwest Total.

(Source: U.S. Forest Service, Preliminary RPA Review Draft, 1988)

## PRODUCT SPECIFICATIONS

Each individual timber product has its own specifications. Generally the higher the value of the product, the more stringent or limiting are the specifications; for example, in the case of softwood, the acceptable limits for pulpwood are quite broad, whereas those for poles and piling are quite narrow. With hardwood, the range of material suitable to make railroad crossties is very wide, while that suitable for veneer bolts is very narrow.

### Pulpwood

Virtually all softwoods and hardwoods are now acceptable to pulp and paper mills. A few firms specify particular species. Practically all species of hardwood are purchased by some mills; but volumes are sometimes limited, especially for the hard hardwoods such as the oaks. Figure 11-1 shows a Hahn harvester which can delimb a tree, cut the timber into the proper lengths, and stack it in a single operation.

Fig. 11-1. This Hahn harvester can delimb, cut to length, and stack pulpwood in one operation. (Courtesy American Pulpwood Association)

Minimum-sized pulptimber trees are 5 inches in dbh. Generally these trees are too small to yield enough pulpwood to justify cutting. A practical minimum is more like a 7-inch dbh. The trees must be sound and unburned.

No two pulp and paper mills or U.S. regions have identical pulpwood specifications. Individual mill requirements may be obtained from each firm. Some generalized pulpwood specifications are as follows:

1. Pulpwood is classified as *shortwood* if under 120 inches in length and *longwood* if over 120 inches long. Some general lengths by regions are 48 inches in the Northeast; 4 feet, 5 feet, 5 feet 2 inches, 5 feet 3 inches, and 5 feet 4 inches in the South; 100 inches in the Lake States; and 90 inches in the West. Some paper mills purchase tree length pulpwood.

2. Minimum softwood diameter at the small end, measured inside the bark, must not be less than 4 inches, although a few smaller sticks are allowed by some mills. Minimum hardwood diameters are usually 5 inches. Generally no maximum diameters exist, but a few mills have specified upper limits.

3. All trees must be sawed and limbs trimmed close to the surface of the stick.

4. Sticks must be cut from sound, live trees free from charred or pitch wood and metal.


## Fence Posts

Like pulpwood, fence posts provide good outlets for small timber, especially for that cut in the thinning of softwood plantations. Pines are preferred species because of the ease of treatment with preservatives, but some hardwood, such as sweet gum, is finding increasing use. Trees used for fence posts must be reasonably straight and the wood fairly dense for adequate post strength. Minimum tree size is 5 inches in dbh, but generally posts are harvested from larger timber. The sizes are designated by the top diameter and usually run from 2½ inches to 8 inches, diameter inside bark. Post lengths generally run from 5 to 8 feet.

## Mine Timbers

Some limited markets are still available for timber used in mines as supports in the construction of tunnels, shafts, openings, and chambers. Hardwoods, principally oak, and the southern pines are the main species used. The species used must be high in bending and column strength. Some material is sawn and some used as round timbers.

Mine timbers are usually taken down to 4-inch diameters. This provides an outlet for small-sized and short-length timber. It is a low-valued product receiving minimum prices. A considerable volume of mine timbers are exported to Mexico.

## Railroad Crossties

The demand for railroad crossties, used to support the steel track, has continued to be good in recent years. Only a few ties are still hewn; that is, cut into rectangular shapes with an adz or large axe. Most ties are sawn in small portable sawmills. Ties are produced principally from low-grade hardwood because the higher grades of it and pine have become too valuable and are used for sawtimber.

Larger-sized, low-grade southern pine, Douglas fir, and other softwoods, and virtually all species of low-grade hardwood, such as oaks and gums, are suitable for ties. Generally trees not suitable for other uses are best sold for this product. In recent years sawn crosstie prices have increased appreciably. Minimum-sized trees are those suitable for sawtimber, that is, 9 inches dbh.

Railroad ties are produced in rectangular shapes in sizes from 6 by 7 inches to 7 by 9 inches. Lengths vary from 6½-foot narrow gauge ties to 8-, 8½-, and 9-foot standard gauge ties. Most ties are pressure treated with coal-tar creosote to increase their service life.

## Sawtimber

Sawtimber trees are generally those cut into sawlogs to produce lumber, veneer, and plywood. Demand for both softwood (pines, firs, etc.) and hardwood sawtimber continues to reach all-time highs. Virtually all softwoods are harvested for sawtimber with the southern pines, Douglas fir, and ponderosa pine especially desirable for lumber production. Virtually all species of hardwood of adequate quality can be used to produce lumber. Lower grades of hardwood may be used to produce board road—a low-grade lumber used to build roads for oil well drilling rigs.

Sawtimber trees are usually at least 8 inches dbh, but generally are of larger diameter. Sawtimber values, however, vary greatly with species and size. A 16-inch, three 16-foot log tree will scale about 10 times as many board feet as a 10-inch, one 16-foot log tree, and the grade and value of the logs will be much higher.

Due to the nature of volume tables, tree volumes practically double with each 2-inch increase in dbh from 8- through 16-inch trees. This has led to the statements that a 10-inch tree has twice the volume of an 8-inch tree, a 12-inch tree twice that of a 10-inch tree, a 14-inch tree twice that of a 12-inch tree, and a 16-inch tree twice that of a 14-inch tree. This phenomenon occurs because of the loss in slab and edging in producing lumber from small diameters. Since the smaller-diametered trees virtually double in volume and value between each 2-inch diameter class, it makes them especially valuable. Under average southern and some western coastal sites growing conditions, these trees will grow into the next larger 2-inch diameter class in less than six years. The rate of annual volume and value increase may be as high as 15 to 20 per cent or more per year. This is one reason why intermediate cuttings should be done with the smaller diameters. This increase in volume and value is illustrated in Table 11-2.

**TABLE 11-2**

**AVERAGE VOLUME AND VALUE INCREASES IN
SMALL-DIAMETERED TREES FROM 8 TO 18
INCHES, SCRIBNER RULE**

| | Tree dbh | | | | | |
|---|---|---|---|---|---|---|
| | 8″ | 10″ | 12″ | 14″ | 16″ | 18″ |
| Average Volume, Board Feet, Scribner Rule | 14 | 28 | 61 | 114 | 211 | 306 |
| Stumpage Values, Dollars | | | | | | |
| $70/MBF | $0.98 | $1.96 | $4.27 | $ 7.98 | $14.77 | $21.42 |
| $80/MBF | 1.12 | 2.24 | 4.88 | 9.12 | 16.88 | 24.48 |
| $100/MBF | 1.40 | 2.80 | 6.10 | 11.40 | 21.11 | 30.60 |

Markets also exist for high-quality hardwood sawtimber to be used to make cooperage for barrels, baskets, and boxes. Cooperage material includes top-quality white oak, cow oak, overcup oak, and post oak. Basket and box industries utilize quality black gum, sweet gum, sycamore, cottonwood, and some of the big-leaf elms such as American and slippery elms. The demand and price for black walnut is very high.

Sawlogs are measured in terms of diameters inside the bark at the small end to the nearest inch. This material is cut into lengths in increments of 2 feet. Minimum diameter for sawlogs is generally 6 inches and minimum length is 8 feet. Smaller-sized plywood log cores are sometimes cut into lumber with specialized mills.

Lumber is usually cut as boards of up to but not including 2-inch thickness, dimensions of 2-inch thickness up to but not including 5 inches, and timbers of a 5-inch thickness or larger. Lumber widths are generally in even 2-inch units such as 2-inch, 4-inch, 6-inch, 8-inch, etc. Lumber lengths are usually in even 2-foot units such as 8-foot, 10-foot, 12-foot, 14-foot, etc. Hardwood lumber thickness is commonly cut into fifths of an inch and both even- and odd-inch widths. All measurements are prior to planing.

In 1970, the U.S. Department of Commerce Standard (PS20-70) stated that sawmills must produce green lumber to one size schedule and dry lumber to another slightly smaller set of sizes. Two-inch southern yellow pine lumber is now sawn 1⅞ inches thick and 1-inch lumber ⅞ inch thick.

## Poles

The demand for preservative-treated and some untreated utility poles has remained high despite the trend to put electric communication cables underground. Most utility and telephone poles are produced from pine, Douglas fir, cedar, and western larch timber. Pine species generally used are longleaf, lodgepole, shortleaf, loblolly, slash, and ponderosa pines. Poles and piling represent a high-value product for pine, cedar, fir, and larch. Occasionally some tall, straight hardwood species such as sweet gum may be used also for poles.

The specifications on pole timber are very high. Generally only about 5 per cent of the trees in a normal stand are suitable for poles. The most limiting factor is the form of the tree. If the tree has sweep or bend in one plane or direction, it cannot be more than 1 inch for each 6 feet of length. If the sweep is in two directions or planes, it cannot fall outside the surface of the pole when a straight line is run connecting the midpoint at the base of the pole and a midpoint at its top.

Poles must also be free of defects such as crossbreaks or cracks, bird holes, hollow butts or tops from red heart or other decay, or splits in the butt or top; they must also be free of metal. Each pole has to be free of scars or turpentine faces within two feet of the ground line. Limitations are placed also on the extent of spiral grain and on allowable knot sizes. Figure 11-2 shows debarked poles prior to treatment with chemical preservatives.

Pole lengths generally run from 25 feet in length to 75 feet in 5-foot intervals. A few shorter or longer poles are cut for special orders, such as barn poles. Shorter lengths are cut in 2-foot intervals. Minimum allowable circumferences are established for poles near the butt and top by classes. Pole classes are established running from 1 through 10, with Class 1 the highest or most valuable in terms of classes, and 10 the lowest. The minimum circumfer-

Fig. 11-2. These poles have been debarked and knots trimmed prior to entering the pressure treating cylinder for preservative treatment. (Courtesy Mississippi Cooperative Extension Service)

ence is measured 6 feet from the butt (except for Classes 8, 9, and 10) and at the top. Also, the circumference at 6 feet from the butt of a pole in Classes 1 through 7 is not to be more than 7 inches larger than the specified minimum. The top dimensional requirements apply at a point corresponding to the minimum length permitted for the pole. Table 11-3 indicates dimensions for some pole classes and lengths established by the American Standards Association, 1963.

TABLE 11-3

DIMENSIONS FOR PINE POLES, CLASSES 1, 3, 5, AND 7

|  |  | Length in Feet | | | | | |
|---|---|---|---|---|---|---|---|
|  | Class | 25 | 35 | 40 | 45 | 50 | 60 |
| Min. Top Cir. in Inches | 1 | — | — | — | 27 | — | — |
| Min. Cir. 6 Feet from Butt | 1 | 33.5 | 39.0 | 41.0 | 43.0 | 45.0 | 48.0 |
| Min. Top Cir. in Inches | 3 | — | — | — | 23 | — | — |
| Min. Cir. 6 Feet from Butt | 3 | 29.5 | 34.0 | 36.0 | 37.5 | 39.0 | 42.0 |
| Min. Top Cir. in Inches | 5 | — | — | — | 19 | — | — |
| Min. Cir. 6 Feet from Butt | 5 | 25.5 | 29.0 | 31.0 | 32.5 | 34.0 | 36.0 |
| Min. Top Cir. in Inches | 7 | — | — | — | 15 | — | — |
| Min. Cir. 6 Feet from Butt | 7 | 21.5 | 25.0 | 26.5 | —— | —— | —— |

Most poles are sold on a percentage of the delivered price. The stumpage price will generally average about 50 per cent of the cut, peeled, and delivered price to the treating plant. For larger poles, the stumpage may run as high as 65 per cent of the delivered price with the smaller poles averaging less than 50 per cent.

In areas of high competition for sawlogs and veneer bolts, some pole buyers will bid on entire timber stands and offer an overall price per thousand board feet for poles and sawtimber. This technique has been received with favor by timber growers because it aids them in comparing buyer price offers.

### Piling

Piling is a specialty item generally pressure treated with creosote for use in the construction of bridges, docks, wharves, and foundations, and in other heavy general construction. Under wet or submerged conditions, creosote has proven to be the most effective preservative. The demand for piling is now limited, due to a shift to steel and concrete for much of the construction formerly done with wood piling. The current use for piling is principally for docks and wharves, so demand is best near coastal ports.

The same requirements in selecting poles are employed in selecting piling, with the addition that piles must be shock resistant and generally straighter in form. Prices paid for piling are somewhat higher than those paid for poles.

Piling may be of any species of wood which will withstand driving and will support the required loads. Common piling species include southern pine, Douglas fir, elm, oak, maple, and cypress. Some western larch, tamarack, cedars, hemlock, and spruces are also used for this purpose.

Timber piles are classified under three general classes, according to their intended use, such as A, B, and C. Class A, the highest, includes piling suitable for railway bridges and other heavy construction. The minimum diameter of the butt permits the use of load-bearing timber caps 14 inches in width. Class B piling is suitable for use in docks, wharves, bridges, and foundations, and for general construction. The minimum diameter of the butt permits the use of load-bearing timber caps 12 inches in width. In some cases smaller sizes than those stipulated for Class B may be used, but the Class B quality is desired for use with light bearing values or special cases such as the use of concrete caps. Class C piling is suitable for use in foundations which will be completely submerged for cofferdams, falsework, or light construction.

### Veneer Timbers

Veneer timbers generally refer to large, high-quality hardwood species to produce face veneers for paneling; commercial veneers for crossbands, cores, backs, and concealed furniture parts; and container veneers for baskets and boxes. In the broad sense, timber used to produce softwood plywood also falls into this category. Softwood plywood timber is generally purchased as sawtimber.

Virtually all species of hardwood timber of sufficient size and quality are used for veneer. This includes not only the gums, oaks, walnuts, ashes, and maples but also such minor species as hickory, box elder, persimmon, catalpa, and sassafras. The demand for veneer timber has been strong. This has been reflected in steadily rising prices. Stumpage prices for pecan, cherry, and walnut are especially high.

For some years the demand for hardwood plywood, particularly for paneling, doors, furniture, and certain construction uses has been met to a considerable extent by imports of "Philippine mahogany" or "Luan" from Southeast Asia. Fifty to 60 per cent of current consumption of hardwood veneer and plywood is met by imports. However, demand for native hardwood veneers, especially for furniture and paneling, continues to be very high.

Veneer timber is generally cut from large-diametered trees, that is, larger than 20 inches in dbh. The portion of the tree used for veneer must be free of defects, including rot and limbs. Frequently veneer logs will be cut from the lower portion of the tree stem and a sawlog from the remaining merchantable portion. The size of timber suitable for veneer has been dropping due to a shortage of larger timber and also to improvements in veneer-cutting machines. Veneer logs are cut from trees 16 inches in dbh and in some instances even smaller. The trend toward use of smaller-diametered timber for veneer will continue.

Veneer is a thin sheet of wood of uniform thickness produced by peeling, slicing, or sawing logs, bolts, and flitches. It may be cut thick enough to be used as is or glued together as thin sheets to form plywood. Thickness ranges from ⅛ to 1 inch of varied plies. Plywood is usually measured in terms of square feet of surface.

## HARVESTING

Harvesting or logging has been called the key to forestry. The best silvicultural plan depends upon logging to make it work. On the other hand, the productivity of timber stands can be virtually destroyed by poorly planned or careless logging. Even in forests managed primarily for purposes other than timber production, some cutting is often inevitable.

The cost of logging is a major item in the production of wood products. Timber is heavy, hard, and difficult to handle. It is generally utilized within 50 miles of its growing site, but sometimes it is hauled by railroad several hundred miles. Logging work is usually considered in the general grouping of dangerous occupations. The activities associated with it require persons skilled in woods work and the operation of logging equipment.

Logging costs are rising, so efficient and economical harvesting is essential to sustained yield forest management. As a result, logging must be carefully planned. It must be integrated with the silvicultural and forest protection activities. The logging plan should be a part of the forest management plan.

Some state forest practice acts, for example California and Massachusetts, require timber harvest plans. The U.S. Environmental Protection Agency is recommending that all states adopt such acts which require prior approval of harvest plans by state boards. The major concern is an attempt to design logging activities which will minimize soil erosion and other types of nonpoint source pollution.

A logging plan may be as comprehensive as the forest management plan. Some of the general considerations are as follows:

1. The location of cutting boundaries for the stand to be cut.
2. The marking of timber to be harvested except for clear cuts.
3. The cruise of timber to be removed to estimate volume by species and products, timber size, and its location.
4. The location of the most efficient log-loading sites.
5. The location of skid trails and haul roads.
6. The description of equipment to be used and the type of logging to be done; that is, short logs, long logs, or tree lengths.
7. The location of equipment storage points including fire-fighting tools, first aid containers, and other emergency equipment.

Logging involves the cutting of the tree, limbing, cutting into lengths, loading at that point for pulpwood bolts, or skidding to a central point for loading onto trucks or railroad cars and hauling to a mill. Each of these operations requires special skills and equipment. Due to rising labor costs, equipment is replacing people wherever possible in woods work.

## Felling and Bucking

Felling is the act of cutting or severing the tree from the stump, whereas bucking is the next step of limbing and cutting the tree stem into log or bolt lengths suitable for skidding and/or loading and hauling. The principal tools used are the power saw and axe; the use of the former has just about doubled the work-day output of felling and bucking crews over the use of hand saws. Large tree combines use huge hydraulic shears to fell and buck small trees. Other devices fit around tree trunks and limb them prior to felling. Crane or tractor-mounted shears will cut large sawtimber.

The average sawtimber felling and bucking output with a power saw in the South is from 4,000 to 8,000 board feet (MBM) per work day. The average pulpwood power saw output is from 3 to 10 cords per work day. These production ranges are similar for the North. Large western sawtimber outputs are up to five times higher. Some of the important factors affecting felling and bucking outputs are:

1. The volume of timber per acre to be cut and its size.
2. The skill of felling and bucking crews.
3. The terrain in terms of amount of brush, steepness, and drainage; that is, wet or dry sites.
4. The amount of defect in the timber.
5. The seasons of the year.

## Skidding

Skidding is that portion of the logging operation in which the logs are dragged from the point of bucking to a central location for loading onto trucks or railroad cars. In some cases this step is bypassed. For example, in the case of short pulpwood bolts they are hand carried and loaded directly onto the truck from the point where the tree was cut into bolts. Small sawlogs are sometimes loaded directly onto the hauling truck with special loading devices mounted on the truck.

Principal skidding equipment includes tractors, animals, and cables from powered drums. Average skidding output in the South and North with tractors is from 5 to 20 MBM of sawtimber and 6 to 14 cords for pulpwood—each on a per work-day basis. Production in the West may range 5 to 10 times higher in larger timber with big equipment. Figure 11-3 illustrates the use of a farm tractor to skid

Fig. 11-3. Farm tractors are used on small operations to skid sawlogs. Skidding output varies according to the terrain, size of logs, equipment used, and distance to the loading point. (Courtesy Mississippi Cooperative Extension Service)

sawlogs in the South. Balloon yarding (skidding) of logs was first experimented with in the United States in Oregon in 1964. Some very complex yarding systems have been developed using balloon techniques. While not competitive with conventional methods, balloon logging has promise in past inoperable, mountainous areas of the West and Alaska.

Factors involved in skidding are similar to those for felling and bucking but also include:

1. The difference in weight of logs; that is, hardwood is generally heavier by 50 per cent or more than softwood.
2. The distance to skid, with shorter distances being more efficient.
3. The amount of time required to bunch logs prior to skidding.

### Loading

Loading is the lifting of logs or bolts from the ground and placing them on trucks, trailers, and railroad cars. This is carefully done so they will withstand the jostling action during hauling and will make a compact load. Small pulpwood bolts are loaded by hand. Large logs are loaded with drum-powered cable devices on trucks, hydraulic cranes, front end hydraulic loaders, large cable cranes, and cables attached to the tractor skidders.

The average loading output in the East with cranes is from 8 to 40 MBM of sawtimber per work day with some western output higher. It is affected by weight, number of pieces, and effective loading time. Tree length logging has reduced the number of pieces to be loaded. The number of trucks and length of the haul are related to the effective loading time.

## Hauling

Most logs and bolts are hauled from the woods by the use of trucks to a wood-using mill or railroad siding for reloading for shipment of some distance to a mill. A few logs continue to be skidded directly to rail sidings, but this practice is fast disappearing. Every size and type of truck manufactured, from pick-up trucks to huge tractor-multi-trailer rigs, is used to haul bolts and logs. State laws establish the size of loads which may be carried in terms of length, width, and weight.

Generally 50 miles has been considered as a maximum trucking distance. Larger trucks with larger loads and improved roads and highways are increasing this distance so that 100 miles or more is no longer considered prohibitive for high-value timber.

The average hauling output in the East is about 3 to 10 cords of pulpwood and 4 to 20 MBM of sawlogs per work day with output in the West several times higher in larger timber. This statistic is increasing with improved trucks and highways. Hauling output is affected by the size of the load, length of the haul, quality of the road, and effective hauling time. The last factor refers to waiting time and loading and unloading time.

## Whole Tree Harvesting

A new concept of whole tree utilization on the logging site has caught the imagination of the U.S. forest industry. When conventional harvest systems are used, about 60 per cent of the total tree weight is utilized. The remaining tree parts such as tops, branches, stumps and roots, and needles or leaves are left in the forest. New logging equipment, commonly called whole tree chipper systems, is being used to cut, chip, and haul the stem, branches, and bark to pulp and paper mills, building board plants, cedar oil mills, and other units using tree chips in their manufacturing process. Figure 11-4 illustrates one of the tree chipping machines.

Fig. 11-4. A whole tree chipper unit chews up a 20-inch diameter tree in less than a minute—limbs, leaves, and all. Wood chips produced by this unit may be stockpiled for later loading or blown directly into large truck vans for transport to mills. This system not only increases forest production but also removes tops and limbs as forest debris, eliminates air pollution caused by slash burning if this practice is necessary or fire hazard if not used. Tree planting is also made easier. (Courtesy Department of Forestry, University of Illinois)

When tree farmers utilize this process, total forest yields are expected to increase by several tons of "wood" fiber per acre. Tree farmers will profit from whole tree harvest by receiving extra income from timber sales. This system is very popular with environmentally conscious landowners who are concerned with traditional logging debris.

Machines are being used in the South to lift the entire tree from the ground to utilize the stump and most of the roots in addition to the above-ground portion. Tests of building board manufactured from root wood have compared favorably with stem wood.

## MANUFACTURING

Once logs or bolts reach a wood-using firm, they may be handled in a variety of ways to manufacture one of the many wood products. They may be debarked, sawed, chipped, shaped, peeled, cooked, burned or glued, and dried. These treatments result in the production of lumber, paper, plywood, building boards, poles and piling, railroad crossties, fence posts, furniture, handles, and charcoal, to name some of the important items.

The South and the West are the major producers of all wood products while the Lake States and the Northeast are major producers of pulp and paper products and lumber; however, many projections for timber needs indicate the South is rapidly becoming the major production area for all wood products.

### Lumber

The nation's sawmills produced an estimated 41.7 billion board feet of lumber in 1986. This output is close to U.S. lumber production in 1927, over a half century earlier, and evidence that forest resources are renewable.

The 1986 lumber output would be enough lumber to build about 3.3 million new homes each year if all of this lumber were so used. Today, most sawmills are medium- or large-sized units and are permanently located. Lumber production methods are becoming more complex.

When logs arrive at a sawmill, they are generally stored until needed for processing. Tree-length logs at fully integrated operations are utilized for their most efficient use such as lumber, plywood, poles, chips, etc.

From the storage deck, logs are moved by bull chains or jack ladders or rolled into the mill. At larger mills, the logs are debarked prior to entering the mill so that slabs and edgings may be "hogged," or chopped, into pulp chips. The logs are rolled, one at a time, onto a carriage or holding device for sawing. An individual called a sawyer controls the headsaw to get the most and best lumber from each log. The headsaw removes slabs or the outer portion in reducing logs from the shape of cylinders to rectangles. It may further reduce the rectangle to boards and cants which move into a gangsaw or resaw. Figure 11-5 illustrates a chip-n-saw machine. Logs are stripped at bark, sawn into boards by gangsaws, and the slabs are chipped for use in paper and board mills. The sawdust will be conveyed to a storage bin and is also for sale to pulp and paper mills. With energy shortages, more and more mill residue is also burned to generate power.

Fig. 11-5. A chip-n-saw machine now used in many modern sawmills. Logs are stripped at bark, sawn into boards by gangsaws, and the slabs are chipped for use in paper and board mills. (Courtesy Department of Forestry, University of Illinois)

Headsaws traditionally have been flat, circular saws with teeth on their entire circumference or have been band-type saws. In recent years, special chipping headsaws have been developed which chip out the rectangular profile from the log while directly reducing the outside or slab to pulp chips. The logs may move back and forth on the carriage while being cut by the headsaw or go straight through the headsaw and then on to a resaw or edger. The saws of the edger cut boards (1-inch lumber) and dimensions (2-inch lumber plus) into proper widths. Finally the trimmer cuts the lumber into proper lengths. Wood cut off by the edger and trimmer goes to the hog, where pulp chips are produced, or for energy production (Chapter XV).

From the trimmer the lumber is carried by a "green chain" into a long sorting shed. Here experts grade the lumber according to specifications for quality adopted by the lumber manufacturing industry. The lumber may be stacked in the yard for air drying or loaded onto special cars to enter dry kilns. In kilns the lumber is rapidly seasoned under controlled conditions to reduce the moisture levels to those suitable for the area in which it will be used.

Larger mills have planing units which surface or smooth the rough lumber. In this case, grading takes place after surfacing, and the lumber is sorted into similar pieces and grades. Special products such as flooring, siding, and molding also are finished in the planing mills. Shavings from these mills, once used for poultry house litter, now find a strong demand for making building boards.

New innovations are automating sawmill operations. Electronic sorters automatically stack the lumber by size at very high rates of speed. Closed circuit TV allows machine operators to control equipment hundreds of feet away. X-ray machines and computers scan logs and instantly decide the most profitable way for headsaws to cut them. Computerized headsaws boost rough lumber recovery to 60 per cent. Thin saw blades reduce sawdust volumes by 5 per cent. Laser beams and water-jet headrigs may eliminate most sawdust and the need for some lumber planing.

Some modern mills are equipped with electro-mechanical machines which can measure the stiffness and strength characteristics of individual pieces of lumber and stamp a strength value on each piece as it passes through the machine. Lumber processed this way is marketed as "stress rated" or "stress graded" and can be used more efficiently and safely in construction components requiring materials which meet certain stress-bearing specifications.

## Paper

Paper and paper board production is one of the fastest growing industries in the United States, which produces about half of the world's pulp and paper. Paper and paperboard production reached 73 million tons in 1986. Per capita consumption of paper and paperboard in this nation has almost doubled in the last three decades to about 660 pounds per person each year. In the past 30 years, the nation's pulpwood consumption increased by 3 times, rising to 94 million cords in 1986.

Paper mills turn out a variety of different materials, from raw pulp to attractive gift wrapping paper, with kraft, newsprint, magazine and book stock, writing paper, milk carton stock, bond, mimeograph, and wax paper in between, to name a few. Some building materials such as roofing felt and fiberboard are also made by the pulping process. In addition, wood pulp is used to manufacture other non-paper products such as rayon, cellophane, nitrocellulose, acetate plastics, photographic film, smokeless powder, tire cord, Scotch tape, telephone parts, and plastic handles and toys.

Paper was first made by the Chinese from the ground-up bark of mulberry about 2,000 years ago. An American chemist named Benjamin Tilghman discovered a chemical means to treat wood to reduce it to pulp in 1865. Since then the cooking of wood fiber in a chemical solution has been the most widely used pulp-making method.

When pulpwood bolts or logs arrive at a mill, they are stored in huge piles for later use. Figure 11-6 shows the method for handling tree-length pulpwood at a modern pulp and paper mill. From the stacks the pulpwood moves by conveyors to debarking machines where the logs are tumbled together in huge drums or sprayed with high-pressure jets to remove the bark. Next, the bolts move to large chippers to slice off small wood chips for the chemical process or to large, coarse grindstones to reduce the bolts to

Fig. 11-6. Tree-length pulpwood enters a "slasher" to be cut into pulpwood bolts. A series of trimmer saws makes quick work of converting tree-length logs into short bolts which can be handled by debarking drums. (Courtesy American Forest Council)

short fibers for the ground wood process; the latter is used to make much of the country's newsprint.

To make paper, the wood fiber or cellulose must be chemically separated from the lignin binder by cooking the wood in sulfite, soda, or sulfate solutions. This is done in digesters or huge pressure cookers where the wood and chemicals are cooked under steam pressure, reducing the whole to a mass of wet pulp of individual fibers. The chemicals are removed and the pulp thoroughly washed.

From this stage the wood pulp goes through beaters which separate the individual fibers to make uniform sheets of pulp. Often sizing for smoothness and water resistance, bleach, and color are added during this process.

The final step is for the wet pulp to enter the Fourdrinier paper machine. It is sprayed onto an endless wire screen to interlace the wood fibers while drawing off the water. From the screen the continuous mat moves onto a belt of wool felt and then through a series of rollers which squeeze out more water. The material then moves into the dry end of the Fourdrinier through a series of heated rollers called dryers. Finally it is wound onto rollers which vary in width from a few feet to 25 feet and may weigh a ton or more.

Recycling of paper in the manufacture of paper and paperboard has been under way in the United States for many years, with the current recycle rate nearly 21 per cent. Much paper used in the United States is not recoverable. Studies indicate that the tonnage recycled may rise to 25 to 30 per cent in the future.

### Veneer and Plywood

The U.S. veneer and plywood industries are growing rapidly. Domestic softwood plywood production in 1986 was 22.1 billion square feet (⅜ inch basis), while hardwood plywood production reached almost 1.1 billion square feet. The South was responsible for over 50 per cent of total softwood plywood production and about 80 per cent of hardwood plywood production in that year.

Veneer is a thin sheet of wood, ¼ inch in thickness or less, and is used to make containers such as baskets, boxes, and furniture items. Plywood is manufactured from three or more sheets of veneer glued together, with the grain of alternate sheets running at right angles for strength. It is used for paneling, sheathing, furniture, concrete forms, sporting equipment, and for hundreds of other uses.

When veneer or plywood logs arrive at a plant, they are cut into lengths to fit the lathe or veneer-cutting equipment. The bolts are usually heated in vats to facilitate removal of bark and to soften the wood for easy cutting. They are heated for several hours in hot water or steam chests, after which they are debarked and then moved to the lathe or veneer-cutting machine with a mechanical hoist. The bolt is turned in the lathe to peel a thin sheet of continuous rotary veneer, or it is sliced or sawed into sheets by veneer-cutting machines. Rotary veneer moves down a conveyor to large knives or clippers where it is cut into required sizes, and defective portions are removed. Figure 11-7 shows veneer being stacked after it comes from the clippers in a southern pine plywood plant. The bolts are peeled to small diameters, limited only by the size of the lathe chucks. The cores are either sawn for lumber, sold for pulpwood or fence posts, or hogged for pulp chips.

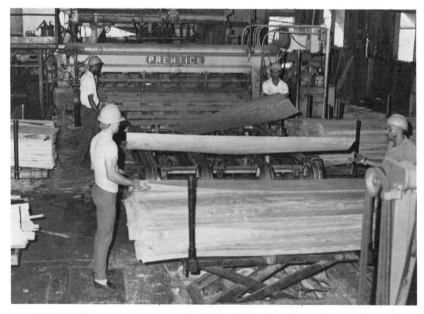

Fig. 11-7. Rotary pine veneer is graded and stacked after being cut into widths by a clipping machine in a southern pine plywood plant. (Courtesy Mississippi Cooperative Extension Service)

The sheets of veneer are seasoned in dryers, run through glue machines, and assembled in sets, depending on the number of plies or sheets in the plywood. The sheets are inserted into hot presses to glue together. From the presses the sheets are trimmed to size, patched for defects for higher grades, and finally sanded on one or both sides if required.

## Poles and Piling

Pole and piling production in the United States has been relatively stable in recent years despite a shift to underground utilities and other piling materials.

When poles and piling arrive at a treating plant, they are run through a debarking and rossing machine to remove the bark and smooth the surface before treatment. Some poles are hand peeled in the woods and some are debarked and rossed at central concentration points before arriving at the treating plant.

From the debarking and rossing machine, the poles are cut to length and stacked onto small railroad cars for loading into pressure-treating vats. Virtually all southern pine poles and piling are pressure treated.

## Railroad Crossties

The use of crossties fluctuates considerably. While the overall use trend was definitely down until the mid-1960's, the recent tie consumption has been upward. Annual total U.S. tie production was 95 million cubic feet in 1985.

A few hewn ties are cut in the woods, usually from the tops of sawlog trees or from low-quality sawlogs. They are shaped on two sides with an axe or adz. Most ties are produced by small sawmills from lower-quality hardwood logs. Generally some low-grade lumber is produced as a by-product from larger logs. Ties are usually stacked and air dried prior to shipment to a treatment plant.

## Miscellaneous Products

There are many other products made from wood, but they generally represent only a small fraction of the total timber harvested. One of the largest in this category is fuelwood. After declining for a number of years, the use of fuelwood for home heating is increasing in response to rapidly rising costs of fossil fuels such as oil and natural gas. Wood for energy will probably play a more important role in meeting the nation's future energy needs (Chapter XV). Hardwood species such as the oaks and hickories are the preferred fireplace woods. Production is by small operations, and delivery is generally made directly to home owners. Some prices for fireplace and stove wood, delivered and stacked, have reached $150 or more per cord.

Cooperage, the material to make wood barrels, continues to decline as other packaging materials supplant barrels and kegs. Two types of cooperage are recognized. These are (1) tight cooperage or wooden staves which hold liquids and (2) slack cooperage used for shipping fruits, vegetables, and hardware.

Pallet production, on the other hand, doubled from 1960 to 1970 to a total output of 126 million. In 1985, 450 million pallets were produced and the number continues to rise. Pallets, constructed from lumber and plywood, have greatly mechanized product shipment by truck, rail, water, or air travel.

Furniture and fixtures find considerable use for hardwoods and softwoods, the latter generally in use for low-cost unfinished furniture. Treated fence posts have found increased outlets not only for fences on farms and ranches but also for residential fencing. Wood charcoal for barbecues has provided additional outlets for this product, but it has not made up the decline in industrial charcoal use. Quality hickory and ash are still in demand for handle stock. Specialty item production varies greatly. Items such as dogwood shuttle blocks have been generally replaced by plastics, for example.

## Bark

Formerly a waste material, bark has recently become a product in short supply. Due to energy shortages, bark is now being used for fuel for many mill operations. Some high-value bark use continues for decorative purposes and soil mulches. The continued energy crunch has made it economical to chip whole low-grade trees and logging residues for fuel sale. Some wood-using mills are operated on this fuel, while a new utility plant in the Northeast has been constructed to operate on wood fuels.

## *BIBLIOGRAPHY*

American Pulpwood Association. *Timber Harvesting.* Fourth Edition. Danville, Ill.: The Interstate Printers & Publishers, Inc., 1988.

American Wood Preservers Association. *Proceedings Eighty-Third Annual Meeting,* Vol. 83, 1987.

*The Demand and Price Situation for Forest Products, 1976-1977.* Miscellaneous Publication No. 1357. Washington, D.C.: U.S. Forest Service, 1977.

*Forest Farmers, Manual Edition.* Atlanta, Ga.: Forest Farmers Association, 1975.

*Forest Industries 1987-88. North American Fact Book.* San Francisco, Calif.: Miller-Freeman Publications, Inc., 1987.

*Forest Statistics of the United States.* Washington, D.C.: U.S. Forest Service, 1977.

*Historical Statistics of the United States.* Statistical Bulletin 228. Washington, D.C.: U.S. Forest Service, 1958.

Koch, P. *Utilization of Southern Pines.* Vols. 1 and 2. U.S.D.A. Washington, D.C.: Superintendent of Documents, U.S. Government Printing Office, 1972.

McCurdy, D. R., and Ewers, J. T. *The Pallet Industry in the U.S. 1980-1988.* Carbondale, Ill.: Department of Forestry, Southern Illinois University, 1986.

Pearce, J. K., and Stenzel, G. *Logging and Pulpwood Production.* New York, N.Y.: The Ronald Press Company, 1972.

U.S. Forest Service. *The Outlook for Timber in the United States.* FRR-20. U.S.D.A. Washington, D.C.: Superintendent of Documents, U.S. Government Printing Office, 1973.

U.S. Forest Service. *Timber: The Renewable Material.* U.S.D.A. Washington, D.C.: Superintendent of Documents, U.S. Government Printing Office, 1973.

U.S. Forest Service. *U.S. Timber Production, Trade, Consumption and Price Statistics 1950-1986.* Miscellaneous Publication No. 1460, 1988.

CHAPTER XII

# Wood Preservation

Wood deteriorates in use just like any other material. Iron and steel rust upon exposure to the air; wood deteriorates through the action of fungi in damp or moist places, or through action by insects. Most of the wood used in homes should not cause concern, as it does not come in contact with the ground. There are, however, some danger points such as house steps, framework of porches, and siding near the ground. Fence posts and other wood material in the ground, or near the surface, are very susceptible to decay and deterioration by insects. In general, all wood exposed to weather or in contact with the ground should be treated. Particularly is this most important in regions of high rainfall and mild climate (Figure 12-1).

To promote a long service life from wood, these precautions should be considered:

1. The conditions that present a decay or insect problem for wood should be recognized.
2. When new construction is planned, wood should be protected from moisture and decay hazard and insects, such as termites, through proper design and treatment.
3. For above-ground use, where wood cannot be kept at least 18 inches above the surface of the ground and thus protected from excessive moisture, treated wood should be used. Particularly should large exposed load-bearing beams be preservative-treated.
4. Where wood in permanent structures is in contact with the ground, the use of a preservative is essential.
5. When decay in wood is detected, immediate corrective action to stop the wetting of wood should be taken. If not done, decay will only get worse. Decay fungi need only a

little moisture on the surface of wood cells in order to grow.

6. If needed, professional advice may be obtained through the local state forestry agency.

Wood that is commercially pressure treated with a good preservative can be expected to give the most dependable service. However, wood that is "home treated" with a good preservative can be expected to give much service life. This assumes that the wood is properly treated with a recognized toxic preservative. Good preservatives and poor treatment or poor preservatives and good treatment are of little value. The purpose of treating wood is to protect it against insects and decay organisms.

Pressure treatment requires expensive equipment and highly technical skills. In operation, the wood to be treated is placed in a steel cylinder and sealed up. A preservative is pumped into the cylinder to cover the material, and pressure and/or vacuum is applied so that the wood takes up the desired amount of preservative. There are several ways in which wood can be treated in the

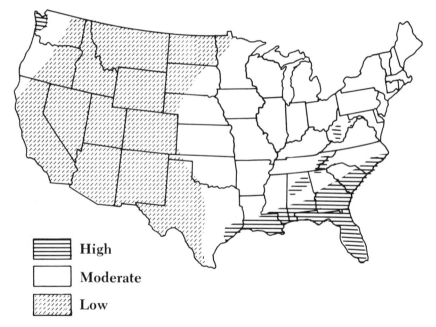

High

Moderate

Low

Fig. 12-1. Shown on the map are three zones of decay hazard for wood used above ground. Decay hazard is greatest in regions of high rainfall and mild climate. The Southeast and Northwest are more vulnerable. (Courtesy U.S. Forest Service)

cylinder, but a detailed discussion of these will be omitted from this text since they have little application to a woodland owner.

In 1985 there were 569 wood-treating plants in the United States. Almost 60 per cent were located in the South; 16 per cent were located in the North Central Region, 10 per cent in the Northeast, 8 per cent on the Pacific Coast, and the rest in the Rocky Mountains. Total wood treated in 1985 was 519.3 million cubic feet. Lumber made up most of this volume (260.3 million cubic feet), followed by crossties (85.9 million cubic feet), poles (76.8 million cubic feet), timbers (29.2 million cubic feet), fence posts (12.4 million cubic feet), piling (10.5 million cubic feet), and other products (44.2 million cubic feet).

## QUALITIES OF A GOOD WOOD PRESERVATIVE

In the past some chemical products have been recommended and sold as wood preservatives that have had little preservative qualities. For this reason, a woodland owner should become knowledgeable as to those preservatives which, over a period of years, have demonstrated their value by actual field test.

To preserve wood from wood-destroying fungi and insects, such as termites, a good preservative must be toxic. It must penetrate the wood in sufficient depth to form an exterior shell of poisonous wood that will prevent attacks by fungi and insects, even in surface checks that may later develop. And, it must retain its toxic effect under field conditions for a number of years to justify its use. It must not leach out of the wood too easily while in service.

A good preservative is also one that can be safely handled and is not dangerous in small concentrations to animals and humans. It must not be inflammable or injurious to the wood, nor must it corrode metal.

With the foregoing qualities, its usefulness will be determined by its cost and availability.

There are, today, many good preservatives. They include coal-tar creosote, solutions of creosote with other toxic chemicals, pentachlorophenol (more commonly called "penta") solutions, and water-borne materials containing one or more compounds of copper, zinc, arsenic, fluorine, and chromium. Their values have been shown through experience. However, coal-tar creosote and pentachlorophenol are available for purchase from and use by only properly licensed users.

The mention of a chemical preservative in this chapter does not necessarily connote a recommendation. Only those chemicals registered by the U.S. Environmental Protection Agency (EPA) can be recommended. Registration of preservatives is under constant review by the EPA and the U.S. Department of Agriculture. Only those preservatives that bear an EPA registration number and carry specific instructions for use are acceptable. Preservatives such as creosote and pentachorophenol should not be applied to the interior of dwellings. Because all preservatives are under constant review by the EPA, a responsible state or federal agency representative (extension forester or representative of a state forestry agency) should be consulted as to the current status of any particular preservative.

New and better wood preservatives are constantly being sought. Extensive research in this area is being conducted at the Forest Products Laboratory, U.S. Forest Service, Madison, Wisconsin, and at several U.S. Forest Service forest experiment stations. Research is also being conducted by various state forestry agencies and by state agricultural experiment stations.

## NATURAL DURABLE WOODS

As a general rule, the sapwood of trees is not durable in contact with the soil. The heartwood of some species is durable— some being more durable than others. Heartwood does resist decay better than sapwood within a given species, however.

Heartwood is difficult to treat with preservatives while the sapwood is more easily treated.

The heartwood of the following species is considered naturally durable and will give good service in contact with the ground without treatment: bois d'arc, black locust, cedar, "lighter" or "pitchy" pine, catalpa, red mulberry, chestnut, chinkapin, juniper, black walnut, sassafras, Pacific yew, and the white oak species. Of these, black locust, "lighter" pine, red mulberry, Pacific yew, and bois d'arc are considered as being most durable.

Bald cypress, redwood, and western red cedar, often considered as being naturally durable, have been found to decay and succumb to termites in just a few years in the South.

## WOOD PRESERVATIVES

Wood preservatives can be divided into two groups: (1) preservative oils such as creosote and pentachlorophenol in petroleum solutions and (2) water-borne salts that are applied as water solutions.

Since oils have higher resistance to leaching, they are more suitable for outdoor exposure. However, odor, paintability, color, and combustibility are factors to consider in the use of such preservative oils for certain purposes.

Water-borne salts are principally used where wood will not be in contact with the ground. They do not perform so satisfactorily as the preservative oils under conditions favorable to leaching. However, some have been developed to the point where good performance can be expected in contact with the ground. The double-diffusion process, described later, is an example. Wood treated with water-borne preservatives is relatively clean, paintable, and free from objectionable odor.

Wood preservatives used in water solution include zinc chloride, chromated zinc chloride, tanalith or fluor-chrome-arsenic-phenol (Wolman Salts® or Osmosalts®), acid copper chromate (Celcure®), ammoniacal copper arsenate (Chemonite®), zinc meta arsenate, chromated copper arsenate (Erdalith® or Greensalt®), and chromated zinc arsenate (Boliden salt®).

Chromated zinc chloride and zinc chloride have been used as fire retardants for wood; however, the amount of retention for this purpose is much higher than for wood preservation alone.

A summary of the characteristics of some of the more widely used wood preservatives is presented in Table 12-1.

The relative effectiveness of various treatments for which average service life has been determined is shown in Table 12-2.

### Preservative Oils

*Coal-tar creosote.* Coal-tar creosote, the most widely used preservative, is a brownish or black oil made by distilling coal tar. It is practically insoluble in water and has proven to be best under conditions of water use. Its characteristics may vary due to the method of distillation and the temperature range at which the fraction of creosote is collected; however, small differences in its character do not prevent it from giving good service if the standard specifications are met.

Some of the advantages of coal-tar creosote are:

1. It is toxic to fungi and insects.
2. It is insoluble in water and makes the treated wood more resistant to weathering.

## TABLE 12-1

### PRESERVATIVE CHARACTERISTICS OF SOME OF THE MOST WIDELY USED WOOD PRESERVATIVES[1]

| Preservative | Paintability | Color | Odor | Intimate Contact with Plants | Intimate Contact with Animals | Handling Characteristics | Indoor Use | Effectiveness in Preventing Attack |
|---|---|---|---|---|---|---|---|---|
| Creosote | NR | brown to black | P | NR | NR | P | NR | E |
| Penta in — Light oil | V | tan | V | NR | NR | V | NR | E |
| Penta in — Heavy oil | NR | brown | P | NR | NR | P | NR | E |
| Water-borne treatments (CCA)[2] | E | green | E | G | F | G | G | E |
| Copper naphthenate | F | green | P | V | V | G | F | F |

### Legend

E - excellent    F - fair    V - variable    NR - not
G - good    P - poor                          recommended

[1]These characteristics are for treated wood following three months of storage or service.
[2]When oil based paints are used, water-borne preservative-treated wood must be dried before painting.

(From General Report SA-GR2, Southeastern Area, State and Private Forestry, U.S. Forest Service)

3. It does not corrode metal.
4. It is generally available.
5. It has a long record of satisfactory use.

Some of the disadvantages of coal-tar creosote are:

1. It is naturally oily and causes the treated wood to bleed.
2. It irritates the skin of some persons.
3. It has an unpleasant odor which is offensive to some persons.
4. It causes treated wood to be difficult to paint.

## TABLE 12-2

### RELATIVE EFFECTIVENESS OF VARIOUS WOOD PRESERVATIVE TREATMENTS[1]

| Preservative | Average Retention (Pounds/Cubic Foot)[2] | Average Life in Years | Condition at Last Inspection |
|---|---|---|---|
| Untreated stakes .................. | | 1.8 to 3.6 | |
| | 0.13 | 11.6 | |
| | 0.14 | 6.1 | |
| Acid copper chromate | 0.25 | — | 60 per cent failed after 15 years |
| | 0.26 | — | 20 per cent failed after 36 years |
| | 0.29 | 4.6 | — |
| | 0.37 | — | 40 per cent failed after 36 years |
| | 0.50 | — | 40 per cent failed after 15 years |
| | 0.76 | — | 20 per cent failed after 15 years |
| | 0.24 | — | 40 per cent failed after 37 years |
| | 0.25 | — | 10 per cent failed after 15 years |
| Ammoniacal copper arsenate | 0.51 | — | No failures after 37 years |
| | 0.97 | — | No failures after 37 years |
| | 1.25 | — | No failures after 37 years |
| Chromated copper arsenate, Type I | 0.15 | — | 70 per cent failed after 36 years |
| | 0.22 | — | 20 per cent failed after 15 years |
| | 0.29 | — | No failures after 36 years |
| | 0.44 | — | No failures after 36 years |
| Type II | 0.23 | — | 20 per cent failed after 15 years |
| | 0.26 | — | No failures after 32 years |
| | 0.37 | — | No failures after 32 years |
| | 0.52 | — | No failures after 32 years |
| | 0.79 | — | No failures after 32 years |
| | 1.04 | — | No failures after 32 years |

(continued)

**TABLE 12-2 (Continued)**

| Preservative | Average Retention (Pounds/Cubic Foot)[2] | Average Life in Years | Condition at Last Inspection |
|---|---|---|---|
| | 0.30 | 14.2 | — |
| | 0.47 | 20.2 | — |
| | 0.46 | — | 60 per cent failed after 15 years |
| | 0.62 | 20.1 | — |
| Chromated zinc chloride | 0.62 | — | 40 per cent failed after 15 years |
| | 0.92 | — | 80 per cent failed after 30 years |
| | 0.96 | — | 40 per cent failed after 15 years |
| | 1.78 | — | 40 per cent failed after 30 years |
| | 3.67 | — | No failures after 30 years |
| Copper naphthenate | | | |
| 0.11 per cent in No. 2 fuel oil | 10.3 | 15.9 | |
| 0.29 per cent in No. 2 fuel oil | 10.2 | 21.8 | |
| 0.57 per cent in No. 2 fuel oil | 10.6 | 27.2 | |
| 0.86 per cent in No. 2 fuel oil | 9.6 | — | 80 per cent failed after 40 years |
| Copper-8-quinolinolate | | | |
| 0.1 per cent in Stoddard solvent | 0.01 | 5.3 | |
| 0.2 per cent in Stoddard solvent | 0.02 | 4.2 | |
| 0.6 per cent in Stoddard solvent | 0.06 | 5.6 | |

(continued)

**TABLE 12-2 (Continued)**

| Preservative | Average Retention (Pounds/Cubic Foot)[2] | Average Life in Years | Condition at Last Inspection |
|---|---|---|---|
| 1.2 per cent in Stoddard solvent | 0.12 | 7.8 | |
| 0.15 per cent in AWPA Pg heavy oil | 0.01 | — | 10 per cent failed after 18 years |
| 0.3 per cent in AWPA Pg heavy oil | 0.03 | — | No failures after 18 years |
| 0.6 per cent in AWPA Pg heavy oil | 0.06 | — | No failures after 18 years |
| 1.2 per cent in AWPA Pg heavy oil | 0.12 | — | No failures after 18 years |
| | 3.3 | 29.4 | |
| | 4.1 | 14.2 | |
| | 4.2 | 17.8 | |
| | 4.6 | 21.3 | |
| Creosote, coal-tar (regular type) | 7.8 | — | 60 per cent failed after 40.5 years |
| | 8.0 | — | 60 per cent failed after 41.5 years |
| | 8.3 | — | 20 per cent failed after 32 years |
| | 10.0 | — | 70 per cent failed after 41 years |
| | 11.8 | — | 20 per cent failed after 41.5 years |
| | 13.2 | — | 20 per cent failed after 40.5 years |
| | 14.5 | — | No failures after 41 years |
| | 16.5 | — | No failures after 41.5 years |

(continued)

**TABLE 12-2 (Continued)**

| Preservative | Average Retention (Pounds/Cubic Foot)[2] | Average Life in Years | Condition at Last Inspection |
|---|---|---|---|
| Creosote, coal-tar (special types) | | | |
| Low residue, straight run | 8.0 | 17.8 | |
| Medium residue, straight run | 8.0 | 18.8 | |
| High residue, straight run | 7.8 | 20.3 | |
| Medium residue | | | |
|   Low in tar acids | 8.1 | 19.4 | |
|   Low in naphthalene | 8.2 | 21.3 | |
|   Low in tar acids and naphthalene | 8.0 | 18.9 | |
| Low residue, low in tar acids and naphthalene | 8.0 | 19.2 | |
| High residue, low in tar acids and naphthalene | 8.2 | 20.0 | 80 per cent failed after 34 years |
| | 5.3 | 18.9 | 50 per cent failed after 34 years |
| | 8.0 | — | No failures after 34 years |
| | 10.1 | — | |
| | 15.0 | | |

[1]Tests were based on 2″ × 4″ × 18″ stakes of southern pine sapwood. Site of the study was the Harrison Experimental Station in Mississippi.
[2]All water-borne salt preservative retentions are based on oxides.

(Source: *Wood Handbook: Wood as an Engineering Material*, Agricultural Handbook 72, U.S. Forest Service, 1987)

5. It darkens the wood surface to an unsightly dark brown or black.
6. It is of a varied chemical composition.
7. It causes treated wood to become more susceptible to fire than untreated wood until such time as the light oils have evaporated.
8. It can only be purchased and used under a license because of its toxicity.

If handled properly, creosote has no effect on the handler's health or on the health of occupants of buildings in which it is used. Treated lumber can be used in sills and foundations with little danger of the odor's becoming objectionable.

While coal-tar creosotes vary in quality, satisfactory results may be obtained from any good grade, provided a sufficient quantity is taken up by the wood. Those which contain a high percentage of oils which boil at a low temperature are not so suitable to a woodland owner for wood treating as those which contain less of these oils. The reason is that up to 20 per cent may evaporate during treatment. This loss may be offset, however, by the lower price that is paid for low-boiling creosote.

Landowners who wish to use either coal-tar creosote or pentachlorophenol in wood preservation should contact a person who is qualified and licensed to use these materials. An extension forester or representative of a state forestry agency can help in locating a qualified person.

*Coal-tar creosotes for non-pressure treatments.* There is a so-called crystal-free coal-tar creosote. In the process of manufacture, the crystal-forming chemicals have been removed. This type of creosote is used where brush or spray applications are desired. The oil flows freely at ordinary temperatures. Properties and effectiveness are similar to ordinary coal-tar creosote. This creosote is covered by Federal Specification TT-C-655.

*Other creosotes.* Wood-tar creosote, water-gas-tar creosote, and oil-tar creosote, when of quality and properly used, have some wood-preserving properties but are generally less effective than coal-tar creosote.

*Coal tar.* Coal tar is not a good preserver. Unlike creosote, it is not very poisonous to fungi, and it does not penetrate wood very well. Tests have shown that surface coatings of tar are of little value.

*Creosote mixtures.* Creosotes made from coal tar are usually so toxic to fungi that they can be diluted up to 50 per cent or more with other oils to lower the cost of the preservative. Generally a 50-50 solution of creosote and diesel oil is used in the cold soaking process. Some commercial users use such toxic materials as pentachlorophenol and copper naphthenate to increase the wood preservative effectiveness.

*Pentachlorophenol solutions.* Of the chlorinated phenols, pentachlorophenol, more popularly known as "penta," has gained wide acceptance as an effective wood preservative in cold soaking and hot and cold bath processes. In use, it is put in solution with diesel or other petroleum oil.

Pentachlorophenol is available as a dry flake, a concentrated solution, or a ready-to-use solution. It does irritate the skin of workers, but with careful handling and protective clothing, one can avoid its effects. Dry flake is difficult to dissolve in a carrier.

For a woodland owner, it would be cheaper to buy a concentrated solution and dilute it with petroleum oil to make a 5 per cent solution. Concentrates are available which call for mixing with 2 to 12 or more parts of solvent, by volume, to make the desired 5 per cent. Current research shows that best results are obtained by using fairly heavy oils of low volatility. The heavier oils however may interfere with painting of the treated product. For paintability, mineral spirits or highly volatile carriers are needed. Generally, diesel oil is used as a carrier for the penta.

*Copper naphthenate.* Concentrated and ready-to-use solutions of copper naphthenate are available for mixing with petroleum oils to make a treating solution that is effective against termites and decay. The solution should contain a copper metal equivalent of at least 1 per cent. Copper naphthenate gives wood a green color. This preservative is covered by Federal Specification TT-W-572.

## Water-Borne Salts

*Zinc chloride.* This preservative is relatively cheap, has no color, is uniform in quality, and is not a fire hazard. It will however leach out of wood in contact with the soil and does not give so satisfactory a performance as other preservatives. Its use is not recommended where the treated wood is in contact with the soil.

*Chromated zinc chloride.* As an improvement over zinc chloride, chromated zinc chloride and copperized chromated zinc chloride were developed. These chemical formulations on wood result in more resistance to leaching than zinc chloride, according to the manufacturer.

*Trade name preservatives.* There are a number of commercially available patented preservatives on the market under the trade names of Wolman Salts®, Osmosalts®, Celcure®, Chemonite®, Boliden salt®, Greensalt®, and Erdalith®. As with other water-borne preservatives, they are principally used for the treatment of wood where there is no ground contact and where the treated wood requires painting. Some show leaching resistance, but they are not equal to creosote. Information on these preservatives may be obtained from the manufacturer.

### Preparing Timber for Treatment

*Cutting.* Posts may be cut and peeled in the late fall or winter so that when warm weather arrives they will be partially seasoned. Post material peels best in the spring or early summer; however, it is more likely to check.

*Peeling.* In the treatment of posts by the non-pressure oil preservative process, it is essential that all bark be removed from the material. This permits the posts to be seasoned properly and penetrated satisfactorily by the preservative. Patches of inner bark left on material will prevent the preservative from entering the wood. Eventually the patch will fall off, leaving exposed untreated wood in which decay can enter.

There are several types of efficient bark-peeling machines on the market, but they are usually too expensive for a small operation. Some owners of bark-peeling machines will exchange a certain number of peeled posts for a certain number of posts with bark on.

A peeling tool can be made by straightening a gooseneck hoe. Such a tool could be effectively used in the spring. If peeling is done in the winter, a draw-knife may be necessary.

*Seasoning.* For treatment with preservative oils, seasoning of wood is essential in order to obtain the best absorption and penetration of the preservative. Seasoning takes out the water and leaves room for the preservative.

The length of time to air-dry or season wood depends upon such factors as climate, method of stacking, and time of the year, and the wood's size, species, location, and protection. Small pieces of wood season more quickly than larger sizes, and sapwood seasons more quickly than heartwood.

Southern pine posts cross-stacked on high, well-drained ground so as to allow the free flow of air around each post will usually dry in about 40 to 60 days of good seasoning weather. It is desirable that they be stacked at least 12 inches above the ground, preferably on concrete or treated piers. They should also be covered to prevent excessive checking and to protect them from the rain (Figure 12-2).

*Cutting and framing.* Before any wood is treated, it should be cut and framed. This also applies to the boring of holes. Cutting

Fig. 12-2. For treatment of wood with preservative oils, seasoning of wood is essential. Wood must be stacked loosely above ground for air circulation. A cover also should be provided to prevent excessive checking and to protect material from the rain. (Courtesy Forest Products Laboratory, Texas Forest Service)

after treatment exposes the untreated wood and permits entrance of fungi or insects. Where such cutting is done following treatment, a thorough brush treatment with preservative should be made to the exposed portion.

*Incising.* Since a preservative penetrates wood much farther in a longitudinal direction (through the cells) than in a direction perpendicular to its face, some woods are incised to provide for deeper penetration. By exposing end-grain surfaces by puncturing the wood to a depth of about one-half inch, more longitudinal penetration can be obtained (Figure 12-3). This practice is usually followed in the pressure treatment with "hard to treat" woods. It is not practical with southern pine. Incising is practiced on Douglas fir, western hemlock and western larch ties and timbers for pressure treatment, and on poles of cedar and Douglas fir.

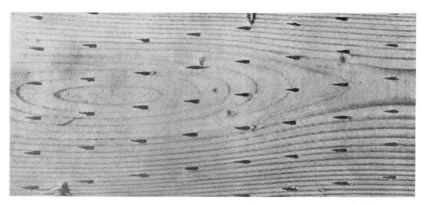

Fig. 12-3. Incisions made in a piece of wood to provide deeper penetration of preservative.

## Non-pressure Treating Processes

*Superficial applications.* As a general rule, the superficial application of oil preservatives to wood by brushing, spraying, and brief dipping or soaking will prolong its service life by two to three times. Such applications are recommended only where more effective treatments cannot be used. For example, brushing or spraying would be applicable to existing structures that are on or near the ground; it should not be employed to treat posts.

In brushing or spraying, the wood to be treated should be

flooded, rather than given a light coat. It is important to fill every check in the wood, and it is best to apply several coats after the first one has dried.

For application of oil preservatives, a 5 per cent penta-chlorophenol coal-tar creosote solution can be used.

Treatment in this manner with water-soluble preservatives is not recommended where wood is to be exposed to weather, soil, or water.

For exterior woodwork and millwork that is to be painted, a three-minute dip application in a preservative with a water-repellent additive such as penta-WR will be beneficial in preserving the wood. It may be purchased in the concentrated form and mixed with mineral spirits, or in the ready-mix form. The water-repellent additive is important for this purpose.

*Cold-soaking.* The cold-soaking process involves the submerging of wood in a preservative solution for about two to three days (Figure 12-4). The submersion time will be about 48 hours

Fig. 12-4. Posts being treated for home use in a small fence post treating plant. Note the overhead roof which protects the treating solution from rain. (Courtesy South Carolina Extension Service)

in summer to 72 hours in winter. If the wood is to be treated with an oil preservative, it should first be dried to a moisture content of 20 to 30 per cent. If treatment is to be with a water-borne preservative, such as zinc chloride, green or seasoned wood may be used.

Good success in terms of service life has been obtained where pine posts were soaked in a 5 per cent solution of pentachlorophenol in No. 2 fuel oil from one to two days. The treatment can also be used with creosote, but the cost of treatment is much higher.

The important thing is to soak the posts, or other wood, until good penetration is obtained, particularly in the sapwood. For some wood species this may be several days. Hardwoods can seldom be overtreated, while pine is easily overtreated. A 12-hour soaking is generally sufficient.

Among the woods most easily treated are the southern yellow pines, white oak, southern red oak, and red and black oaks with a high sapwood content. Retention of preservative is fair to good, while penetration in the sapwood is reasonably good. Retention and penetration of preservative are poor to fair in beech, birch, ash, elm, hackberry, and hickory. Such species as hard and soft maple, willow, sweetbay, birch, basswood, and cottonwood have good retention of the preservative, but the transverse sapwood penetration is generally poor. In general, cold-soaking works best with pine posts that are well seasoned.

Retention in posts (Table 12-3) or other wood can be observed by cutting a section of the wood during the treating process.

TABLE 12-3

APPROXIMATE VOLUME (QUARTS) OF
PENTACHLOROPHENOL SOLUTION REQUIRED PER POST

| Length Post (ft.) | Diameter at Small End of Post (in.) | | | | |
|---|---|---|---|---|---|
| | 2½ | 3 | 4 | 6 | 8 |
| 5½ | ¾ | 1 | 1½ | | |
| 6 | 1 | 1 | 2 | 4 | |
| 7 | 1¼ | 1¼ | 2½ | 5 | 9 |
| 8 | | 1½ | 3 | 6 | 10 |
| 10 | | 2 | 3½ | 7½ | 12½ |

Cold-soaking of wood in coal-tar creosote and penta-chlorophenol solutions should preferably be done during warm weather, using oils that are low in viscosity. This will result in more satisfactory penetration of the preservative.

Cold-soaking calls for a tank or oil drums welded together to form the container in which the wood is submerged; however, provision must be made to keep materials submerged during the treatment period.

*Double-diffusion.* This process involves soaking green, unseasoned wood in one chemical solution and then placing it in another. The two chemicals react in the wood, producing a compound that is very insoluble in water and is toxic to fungi and insects.

Two of the most reasonably priced chemicals for use in this treatment are technical copper sulfate and technical sodium fluoride in water solutions.

Because the copper sulfate solution is corrosive to iron, it must be placed in a wooden barrel or some other non-metal container. A steel drum could be used if coated first, inside and out, with a corrosive-resistant material such as roofing pitch. Any suitable container can be used for the sodium fluoride solution.

As with any chemical, care should be exercised in handling. The copper sulfate solution is somewhat irritating to the skin. Rubber gloves and goggles should be used. Animals should be kept away from the solution.

Posts should be treated not later than one week after they are cut, with bark being removed just prior to treatment. If posts are held for a week before treatment, the ends should be cut off about 4 inches to expose a fresh surface.

The sodium fluoride solution is prepared by adding 9 pounds of the chemical to 26 gallons of water. This should be thoroughly stirred. In the other container 18 pounds of copper sulfate should be added to 24 gallons of water and stirred until the crystals are dissolved.

In practice, the posts or other wooden material is first placed in the sodium fluoride solution and allowed to remain three days. It is then removed and placed in the copper sulfate solution. Here it remains an additional three days, following which it is rinsed off with clear water. The rinsing will enable one to handle the wood more safely without gloves.

Fig. 12-5. Stacked lumber after treatment with wood preservative. (Courtesy Department of Forestry, University of Illinois)

It is recommended that upon treatment the wood be stored in a shady location for a rest period of several weeks so that chemical action may continue and the chemicals may become more evenly distributed in the wood (Figure 12-5).

A recent process involves chromated copper arsenate or copper-chrome-arsenic. It is applied under pressure. When applied properly, with essential retention, it is an effective preservative.

*Hot-cold bath.* This treatment process, using coal-tar creosote and other oil preservatives, is the most effective of all nonpressure processes. It consists of heating seasoned wood in a preservative for several hours and then quickly submerging it in a cold preservative and allowing it to remain several hours more.

There are several means by which this can be done. First, the wood could be transferred from the hot-bath tank to a cold-bath tank. Second, the hot-bath tank could be drained of the hot preservative and the tank immediately filled with cold preservative. And third, the wood could remain in the tank following the heat treatment, until the solution is cool.

In principle, the hot bath causes air in the wood to expand, forcing some out. It also helps to improve the penetration of the preservative. In the cold bath the air in the wood contracts, creating a partial vacuum and causing the preservative to be absorbed.

In the hot bath in which creosote is used the wood is heated to a temperature of from 210° to 220° F. In the cold bath a temperature of 100° F. is desired to keep the solution fluid. With pentachlorophenol, a hot-bath temperature of from 170° to 180° F. will suffice when light oils are used. The cold bath can be normal air temperature.

A water-soluble solution may be used in this process if it is kept at uniform strength and if it is not adversely affected by heating.

A tank for treating purposes can be made at a reasonable cost from a used gasoline storage drum of about 500-gallon capacity. This will treat about 45 posts at a time. A wholesale distributor of oil products should be consulted.

### Assistance on Wood-Treating Problems

Assistance on wood-preservation problems may be obtained from a state forester, state extension forester, and manufacturers of wood preservatives. One important source of information is the U.S. Forest Products Laboratory, Madison, Wisconsin, which has done extensive research on this subject.

#### BIBLIOGRAPHY

Baechler, R. H., and Roth, H. G. "The Double-Diffusion Method of Treating Wood: A Review of Studies." Reprint from *Forest Products Journal.* Madison, Wis.: U.S. Forest Products Laboratory, 1964.

Blew, J. Oscar, Jr. *Treating Wood by the Cold-Soaking Method.* Report No. 1445. Madison, Wis.: U.S. Forest Products Laboratory, 1963.

De Groot, Rodney C. *Your Wood Can Last for Centuries.* Washington, D.C.: U.S. Forest Service, 1976.

*Dividends from Wood Research.* Madison, Wis.: U.S. Forest Products Laboratory, 1979.

*Forest Products Laboratory List of Publications on Wood Preservation.* Madison, Wis.: U.S. Forest Products Laboratory, 1978.

Gjovik, L. R., and Baechler, R. H. *Selection, Production, Procurement and Use of Preservative-Treated Wood.* General Technical Report FPL-15. Madison, Wis.: U.S. Forest Products Laboratory, 1977.

Levi, M. P. *Wood Tip-Pressure-Treated Southern Pines: Some Questions and Answers.* Publication AG-99. Raleigh, N.C.: North Carolina Extension Service, 1977.

Little, Robert L., Wagner, Francis G., Jr., and Beals, Harold O. *Preservative Treatment of Posts, Timber, and Lumber.* Asheville, N.C.: Southeast Forest Experiment Station, 1978.

McKean, A. S. *Give Your Fence Posts a Treat.* Baton Rouge, La.: Louisiana Extension Service, Louisiana State University, 1969.

Scheffer, T. C., and Verrall, A. F. *Principles for Protecting Wood Buildings from Decay*, Publication FPL 190. Madison, Wis.: U.S. Forest Products Laboratory, 1973.

Smythe, Richard V., and Williams, Lonnie H. *Structural Pest Control Regulations.* Forest Service Research Paper SO-93. New Orleans, La.: Southern Forest Experiment Station, 1974.

St. George, R. A. *Protecting Log Cabins, Rustic Work, and Unseasoned Wood from Injurious Insects in Eastern United States.* Farmers Bulletin 2104. Washington, D.C.: U.S.D.A., 1962.

Verrall, Arthur F. *Preserving Wood by Brush, Dip and Short-Soak Methods.* Technical Bulletin No. 1334. Washington, D.C.: U.S.D.A., 1965.

*Wood Handbook.* Agricultural Handbook 72. Madison, Wis.: U.S. Forest Products Laboratory, 1987.

CHAPTER XIII

# Fire in the Forests

Uncontrolled forest fires, called wildfires, have been a major influence upon the type and extent of forest resources in this nation. Prior to the coming of Western Civilization, wildfires burned uncontrolled over hundreds of square miles of land. These blazes, frequently set by lightning, were limited only by fuel, topographic barriers, and weather. As a result, wildfires destroyed tree species of lesser heat resistance and favored the more resistant ones that could survive under the conditions created by fires. In areas where a large number of nature's fires occurred, the thick-barked coniferous species, with its seed protected in fibrous cones, generally proved more fire resistant than hardwoods.

The American Indian set wildfires to improve the hunting of game. Early settlers used wildfires to help clear the land for cultivation. In later years, wildfires were improperly used to rid the woods of pests, to green-up the grass, and even to get revenge on a neighbor. Due to the effectiveness of the U.S. Forest Service fire prevention and educational programs, only 47 per cent of present wildfires in the United States are caused by people as compared to nearly 90 per cent in recent decades.

A raging forest fire can be the most awesome of natural phenomena. Fed by fuel in the form of vegetation and whipped on by high winds, wildfires destroy natural resources, improved property, and human life. Under very dry, windy conditions, little can be done to contain them. The Peshtigo fire in eastern Wisconsin and central Michigan in 1871 took 1,500 lives and burned over 4 million acres. The Hinckley fire in central Minnesota took 418 lives. The Tillamook burn in Oregon in 1933 burned over 310,000 acres. In recent years, wildfires in southern California have destroyed hundreds of homes and have done untold property damage.

Fires are still common in the forests of the United States.

They constitute one of the principal hazards to the forest resources and the business of timber growing. Protection of the forest from fire is one of the primary factors in instituting the plans for the scientific management of forest lands.

Public forestry agencies have had the principal responsibility of forest protection. Figure 13-1 shows the use of fire lookout towers and aerial surveillance to detect forest wildfires. In the early years of forestry efforts in the United States, virtually all the emphasis was on fire protection. In recent years, these activities have been expanded to include considerable emphasis on insects and diseases. Private timber growers, especially the wood-using industry, are taking over more and more of their protection responsibility with additional emphasis on wildfires. The concerted public and private fire protection efforts have considerably reduced the risk from wildfires. The status

Fig. 13-1. Strategically located fire lookout towers supplemented with aerial surveillance provide rapid detection of forest wildfires. Today, greater emphasis is being given to aerial detection. (Courtesy Texas Forest Service)

of forest fire protection is shown in Table 13-1. Improved knowledge of the behavior of wildfires, better equipment, and more adequately trained personnel have resulted in a sharp reduction in the damage caused by forest fires. Continuous efforts, however, are required to keep this damage at a reduced rate. The recent significant fire problems caused by the extreme drought during the summer of 1988 offer substantial evidence that we must remain diligent in our effort to control fire. A policy has been in effect for certain areas of national parks and wilderness areas which allows wildfires to burn uncontrolled; following the disastrous fires of 1988, this policy is now being reviewed.

**TABLE 13-1**

**AREA QUALIFYING FOR PROTECTION, 1983**

| Region | Total Qualifying Area | Total Area Protected | Per Cent Protected |
|---|---|---|---|
| | . . . . . . . . . . . *(thousand acres)*. . . . . . . . . . | | |
| *United States* | | | |
| Federal | 736,448 | 682,216 | 93 |
| State & Private | 1,052,196 | 851,463 | 81 |
| Total | 1,788,644 | 1,533,679 | 86 |
| *Pacific Northwest* | | | |
| Federal | 47,038 | 46,867 | 99 |
| State & Private | 40,206 | 26,276 | 65 |
| Total | 87,244 | 73,143 | 84 |
| *Pacific Southwest* | | | |
| Federal | 39,746 | 39,746 | 100 |
| State & Private | 36,221 | 36,221 | 100 |
| Total | 75,967 | 75,967 | 100 |
| *Northern* | | | |
| Federal | 72,273 | 72,273 | 100 |
| State & Private | 105,097 | 73,461 | 70 |
| Total | 177,370 | 145,734 | 82 |
| *Inter-mountain* | | | |
| Federal | 92,742 | 92,742 | 100 |
| State & Private | 23,501 | 23,501 | 100 |
| Total | 116,243 | 116,243 | 100 |

(Continued)

**TABLE 13-1 (Continued)**

| Region | | Total Qualifying Area | Total Area Protected | Per Cent Protected |
|---|---|---|---|---|
| | | . . . . . . . . . . (*thousand acres*). . . . . . . . . . | | |
| *Rocky Mountain* | | | | |
| | Federal | 69,978 | 69,978 | 100 |
| | State & Private | 127,831 | 120,062 | 94 |
| | Total | 197,809 | 190,040 | 96 |
| *Southwestern* | | | | |
| | Federal | 76,159 | 76,159 | 100 |
| | State & Private | 58,527 | 58,527 | 100 |
| | Total | 134,686 | 134,686 | 100 |
| *Alaska* | | | | |
| | Federal | 307,387 | 253,326 | 82 |
| | State & Private | 67,500 | 66,301 | 98 |
| | Total | 374,887 | 319,627 | 85 |
| *Southern* | | | | |
| | Federal | 16,746 | 16,746 | 100 |
| | State & Private | 380,757 | 250,120 | 66 |
| | Total | 397,503 | 266,866 | 67 |
| *Northeastern* | | | | |
| | Federal | 14,379 | 14,379 | 100 |
| | State & Private | 212,557 | 196,994 | 93 |
| | Total | 226,936 | 211,373 | 93 |

(Source: *1983 Forest Fire Statistics*, U.S. Forest Service)

## FIRE EFFECTS AND BEHAVIOR

A knowledge of the effects and behavior of forest wildfires is essential to their prevention and control. The ability to protect the forest from fire requires a knowledge of combustion, fire effects and behavior, weather, and fuels.

### Fire Combustion

Fire is a common chemical and physical phenomenon resulting from the quick combustion of oxygen with another substance. It is characterized by heat, some light, and usually a flame, but not always. In the case of forest wildfires, combustion is unenclosed and freely spreading and consumes forest litter, grass, weeds, brush, and trees.

Fire is both a physical and a chemical process. It quickly breaks up plant substances into their chemical parts. This breaking up is accompanied by the release of energy in the form of heat. The fire process is described as follows:

| Fuel | + | Oxygen | + | Heat | → | Fire |
|------|---|--------|---|------|---|------|
| (Wood cellulose or other plant material) | | | | (Heat to reach kindling temperature) | | (Carbon dioxide, water and heat) |

## Types of Forest Fires

There are three general types of forest fires as defined by the U.S. Forest Service. They include ground, surface, and crown fires. Each of these may occur in the same fire. The three types are defined as:

1. Ground fires are those that burn the organic materials beneath the surface litter; that is, needles, leaves, and twigs on the forest floor. These fires burn in the organic material, which is in various stages of decomposition and which builds up on top of the mineral soil. While not too common in the South, they sometimes occur in bottomland hardwood forests and in the coastal forest area of the East Coast. In peat bogs or swamps, fires may burn many feet below the ground surface in this deep organic material.
2. Surface fires are those that burn surface litter of loose debris on the forest floor and small vegetation. These are the most common kind of fires. If there is an abundance of surface fuel, these fires may burn up into the upper portion of trees. This is called "crowning out."
3. Crown fires are those that burn from top to top of trees or shrubs, sometimes independently of the surface fire. However, crown fires always start as surface fires. Crown fires are the fastest spreading of all types of fires.

## Fire Effects

The effects of wildfires on the forest vary considerably depending upon such factors as (1) the size, intensity, and duration of the fire; (2) the size and composition of the timber stand; (3) the nature of the fuel burned; (4) the frequency of fire on the area; and (5) the character of the soil. Fire consumes woody and vegetative material. It is used in prescription burning to reduce the risk of fire or in land clearing in the direct application of combustion to remove large quantities of forest litter. In addition, the effects of heat damage or kill plant and animal life and alter the soil. Fire also produces certain mineral products which are usually leached away through the soil. Frequent and intense fires expose the soil to severe erosion and excessive water runoff.

Very hot fires can kill all trees, although some species have a higher resistance to fire than others. Lethal temperatures occur when they are hot enough to kill the phloem or cambium tissues at the base of the tree. Small trees such as seedlings may be completely consumed by fire. More important is the injury to larger trees. This may take the course of direct injury to the tree roots, the lower portion of the stem, the upper stem, and the tree crown. Information is lacking on the exact internal temperatures necessary to kill living woody tissue in trees. Some damage and killing of tissue occurs, however, with temperatures as low as 120° F. of about one hour in duration.

In recent years some public controversy has occurred with wildlife biologists who stress the wildfire advantages to game animals. Fire kills the overstory plants and eventually lowers the plant browse line to, at, or near ground levels. Some fire advocates suggest that wildfires should not be controlled but left to burn. While some wildlife benefits have long been recognized by students of fire control, the problem is how to determine in advance whether or not a wildfire will be another Peshtigo fire or a Tillamook burn. In 1977 the U.S. Forest Service changed its policy for dealing with fires in the national forests from strict fire control to fire management. The change is based on the knowledge that fire can benefit wild land resources. Land managers now make fire management a part of the forest planning process. The objective is to weigh the costs against the benefits involved in controlling any particular wildfire beyond a certain size.

### Fire Behavior

Fire behavior relates to what a fire does. Wildfires are capable of doing many things under a wide range of conditions. They may burn very slowly, only a few feet a day, or they may whip through the tops of trees or brush at up to 5 miles per hour. For this reason, a knowledge of fire behavior is essential to fire control activities, especially for the "blowup" or conflagration-type wildfire.

The behavior of fires is related to the intensity of the fire itself and its rate of speed. Fortunately most fires are of relatively low intensity. Their behavior, in a general sense, can be predicted. The blowup fire, however, may create energy equal to a summer thunderstorm and be quite unpredictable.

Several factors of fire behavior may be considered. These would include the time of occurrence of the fire season, air movements, and topography.

Fire seasons vary by areas of the United States. In the North and West the summer months are generally the period of most fires, while in the South the fall or spring may be the "hottest" wildfire period. The "season" is related to the buildup of fuels and the occurrence of extended dry periods. In the South, the forest vegetation is "green" and contains a considerable amount of moisture in the summer, while in the North and West, vegetation may become tinder dry during this period. Killing frosts in the fall, followed by strong winds, dry out the vegetation and increase the number and size of wildfires. Prolonged droughts and dry weather have a similar effect upon forest fuels.

Fires are most likely to occur and burn most intensely during the middle of the afternoon on sunny days. This is the time when the vegetation is the driest and the wind generally the highest. Some fires have burned the hottest at night.

### Air Movements

The speed and direction of the wind at different levels, including both horizontal and vertical air movements, governs the duration and rate of speed of a fire. Winds are also important in drying out the vegetation. In the South, "northers," or strong, dry winds from the North, are important in both the occurrence and the spread of fires. In the West, hot, dry "East" winds tend to increase fire occurrence and intensity.

Since hot air rises, fires will tend to create their own winds or updrafts. These updrafts may carry sparks into upper winds which will scatter them out into unburned areas causing "spotting," or spot fires. The updrafts increase the intensity of the fire, and spotting greatly accelerates its rate of spread.

There are special types of winds associated with local mountain systems. The most critical fire situations are caused by local winds which blow over mountain ranges and drop down the slopes as warm, dry, down-flowing winds.

### Topography

Like air movement, topography has an important influence on the rate of spread of wildfires. It has the effect of putting the fuel in contact with the flames of the spreading fire. The steeper the terrain, the more rapidly the fuel comes in contact with the flames. Steep slopes also increase the updraft, further speeding up the fire's spread.

Generally fires will spread or move up slope. In cases of some blowup fires, they have spread both directions. Streams, highways, fields, and other areas serve as natural barriers to fires. Fires of high intensity, however, will sometimes cross these as though they did not exist.

### FIRE WEATHER

Basically the conditions which start and spread fires are related to weather conditions. Although weather may bring more severe burning conditions to wildfires, it may also create conditions which reduce the rate of spread and aid fire control. Examples are rains on the fire, wind reverses which blow the fire back into burned areas, and increases in relative humidity which increase the fuel moisture.

Temperature is one of the basic elements of weather. It is a measure of the degree of hotness or coldness of the air. The capacity of the air to contain moisture in the form of water vapor increases with increases in temperature. For example, for 100 per cent saturation, air at 100° F. must contain over 40 times more water vapor than air at 0° F.

The amount of water vapor in the air is measured in terms of relative humidity. It is the ratio in per cent between the amount of water vapor in the air at the temperature measured and the amount of water vapor the air can contain at that temperature. Relative humidity has a direct effect upon the amount of moisture in the fuel; that is, a high relative humidity means a high fuel moisture.

### Air Mass

Air is constantly being cooled or heated by its contact with the earth. Surface air expands and rises under warming conditions and is replaced by other air. Cooled air at the surface is denser or heavier, so it does not tend to rise. Since air has weight, its pressure increases as large amounts sink toward the earth's surface. These are referred to as "highs." When air becomes quite warm from the surface upward or where large amounts of air are rising, the air pressure becomes quite low at the earth's surface, and these are called "lows."

Winds, or air in motion, move in both horizontal and vertical directions. All winds are caused by unequal distribution of temperatures over the earth's surface. Some of the vertical or upward movements of air may be caused by air movement over steep terrain. Surface friction reduces the force of wind at or near the ground level.

### Thunderstorms

Another element to consider in fire weather is thunderstorms with their accompanying lightning. They are extremely unstable developments. Thunderstorms develop where there is adequate air moisture to condense and form clouds and where there is sufficient atmospheric temperature change. In terms of fires, thunderstorms are important because of rainfall, high winds, and lightning. The latter is of major concern in the West, where over 30 per cent of the forest area burned over in a recent 15-year period was caused by fires set by lightning.

### Weather Control

No discussion of fire weather would be complete without mention of experiments in weather modification. From a standpoint of fires in the forest, artificial rainfall and lightning prevention are of interest.

The seeding of clouds with silver iodide or dry ice crystals will trigger the release of rainfall from existing clouds. It does require, however, the existence of moist air currents and active cloud-forming processes similar to those when natural rainfall occurs. For this reason, cloud seeding will only hasten rainfall which may occur naturally.

On the other hand, overseeding potential thunderstorm clouds may prevent the formation of precipitation. This would, in turn, prevent the growth of these clouds to the thunderstorm stage and prevent the distribution of electrical charges necessary for lightning discharges.

## FUELS IN THE FOREST

Forest fuels are the result of vegetative growth in the forest complex and are composed of woody and other plant material. The nature and extent of fuel actually follow the development of the forest from the seedling through the mature or even overmature stage. In the seedling and sapling stages, grasses, weeds, and shrubs are the major fuel components. As the forest canopy closes, these fuels are gradually replaced by leaves, needles, limbs, and fallen trees.

### Types of Fuel

There are two basic types of fuel: ground fuels lying on the forest floor and aerial fuels represented by stems and crowns of woody plants. Ground fuels include such things as peat (common in forests of the North), duff, tree roots, tree leaves, dead grass and weeds, low shrubs and brush, tree seedlings, small pieces of dead wood, large limbs, downed tree trunks, and stumps. The smaller of these fuels influence the rate of fire spread. The larger fuels are slower burning and generally result in persistent small fires or "smokes" within the large fire. If sufficient volume of the larger fuels is present, as may occur during or shortly after a logging operation, then these fuels generate tremendous heat which accelerates spotting and fire spread.

Aerial fuels include all burnable fuels located in the tree canopies above 6 feet from the ground. The types of aerial fuels are tree branches, foliage, dead standing trees called snags, vines, and lichens and mosses. With the exception of large tree limbs and snags, these represent fast-burning fuels. All contribute to a rapid rate of spreading of fires. Crown fires generally are restricted to coniferous forests and rarely occur in hardwood forest types.

## FOREST FIRE PROTECTION

Protection of the forest resources from the ravages of wildfires is essential to their systematic management. This topic is frequently called fire control and is divided into two main headings: prevention and suppression. Fire-prevention activities include those associated with keeping the fire from occurring while suppression includes those efforts involved in fighting the fire once it has started. In the latter case, certain presuppression activities such as weather prediction, detection, and planning are essential if wildfires are to be most effectively fought.

### Fire Prevention

The prevention of wildfires involves a knowledge of how they are started. Virtually all fires are caused either by people or by lightning. Since lightning is a natural process, programs must be directed toward people in an attempt to prevent wildfires.

Nearly all fires which occur on timberland in the United States are investigated to determine the causes. These are classified by standards established by the U.S. Forest Service and are arranged under nine headings: (1) lightning, (2) campfires, (3) smoking, (4) debris burning, (5) arson, (6) equipment use, (7) railroads, (8) children, and (9) miscellaneous. Most of these classes are self-evident. Debris burning refers to fires set to clear land or burn rubbish, garbage, ranges, or field stubble. Arson fires are those willfully set to burn the property of another without the owner's consent. Miscellaneous fires are those of a known cause which cannot be classified under the other headings. Table 13-2 shows the causes of wildfires in the United States in 1986.

### Educational Programs

A careful study of fire causes coupled with an understanding of basic motivations provides the necessary background information for planning fire-prevention programs. These activities are conducted principally by the state forestry agencies in cooperation with the U.S. Forest Service. One of the best known of these ef-

**TABLE 13-2**

**NUMBER OF WILDFIRES BY CAUSE, 1986[1]**

| Region | | Light- ning | Camp- fires | Smoking | Debris Burning | Arson | Equip- ment Use | Rail- roads | Chil- dren | Misc. | Total |
|---|---|---|---|---|---|---|---|---|---|---|---|
| *Northern* | | | | | | | | | | | |
| | Federal | 1,252 | 86 | 34 | 31 | 10 | 26 | 0 | 5 | 40 | 1,484 |
| | State & Private | 597 | 52 | 123 | 127 | 16 | 116 | 71 | 39 | 187 | 1,328 |
| | Total | 1,849 | 138 | 157 | 158 | 26 | 142 | 71 | 44 | 227 | 2,812 |
| *Rocky Mountain* | | | | | | | | | | | |
| | Federal | 406 | 67 | 16 | 9 | 6 | 23 | 2 | 12 | 58 | 599 |
| | State & Private | 543 | 167 | 463 | 1,752 | 230 | 877 | 735 | 218 | 3,770 | 8,755 |
| | Total | 949 | 234 | 479 | 1,761 | 236 | 900 | 737 | 230 | 3,828 | 9,354 |
| *Southwestern* | | | | | | | | | | | |
| | Federal | 1,713 | 204 | 127 | 153 | 418 | 82 | 6 | 56 | 311 | 3,070 |
| | State & Private | 142 | 48 | 84 | 106 | 49 | 24 | 15 | 27 | 152 | 647 |
| | Total | 1,855 | 252 | 211 | 259 | 467 | 106 | 21 | 83 | 463 | 3,717 |
| *Inter-mountain* | | | | | | | | | | | |
| | Federal | 173 | 34 | 7 | 2 | 5 | 7 | 2 | 5 | 5 | 240 |
| | State & Private | 144 | 18 | 10 | 65 | 32 | 32 | 35 | 20 | 82 | 438 |
| | Total | 317 | 52 | 17 | 67 | 37 | 39 | 37 | 25 | 87 | 678 |
| *Pacific Southwest* | | | | | | | | | | | |
| | Federal | 1,402 | 199 | 125 | 63 | 190 | 81 | 14 | 44 | 158 | 2,276 |
| | State & Private | 551 | 363 | 431 | 1,152 | 1,286 | 1,964 | 55 | 863 | 1,344 | 8,009 |
| | Total | 1,953 | 562 | 556 | 1,215 | 1,476 | 2,045 | 69 | 907 | 1,502 | 10,285 |

(Continued)

**TABLE 13-2 (Continued)**

| Region | Light-ning | Camp-fires | Smoking | Debris Burning | Arson | Equip-ment Use | Rail-roads | Chil-dren | Misc. | Total |
|---|---|---|---|---|---|---|---|---|---|---|
| **Pacific Northwest** | | | | | | | | | | |
| Federal | 827 | 149 | 59 | 48 | 9 | 38 | 3 | 9 | 69 | 1,211 |
| State & Private | 447 | 128 | 101 | 406 | 57 | 88 | 24 | 145 | 274 | 1,670 |
| Total | 1,274 | 277 | 160 | 454 | 66 | 126 | 27 | 154 | 343 | 2,881 |
| **Southern** | | | | | | | | | | |
| Federal | 94 | 44 | 28 | 28 | 620 | 28 | 7 | 13 | 129 | 991 |
| State & Private | 871 | 541 | 4,574 | 19,979 | 26,350 | 1,711 | 1,430 | 2,790 | 4,332 | 62,578 |
| Total | 965 | 585 | 4,602 | 20,007 | 26,970 | 1,739 | 1,437 | 2,803 | 4,461 | 63,569 |
| **Northeastern** | | | | | | | | | | |
| Federal | 11 | 44 | 27 | 11 | 134 | 24 | 10 | 8 | 2 | 271 |
| State & Private | 175 | 706 | 1,259 | 5,567 | 5,140 | 949 | 864 | 3,383 | 2,427 | 20,470 |
| Total | 186 | 750 | 1,286 | 5,578 | 5,274 | 973 | 874 | 3,391 | 2,429 | 20,741 |
| **Alaska** | | | | | | | | | | |
| Federal | 2 | 6 | 1 | 0 | 0 | 0 | 1 | 1 | 7 | 18 |
| State & Private | 26 | 50 | 14 | 160 | 3 | 17 | 7 | 16 | 83 | 376 |
| Total | 28 | 56 | 15 | 160 | 3 | 17 | 8 | 17 | 90 | 394 |
| **United States** | | | | | | | | | | |
| Federal | 5,880 | 833 | 424 | 345 | 1,392 | 309 | 45 | 153 | 779 | 10,160 |
| State & Private | 3,496 | 2,073 | 7,059 | 29,314 | 33,163 | 5,778 | 3,236 | 7,501 | 12,651 | 104,271 |
| Total | 9,376 | 2,906 | 7,483 | 29,659 | 34,555 | 6,087 | 3,281 | 7,654 | 13,430 | 114,431 |

(Source: *National Forest Fire Report, 1986*, U. S. Forest Service)

¹Protected area only.

forts is the Smokey Bear program which has served as the national symbol of forest fire prevention for over three decades.

Most prevention educational activities use certain advertising principles to urge the safe use of fire out-of-doors. These include (1) gaining attention and recognition, (2) repetition and continuity, and (3) accuracy and timeliness. These principles are applied through a variety of means and educational media. Some of the most frequently used are posters, signs, exhibits, and advertisements. Written material in newspapers, magazines, and leaflets is also common. Also effective in reaching large numbers of people are television, radio, and motion pictures. Group contacts utilize audio-visual materials like motion picture films to convey prevention messages to groups. Finally, individual contacts on a person-to-person basis provide the foundation for prevention programs, especially in areas of high fire occurrence.

### Law Enforcement

State and federal legislation serves as a deterrent to persons causing a forest wildfire. These laws may result in civil or criminal legal action against the individuals involved. A fire accidentally set, for example, in allowing a brush fire to escape to the property of another, is usually considered a misdemeanor. Arson is a felony under federal and most state laws and is subject to a fine and imprisonment. Many states have laws requiring permits for doing outdoor burning, especially during periods of high fire occurrence.

The enforcement of fire laws is an essential part of fire prevention efforts. It is an educational tool which, when coupled with other educational activities, serves to reduce wildfires. To be successful, however, it must have the local support of the general public.

## FOREST FIRE SUPPRESSION

Fighting forest fires is the most spectacular but most difficult of the protection jobs. When a fire occurs, it means that forest resources are being damaged or destroyed, and money is being spent—usually quite rapidly. Before the wildfires can be fought effectively, certain presuppression or detection activities must be undertaken.

## *Presuppression*

Presuppression includes those advance efforts made before the fire starts so that it can be readily controlled and extinguished. It includes advance planning or the use of personnel and equipment most effectively under virtually any fire situation. An important phase is weather prediction to anticipate periods when large numbers of fires or large fires are likely to occur. Detection of fires is an essential element utilizing lookout towers, airplanes, and the general public to spot and report wildfires. It is the first step in suppression activities. Good detection efforts attempt to reduce the time from the start of the fire to the arrival of fire-fighting crews. Innovations in detection include the use of closed-circuit television in lookout towers for continuous vigil for fires.

## *Suppression*

The basic jobs of fire suppression are to (1) rob the fire of fuel, (2) reduce the fire's temperature, and (3) cut off the oxygen from the fire. These may be accomplished in a variety of ways.

For example, the fire may be robbed of fuel by plowing a firebreak between it and the unburned fuel. Figure 13-2 shows a tractor plowing a firebreak on industrial forest lands in Florida. Then the area between the break and the fire is "backfired," or burned out, to remove the fuel in front of the fire. This is a common technique of forest fire suppression in the South and North. Tractor-plow units, mounted on heavy-duty trucks, provide the power and mobility to cut suitable firebreaks. Streams, logging roads, and highways frequently serve as natural firebreaks. Other means of fuel removal include felling snags in advance of fires and making fuels nonflammable through applications of dirt, water, or chemicals.

In mountainous terrain much of the fire-fighting effort has to be done by people. Cutting fire lines, felling snags, carrying water pumps and hoses, and putting out burning spots within the fire have to be done by large numbers of people.

The temperature of fuels may be reduced also through the application of dirt, water, or chemicals and even through the partial removal or separation of fuels. The oxygen may be cut off by burying the fuels in dirt or smothering them with water or chemicals. The last two methods are generally accomplished by the use of

Fig. 13-2. A tractor plows a firebreak to separate the fire from unburned fuels on wood-using industry lands in Florida. The firebreak serves as a point to back-fire or burn out the fuel between the oncoming fire and the firebreak. (Courtesy American Forest Institute)

hand tools such as shovels and back-pack water pumps in "mopping up" activities, once the fire is contained.

Aircraft are sometimes used to make aerial drops of fire retardants. They are used in advance of fires to slow down the rate of spread prior to the arrival of conventional fire-fighting forces. Helicopters are also effectively used to rapidly move fire-fighting crews to suppress hot spots. Figure 13-3 shows a plane dropping a fire-retardant chemical on a fire.

### Fire-Fighting Methods

There are two general methods for fighting fires: the direct and the indirect methods. The particular method used is dependent upon the fuels, rate of fire spread, and topography.

The direct method (Figure 13-4) attacks the fire at the burning edge, or fire line. It is used when fires are small and slow-burning.

Fig. 13-3. A plane drops a fire-retardant chemical on the leading edge of a wild-fire. (Courtesy U.S. Forest Service)

The heat is usually low enough to permit fire fighters to work at the fire's edge.

The indirect attack is used on fast-burning fires which are too hot to control near the edge of the fire (Figure 13-5). This method involves cutting a firebreak some distance from the fire and backfiring the intervening area. In many cases, both methods will be used on a single fire. The indirect attack will be used on the fire's head or fast-moving front, and the direct attack will be used on its flanks or sides.

## PROTECTION OF TIMBER STANDS FROM FIRE

Firebreaks about 5 feet wide may be plowed or disced around timber stands to protect them from fire. These may be constructed adjacent to roads or highways and along property boundaries to prevent fires from spreading into timber stands, but most important, as a backfire point for oncoming fires. Streams and rivers may be used

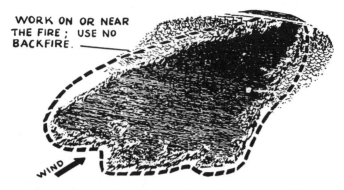

Fig. 13-4. The direct method of attacking forest wildfires.

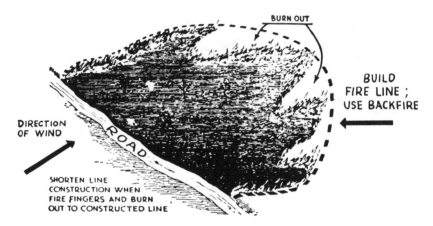

Fig. 13-5. The indirect method of attacking forest wildfires.

as natural barriers. Firebreaks should be constructed also through young plantations at about one-quarter-mile intervals to help reduce damage in the event of a fire in the plantation. Small trees are especially susceptible to fire damage. Some states provide cost-sharing assistance through the Rural Environmental Conservation Program. See your local forester for assistance.

### BIBLIOGRAPHY

Alexander, M. E. *Let the Forests Burn?* Technical Session Proceedings. Fort Collins, Colo.: Department of Forest and Wood Sciences, College of Forestry and Natural Resources, 1974.

Chandler, C., *et al*. *Fire in Forestry*. Volumes I and II. New York, N.Y.: John Wiley and Sons, Inc., 1983.

Deeming, J. E., *et al*. *National Fire-Danger Rating System*. Research Paper RM-84. Ft. Collins, Colo.: Rocky Mountain Forest and Range Experiment Station, 1972.

Dunkelberger, J. E., and Altobellis, A. T. *Profiling the Woods-Burner: An Analysis of Fire Trespass Violations in the South's National Forests*. Bulletin 469. Auburn, Ala.: Agricultural Experiment Station. 1975.

Grigel, J. *Role of Helitanker in Forest Fire Control*. Informational Report NOR-X-123. Edmonton, Alberta, Canada: Northern Forest Research Centre. 1974.

Nelson, Thomas C. "Fire Management Policy in the National Forests—A New Era." *Journal of Forestry*. Volume 77:11, November, 1979.

U.S. Forest Service. *Fire in Land Management*. Undesignated. Missoula, Mont., 1975.

U.S. Forest Service. *Fire Weather*. Agricultural Handbook 360. U.S.D.A. Washington, D.C.: Superintendent of Documents, U.S. Government Printing Office, 1970.

U.S. Forest Service. *National Forest Fire Report—1986*. Washington, D.C., 1987.

U.S. Forest Service. *Wildfire—A Story of Modern Fire-fighting*. PA 933. U.S.D.A. Washington, D.C.: Superintendent of Documents, U.S. Government Printing Office, 1972.

CHAPTER XIV

# Protecting Forests from Other
# Destructive Agents

In addition to protection from fire, forests must have protection from other destructive agents including insects, diseases, air pollutants, and mechanical injuries. Much more timber is destroyed by diseases and insects, commonly grouped together as forest pests, than by wildfires. Mechanical injury to forests may be inflicted by weather, domestic animals, wildlife, and even people. Air pollutants cause extensive damage to forests in some parts of the nation, and damage through acidification of soils by heavy metal emissions can be severe. A rough approximation of the loss of timber by destructive agents is shown in Table 14-1.

Not only do insects and diseases damage timber but they also cause serious damage to wood products. The damage or destruction of wood-in-use caused by termites, marine borers, powder post beetles, fungi or decay, and other wood deteriorators amounts to billions of dollars each year in the United States. This is the reason for the use of chemical preservatives in treating wood.

TABLE 14-1

**RELATIVE IMPORTANCE OF VARIOUS DESTRUCTIVE AGENTS
AFFECTING FORESTS IN THE UNITED STATES**

| Cause | Timber Volume | |
|---|---|---|
| | (million cubic feet) | (per cent) |
| Fire | 260 | 4 |
| Insects | 1,450 | 24 |
| Disease | 1,450 | 24 |
| Weather and Other | 1,950 | 32 |
| Unknown | 1,000 | 16 |
| All causes | 6,110 | 100 |

(Source: U.S. Forest Service)

309

## FOREST PESTS

Identification and control of insects and diseases is an extremely important part of forest management activities. Large-scale systematic surveys are undertaken at frequent intervals to maintain constant vigils on the extent and nature of forest pests. Biological evaluations and cost-benefit analyses are made on each outbreak, when located, as a basis for treatment decisions. When outbreaks become serious, concerted efforts are made by public and private forest interests to keep them under control. Many states now have laws relating to the control of forest pests. While much attention has been focused upon the more spectacular effect of the most evident insects, equal efforts are being directed to the silent killers—forest diseases.

Millions of dollars are expended annually for the control of insects and diseases in the United States. Approximately 80 per cent is provided by the federal government, with the balance provided by cooperating states and private organizations. Needless to say, control decisions are difficult to make, especially considering economic and environmental considerations.

Fig. 14-1. Aerial surveillance flown over forest pest outbreak areas reveals discolored tree crowns such as in the light area in the center of this aerial photograph. (Courtesy Texas Forest Service)

In the South, much attention has been directed at locating and controlling the southern pine beetle, the most damaging insect in these forests. Figure 14-1 shows how a pine beetle infestation and other forest pest outbreaks can be detected from aerial surveys. Emphasis has also been directed to controlling other bark beetles, tip moths, leaf-cutting ants, twig borers, sawflies, leaf miners, webworms, and other insects.

As a result of tree improvement work and the establishment of many seed orchards throughout the nation, more and more attention is being directed to insects which attack flowers, cones, and seeds of both softwoods and hardwoods.

Some of the more common insects affecting trees in the East, Northwest, and Southwest are noted in Tables 14-2, 14-3, and 14-4, respectively.

Diseases also cause considerable mortality in forest stands. A reduction in growth rate and the outright killing of trees are substantial and widespread. The more serious pine diseases include fusiform rust on loblolly and slash pine and brown spot on longleaf pine. A silent killer, *Fomes annosus*, attacks plantations and some natural stands across the South and into the lower Midwest. Other species of *Fomes* attack and do similar damage to tree species throughout the United States. Dutch elm disease has reached serious proportions all across the Eastern United States. This disease has almost eliminated the use of elm as shade trees in the Northeast and Midwest and as a commercial timber species, except in the northern parts of the Lake States and Maine. Its present distribution is shown in Figure 14-2.

The more common diseases affecting pine and hardwood trees in the East, Northwest, and Southwest are shown in Tables 14-5, 14-6, and 14-7, respectively.

In the Northeast, the most serious insects are the spruce budworm, gypsy moth (Figure 14-3), and forest tent caterpillar. The major diseases are the Dutch elm disease and beech bark disease.

In 1977 alone, the spruce budworm defoliated over 10.2 million acres, the gypsy moth over 1.6 million acres, and the forest tent caterpillar 3 million acres. Repeated defoliation has resulted in much mortality representing millions of board feet of timber loss.

In the West the major insects are represented by the western spruce budworm (Figure 14-3), mountain pine beetle, Douglas fir tussock moth, western pine beetle, and larch casebearer. Dwarf mistletoe is still the most destructive pathogen affecting conifers.

Dutch elm disease (Figure 14-2) is spreading rapidly west and

TABLE 14-2

**SOME COMMON INSECTS AFFECTING PINE AND HARDWOOD TREES
IN THE EASTERN REGIONS**

| Conifers | Hardwoods |
|---|---|
| Ambrosia beetle | Beech blight |
| Arkansas pine sawfly | Carpenterworm |
| Bagworm | Columbian timber beetle |
| Balsam wooly adelgid | Cottonwood borer |
| Blackheaded pine sawfly | Cottonwood twig borer |
| Black turpentine beetle | Cottonwood leaf beetle |
| Coneworms | Eastern tent caterpillar |
| Deodar weevil | Elm spanworm |
| Introduced pine sawfly | Fall cankerworm |
| *Ips* engraver beetle | Fall webworm |
| Jack pine budworm | Forest tent caterpillar |
| Larch sawfly | Fruit tree leaf roller |
| Loblolly pine sawfly | Gypsy moth |
| Nantucket pine tip moth | Hickory bark beetle |
| Pales weevil | Locust leaf miner |
| Pine colaspis | Looper complex |
| Pine engraver beetle |    Lindem looper |
| Pine needle midge |    Eastern oak looper |
| Pine sawfly | Oak leaf tier |
| Pine seedworms | Small European elm |
| Pine webworm |    bark beetle |
| Pitch-eating weevils | Sycamore lace bug |
| Pitch pine tip moth | Variable oakleaf caterpillar |
| Redheaded pine sawfly | Walking stick |
| Scale insects | Walnut caterpillar |
| Seedbugs | White flies |
| Slash pine thrips | Whitemarked tussock moth |
| Southern pine beetle | White oak borer |
| Southern pine sawyer | |
| Texas leaf cutting ant | |
| Virginia pine sawfly | |
| Webbing coneworm | |
| White pine weevil | |

## TABLE 14-3

**SOME COMMON INSECTS AFFECTING PINE AND HARDWOOD TREES
IN THE NORTHWESTERN AND ROCKY MOUNTAIN REGIONS**

| Conifers | Hardwoods |
| --- | --- |
| Balsam woolly adelgid | Ash borer/lilac borer |
| Black pineleaf scale | Cecropia moth |
| Cerambycid wood borer | Cerambycid wood borer |
| Cooley spruce gall aphid | Cottonwood twig gall aphid |
| Cranberry girdler moth | Elm leaf beetle |
| Cylindrical bark beetle | Fall webworm |
| Douglas fir beetle | Forest tent caterpillar |
| Douglas fir engraver | Fruit tree leaf roller |
| Douglas fir tussock moth | Fungus gnat |
| Fir engraver | Gray willow leaf beetle |
| Gypsy moth | Gypsy moth |
| Jack pine budworm | Honey locust podgall midge |
| Larch budworm | Large aspen tortix |
| Larch casebearer | Peach tree borer |
| Lodgepole pine terminal | Poplar and willow borer |
|   weevil | Spring cankerworm |
| Mites | Twig girdler |
| Modoc budworm | Variable oakleaf caterpillar |
| Mountain pine beetle | Western tent caterpillar |
| Pine bark aphid | |
| Pine budworm | |
| Pine butterfly | |
| Pine engraver beetles | |
| Pine moths | |
| Pine needle miner | |
| Pine needle scale | |
| Pine needle sheath miner | |
| Pine tip moths | |
| Silver-spotted tiger | |
|   moth | |
| Spider mites | |
| Spruce beetle | |
| Spruce mycorrhizal aphid | |
| Western balsam bark beetle | |
| Western conifer seed bug | |
| Western pine beetle | |
| Western pine shoot borer | |
| Western spruce budworm | |

TABLE 14-4

**SOME COMMON INSECTS AFFECTING PINE AND HARDWOOD TREES
IN THE SOUTHWESTERN REGIONS**

| Conifers | Hardwoods |
|---|---|
| Black pineleaf scale | Fruit tree leaf roller |
| Douglas fir beetle | Gypsy moth |
| Douglas fir tussock moth | Large aspen tortix |
| Eurasian pine aphid | Tent caterpillar |
| Fir engravers | |
| Grasshoppers and crickets | |
| Greenhouse thrips | |
| Jeffrey pine beetle | |
| Jeffrey pine needle miner | |
| Larch casebearer | |
| Lodgepole pine needle miner | |
| Modoc budworm | |
| Mountain pine beetle | |
| Pandora moth | |
| Pine butterfly | |
| Pine engraver beetle | |
| Pine needle sheath miner | |
| Spruce beetle | |
| Sugar pine tortix | |
| True fir bark beetles | |
| Western pine beetle | |
| Western pine shoot borer | |
| Western spruce budworm | |

poses a serious threat. Among other diseases of concern are the shoe-string root rot, black stain root disease, laminated root rot, and annosus root rot. These cause significant amounts of tree mortality in managed coniferous stands.

## INSECTS OF THE FOREST

The study of forest insects, called *forest entomology*, involves an investigation and understanding of the life cycle of forest insect species. This facilitates the development of effective control techniques. Forest entomology generally includes those insects which attack trees, forests, and wood products. This discussion is limited to those which attack trees and forests.

Not all insects of the forest are harmful. Some are predators, seeking out and destroying destructive insect species. Sometimes,

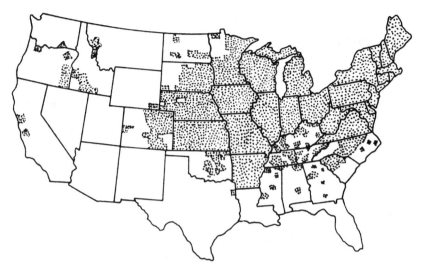

Fig. 14-2. Distribution of Dutch elm disease in the United States in 1977. This disease was introduced from Europe about 1930. (Courtesy U.S. Forest Service)

Fig. 14-3. (Left) Full-grown gypsy moth caterpillar. (Right) Egg mass of spruce budworm. Over $100 million has been spent to suppress and control the spread of gypsy moth in the northeastern states. The spruce budworm occurs in the Northeast, throughout Canada, and in the northwestern portion of the United States. The magnitude of loss to timber is great in widespread outbreaks.

TABLE 14-5

## SOME COMMON DISEASES AFFECTING PINE AND HARDWOOD TREES IN THE EASTERN REGIONS

### CONIFER DISEASES

| Foliage | Stem and Branch | Root | Vascular Wilts |
|---|---|---|---|
| Brown spot | Comandra blister | Annosus root | Pinewood |
| Cedar apple | rust | disease | nematode |
| rust | Cone rust | Brown cubical | |
| Cedar blight | Diplodia tip | rot | |
| Needle casts | blight | Little leaf | |
| of pine | Eastern dwarf | disease | |
| Pine needle | mistletoe | Red root and | |
| rust | Eastern gall | butt rot | |
| | rust | Root decay | |
| | European larch | Root decline | |
| | canker | | |
| | Fusiform rust | | |
| | Pitch canker | | |
| | Red heart | | |
| | Scleroderris | | |
| | canker | | |
| | Stem decay | | |
| | Basidomycetes | | |
| | Wood decay | | |

### HARDWOOD DISEASES

| Foliage | Stem and Branch | |
|---|---|---|
| Anthracnose | Beech bark disease | Septoria canker |
| Black knot | Botrysphaeria canker | Shoot dieback |
| of cherry | Canker rot | Slime flux |
| Cottonwood | Chestnut blight | Spiculosa canker |
| rust | Cytospora canker | Stem canker |
| Oak leaf | Hispidus canker | Stem decay |
| blister | Hypoxylon canker | Strumella canker |
| | Irpex canker | Witches broom |
| | Nectria canker | |

### HARDWOOD DISEASES

| Root Diseases | Vascular Wilts |
|---|---|
| Amillaria root rot | Dutch elm disease |
| Cylindrocladium root rot | Elm phloem necrosis |
| Lucidus root and butt rot | Mimosa wilt |
| Root decay | Oak wilt |
| | Sycamore leaf scorch |
| | Verticillium wilt |

## TABLE 14-6

## SOME COMMON DISEASES AFFECTING PINE AND HARDWOOD TREES IN THE NORTHWESTERN REGIONS

| CONIFER DISEASES | | |
|---|---|---|
| Foliage | Stem and Branch | Root |
| Diplodia tip blight | Atropellis canker | Annosus root |
| Douglas fir tip | Comandra blister rust | disease |
| blight | Dwarf mistletoes | Armillaria root |
| Elytroderma disease | Stem decay | disease |
| Fusarium root | Western gall rust | Black stain root |
| disease | White pine blister | disease |
| Juniper blight | rust | Laminated root |
| Larch needle disease | | rot |
| Meria needle disease | | Phytophthora |
| Needle cast diseases | | root rot |
| Red band needle | | Red-brown butt |
| blight | | rot |
| Rhabdocline needle | | |
| blight | | |
| Scotch pine needle | | |
| cast | | |
| Spruce needle blight | | |
| Swiss needle cast | | |
| White pine needle case | | |

| HARDWOOD DISEASES | | |
|---|---|---|
| Foliage | Stem and Branch | Vascular Wilts |
| Anthrocnose | Siberian elm canker | Dutch elm |
| Ink spot | Thyronectria canker | disease |
| Marssonina blight | | |

tree killing by insects benefits people. Stand composition may be improved when insects kill undesirable species. They may contribute also to "natural" thinning of overcrowded stands, speed up the rate of pruning of others, and hasten the decomposition of logging slash; however, in the main, they are harmful.

On the other hand, forest trees have an eternal struggle to survive insect attacks. Some insects infest seedlings shortly after they emerge from the ground. Others destroy young and mature trees by girdling the cambium layer. Certain insects attack tree roots, while others destroy the seed and fruit.

Over the last 15 to 20 years, more than 180 different insects

TABLE 14-7

**SOME COMMON DISEASES AFFECTING PINE AND HARDWOOD TREES
IN THE SOUTHWESTERN REGIONS**

| CONIFER DISEASES | | |
|---|---|---|
| **Foliage** | **Stem and Branch** | **Root** |
| Dothistroma needle blight | Comandra blister rust | Annosus root disease |
| Elytroderma disease | Cone rust | Armillaria root disease |
| Fir broom rust | Dasyscypha canker | Black stain root disease |
| Lodgepole pine needle cast | Dwarf mistletoes | Inonotus tomentosus |
| Meria needle disease | Fir broom rust | Laminated root rot |
| Needle casts of true fir | Fir mistletoes | Phytophthora root rot |
| Needle rust of fir | Indian paint fungus | Red-brown butt rot |
| Needle rust of pine | Juniper rust | |
| Needle rust of pinyon pine | Limb rust | |
| Rhabdocline needle blight | Red ring rot | |
| Spruce broom rust | Spruce broom rust | |
| Subalpine fir needle cast | Stalactiform rust | |
| | Twig dieback | |
| | Western gall rust | |
| | White pine blister rust | |

| HARDWOOD DISEASES | | | |
|---|---|---|---|
| **Foliage** | **Stem and Branch** | **Root** | **Vascular Wilts** |
| Marssonina blight | Cytospora canker | Ganoderma applanatum | Dutch elm disease |
| Melampsora rust | False tinder fungus | | |
| Shepherd's crook | Stem canker | | |
| | True mistletoes | | |

have been recorded in outbreak status in the eastern forests of the United States. Fortunately, the majority of these outbreaks were small and short-lived.

Lack of space does not permit a discussion of all insects of economic importance. Some typical examples have been selected for discussion. Additional information is available in various references included in the bibliography at the end of the chapter.

Control measures, by use of chemicals, have been purposely limited in the discussion which follows. The rapid changes occurring in the development and use of pesticides in forest insect and disease control make this step advisable. All pesticides are under constant review by the U.S. Environmental Protection Agency, which controls and registers pesticides that can be used. Your state forestry agency or state agricultural experiment station should be contacted for current recommended control measures, as these are changing constantly.

## TYPES OF FOREST INSECTS
## BASED ON TREE DAMAGE

*Bark beetles*—insects that destroy the phloem and cambium tissues by chewing their way through the outer and inner bark, girdling the tree, and introducing wood-destroying fungi.

*Leaf eaters*—insects that eat all or part of the foliage by chewing or that cause discoloration or malformation by sucking plant sap.

*Wood borers*—insects that bore into the wood of the main bole, large branches, dried wood, and roots by chewing their way through woody tissue.

*Tip feeders*—insects that feed on the growing tips by boring, eating the bark, or girdling the twig.

*Cone and seed feeders*—insects that bore into the seed or chew holes through the cones, nuts, or other fruit.

*Gall formers*—insects that injure the plant tissue so that various types of abnormal swelling, or galls, are formed on the leaves, twigs, trunks, or roots.

### Bark Beetles

Bark beetles are the most destructive of all forest insects. In the nation, it is estimated that about 90 per cent of all insect-caused tree deaths and over 60 per cent of the total loss of tree growth are due to bark beetles. There are several hundred different kinds of bark beetles in the United States, including those which attack western firs, western pines, spruces, poplars, and southern pines. Three typical bark beetles are shown in Figure 14-4.

In addition to killing trees by girdling and allowing air to reach the water-conducting tissue, bark beetles also act as carriers of blue stain fungi. Although not a deadly disease, it plays some role in causing rapid foliage death following bark beetle attacks. Blue stain coloration is a characteristic of beetle-attacked timber. It causes a loss of grade in lumber but no reduction of strength.

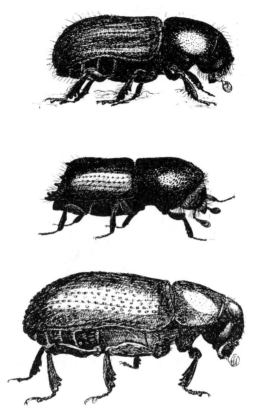

Fig. 14-4. Three principal bark beetles which attack southern pine. Top to bottom: southern pine beetle *(Dendroctonus frontalis)*, *Ips* engraver beetle *(Ips avulsus, Ips grandicollis, Ips calligraphus)*, and the black turpentine beetle *(Dendroctonus terebrans)*. Adult beetles are shown.

### Southern Pine Beetles

The southern pine beetle is an excellent example of one of the most destructive of forest pests. It has frequently reached epidemic proportions in many states in the South since 1958. The worst outbreak occurred in southeast Texas where this beetle had infested a gross area of 6 million acres. Every state in the South (Figure 14-5) has had southern pine beetle outbreaks.

This insect is sporadic in its behavior, killing groups of trees here and there in the forest. Occasionally the infestation dies out,

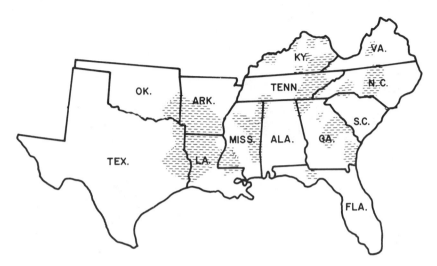

Fig. 14-5. Distribution of the southern pine beetle, 1977. (Adapted from U.S. Forest Service report titled *Forest Insect and Disease Conditions in the United States, 1977*)

but sometimes it jumps about in "popcorn" fashion. A constant vigil is required on this pest following ice, hail, windstorms, intense fires, extended droughts, and other major forest disturbances.

The beetle is a small, inconspicuous insect, brown to black in color, and somewhat smaller than a grain of rice. Figure 14-4 illustrates an artist's conception of the southern pine bark beetle. One early symptom of its presence is the tree crown, which begins to turn grayish-yellow to reddish-brown. Usually the first evidence that living trees are being attacked is the presence of numerous dime-size pitch tubes generally on the middle or upper trunk. Reddish boring dust may also be found lodged in the bark crevices and around the base of the tree. On the inner bark of recently attacked or dying trees, the tunnels (Figure 14-6) are distinct, winding, and crisscrossed, making S-shaped engravings. The last may be associated with the "s" in the word "southern," used to name this insect.

## Ips *Engraver Beetles*

The *Ips* engraver beetles are another destructive example of pine bark beetles. They are common in almost all forested regions of the country and normally attack trees which are weakened, dying, or

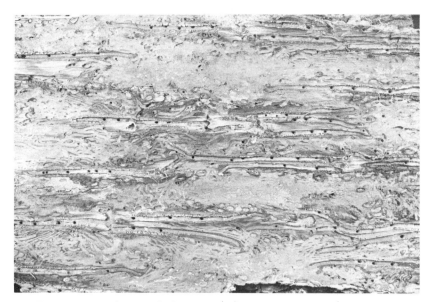

Fig. 14-6. Top photograph shows the gallery pattern formed in the inner bark by the southern pine beetle. Lower photo is pattern of the *Ips* beetle. Note typical I-shape tunnels.

recently felled or adjacent to felled trees or logging slosh. Generally infestations involve scattered individual trees or small groups throughout the forest. Epidemics sometimes develop in timber stands stressed by drought, windstorms, or wildfires.

The *Ips* beetle (Figure 14-4) is a variable tan to brown in color and between $\frac{1}{16}$ and $\frac{5}{16}$ of an inch in length. The scooped out or shovel-shaped rear body is an easy way to distinguish them from other types of beetles.

Mature beetles make radiating or forked egg galleries in the inner bark which are often straight up and down in an "I" shape (Figure 14-6).

Various factors affect the severity of bark beetle outbreaks. Among these are tree vigor, competition for food and space, and attacks upon bark beetles by parasites and predators. Predators play an important role in keeping bark beetle populations under control under most conditions. The most important predators are checkered beetles (*Cleridae*), southern pine sawyers (*Monochamus*), ostomid beetles (*Ostomidae*), ants, and woodpeckers.

Two means of direct control for bark beetle infestations are spraying with an insecticide and logging the infested trees before the bark beetles emerge (Figure 14-7). Rapid removal of *Ips*-infested trees following wildfires, windstorms, and other disasters is also necessary to prevent population buildups.

Sex attractants are being given increased research attention to open up new opportunities for the control of bark beetles and other destructive insects.

## Leaf Eaters

Many insects defoliate or feed upon the leaves of trees. The damage can be readily recognized from the absence of foliage or from uneaten leaf parts. The degree to which a tree is injured depends upon the frequency and extent of defoliation, the species, and the season of the year. Conifers generally suffer more severely or are more readily killed than the hardwoods. Occasional epidemic conditions will occur which will severely defoliate and kill large stands of timber. Spruce budworm attacks on coniferous forests of the Northeast and West and tent caterpillar epidemics on hardwood forests are examples; however, any serious defoliation reduces the growth of timber. Leaf-eating insects can be divided into three subgroups:

Fig. 14-7. Direct control of the southern pine bark beetle involves cutting the trees while they are still green and quickly removing them from the forest. (Courtesy Texas Forest Service)

chewers, leaf miners, and skeletonizers, depending on the location and kind of feeding activity. Chewers consume entire leaves or portions of leaves. "Leaf miners," as the term implies, live within the leaf and consume inner tissues. Skeletonizers consume leaf tissue from the lower side of the leaf, leaving only the upper layer, or vascular tissue.

The gypsy moth and the forest tent caterpillar are typical examples of forest insect pests which are defoliators. The gypsy moth occurs over large areas of the northeastern United States with infestations also occurring in the midwestern, southern, and western states. Trees may be partially or completely defoliated. Many hardwoods which are significantly defoliated refoliate during late summer, but a single defoliation frequently kills conifers. Trees growing under a wide range of conditions are attacked; however, poor site conditions do not seem particularly to trigger attacks.

The gypsy moth does very well on white and chestnut oak and attacks almost all forest tree species with the exception of yellow-poplar and ash. A thin canopy with many partially consumed leaves or needles is typical.

The forest tent caterpillar thrives throughout most of the United States and Canada. Bottomland forests along waterways are particularly susceptible. The caterpillar attacks mainly species of hardwoods but prefers trembling aspen, sugar maple, black gum, tupelo, and sweet gum. Various species of oaks are commonly attacked in the southern states. Frequently large acreages of bottomland hardwoods are attacked and occasionally upland oak stands.

Young larvae of the tent caterpillar sometimes skeletonize leaves, while mature larvae typically consume the entire leaf. Defoliated forests appear silvery gray from a distance or from the air and have very sparse canopies. Despite its name, the forest tent caterpillar does not form tents of webbing but lays down a silky trail or mat on foliage or bark.

Control measures for leaf-eating defoliators often consist of the application of a suitable insecticide. Appropriate information can be obtained from the district forester or extension advisor.

### Wood Borers

Many insects attack wood by boring into it for food and shelter or merely for a place to live. Some wood borers attack only living trees; others are found chiefly in freshly felled or dying trees; a few infest only dry, seasoned lumber; and some borers attack only old, moist wood.

Typical hardwood borers are the bronze birch borer, the bronze poplar borer, and the locust borer. The galleries of these borers are flat and usually packed with sawdust-like material. These larvae initially feed just beneath the bark and then bore into the wood. Living trees are attacked; however, those which are under stress due to drought, defoliation, or other factors are most likely to be attacked.

The southern pine sawyer is an important conifer wood borer. It invades both live trees and dying or freshly felled trees. The sawyer often attacks shortly after bark beetles have become established.

Borers are also common in the western pine forests and Douglas fir of the Northwest but are of less concern than in the South and East. Damage to trees by borers and beetles can be reduced by a salvage cut to harvest the logs which should be quickly sawed into lumber.

Of significant concern is the pine nematode (eel worm). This pest kills loblolly, Scotch, Austrian, and Japanese black pine as well as other conifer species. Several eastern states have reported damage. Reportedly nematodes are carried from infested to healthy trees by long-horned beetles.

### Tip Feeders

A wide variety of forest insects damage the growing tips of trees. These include weevils and caterpillars. Most damage is caused by borers, but some species eat the bark and girdle twigs. The females of a few of these insects cut small slits in the twigs in which they place their eggs.

One of the most serious of the tip feeders in the East and South is the Nantucket pine tip moth. The tip moth caterpillars bore into buds and destroy them. They often extend their tunnels into the twig for a distance of a few inches. Seedlings of shortleaf, loblolly, and Virginia pines frequently appear seriously damaged, but each spring the trees recover and eventually outgrow the attacks. There can be two to five generations per year, depending on latitude. The loss of height growth may be ½ foot or more, but this may be recovered by more vigorous growth the following spring. Wholesale control of entire stands may be impractical. Where high-valued trees are involved, such as in special tree seed orchards or in Christmas tree plantings, systemic insecticides can provide good control; however, they must be used with extreme care.

### Gall Formers

Many forest insects feed only on plant sap. The injury may consist of enlarged growths in the form of galls or in foliage deformation. Under forest conditions, the conifers are more severely attacked than hardwoods.

Some of the more common gall-producing insects are wasps, midges, aphids, mites, and some beetles. Their attack stimulates plant tissue so that a variety of galls or abnormal swellings occur on the twigs, leaves, and roots. No chemical control is used under forest conditions.

## DISEASES OF FOREST TREES

The study of forest tree diseases for the purpose of preventing and controlling them is called *forest pathology*. A tree disease is the sustained functional and structural damage of living plant tissue which may bring about the tree's death. It may be caused by the physical environment such as the weather, air pollution, or unfavorable soil conditions, by little understood viruses, or by living organisms such as fungi, bacteria, mold, or parasitic plants. Although they are silent killers, diseases destroy more timber than wildfires do.

Some typical forest tree diseases of significance have been selected for brief discussion. For more complete information, please consult the Bibliography at the end of the chapter.

### Annosus Root Rot

One of the most serious diseases attacking young pine stands is annosus root rot (*Fomitopsis annosa*). This disease also attacks a wide range of conifers and is often severe on red cedar. The infection starts when the fungi enter the surface of a freshly cut pine stump. The disease is spread by means of root contacts to adjacent trees. An indication of the disease is the presence of fungus-fruiting bodies at the base of the trunk (Figure 14-8). These "conks" range in size from ¼ inch to several inches in width and are gray-brown above and whitish below. Some infested trees do not have observable fruiting bodies.

The foliage of infected trees may appear healthy or may be colored from light green to yellow-brown. Branches may have only current year needles that are shorter than normal. This gives the crown a thin, tufted appearance.

The greatest damage from annosus root rot has occurred in areas with light, sandy soils and in planted rather than in natural stands.

Dry, granular borax has been found to provide an effective protection against both stump surface colonization by spores and residual tree infection and mortality. The material is applied to the stump surface immediately after a tree is cut. It reduces the possibility of infection. No stump treatment is effective once the disease is present and trees are dying. Under this situation, the fungus is well established in the root systems.

Fig. 14-8. Fruiting body of annosus root rot at base of pine tree. This is one of the most serious diseases attacking young pine stands in the South. (Courtesy Texas Forest Service)

## Wood Rots

A wide variety of wood-destroying fungi cause a large number of wood rots or decays. Some fungi, such as annosus root rot, attack the roots, while others attack the stem and limbs of trees. Some of the rots attack the living tissue of the sapwood and inner bark, while others attack only the heartwood. Some fungi play an important role in decomposing forest litter by attacking the wood of dead trees.

Fungi reproduce by means of minute spores. These are single cells or a small number of united cells specifically adapted for reproducing the plant. Spores are produced by special fruiting bodies from very small structures to large ones such as mushrooms, puffballs, and conks, or brackets, on decaying wood. The fruiting body is used to identify the specific fungus attacking trees, as in the case of annosus root rot. Spores penetrate trees through bark injury or broken limbs.

There is no control for the wood rots. Some prevention can be accomplished by reducing wounding to the trees resulting from logging, fire, or other means. When pruning is done, it should be restricted to smaller limbs, preferably under 1 inch in diameter. Since decay losses increase with advancing age, the rotation or final harvest cutting age may be shortened to remove timber prior to the most damaging periods.

### Gall Rusts

Another important stem disease causes galls, or cankerlike protrusions, in the trunks or branches of scattered individual pine trees. These are particularly noticeable in the early spring when the galls develop readily visible yellowish spores. These "wart-like" growths are caused by fungi (Figure 14-9).

Fusiform rust (*Cronartium fusiforme*) is destructive from Maryland to Texas, especially in slash and loblolly pine plantations. Comandra blister rust (*C. comandrae*) has been especially destructive in shortleaf stands in Arkansas, Oklahoma, and Tennessee. White pine blister rust (*C. ribicola*) has attacked this species across the East and is of economic importance throughout the range of white pine. The eastern gall rust (*C. cerebrum*) has been particularly destructive on Virginia pine and shortleaf pine. Trees with galls should be removed in thinnings or improvement cuttings.

Fig. 14-9. Two types of galls on the trunks of pine trees caused by a cronartium disease. (Courtesy U.S. Forest Service)

### Leaf Diseases

Forest trees exhibit numerous leaf diseases. Those which result from a fungal attack usually show evidence of some typical fruiting structure or a distinctive symptom pattern. Several leaf diseases of interest include anthracnose, leaf blister of oak, leaf rust of poplar, powdery mildew, tobacco mosaic virus of ash, and line pattern of birch.

Anthracnose is a typical leaf disease which is characterized by sharply defined areas of dead tissue on affected leaves. These areas are usually adjacent to a leaf vein, but in severe instances entire leaves may die. Sycamores are particularly susceptible to infection by the anthracnose fungus, but most hardwood species are subject to attack. Anthracnose is found throughout the United States but is of primary concern in the eastern, southern, and central hardwood forests.

### Oak Wilt

Another serious stem disease is oak wilt (*Ceratocystis fagacearum*) which attacks most oak species (*Quercus spp.*) but primarily those in the red oak group. It has spread over much of the eastern United States and as far south as South Carolina and as far west as Texas and Kansas. Symptoms are most notable during the late spring and early summer, with leaves dying from the outside edge toward the midrib and defoliation from the outer limbs inside and downward. It is commonly spread through wounds and underground root grafts. No effective control is known, although physical removal of the infected tree and herbicide treatment of the stump are recommended.

### GRAZING DAMAGE

Some damage is done to forest trees by both domestic and wild animals. Damage may be done in the form of browsing on the foliage or of trampling in the case of seedlings. Damage is more severe in hardwood stands than in conifer stands; however, hardwoods recover more quickly than do the conifers. Browsing damage by livestock and deer generally occurs during the winter months when there is a shortage of green plant material. Some damage occurs to forest trees through the gnawing of animals such as rabbits, beavers, and rats. In addition to the trampling of seedlings, overgrazing frequently causes soil compaction which disrupts the soil-moisture relationships.

All grazing should be excluded from hardwood stands because the most desirable timber trees are the browse species preferred by livestock. Adequate fences should be maintained around bottomland hardwood stands. On the other hand, regulated cattle grazing can be permitted in pine stands to utilize available forage. Cattle must be fenced out of pine plantations until the trees are two years old or until the seedlings are large enough to avoid trampling. Sheep and goats should be excluded from all young pine timber stands until the trees reach 15 feet or more in height. Soil compaction around cattle feeding areas may damage trees and result in serious soil erosion. Frequent moving of feed troughs and salt blocks will help reduce this problem. Sufficient harvest of deer herds will prevent overpopulations and excessive browse damage.

High value forest crops such as Christmas trees deserve particular attention. Deer browse can easily result in thousands of dollars in revenue loss. Deer repellents, electric fencing, and regular fencing have all been used to reduce browse damage in these instances.

## WEATHER DAMAGE

Damage caused by severe or unusual weather may reach serious proportions. Those elements exerting a direct influence upon the forest include wind, ice, frost including winter kill, floods, sun, lightning, erosion, and shifting sands; however, only under severe conditions will these elements cause widespread damage to forest stands.

High wind damage from hurricanes or tornadoes occurs in both coniferous and hardwood stands. Damage is greatest in overcut pine stands. It includes the uprooting and windthrowing of both young and mature trees and the destroying of reproduction under felled trees.

Ice damage is also serious in forest stands, especially in young even-aged stands where the crowns are nearly the same height. Interlacing branches of young trees are more apt to hold large quantities of ice glaze and snow. The greatest damage occurs during rains at or just below freezing. Trees may be crushed or bent to the ground or their crowns twisted. Even though some may continue to grow, the trunks remain crooked. Compression wood is formed on the lower side of leaning trees, making them unsuitable for lumber. Similar damage occurs with wet snow. Occasionally, severe hailstorms will cause blowdown and will completely defoliate and damage limbs and leaders on both hardwoods and pines.

The freezing of seedlings causes outright death, called winterkill. The formation of cankers is also a problem. Freezing may winterkill large trees by destroying the buds or leaves or may cause serious die-back. Damage is more severe when early heavy frosts occur in the fall or in the late spring.

Flooding becomes a significant problem where inundation occurs over a period of several weeks. Some species, such as cypress, are more flood-tolerant, but most bottomland hardwoods will not survive flooding beyond two or three weeks.

Lightning damage generally occurs to the tallest and best trees in the stand. Severe strikes will kill a tree outright. Many trees will be damaged by stripping of the bark along the trunk, as this makes them very susceptible to attacks by insects or diseases.

Timber blown down by high winds or broken or bent by heavy ice or snow should be salvage-harvested as soon as possible. Dead or dying timber caused by frost, flooding, extended dry spells, or lightning should be removed from forest stands. Windfalls or dead trees create a fire hazard and make a breeding ground for insects and diseases. Early salvage is essential to remove the timber before it starts to deteriorate and total loss occurs.

## AIR POLLUTION

While the role of trees in our lives is becoming more important, trees are, today, increasingly threatened by air pollution from a variety of sources.

Some trees are injured by gases and particles in the air. Others absorb and use some contaminants without apparent harm. Pollutants are absorbed in the process of photosynthesis. The exchange occurs through stomata, or pores, in the leaf's surface (Figure 3-4). These include pollutants such as sulfur dioxide, chlorine, fluoride, and ozone and are known to be major tree despoilers. Scientists are of the opinion that these differences in response to injury are due to the kind of tree and its genetic makeup; however, other factors, such as tree growth stage, nearness to pollution source, pollutant concentration, and the duration of exposure, are also important. Thus, whether or not a tree dies as a result of pollution will depend on a combination of host and environmental factors.

Generally, trees are injured through the foliage. Foliar damage is more severe in conifers than in hardwoods; pollution damage in conifers can cause premature needle drop. As such, the trees cannot maintain their food production level. Becoming undernourished and weakened, they become susceptible to attack by insects, diseases, and environmental stresses. Death frequently follows.

Pollution may cause hardwood trees to lose their leaves; however, since they bear their leaves for only a portion of the year and replace them the following year, injury from pollution may not be severe.

Recently, sulfates and nitrates (acid deposition) have attracted widespread interest. Eastern forests, especially those in mountainous areas, are showing widespread damage which may be partially attributable to acid deposition; however, the situation is a very complex problem which is not likely due to a single causal factor. Much research must be done to correctly assess this important problem. Generally, acid deposition shows significant foliar damage only where trees are directly in the vicinity of a pollutant source, that is, in a direct plume dispersion pathway.

Presently, much research is being conducted on the effect of pollutants on tree growth and mortality.

### BIBLIOGRAPHY

Anonymous. *A Guide to Common Insects and Diseases of Forest Trees in the Northeastern United States*. FIDM NA-FRA. Washington, D.C.: U.S. Government Printing Office, 1979.

Baker, Whiteford L. *Eastern Forest Insects*. Miscellaneous Publication 1175. Washington, D.C.: U.S. Forest Service, 1972.

Bennett, William H., and Ostmark, H. Eugene. *Insect Pests of Southern Pines*. Unnumbered Publication. New Orleans, La.: Southern Forest Experiment Station, 1972.

Campbell, R. W. *The Gypsy Moth and Its Natural Enemies*. Agriculture Information Bulletin 381. Washington, D.C.: U.S. Forest Service, 1974.

*Diagnosing Injury to Eastern Forests*. Washington, D.C.: U.S. Forest Service, 1987.

Dix, Mary Ellen. *Protection of Great Plains Shelterbelts from Insects*. Publication 78. Denver, Colo.: Great Plains Agricultural Council, 1976.

Doane, C. C., and McManus, M. L., editors. *The Gypsy Moth: Research Towards Integrated Pest Management*. Technical Bulletin 1584. U.S.D.A., 1981.

Ebel, Bernard H., et al. *Southern Pine Seed and Cone Insects*. General Technical Report SE-8. Asheville, N.C.: Southeastern Area, State and Private Forestry and Southeast Forest Experiment Station, 1975.

*Forest Insect and Disease Conditions in the United States, 1977*. Unnumbered. Washington, D.C.: U.S. Forest Service, 1978.

French, D. W., et al. *Diseases of Forest and Shade Trees*. St. Paul, Minn.: Department of Plant Pathology, University of Minnesota, 1975.

Furniss, M. M., and Barr, W. F. *Insects Affecting Native Shrubs of the Northwestern United States*. General Technical Report INT-19. Ogden, Utah: Intermountain Forest and Range Experiment Station, 1975.

Hepting, George H. *Diseases of Forest and Shade Trees of the United States*. Agricultural Handbook 386. Washington, D.C.: U.S. Forest Service, 1971.

*Insects of Eastern Forests*. Miscellaneous Publication 1426. Washington, D.C.: U.S. Forest Service, 1985.

Johnson, Warren T., and Lyon, Howard H. *Insects That Feed on Trees and Shrubs*. Ithaca, N.Y.: Cornell University Press, 1976.

Jones, Thomas W., and Phelps, William R. *Oak Wilt*. Forest Pest Leaflet 29. Washington, D.C.: U.S. Forest Service, 1972.

Loomis, Robert C., and Padgett, William H. *Air Pollution and Trees in the East*. Atlanta, Ga., and Upper Darby, Pa.: State and Private Forestry, U.S. Forest Service, 1973.

Martineau, R. *Insects Harmful to Forest Trees*. Ottawa, Canada: Multiscience Publishers, Ltd., 1984.

Musselman, Lytton J., and Mann, William F., Jr. *Root Parasites of Southern Forests*. General Technical Report SO-20. New Orleans, La.: Southern Experiment Station and Southeastern Area, State and Private Forestry, 1978.

Partridge, Arthur D. *Major Decays of Wood in the Inland Northwest*. Bulletin No. 2. Moscow, Ida.: University of Idaho, 1968.

Peterson, Glenn W., and Riffle, Jerry W. *Protection of Windbreaks from Diseases*. Publication 78. Denver, Colo.: Great Plains Agricultural Council, 1976.

Rose, A. H., and Lindquist, O. H. *Insects of Eastern Pines*. Publication 1313. Ottawa: Department of the Environment, Canadian Forestry Service, 1973.

Sanders, C. J., et al., editors. *Recent Advances in Spruce Budworms Research*. Ottawa: Canadian Forest Service and U.S.D.A., 1985.

Stein, John D., and Kennedy, Patrick C. *Key to Shelterbelt Insects in the Northern Great Plains*. Research Paper RM-85. Ft. Collins, Colo.: Rocky Mountain Forest and Range Experiment Station, 1972.

Tatter, Terry A. *Diseases of Shade Trees*. New York, N.Y.: Academic Press, Inc., 1978.

Thatcher, R. C., et al., editors. *The Southern Pine Beetle*. Technical Bulletin 1631. U.S.D.A., 1980.

U.S. Forest Service. *Forest Insect and Disease Handbook: Renewable Resources Evaluation*. General Report SA-GR 14, 1980.

U.S. Forest Service. *Insects and Diseases of Trees in the South*. General Report R8-GR5. Atlanta, Ga.: Southern Regional Forest Service, 1985.

U.S. Forest Service. *Insects of Eastern Forests*. Miscellaneous Publication 1426. 1985.

U.S. Forest Service. *Oak Pests: A Guide to Major Insects, Diseases, Air Pollution, and Chemical Injury*. General Report SA-GR 11. Stoneville, Miss.: Southern Forest Experiment Station, 1980.

Wilson, L. F. *A Guide to Insect Injury of Conifers in the Lake States*. Agricultural Handbook 501. U.S.D.A., 1977.

CHAPTER XV

# Wood for Energy

Forests of the continental United States represent about one-fourth of the total land area (Table 1-2). They are being increasingly considered as a fuel source capable of providing more of our need for heat and energy at a cost less than that of present fossilized fuels. The forests of this nation can provide a significant portion of our energy needs.

## WOOD FOR FUEL

There has been an increasing interest in the United States relative to the use of wood to help alleviate energy costs. Many home owners are installing the latest, more efficient wood-burning stoves for heating in order to offset the escalating cost of other fuels. Some utility companies which formerly put wood residue from utility line clearances in landfills are now using this product for fuel. Many sawmills have switched from natural gas and oil to dry wood waste in firing dry kilns. Others generate their own electricity from wood waste, and there are instances in which municipal utilities now generate electricity from wood at a lower cost than from other fuels. These are but a few cases in which individuals and companies are converting to wood use.

While reduction in cost is the major economic factor in the switch-over to wood, there can be an independence associated with it. It means that a locally supplied fuel can provide heat and power without interruptions due to storms, strikes, and embargoes.

While wood may be used advantageously for energy, there are limitations to its use in various parts of the nation, depending upon local availability and price. Notwithstanding, it is evident that wood as energy promises to help provide, at least in part, the nation's energy needs. To many forest landowners, fuelwood will provide a marketable forest product. Indications for the future are that harvesting of energy wood from the total tree may become as common as harvesting other forest products (Figure 15-1).

One term that is encountered in dealing with wood for energy is "biomass." Biomass is the weight of the complete tree, including the roots, stem, limbs, branches, and leaves, all of which can be used to produce energy. The reason for the use of weight is that the heating value of wood, like that of coal, can be more conveniently expressed in units of weight than in units of volume. Tree weight data will allow for the assessment of the energy potential of forests and forest growth.

Above-ground biomass on the commercial forest lands of the United States is estimated at 36 billion tons green weight. This material is distributed approximately as 80 per cent wood, 12 per cent bark, and 8 per cent foliage. The underground biomass made up of stumps and roots is said to add perhaps 20 per cent more to the wood

Fig. 15-1. Scattered debris left after a logging operation. In the foreseeable future, debris such as this, including leaves and other small trees, may be used to make other forest products or used for fuel and energy production. Some consideration is being given to the utilization of stumps and roots. (Courtesy Texas Forest Service)

and bark tonnages but has relatively little potential for use except in a few special cases. This 36 billion tons is divided about equally between hardwoods and softwoods and includes all sizes and types of trees in the forest. It is further reported that the commercial forests of the nation grow 490 million tons of tree biomass annually, above that currently used for forest products. This is potentially available for energy.

The production of residues produced in the manufacture of lumber and wood products annually in the United States is reflected in Table 15-1. (See also Figure 15-2.)

TABLE 15-1

**WEIGHT OF WOOD AND BARK PRODUCED IN THE
MANUFACTURE OF LUMBER AND OTHER
PRODUCTS, 1987**

| Type of Use | Wood Residue[1] | Bark Residue | Total Residue |
|---|---|---|---|
| | . . . . . . . . . . . . . . . . . (*thousand dry tons*) . . . . . . . . . . . . . . . . . | | |
| Fiber production[2] | 38,724 | 289 | 39,013 |
| Fuel | 19,630 | 17,575 | 37,205 |
| Other uses | 7,970 | 3,031 | 11,001 |
| Not used | 1,936 | 1,029 | 2,965 |
| Total | 68,260 | 21,924 | 90,184 |

[1]Includes slabs, edgings, trim, spur ends, planer shavings, and sawdust.
[2]Pulp and board, including wood chips for export.

(Source: U.S. Forest Service, Preliminary RPA Review Draft, 1988)

While the use of wood for energy may appear to be of recent origin, such is not the case. Wood has been used for fuel more than any other material since the beginning of history. Even today, over half of all the wood harvested in the world is for fuel.

## HISTORICAL BACKGROUND OF WOOD
## USED AS FUEL

About 100 years ago, the use of wood as fuel reached its peak in the United States. At that time, wood provided 3 of the 4 quadrillion BTU's (British Thermal Units) consumed. By 1984, the nation's consumption of energy had climbed to over 74 quadrillion BTU's, while the contribution of wood decreased to 2.6 quadrillion (or quads), 3.4 per cent of the total.

Fig. 15-2. Small sawmill operation in Kentucky. In the production of lumber at a mill, slabs, edgings, and sawdust are by-products. While such by-products formerly were burned, greater use is made of them today for manufacturing paper, mulch, and other goods and for producing energy. Large mills debark logs prior to producing lumber in the mill. This allows for chipping the bark-free slabs and edges for use in other products, such as newsprint, and for utilizing the bark for mulch or fuel. (Courtesy Kentucky Division of Forestry)

A BTU is the amount of heat required to raise the temperature of a pound of water 1 degree. Presently, 8,300 BTU's per pound of oven-dry hardwood is the energy conversion factor in general use.

Several events contributed to the reduction in wood fuel use. One was the development of the coal industry in the Northeast. Another was the beginning of the oil industry in the Northeast and its subsequent development in the Southwest. These events led to a switch from wood to the more economical and more convenient fossil fuels. Energy consumption by fuel type for the United States is given in Table 15-2.

Favorable price regulations on natural gas eventually encouraged many industries to convert to gas. Yet, these same regulations discouraged profit opportunities on the part of the oil and gas industries. The result was that exploration and development for new sources came to a standstill in the United States. Air quality regulations also encouraged a switch from high-sulfur coal to oil and gas so that more and more, this nation became dependent on foreign nations for its energy needs.

Its dependence on foreign oil supplies came into focus with the 1973 and 1979 Arab oil embargoes and the radical increases in price that subsequently followed. This placed the nation in a serious situation. It was faced with ever-increasing prices and a supply that could be interrupted by political events.

The severe winter of 1976-77 emphasized the fact that the nation was facing an energy crisis. The shutdown of many industrial plants and schools made this evident. As a result, industry and other users of fossil fuels have looked to other sources of energy to avoid costly plant shutdowns and to provide heat and energy at a more economical price. Wood is one of these sources.

## NON-FOSSIL FUELS

The principal non-fossil, fuel-derived sources of energy include organic gas, solar energy, geothermal water and steam, the wind, ocean tides, and wood.

Wood, due to its value, renewability, availability, and clean-burning characteristics, ranks high among this list as an extremely viable source of energy. It is a low-sulfur fuel that can be burned for energy without costly antipollution devices. A wood-fueled system also has less total emissions per unit of energy output than a system using cleaned coal or low-sulfur coal.

Sawdust contains about 6 per cent hydrogen, 52 per cent carbon, 1 per cent nitrogen, 43 per cent oxygen, 0.7 per cent ash, and relatively little sulfur. These proportions do not vary greatly among wood species.

## TABLE 15-2

## ENERGY CONSUMPTION IN THE UNITED STATES, BY CONSUMING SECTOR AND FUEL, 1985

| Consuming Sector | Coal | Natural Gas | Petro-leum | Hydro-power | Nuclear | Gas Thermal | Total Fuel Inputs | Elec-tricity Purchased | Total Energy Consumed (Three Sectors) |
|---|---|---|---|---|---|---|---|---|---|
| | | | | | | *(quadrillion BTU's)* | | | |
| Industrial | 2.60 | 6.80 | 8.65 | — | — | — | 18.05 | 8.99 | 27.04 |
| Residential and commercial | 0.18 | 6.80 | 2.92 | — | — | — | 9.90 | 16.89 | 26.79 |
| Transportation | — | 0.50 | 21.11 | — | — | — | 21.61 | — | 21.61 |
| Electric utilities | 15.41 | 3.00 | 1.03 | 3.38 | 4.14 | 0.20 | 27.16 | | |
| Total fuel inputs | 18.19 | 17.10 | 33.71 | 3.38 | 4.14 | 0.20 | 76.72 | | |

(Courtesy U.S. Department of Energy, 1985)

Wood, in general, contains about 77 per cent of volatile matter, about 20 per cent fixed carbon, and about 2 per cent ash.

Oven-dry wood averages about 8,300 BTU's per pound for most species; however, woods which contain resin have higher BTU values than woods which do not. About the same relationship exists between softwood bark and hardwood bark; however, softwood bark does contain a higher percentage of ash than does hardwood bark. Burning efficiency of bark is reduced somewhat because of the ash content.

It is generally accepted that a mixture of wood, bark, and foliage will also have a value of approximately 8,300 BTU's per oven-dry pound, the same as wood.

As reported by the U.S. Forest Service's Forest Products Laboratory, wood can be pelletized, pulverized, liquefied, and gasified and used to generate electrical energy.

More energy is derived from dry wood than from green wood. This is reflected in Table 15-3, which shows the heating value of various species of trees. This is because the water in wood must first be

TABLE 15-3

**APPROXIMATE HEATING VALUE PER STANDARD CORD
OF SELECTED SPECIES**

| Species of Wood | Green | Air-Dried |
|---|---|---|
| | . . . . . . . . . . *(million BTU's)*. . . . . . . . . . | |
| Hickory | 23.1 | 24.8 |
| Black locust | 23.1 | 24.6 |
| Oak, white | 22.4 | 23.9 |
| Apple | 22.3 | 24.3 |
| Pine, southern | 21.1 | 22.0 |
| Maple, sugar | 20.4 | 21.8 |
| Beech | 19.7 | 20.9 |
| Oak, red | 19.6 | 21.7 |
| Birch, yellow | 19.4 | 20.9 |
| Ash, white | 19.0 | 20.5 |
| Walnut, black | 18.6 | 20.8 |
| Maple, red | 17.6 | 19.1 |
| Elm | 15.8 | 17.7 |
| Cherry | 15.1 | 18.8 |
| Pine, white | 12.9 | 14.2 |
| Cottonwood | 12.7 | 15.0 |
| Basswood | 10.0 | 11.7 |

(Source: *Industrial Wood Energy Handbook*, 1984)

heated and vaporized in a heater or furnace, thus reducing the heat that can be recovered from a given weight of wood.

The moisture content of wood in its natural state varies among species. Moisture content may vary from 40 to 130 per cent compared to the solid content. This moisture dramatically affects the amount of heat that can be recovered from wood. Oven-dry wood, for example, contains 8,300 BTU's per pound and burns at about 80 per cent efficiency. This produces 6,600 BTU's of recoverable heat. In contrast, wood at 80 per cent moisture content burns at about 66 per cent efficiency and produces only 1,700 BTU's per pound. Thus, it can be seen that the moisture content is the most important factor in considering the burning efficiency of wood.

Extensive research is currently being undertaken by the federal government to assess the potential of wood biomass for producing energy products. One location for this research is the Short Rotation Woody Crops Program being conducted at the Oak Ridge National Laboratory in Oak Ridge, Tennessee. At this point, the plan is to develop experience in energy crop management, refine energy farming operations, test specialized equipment, and conduct basic studies. In general, it will be a study in short-rotation forestry.

Other research work in wood energy is being conducted by the U.S. Forest Service, by several universities and state agencies, and by industry.

## ROLE OF WOOD IN ENERGY PRODUCTION

The use of wood for energy cannot be considered as a panacea for the nation's energy problem. Yet, it can play a prominent role locally and on a regional basis; for example, in the Northeast especially, an area removed from coal and oil, the harvesting and burning of wood may be an economically viable alternate for generating electricity.

Forest Service scientists report that in the near future, an additional 5 quads of energy could come from currently unused forest biomass. This is about 7 per cent of the nation's current energy needs. With predicted increases in tree harvesting and processing technology, potential contributions to energy needs could be even more significant.

A study in West Virginia, based on that state's energy needs, reported that the forests of that state could supply about one-eighth of that state's energy needs without depleting the capital growing stock.

Today, the pulp and paper industry has achieved 58 per cent energy self-sufficiency. Limited data on sawmilling indicates a range of from 20 to 50 per cent. The plywood industry has an energy self-sufficiency of about 50 per cent.

## VALUE OF ENERGY WOOD

The value of energy wood, based on BTU content, will always be relative to the values of alternate fuels; for example, if natural gas costs $2.00 per thousand cubic feet, or 28.3 cubic meters (Table 15-4), energy wood would be worth $14.75 per wet ton, or $16.26 per metric ton. On this basis, energy wood can compete economically with sawtimber and pulpwood. Sawtimber would be worth $132.75 per MBF, Doyle scale, while pulpwood would be worth $36.87 per cord, delivered, assuming these products were burned as fuel. Other interesting comparisons can be made upon review of Table 15-4.

TABLE 15-4

**THE VALUE OF ENERGY WOOD, SAWTIMBER, AND PULPWOOD,
IF USED AS FUEL**

| Natural Gas Costs | Energy Wood[1] | Sawtimber[2] | Pulpwood[3] |
|---|---|---|---|
| ($/MCF) | ($/Ton) | ($/MBF Doyle) | ($/Cord) |
| 2.00 | 14.75 | 132.75 | 36.87 |
| 2.25 | 16.59 | 149.31 | 41.75 |
| 2.50 | 18.44 | 165.96 | 46.10 |
| 2.75 | 20.28 | 182.52 | 50.70 |
| 3.00 | 22.13 | 199.17 | 55.32 |

[1]From *Fuel Value Calculator*.
[2]Calculated on the basis of 18,000 lbs./MBF Doyle scale.
[3]Calculated on the basis of 5,000 lbs./cord.

(Courtesy U.S. Forest Service)

Information on energy fuel values is contained in a Fuel Value Calculator developed by the U.S. Forest Service. It is designated as Publication No. 76-19 and is available without charge from this agency. The address is Information Center, Room 816, 1720 Peachtree Road, Atlanta, Georgia 30309.

The heating values for wood and bark of Rocky Mountain species will be noted in Table 15-5. Ordinarily, the heating value of the bark of most species of trees is higher than that of wood.

**TABLE 15-5**

**TYPICAL HEATING VALUES FOR WOOD AND BARK
OF ROCKY MOUNTAIN SPECIES**

| Species | Heating Value per Dry Pound | |
| --- | --- | --- |
| | Wood | Bark |
| | .....................(BTU's)...................... | |
| Douglas fir | 9,200 | 10,100 |
| Lodgepole pine | 8,600 | 10,760 |
| Ponderosa pine | 9,100 | 9,100 |
| Englemann spruce | — | 8,820 |
| True firs | 8,300 | — |

(Courtesy Rocky Mountain Forest and Range Experiment Station)

## *FUTURE OF WOOD AS AN ENERGY SOURCE*

The eventual harvesting and use of above-ground biomass from the forest will depend upon its value in relation to other fuels and demand. While demands for energy wood do not now exist to an appreciable extent, there are indications that they will develop. This is evident in the conversion of many industrial plants—primarily in the forest industry at present—from natural gas and oil to wood waste. And, many home owners are installing wood-burning stoves and fireplaces at a rapid rate. In many urban areas, fireplace wood brings up to $200 per cord.

Should wood be harvested on a large scale for energy production, it would have a tremendous impact on the country's energy budget. Likely, the wood product would take the form of tree chips, total tree-hogged fuel, highly specialized chips for various types of burners, or compressed wood pellets.

At present, the barrier to the increased use of wood for heating homes, small commercial establishments, or institutions is the lack of equipment for using these fuels. The development of equipment that approaches natural gas systems in automation and convenience would spur the demand for wood, especially with the rise of other fuel costs.

Additionally, future levels of timber use for energy will depend upon changes in technology that will allow the harvesting of wood biomass at lower costs. It is predicted that by the year 2000, all primary manufacturing wood residues will either be used as fuel or be

Fig. 15-3. A com-ply stud. Eventually these studs may be used in home construction on an extensive basis. A com-ply stud is a structural sandwich with a particleboard core placed between layers of solid wood veneer. The core is a useable product made from wood residue. (Courtesy Forestry Sciences Laboratory, Athens, Georgia)

converted into salable items. Current trends make this evident (Figure 15-3). This will result in a significant change in the energy economy of the country.

### BIBLIOGRAPHY

*Annual Energy Review 1985.* DOE/EIA-0384(85). Washington, D.C.: U.S. Department of Energy, 1986.

*Energy from Wood.* Bibliography. Madison, Wis.: U.S. Forest Products Laboratory, 1979.

*Estimates of U.S. Wood Energy Consumption 1980-1983.* DOE/EIA-0341(83). Washington, D.C.: U.S. Department of Energy, 1984.

*Firewood for Home Heating.* Publication 87. Charlottesville, Va.: Virginia Division of Forestry, 1979.

*Firewood for Your Fireplace.* Leaflet 559. Washington, D.C.: U.S. Forest Service, 1974.

Grantham, J. B., *et al. Energy and Raw Material Potentials of Wood in the Pacific Coast States.* Station Report 18. Portland, Ore.: Pacific Northwest Forest and Range Experiment Station, 1979.

*The Industrial Wood Energy Handbook.* Atlanta, Ga.: Georgia Institute of Technology, 1986.

LePori, W. A., and Soltes, E. J. *Thermochemical Conversion for Energy and Fuel in Biomass Energy.* College Station, Tex.: Texas A & M University Press, 1985.

Lyons, G. J., Lonny, F., and Pollock, H. P. "A Procedure for Estimating the Value of Forest Fuels," *Biomass*, 8(4):283-300, 1985.

Saeman, Jerome F. *Energy and Materials from the Forest Biomass.* Abstract. Madison, Wis.: U.S. Forest Products Laboratory, 1977.

Sampson, George R. *Energy Potential from Central and Southern Rocky Mountain Timber.* Research Note RM-368. Fort Collins, Colo.: Rocky Mountain Forest and Range Experiment Station, 1979.

Sarles, Raymond L. *Wood Fuel Plentiful in West Virginia.* Research Note NE-279. Broomal, Pa.: Northeast Forest Experiment Station, 1979.

U.S. Forest Service. *A National Energy Program for Forestry.* Miscellaneous Publication No. 1394. Washington, D.C., 1980.

U.S. Forest Service. *Tree Biomass—A State of the Art Compilation.* General Technical Report WO-33. Washington, D.C., 1981.

Youngs, R. L. *Utilization of Hardwood for Energy.* Proceedings, Sixth Annual Hardwood Symposium of the Hardwood Research Council, Cashiers, N.C., 1978.

Zerbe, John I. "The Many Forms of Wood as Fuel," *American Forests*, October, 1977.

Zerbe, John I. "Wood in the Energy Crisis," *Forest Farmer*, November-December, 1977.

# CHAPTER XVI

# Forestry Careers

Exciting developments in forestry and natural resources have opened new career opportunities. The increasing demand for wood products and other forest resources, especially recreation and wildlife, coupled with the need for ecologically and environmentally sound land management policies has resulted in growth in job opportunities.

Scientific knowledge and technical skills from a diversity of disciplines are required to prepare for a natural resource career. As in many scientific fields, growth through new advancements and innovations occurs daily, and the best way to channel this knowledge into the field is through newly educated graduates. A professional forester should acquire a minimum of a B.S. degree in forestry from a four-year college or university fully accredited by the Society of American Foresters (SAF). The curriculum of a forestry major can include training in forest management, wildlife, economics, dendrology, ecology, mensuration, protection, recreation, silviculture, soils, and many other physical and biological sciences. This broad science background provides excellent training for a great variety of positions in natural resource management. Many specialized fields of concentration are often sought in graduate studies: forest business and marketing strategies; computer modeling, simulation, and data analysis; logging and wood-processing techniques; stream, wildlife, and plant biologies; timber stand improvement; genetic engineering; and other creative options.

Forestry and natural resource employment opportunities fall into three areas: public, private, and self-employed. Public employment involves working for the government or educational institutions. Employment can be sought at the federal level (U.S. Forest Service, Bureau of Land Management, Fish and Wildlife Service, etc.); state level (Department of Natural Resources, Conservation, Parks and Recreation, etc.); local, county, and municipal governments (county park managers, urban foresters); and educational institutions (teachers, researchers, extension foresters). Private employment opportunities include working for major wood-based corporations (Weyerhaeuser, International Paper, etc.); marketing and consulting firms or environmental organizations (Sierra Club, Friends of the Earth, Audubon Society). Self-employed foresters work as consulting foresters, tree surgeons, and estate managers. Average starting salaries range from $17,000 to $25,000, and beginning Ph.D. salaries are around $30,000. Salaries eventually range from $35,000 to $75,000 or more depending on education and experience. With forestry enrollments down 50 to 75 per cent in institutions around the country, future demand for foresters is expected to rise. A shortage of forestry graduates is predicted for the early 1990's.

## WHAT DOES A FORESTER DO?

Foresters, because of their broad training in the basic sciences, are involved in many different types of jobs—in the woods, in sawmills, in offices, in laboratories, in classrooms, and in many other diverse activities. The attractiveness of a forestry career lies in the diversity of activity. The forester is always involved with new and exciting challenges relating to management of the forest. Our forests are the one natural resource with many competing uses. This introduces considerable complexity and diversity into forestry as an occupation.

Perhaps the best way to understand the many opportunities available in forestry as a career is to look at typical examples of what foresters do in the management of our valuable forest resource.

Tom is a district ranger on a national forest in Illinois. He manages a large district covering more than 70 square miles of forest and open land. His role is to administer this resource to provide all of the multiple benefits only the forest can provide—wildlife habitat, recreational opportunities, forage production, sustained timber yields, and watershed protection. Tom must draw upon a variety of skills to manage this important resource. He must know technically how to manage the vegetation, but he is also involved daily in planning and budgeting, personnel management, and especially in public relations. Tom has to be a good communicator. He supervises 5 foresters, 4 technicians, and almost 30 other employees and has been with the Forest Service for 11 years. Tom's salary is nearly $40,000 annually.

Susan is an urban forester. With a degree in forestry and supplemental coursework in urban forestry, tree care, communications, planning, and city government, she is one of an increasing number of foresters working in the urban environment. On a typical day, Susan will be preparing a street tree inventory; assessing insect and disease problems, and meeting with the city council to promote an urban tree planting project. Susan must also have strong communication skills to work with the varied personalities she encounters daily. Susan has been employed for three years and makes $23,800 annually.

Jack is a lawyer specializing in natural resources for a southern state. Jack completed a B.S. degree in forestry and then law school to get his law degree. His position with the State Department of Natural Resources involves him in the legal aspects of protecting and managing the forest resource. On a typical day Jack will be reviewing legal briefs on upcoming cases in his office during the morning and will be in court in the afternoon, prosecuting a developer for damages to public land. Jack has been in the position for 15 years and earns $53,000 annually.

Scott is a forestry technician for a state forestry department. He completed a two-year technicians' program and now supervises a field forestry crew after five years on the job. Recently he has been doing timber stand improvement work on a 400-acre forest in the southern part of the state. He works with a crew of five removing low-quality trees. Scott eats many lunches in the field. Following this job he will be supervising a tree-planting crew, developing work schedules, and planting. Scott earns $14,900 annually.

Eileen is a consulting forester in North Carolina. She provides a broad range of services to landowners including farmers, professional people, and forest product companies. Eileen has worked very hard for eight years to build her business and now has one forester and two technicians employed with her company. She stresses that her forestry education was good but needed more coursework in computers, business, and communications. Eileen has recently completed two graduate-level courses in computer programming. On a daily basis, Eileen prepares woodland management plans, administers timber sales, evaluates disease and insect problems, and inventories forest tracts. About 60 per cent of her time is spent outdoors. Eileen is now earning about $37,000 annually but admits it was very difficult to get started.

Tim is a production manager for a large sawmill in the Lake States. He completed a four-year college degree in forestry with a specialization in wood products. Tim's job is to schedule sawing to optimize wood production and meet contractual demands. He is constantly working with timber buyers, who purchase timber to supply the mill with raw material, and with salespeople and lumber brokers who sell the lumber produced in the mill, and lumber brokers on the demand side. Tim also troubleshoots problems with the sawmill equipment including the computerized headsaw, trim saws, and debarkers. He works 50 to 60 hours per week including some evenings and night shifts. Tim earns $33,000 annually after 10 years on the job.

Bill has recently begun working for a tree nursery in California. He earned a B.S. in forestry with specialization in woody plant propagation and soils. Bill will be responsible for procuring tree seed; preparation, seeding, and management of nursery beds; and lifting seedlings. He earns $18,900 annually.

Mark is a forest economist. He recently completed nearly 10 years of college, earning a Ph.D. in forest economics and is employed by a large university. Mark is involved with teaching undergraduate and graduate students about 40 per cent of his time. The rest of his work time is involved in research on the economics of timber production by small private landowners. Mark works extensively with computers and spends nearly 60 hours per week teaching or in his office. He earns $32,000 for a nine-month appointment his first year on the job.

Mary works with the Soil Conservation Service. Her degree is in forestry with a specialization in soils. Mary works on mapping soils in the field and preparing soil maps for several counties which have not been mapped. She also works to a limited extent with farmers and landowners in preparing farm conservation plans. Mary has solid technical skills and is a good communicator. She earns $19,000 annually.

Joe is a district manager for a southeastern pulp and paper company. He is directly responsible for all forest management activities on 25,000 acres of company-owned land. Seven years out of college, he has been promoted to this position after a variety of jobs involving timber sales, timber stand improvement, regeneration, and forest inventory. He has surveyed forest boundaries, estimated timber volumes, marked timber for harvest, supervised tree planting, fought forest fires, and a host of other experiences. He has worked very hard and now supervises all of these activities including budgetary and contractual agreements for his district. Joe earns $34,000 annually.

George is a computer specialist for a large forestry consulting firm. George has a bachelor's degree in forestry and a master's specializing in computers. He manages a large computerized inventory and resource database on lands managed by his firm and prepares reports for foresters and landowners. He began the job two years ago following graduation and earns $26,000 annually.

Denise is employed by the National Aeronautics and Space Administration. With a degree in forestry and specialized training in mapping, she is responsible for analyses of satellite photographs. She has recently developed a computer program to forecast vegetative changes in North America due to depletion of the ozone layer. Denise earns $27,000 annually.

These are just a few examples of the variety of careers available with a forestry degree. Perhaps the most exciting aspect of a career in forestry is the opportunity to work with a renewable, multiple-benefit resource which is constantly changing. It is always exciting, challenging, and rewarding. The Society of American Foresters lists over 700 job categories and more than 14,000 separate employers among its membership. Future opportunities are exceptional.

# Appendices

## *Appendix I*

## *COLLEGES AND UNIVERSITIES OFFERING INSTRUCTION IN FORESTRY*

The Society of American Foresters (SAF) is the official accrediting agency for professional forestry education in the United States recognized by both the Council on Postsecondary Accreditation and the U.S. Department of Education. **The society accredits only the first professional forestry degree offered at an institution.**

The society also designates affiliated institutions. These institutions have certified that they are building toward SAF accreditation.

The society has evaluated only those institutions which have applied for designation as an accredited or affiliated institution. Other institutions listed have not been evaluated by SAF.

The forestry degrees offered at each institution are shown by code: B (Bachelor), M (Master), and D (Doctor). The first year shown indicates the first accreditation or affiliation action by the society; the second year shown indicates the year of last re-examination by the society; the third year indicates the year current accreditation expires. SAF re-examines institutions approximately every 10 years (5 years after initial accrediting).

### *ACCREDITED INSTITUTIONS*

**ALABAMA**

**Auburn University,** School of Forestry, Auburn 36849. B, M, D. 1950. 1983. 1988.

**ARIZONA**

**Northern Arizona University,** School of Forestry, Flagstaff 86011. B, M, D. 1968. 1982. 1992.

**University of Arizona,** School of Renewable Natural Resources, Tucson 85721. B, M, D. 1972. 1984. 1988 (on probation).

**ARKANSAS**

**University of Arkansas at Monticello,** Department of Forest Resources, Monticello 71655. B. 1984. 1984. 1989.

**CALIFORNIA**

**Humbolt State University,** Department of Forestry, Arcata 95521. B, M. 1979. 1984. 1989.

**University of California,** Department of Forestry and Resource Management, Berkeley 94720. B, M, D. 1935. 1981. 1991.

## COLORADO

**Colorado State University,** College of Forestry and Natural Resources, Fort Collins 80523. B, M, D. 1939. 1980. 1990.

## CONNECTICUT

**Yale University,** School of Forestry and Environmental Studies, New Haven 06511. M, D. 1935. 1983. 1988.

## FLORIDA

**University of Florida,** School of Forest Resources and Conservation, Gainesville 32611. B, M, D. 1942. 1983. 1988.

## GEORGIA

**University of Georgia,** School of Forest Resources, Athens 30602. B, M, D. 1938. 1981. 1991.

## IDAHO

**University of Idaho,** College of Forestry, Wildlife and Range Sciences, Moscow 83843. B, M, D. 1935. 1984. 1989.

## ILLINOIS

**University of Illinois,** Department of Forestry, Urbana 61801. B, M. 1963. 1983. 1988.

**Southern Illinois University,** Department of Forestry, Carbondale 62901. B, M. 1975. 1980. 1990.

## INDIANA

**Purdue University,** Department of Forestry and Natural Resources, West Lafayette 47907. B, M, D. 1942. 1980. 1990.

## IOWA

**Iowa State University,** Department of Forestry, Ames 50011. B, M, D. 1935. 1981. 1991.

## KENTUCKY

**University of Kentucky,** Department of Forestry, Lexington 40546. B, M. 1974. 1979. 1989.

## LOUISIANA

**Louisiana State University,** School of Forestry, Wildlife and Fisheries, Baton Rouge 70803. B, M, D. 1937. 1984. 1989.

**Louisiana Tech University,** School of Forestry, Ruston 71272. B. 1984. 1984. 1989 (on probation).

## MAINE

**University of Maine,** College of Forest Resources, Orono 04469. B, M, D. 1937. 1982. 1992.

## MASSACHUSETTS

**University of Massachusetts,** Department of Forestry and Wildlife Management, Amherst 01003. B, M, D. 1950. 1985. 1988.

## MICHIGAN

**Michigan State University,** Department of Forestry, East Lansing 48824. B, M, D. 1935. 1984. 1989.

**Michigan Technological University,** School of Forestry and Wood Products, Houghton 49931. B, M. 1968. 1984. 1989.

**University of Michigan,** School of Natural Resources, Ann Arbor 48109. B, M, D. 1935. 1985. 1990.

## MINNESOTA

**University of Minnesota,** College of Forestry, St. Paul 55108. B, M, D. 1935. 1985. 1990.

## MISSISSIPPI

**Mississippi State University,** School of Forest Resources, Mississippi State 39762. B, M, D. 1966. 1987. 1992.

## MISSOURI

**University of Missouri,** School of Forestry, Fisheries and Wildlife, Columbia 65211. B, M, D. 1950. 1986. 1988.

## MONTANA

**University of Montana,** School of Forestry, Missoula 59812. B, M, D. 1935. 1982. 1989 (on probation).

## NEW HAMPSHIRE

**University of New Hampshire,** Department of Forest Resources, Durham 03824. B, M. 1959. 1983. 1988 (on probation).

## NEW YORK

**SUNY College of Environmental Science and Forestry,** Faculty of Forestry, Syracuse 13210. B, M, D. 1935. 1982. 1992.

## NORTH CAROLINA

**Duke University,** School of Forestry and Environmental Studies, Durham 27706. M, D. 1939. 1987. 1992.

North Carolina State University, School of Forest Resources, Raleigh 27695-8001. B, M, D. 1937. 1984. 1989.

## OHIO

Ohio State University, School of Natural Resources, Columbus 43210. B, M, D. 1986. 1986. 1988.

## OKLAHOMA

Oklahoma State University, Department of Forestry, Stillwater 74078. B, M. 1971. 1986. 1991.

## OREGON

Oregon State University, College of Forestry, Corvallis 97331. B, M, D. 1935. 1989. 1990.

## PENNSYLVANIA

Pennsylvania State University, School of Forest Resources, University Park 16802. B, M, D. 1935. 1982. 1992.

## SOUTH CAROLINA

Clemson University, College of Forest and Recreation Resources, Clemson 29631. B, M, D. 1962. 1982. 1992.

## TENNESSEE

University of Tennessee, Department of Forestry Wildlife and Fisheries, Knoxville 37901. B, M. 1969. 1985. 1990.

## TEXAS

Stephen F. Austin State University, School of Forestry, Nacogdoches 75962. B, M, D. 1965. 1980. 1990.

Texas A & M University, Department of Forest Science, College Station 77843. B, M, D. 1975. 1981. 1991.

## UTAH

Utah State University, College of Natural Resources, Logan 84322. B, M, D. 1937. 1978. 1988.

## VERMONT

University of Vermont, School of Natural Resources, Burlington 05405. B, M. 1971. 1981. 1991.

## VIRGINIA

Virginia Polytechnic Institute and State University, School of Forestry and Wildlife Resources, Blacksburg 24061. B, M, D. 1965. 1985. 1990.

## WASHINGTON

**Washington State University,** Department of Forestry and Range Management, Pullman 99164. B, M. 1965. 1982. 1988.

**University of Washington,** College of Forest Resources, Seattle 98195. B, M, D. 1935. 1985. 1990.

## WEST VIRGINIA

**West Virginia University,** Division of Forestry, P.O. Box 6125, Morgantown 26506. B, M, D. 1947. 1979. 1989.

## WISCONSIN

**University of Wisconsin, Madison,** Department of Forestry, Madison 53706. B, M, D. 1971. 1986. 1988.

**University of Wisconsin, Stevens Point,** College of Natural Resources, Stevens Point 54481. B. 1976. 1981. 1991.

### *PRE-PROFESSIONAL FORESTRY INSTITUTIONS*

Many two-year and four-year institutions in the United States offer pre-professional forestry study programs which may qualify students for transfer to a professional forestry school at the sophomore or junior level. Often these do not include forestry courses but lay a foundation for professional forestry education. Interested persons should contact the forestry school to which they wish to transfer for advice prior to enrolling for pre-professional forestry studies.

### *SAF-RECOGNIZED FOREST TECHNICIAN SCHOOLS IN THE UNITED STATES AND CANADA*

The institutions on the following list have been in contact with the Society of American Foresters and have employed the SAF "Minimum Guidelines for the Training of Forest Technicians" as a self-study. Other institutions beyond those listed may offer similar programs. This list does not constitute accreditation or approval by SAF.

Forest technician graduates of these institutions are eligible for SAF membership category of technician member. Full-time students in forest technology at these institutions are eligible for the student member category.

## CALIFORNIA

**Mount San Antonio College,** Agricultural Sciences Department, 1100 North Grand Avenue, Walnut 91789

**College of the Redwoods,** Forest Technology Program, Eureka 95501

Kings River College, Forest and Park Technology Curriculum, 995 North Reed Avenue, Reedley 93654

Santa Rosa Junior College, Forestry Department, 1501 Mendocino Avenue, Santa Rosa 95401

Sierra College, Forest Technology Department, 5000 Rocklin Road, Rocklin 95677

## FLORIDA

Lake City Community College, Forest Technology Program, Route 7, Box 378, Lake City 32055

## GEORGIA

Abraham Baldwin Agricultural College, Forestry/Wildlife Program, ABAC Station, Tifton 31793

## MAINE

Unity College, Forest Technology Program, Unity 04988

University of Maine, College of Forest Resources, Forest Management Technology, Orono 04469

## MARYLAND

Allegany Community College, Forestry Program, Willow Brook Road, Cumberland 21502

## MICHIGAN

Michigan Technological University, Forest Technology Program, School of Technology, Houghton 49931

## MINNESOTA

Brainerd Area Vo-Tech Institute, Natural Resources Technology Program, 300 Quince Street, Brainerd 56401

Itasca Community College, Forestry Technician Program, 1851 Highway 169 East, Grand Rapids 55744

Vermilion Community College, Natural Resources Program, 1900 East Camp Street, Ely 55731

## MONTANA

Flathead Valley Community College, Department of Forest Technology, One First Street East, Kalispell 59901

## NEW HAMPSHIRE

**University of New Hampshire,** Thompson School, Forest Technician Program, Putnam Hall, Durham 03824

## NEW YORK

**SUNY College of Agriculture and Technology,** School of Agriculture and Natural Resources, Morrisville 13408

**SUNY College of Environmental Science and Forestry,** School of Forestry, Forest Technician Program, Wanakena 13695

**Paul Smith's College of Arts and Sciences,** Forestry Division, Paul Smiths 12970

## NORTH CAROLINA

**Haywood Technical College,** Agricultural and Biological Sciences Department, Freedlander Drive, Clyde 28721

## OHIO

**Hocking Technical College,** Natural Resource Department, Nelsonville 45764

## OKLAHOMA

**Eastern Oklahoma State College,** Forestry Department, Wilburton 74578

## OREGON

**Central Oregon Community College,** Forest Technology Program, N.W. College Way, Bend 97701

**Southwestern Oregon Community College,** Forest Technology Program, Coos Bay 97420

## PENNSYLVANIA

**Pennsylvania State University,** Forest Technician Unit, Mont Alto Campus, Mont Alto 17237

**Williamsport Area Community College,** Natural Resources Management, 1005 West Third Street, Williamsport 17701

## SOUTH CAROLINA

**Horry-Georgetown Technical College,** Forestry Department, Highway 501 East, P.O. Box 1966, Conway 29526

## VIRGINIA

**Dabney S. Lancaster Community College,** Forest Technology Program, Route 60 West, Clifton Forge 24422

## WASHINGTON

**Green River Community College,** Forest Technician Program, 12401 S.E. 320th Street, Auburn 98002

**Spokane Community College,** Natural Resources Department, East 3403 Mission Avenue, Spokane 99202

## WEST VIRGINIA

**Glenville State College,** Department of Forest Technology, Glenville 26351

## Appendix II

### NATIONAL FOREST LAND OWNERSHIP,
### U.S. FOREST SERVICE, 1986

| State | Number of Units | Gross Area Within Unit Boundaries | National Forest System Lands | Other Lands Within Unit Boundaries |
|---|---|---|---|---|
| Alabama | 7 | 1,274,367 | 647,125 | 627,242 |
| Alaska | 2 | 24,018,415 | 22,811,098 | 1,207,317 |
| Arizona | 8 | 11,933,501 | 11,274,109 | 659,392 |
| Arkansas | 5 | 3,502,124 | 2,483,131 | 1,018,993 |
| California | 49 | 24,324,068 | 20,503,111 | 3,820,957 |
| Colorado | 15 | 16,029,552 | 14,445,548 | 1,584,004 |
| Connecticut | 1 | 24 | 24 | — |
| Florida | 4 | 1,224,477 | 1,099,721 | 124,756 |
| Georgia | 6 | 1,855,415 | 866,893 | 988,522 |
| Hawaii | 1 | 1 | 1 | — |
| Idaho | 17 | 21,706,065 | 20,444,224 | 1,261,841 |
| Illinois | 3 | 839,760 | 263,363 | 576,397 |
| Indiana | 3 | 644,198 | 187,733 | 456,465 |
| Kansas | 1 | 116,760 | 108,177 | 8,583 |
| Kentucky | 4 | 2,101,699 | 680,775 | 1,420,924 |
| Louisiana | 1 | 1,022,703 | 600,102 | 422,601 |
| Maine | 4 | 93,553 | 51,237 | 42,316 |
| Michigan | 11 | 4,872,612 | 2,765,673 | 2,106,939 |
| Minnesota | 4 | 5,467,017 | 2,805,482 | 2,661,535 |
| Mississippi | 12 | 2,309,952 | 1,147,234 | 1,162,718 |
| Missouri | 4 | 3,081,618 | 1,471,162 | 1,610,456 |
| Montana | 14 | 19,093,427 | 16,798,058 | 2,295,369 |
| Nebraska | 4 | 441,524 | 351,846 | 89,678 |
| Nevada | 4 | 5,425,964 | 5,161,692 | 264,272 |
| New Hampshire | 2 | 819,387 | 705,798 | 113,589 |
| New Mexico | 16 | 10,383,872 | 9,325,917 | 1,057,955 |
| New York | 1 | 13,232 | 13,232 | — |
| N. Carolina | 9 | 3,165,379 | 1,218,580 | 1,946,799 |
| N. Dakota | 6 | 1,105,768 | 1,105,764 | 4 |
| Ohio | 3 | 832,851 | 178,554 | 654,297 |
| Oklahoma | 3 | 461,265 | 295,505 | 165,760 |
| Oregon | 19 | 17,480,540 | 15,614,102 | 1,866,438 |
| Pennsylvania | 3 | 742,936 | 510,691 | 232,245 |
| Puerto Rico | 1 | 55,665 | 27,846 | 27,819 |
| S. Carolina | 4 | 1,381,542 | 611,196 | 770,346 |
| S. Dakota | 5 | 2,347,467 | 1,997,013 | 350,454 |
| Tennessee | 2 | 1,212,232 | 625,760 | 586,472 |
| Texas | 9 | 1,994,473 | 751,784 | 1,242,689 |
| Utah | 10 | 9,129,523 | 8,043,191 | 1,086,332 |

(Continued)

## *Appendix II (Continued)*

| State | Number of Units | Gross Area Within Unit Boundaries | National Forest System Lands | Other Lands Within Unit Boundaries |
|---|---|---|---|---|
| Vermont | 2 | 629,518 | 325,176 | 304,342 |
| Virginia | 3 | 3,225,721 | 1,637,457 | 1,588,264 |
| Virgin Islands | 1 | 147 | 147 | — |
| Washington | 10 | 10,045,408 | 9,137,251 | 908,157 |
| W. Virginia | 7 | 1,861,189 | 978,347 | 882,842 |
| Wisconsin | 3 | 2,022,809 | 1,506,587 | 516,222 |
| Wyoming | 11 | 9,717,091 | 9,254,762 | 462,329 |
| Totals | 314 | 230,006,811 | 190,832,179 | 39,174,632 |

(Source: U.S. Forest Service Land Areas of the National Forest System
as of September 30, 1986. F.S. 383)

## *Appendix III*

## *STATE FORESTRY AGENCIES IN THE UNITED STATES, 1987*

| Agency | Chief Administrative Officer | Address |
|---|---|---|
| **Alabama** | | |
| Alabama State Forestry Commission | State Forester | 513 Madison Avenue Montgomery, Alabama 36130 |
| **Alaska** | | |
| Division of Natural Resources | State Forester | Division of Forestry, Pouch 7-005 Anchorage, Alaska 99501 |
| **Arizona** | | |
| State Land Department, Forestry Division | State Forester | State Land Department 1624 West Adams Phoenix, Arizona 85007 |
| **Arkansas** | | |
| Arkansas Forestry Commission | State Forester | 3821 West Roosevelt Road Little Rock, Arkansas 72204 |
| **California** | | |
| Department of Forestry, The Resources Agency | Director | Department of Forestry 1416 Ninth Street Sacramento, California 95814 |
| **Colorado** | | |
| State Forest Service | State Forester | Colorado State Forest Service Colorado State University Fort Collins, Colorado 80523 |
| **Connecticut** | | |
| Department of Environmental Protection | State Forester | 165 Capitol Avenue Hartford, Connecticut 06115 |
| **Delaware** | | |
| Department of Agriculture | State Forester | Department of Agriculture, Forestry Section 2320 South Dupont Highway Dover, Delaware 19901 |

**(Continued)**

## *STATE FORESTRY AGENCIES (Continued)*

| Agency | Chief Administrative Officer | Address |
|---|---|---|
| **Florida** | | |
| Division of Forestry, Florida Department of Agriculture and Consumer Services | Director | 3125 Conner Boulevard Tallahassee, Florida 32301 |
| **Georgia** | | |
| Georgia Forestry Commission | Director | P.O. Box 819 Macon, Georgia 31202 |
| **Guam** | | |
| Division of Forestry, Department of Agriculture | Chief | Agana, Guam 96910 |
| **Hawaii** | | |
| Division of Forestry, Department of Land and Natural Resources | State Forester | 1151 Punchbowl Street Honolulu, Hawaii 96813 |
| **Idaho** | | |
| Forestry and Fire, Idaho Department of Lands | Assistant Commissioner | State Capitol Building Boise, Idaho 83720 |
| **Illinois** | | |
| Division of Forest Resources and Natural Heritage, Department of Conservation | Chief | 605 Stratton Office Building Springfield, Illinois 62706 |
| **Indiana** | | |
| Division of Forestry, Department of Natural Resources | State Forester | 608 State Office Building Indianapolis, Indiana 46204 |
| **Iowa** | | |
| State Conservation Commission | State Forester | Wallace State Office Building Des Moines, Iowa 50319 |
| **Kansas** | | |
| Kansas State University | State and Extension Forestry | 2610 Claflin Road Manhattan, Kansas 66502 |

(Continued)

## STATE FORESTRY AGENCIES *(Continued)*

| Agency | Chief Administrative Officer | Address |
|---|---|---|
| **Kentucky** | | |
| Kentucky Division of Forestry, Department for Natural Resources and Environmental Protection | Director | 5th Floor, Capital Plaza Tower Frankfort, Kentucky 40601 |
| **Louisiana** | | |
| Office of Forestry, Department of Natural Resources | State Forester | P.O. Box 1628 Baton Rouge, Louisiana 70821 |
| **Maine** | | |
| Bureau of Forestry | Director | State Office Building Augusta, Maine 04333 |
| **Maryland** | | |
| Forest and Park Services, Department of Natural Resources | State Forester | Tawes State Office Building 580 Taylor Avenue Annapolis, Maryland 21401 |
| **Massachusetts** | | |
| Division of Forests and Parks, Department of Environmental Management | Director | 100 Cambridge Street Boston, Massachusetts 02202 |
| **Michigan** | | |
| Forest Management Division, Department of Natural Resources | Chief | Stevens T. Mason Building Box 30028 Lansing, Michigan 48909 |
| **Minnesota** | | |
| Division of Forestry, Department of Natural Resources | Director | 300 Centennial Office Building P.O. Box 44 St. Paul, Minnesota 55155 |
| **Mississippi** | | |
| Mississippi Forestry Commission | State Forester | Suite 300, 301 Building Jackson, Mississippi 39201 |
| **Missouri** | | |
| Forestry Division, Missouri Department of Conservation | State Forester | 2901 North Ten Mile Drive Jefferson City, Missouri 65101 |

**(Continued)**

## STATE FORESTRY AGENCIES (Continued)

| Agency | Chief Administrative Officer | Address |
|---|---|---|
| **Montana** | | |
| Division of Forestry, Department of State Lands | State Forester | 2705 Spurgin Road Missoula, Montana 59801 |
| **Nebraska** | | |
| College of Agriculture | State Forester | East Campus University of Nebraska Lincoln, Nebraska 68583 |
| **Nevada** | | |
| Division of Forestry, Department of Conservation and Natural Resources | State Forester | 201 South Fall Carson City, Nevada 89710 |
| **New Hampshire** | | |
| Division of Forests and Lands, Department of Resources and Economic Development | Director | P.O. Box 856 856 Christian Mutual Building Concord, New Hampshire 03301 |
| **New Jersey** | | |
| Division of Parks and Forestry, Department of Environmental Protection | State Forester | P.O. Box 1420 Trenton, New Jersey 08625 |
| **New Mexico** | | |
| Forestry Division, Natural Resources Department | Director | Land Office Building P.O. Box 2167 Santa Fe, New Mexico 87503 |
| **New York** | | |
| Division of Lands and Forests, Department of Environmental Conservation | Director | 59 Wolf Road Albany, New York 12233 |
| **North Carolina** | | |
| Office of Forest Resources, Department of Natural and Community Development | Director | P.O. Box 27687 Raleigh, North Carolina 27611 |

(Continued)

## STATE FORESTRY AGENCIES *(Continued)*

| Agency | Chief Administrative Officer | Address |
|---|---|---|
| **North Dakota** | | |
| State Forest Service, North Dakota State University | State Forester | First and Simrall Avenue Bottineau, North Dakota 58318 |
| **Ohio** | | |
| Division of Forestry and Preserves | Chief | Fountain Square Columbus, Ohio 43224 |
| **Oklahoma** | | |
| Forestry Division, Department of Agriculture | Director | 2800 North Lincoln Boulevard Oklahoma City, Oklahoma 73105 |
| **Oregon** | | |
| Department of Forestry | State Forester | 2600 State Street Salem, Oregon 97310 |
| **Pennsylvania** | | |
| Bureau of Forestry, Department of Environmental Resources | Director | 109 Evangelical Press Building Harrisburg, Pennsylvania 17120 |
| **Puerto Rico** | | |
| Department of Natural Resources | Director of the Forest Service | P.O. Box 5887 Puerto de Tierra San Juan, Puerto Rico 00906 |
| **Rhode Island** | | |
| Division of Forest Environment, Department of Environmental Management | Chief | P.O. Box 851, RFD 2 North Scituate, Rhode Island 02857 |
| **South Carolina** | | |
| South Carolina State Commission of Forestry | State Forester | P.O. Box 21707 Columbia, South Carolina 29221 |
| **South Dakota** | | |
| Forestry Division, Department of Game, Fish, and Parks | Director | Sigurd Anderson Building Pierre, South Dakota 57501 |

(Continued)

## STATE FORESTRY AGENCIES (Continued)

| Agency | Chief Administrative Officer | Address |
|---|---|---|
| **Tennessee** Division of Forestry, Tennessee Department of Conservation | State Forester | 701 Broadway Nashville, Tennessee 37219-5237 |
| **Texas** Texas Forest Service Texas A & M University System | Director | College Station, Texas 77843 |
| **Utah** Division of State Lands, Forestry, and Fire Control, Department of Natural Resources | Director | 411 Empire Building 231 East 4th South Salt Lake City, Utah 84111 |
| **Vermont** Department of Forests and Parks, Agency of Environmental Conservation | Director of Forests | State Office Building Montpelier, Vermont 05602 |
| **Virginia** Division of Forestry, Department of Conservation and Economic Development | State Forester | P.O. Box 3758 Charlottesville, Virginia 22903 |
| **Washington** Department of Natural Resources | Supervisor | Public Lands Building Olympia, Washington 98504 |
| **West Virginia** Department of Natural Resources | State Forester | 1800 Washington Street East, Charleston, West Virginia 25305 |
| **Wisconsin** Bureau of Forestry, Department of Natural Resources | Director | P.O. Box 7921 Madison, Wisconsin 53707 |
| **Wyoming** State Forestry Division | State Forester | 1100 West 22nd Street Cheyenne, Wyoming 82002 |

## Appendix IV

## PRINCIPAL HEADQUARTERS OF THE
## U.S. FOREST SERVICE, 1987

| Unit | Chief Administrative Officer | Address |
|---|---|---|
| Headquarters, U.S. Forest Service | Chief Forester | South Building 12th and Independence Avenue, S.W. Washington, D.C. 20250 |
| Northern Region | Regional Forester | Federal Building Missoula, Montana 59807 |
| Rocky Mountain Region | Regional Forester | 11177 West 8th Avenue Box 25127 Lakewood, Colorado 80225 |
| Southwestern Region | Regional Forester | 517 Gold Avenue, S.W. Albuquerque, New Mexico 87102 |
| Intermountain Region | Regional Forester | 324 25th Street Ogden, Utah 84401 |
| Pacific Southwest Region | Regional Forester | 630 Sansome Street San Francisco, California 94111 |
| Pacific Northwest Region | Regional Forester | 319 S.W. Pine Street P.O. Box 3623 Portland, Oregon 97208 |
| Southern Region | Regional Forester | 1720 Peachtree Road, N.W. Atlanta, Georgia 30367 |
| Eastern Region | Regional Forester | 310 West Wisconsin Avenue Milwaukee, Wisconsin 53203 |
| Alaska Region | Regional Forester | Federal Office Building P.O. Box 21628 Juneau, Alaska 99802 |
| Intermountain Forest and Range Experiment Station | Director | 324 25th Street Ogden, Utah 84401 |

(Continued)

## HEADQUARTERS OF U.S. FOREST SERVICE (Continued)

| Unit | Chief Administrative Officer | Address |
|---|---|---|
| North Central Forest Experiment Station | Director | 1992 Folwell Avenue St. Paul, Minnesota 55108 |
| Northeastern Forest Experiment Station | Director | 370 Reed Road Broomall, Pennsylvania 19008 |
| Pacific Northwest Forest and Range Experiment Station | Director | 809 N.E. Sixth Avenue P.O. Box 3141 Portland, Oregon 97208 |
| Pacific Southwest Forest and Range Experiment Station | Director | 1960 Addison Street P.O. Box 245 Berkeley, California 94701 |
| Rocky Mountain Forest and Range Experiment Station | Director | 240 West Prospect Street Fort Collins, Colorado 80526 |
| Southeastern Forest Experiment Station | Director | Post Office Building P.O. Box 2570 Asheville, North Carolina 28802 |
| Southern Forest Experiment Station | Director | U.S. Postal Service Building 701 Loyola Avenue New Orleans, Louisiana 70113 |
| Forest Products Laboratory | Director | P.O. Box 5130 North Walnut Street Madison, Wisconsin 53705 |
| Northeastern Area State and Private Forestry | Area Director | 370 Reed Road Broomall, Pennsylvania 19008 |
| Southeastern Area State and Private Forestry | Area Director | 1720 Peachtree Road, N.W. Atlanta, Georiga 30367 |

## Appendix V

## COOPERATIVE EXTENSION FOREST
## RESOURCE SPECIALISTS, OCTOBER 1987

| State | Address |
| --- | --- |
| Alabama | Head, Extension Natural Resources, Auburn University, Auburn 36830. |
| Alaska | Extension Forestry Specialist, University of Alaska, Fairbanks 99701. |
| Arizona | Range Management Specialist, University of Arizona, Tucson 85721. |
| Arkansas | Extension Forester, P.O. Box 391, Little Rock 72203. |
| California | Extension Forester, 163 Mulford Hall, University of California, Berkeley 94720. |
| Colorado | Extension Forester, Colorado State University, Fort Collins 80523. |
| Connecticut | Extension Forester, Extension Center, Brooklyn, Connecticut 06234. |
| Delaware | Director of Extension Service, University of Delaware, Newark 19711. |
| Florida | Extension Forester, University of Florida, Gainesville 32611. |
| Georgia | Head, Extension Forest Resources Department, University of Georgia, Athens 30602. |
| Hawaii | Department of Land and Natural Resources, Forestry and Wildlife, Honolulu 96813. |
| Idaho | Extension Forestry, College FWR Building, University of Idaho, Moscow 83843. |
| Illinois | Extension Forester, 110 Mumford Hall, University of Illinois, Urbana 61801. |
| Indiana | State Extension Forester, Department of Forestry and Natural Resources, Purdue University, West Lafayette 47907. |

(Continued)

## COOPERATIVE EXTENSION FOREST
## RESOURCE SPECIALISTS *(Continued)*

| State | Address |
| --- | --- |
| **Iowa** | Forestry Extension Coordinator, Iowa State University, Ames 50010. |
| **Kansas** | State and Extension Forester, 2610 Claflin Road, Manhattan 66502. |
| **Kentucky** | Extension Forester, Department of Forestry, University of Kentucky, Lexington 40506. |
| **Louisiana** | Associate Specialist, Forestry, 202 P Knapp Hall, Louisiana State University, Baton Rouge 70803. |
| **Maine** | Extension Forester, 105 Nutting Hall, Orono 04473. |
| **Maryland** | Extension Forester, University of Maryland, College Park 20742. |
| **Massachusetts** | Extension Forester, Department of Forestry and Wildlife Management, University of Massachusetts, Amherst 01003. |
| **Michigan** | Extension Forester, Department of Forestry, Michigan State University, East Lansing 48824. |
| **Minnesota** | Extension Forester, University of Minnesota, St. Paul 55101. |
| **Mississippi** | Leader, Extension Forestry, Cooperative Extension Service, P.O. Box 5426, Mississippi State University, Mississippi State 39762. |
| **Missouri** | Extension Forester and Wildlife Specialist, 1-34 Ag Building, University of Missouri, Columbia 65201. |
| **Nebraska** | Extension Forester, 201 Miller Hall, University of Nebraska, Lincoln 68583. |
| **Nevada** | Extension Range Specialists, Renewable Resource Center, University of Nevada, Reno 89512. |
| **New Hampshire** | Extension Forester, 110A Petee Hall, University of New Hampshire, Durham 03824. |

(Continued)

## COOPERATIVE EXTENSION FOREST
## RESOURCE SPECIALISTS (Continued)

| State | Address |
|-------|---------|
| New Jersey | Specialist in Forest Resources and Recreation Management, 105 Blake Hall, Rutgers University, New Brunswick 08835. |
| New Mexico | Cooperative Extension Service, New Mexico State University, Las Cruces 88003. |
| New York | Extension Forester, 114 Fernow Hall, Cornell University, Ithaca 14850. |
| North Carolina | Extension Forest Resources Specialist, North Carolina State University, P.O. Box 5488, Raleigh 27607. |
| North Dakota | Extension Forester, North Dakota State University, Fargo 58102. |
| Ohio | Extension Forester, The Ohio State University, 2001 Fyffe Court, Columbus 43210. |
| Oklahoma | Extension Forester, Oklahoma State University, Stillwater 74074. |
| Oregon | Coordinator, Forestry Extension, 227 Peavy Hall, Oregon State University, Corvallis 97331. |
| Pennsylvania | Forest Resource Specialist, 111 Ferguson Building, Pennsylvania State University, University Park 16802. |
| Rhode Island | Chairman, Forestry Department, University of Rhode Island, Kingston 02881. |
| South Carolina | Forestry Project Leader, Extension Forestry, 272 Forest and Recreation Resources Building, Clemson University, Clemson 29631. |
| South Dakota | Extension Forester, South Dakota State University, Brookings 57006. |
| Tennessee | Extension Specialist, Department of Forestry, Wildlife and Fisheries, University of Tennessee, P.O. Box 1071, Knoxville 37901. |

**(Continued)**

## COOPERATIVE EXTENSION FOREST
## RESOURCE SPECIALISTS (Continued)

| State | Address |
|-------|---------|
| Texas | Extension Forester, 302 Horticulture & Forest Science Building, Texas A & M University, College Station 77843-2135. |
| Utah | Extension Forester, Utah State University, Logan 84322. |
| Vermont | Extension Forest Management Specialist, School of Natural Resources, University of Vermont, Burlington 05405. |
| Virginia | Extension Forestry, 324 E Cheatham Hall, Virginia Polytechnic Institute and State University, Blacksburg 24061. |
| Washington | Extension Forest Resources Specialist, 131 Johnson Hall, Washington State University, Pullman 99164-6412. |
| West Virginia | Extension Specialist, Forestry, 329 G Percival Hall, West Virginia University, Morgantown 26506. |
| Wisconsin | Extension Forester, Department of Forestry, University of Wisconsin, 1630 Linden Drive, Madison 53706. |
| Wyoming | Plant Science Division, Agricultural Extension Service, University of Wyoming, Laramie 82071. |
| Virgin Islands | Director of Extension Service, P.O. Box L, St. Croix 00850. |
| Washington, D.C. | Extension Forester, Extension Service, U.S.D.A., Washington, D.C. 20250. |

## *Appendix VI*

# RANGE AND CHARACTERISTICS OF MAJOR TREE SPECIES OF THE UNITED STATES

### SPECIES COMMON TO EASTERN UNITED STATES

| Name of Tree | Where the Tree Grows | Descriptive Notes |
| --- | --- | --- |
| Northern white pine *(Pinus strobus)*. | Northeastern and Lake States, Appalachian Mountains. Extensively planted. | Leaves 5 in cluster, 3 to 5 inches long. Cone cylindrical, 4 to 8 inches long. Important timber tree. |
| Red pine, or Norway pine *(Pinus resinosa)*. | Northeastern and Lake States. Extensively planted. | Leaves 2 in cluster, 5 to 6 inches long. Cone 2 inches long, without prickles. Important timber tree. |
| Loblolly pine *(Pinus taeda)*. | Southeastern States, coastal plain Delaware to Texas. | Leaves 3 in cluster, 6 to 9 inches long. Cone 2 to 3 inches long, with stiff sharp prickles. Important timber tree. |
| Pitch pine *(Pinus rigida)*. | Northeastern and Middle Atlantic States. Uplands mostly. (A variety, pond pine *(Pinus rigida serotina)* in the coastal plain from Delaware to Florida.) | Leaves 3 in cluster, 3 to 7 inches long, stout, twisted. Cones short, broad, 2 to 3 inches long, with small prickles. |
| Virginia pine (scrub pine) *(Pinus virginiana)*. | Uplands, New Jersey and Pennsylvania southwest to Alabama. | Leaves 2 in bundle, twisted, 2 to 3 inches long. Cone 2 to 3 inches long; very prickly. |
| Sand pine *(Pinus clausa)*. | Florida and southern Alabama. | Much like Virginia pine. |
| Mountain pine *(Pinus pungens)*. | Scattered in mountains, Pennsylvania to northern Georgia. | Leaves twisted, blue-green, 2 in bundle. Cone 3 inches long with stout curved spines. |
| Shortleaf pine *(Pinus echinata)*. | Middle Atlantic and Southern States, New Jersey to Missouri, Louisiana, and Texas. Uplands. | Leaves 2 or 3 in clusters, 3 to 5 inches long. Cone small, about 2 inches long; fine prickle. Important timber tree. |
| Spruce pine *(Pinus glabra)*. | Coast region South Carolina to Louisiana, along streams. | Leaves 2 in cluster, soft, slender, 2 to 3 inches long. Cones 1 to 2 inches long, with tiny prickles. |
| Jack pine *(Pinus banksiana)*. | Northern States, from Maine to Minnesota. Common on sandy soil. | Leaves 2 in cluster, up to 1½ inches long. Cone 1 to 2 inches long, incurved, irregular in shape. |
| Longleaf pine *(Pinus palustris)*. | Coastal plain, North Carolina to Texas. | Leaves 3 in cluster, 8 to 18 inches long. Cone prickly, 6 to 10 inches long. Important tree for timber and naval stores. |
| Slash pine *(Pinus caribaea)*. | Coastal plain, South Carolina south and west to Louisiana. Planted extensively in Texas. | Leaves 2 or 3 in cluster, 8 to 14 inches long. Cone shiny, 3 to 5 inches long. Important for timber and naval stores. Extensively planted. |
| Tamarack (larch) *(Larix laricina)*. | Northeastern United States, northern Rocky Mountains. | Leaves 1 inch long, in clusters, falling in winter. Cone ¾ inch long. |
| Black spruce *(Picea marianna)*. | Northeastern and Lake States. Crosses continent in Canada. | Leaves blue-green, somewhat blunt-pointed. Cone on incurved stalk, persistent for years; cone scales with rough edges. Twigs finely hairy. Important for pulpwood. |

**(Continued)**

## Appendix VI (Continued)

### SPECIES COMMON TO EASTERN UNITED STATES

| Name of Tree | Where the Tree Grows | Descriptive Notes |
|---|---|---|
| Red spruce (*Picea rubra*). | Northeastern States, high Appalachian Mountains to North Carolina. | Leaves dark yellow-green. Cone falling soon after ripening. Important for pulpwood. |
| White spruce (*Picea glauca*). | Northeastern and Lake States, northern Rocky Mountains (including Black Hills). Extends across the continent in Canada. | Leaves 4-sided, ½ to ¾ inch long, pale blue-green, very sharp, twisting upward. Cone scales rounded. Important for pulpwood. |
| Eastern hemlock (*Tsuga canadensis*). | Northeastern and Lake States south to Ohio River, south in Appalachian Mountains. | Leaves ½ inch long, apparently in flat arrangement on stem, shiny green, lighter below. Cone ¾ inch long. Timber tree; bark for tanning leather. |
| Carolina hemlock (*Tsuga caroliniana*). | Blue Ridge Mountains, Virginia to Georgia. | Resembles above tree. Cone scales longer than broad. Planted for ornament. |
| Southern balsam fir (*Abies fraseri*). | High Appalachian Mountains, Virginia south to North Carolina. | Resembles balsam fir, except cone is covered with protruding bracts (scale-covered). |
| Balsam fir (*Abies balsamea*). | Northeastern States south to Virginia. Great Lakes States. Crosses continent in Canada. | Leaves not sharp-pointed, flexible, flattened, 1 inch long. Cone scales falling when ripe. Pulpwood tree. |
| Southern cypress (*Taxodium distichum*). | Atlantic Coastal Plain, Delaware to Texas, central Mississippi Basin. | Leaves ¾ inch long, feather arrangement, falling in autumn. Cone round, of hard scales. Timber tree. |
| Pond cypress (*Taxodium adscendens*). | Southeastern Virginia to western Florida and southern Alabama. | In shallow ponds or stagnant swamps. Resembles above, except needlelike leaves, few knees. |
| Northern white cedar (*Thuja occidentalis*). | Northeastern and Lake States, south in Appalachian Mountains. Canada. | Leaves scalelike, crowded, resinous, aromatic. Cone resembling an opening scaly bud. |
| Southern white cedar (*Chamaecyparis thyoides*). | Coast, Maine to Florida and Mississippi. Irregularly scattered. | Leaves scalelike, variable, opposite in pairs. Cone persistent, maturing in 1 season. |
| Dwarf juniper (*Juniperus communis*). | Northeastern quarter of United States, across the continent to California. | Leaves sharp, ½ inch long. Sweet aromatic berrylike fruit, ripening in 3 years. |
| Drooping juniper (*Juniperus flaccida*). | Southwestern Texas. | Leaves opposite, long-pointed, spreading at tips. Fruit reddish brown, maturing in 1 season. |
| Red-berry juniper (*Juniperus pinchotii*). | Central and western Texas, central and southern Arizona. | Berries red, ripening in 1 season. Leaves opposite or in threes. |
| Mountain cedar (*Juniperus mexicana*). | Central and western Texas, southwestern Oklahoma. | Fruit 1-seeded, blue or nearly black. Branchlets and leaves small, leaves rough. |
| Eastern red cedar (*Juniperus virginiana*). | Eastern half of United States. | Leaves scalelike, on young shoots awl-like. Berries bluish, ripening in 1 season. Aromatic durable wood. |
| Southern red cedar (*Juniperus lucayana*). | Gulf Coast region, Georgia to Texas. | Leaves tiny, usually opposite. Berries $^1/_{10}$ inch diameter, blue, ripening in 1 season. Drooping branchlets. |

(Continued)

## Appendix VI (Continued)

### SPECIES COMMON TO EASTERN UNITED STATES

| Name of Tree | Where the Tree Grows | Descriptive Notes |
| --- | --- | --- |
| Stinking cedar (*Tumion taxifolium*). | Southwestern Georgia, western Florida (rare and local). | Leaves 1½ inches long, dull green, shiny, pointed. Purple berry. All parts of tree ill-smelling. |
| Florida yew (*Taxus floridana*). | Western Florida, very local. | Leaves ½ inch long, falling after 5 to 12 years. Fruit nearly surrounded by thick cup. |
| Thatch palm (*Thrinax floridana*). | Southern Florida. | Leaves fan-shaped, 2 to 3 feet in diameter, yellow-green, shiny above. Fruit (berry) white. |
| Silvertop palmetto (*Thrinax microcarpa*). | Southern Florida (tropical). | Leaves 1 to 2 feet across, fan-shaped, pale green, shiny above. Fruit (berry) white. |
| Thatch palm (*Thrinax keyensis*). | do. | Leaves 3 to 4 feet in diameter, fan-shaped. |
| Thatch palm (*Thrinax wendlandina*). | do. | Leaves 2 to 3 feet across, fan-shaped, pale green. |
| Thatch palm (*Coccothrinax jucunda*). | do. | Fruit berrylike, black. Leaves fan-shaped nearly round, 1½ to 2 feet in diameter. |
| Cabbage palmetto (*Sabal palmetto*). | Coast from North Carolina to western Florida. | Trees up to 60 feet high and 2 feet in diameter. Leaves 5 to 6 feet long, 7 to 8 feet broad, shiny, fan-shaped. Leaf-buds often eaten as food. |
| Texas palmetto (*Sabal texana*). | Southern Texas. | Generally like the above. |
| Saw cabbage palm (*Acoelorraphe wrightii*). | Southwestern Florida (tropical). | Leaves thin, light green, in curved teeth. Tree often with many stems forming thickets. |
| Saw cabbage palm (*Acoelorraphe arborescens*). | Southwestern Florida. | Leaves 2 feet in diameter, yellow-green, with slight teeth. Trunks often lying on ground. |
| Royal palm (*Roystonea regia*). | Southern Florida (tropical). | Leaves featherlike along the rhacis (or central leaf stem), 10 feet long, no teeth or spines. Fruit blue. Extensively cultivated for its beauty. |
| Hog cabbage palm (*Pseudophoenix vinifera*). | do. | Resembles above, leaves 5 to 6 feet long. Fruit clusters bright scarlet. |
| Spanish bayonet (*Yucca aloifolia*). | Coast from North Carolina to Florida and Louisiana (tropical). | Leaves 1 to 2 feet long, 1 to 2 inches wide, sharply toothed along edges. (This and the next 2 trees belong to the lily family. They differ mostly in their flowers.) |
| Spanish dagger (*Yucca gloriosa*). | South Atlantic Coast. | Leaves thin, flat. Fruit mostly upright or spreading. |
| Spanish bayonet (*Yucca treculeana*). | Coast and Rio Grande River in Texas. | Leaves rough below, concave, finely toothed, bluish-green, 3 feet long. Fruit on stem, fleshy. |
| Spanish bayonet (*Yucca faxoniana*). | Southwestern Texas, desert region. | Leaves 3 to 4 feet long, flat, smooth. Flowers forming narrow tube at base. Fruit shiny, orange-colored. |

(Continued)

## *Appendix VI (Continued)*

### SPECIES COMMON TO EASTERN UNITED STATES

| Name of Tree | Where the Tree Grows | Descriptive Notes |
|---|---|---|
| Butternut (white walnut) (*Juglans cinerea*). | Northeastern States and southern Appalachian Mountains. | Leaves 15 to 30 inches long, of 11 to 17 leaflets. Nut longer than thick. Velvety cushion above leaf scar. |
| Black walnut (*Juglans nigra*). | New York west to Iowa and southward. | Leaves 12 to 24 inches long, of 15 to 23 leaflets. Nut round. Bark rich brown. High-grade cabinet wood. |
| Pecan (*Hicoria pecan*). | Mississippi Valley, Iowa to Texas. | Leaves of 9 to 17 leaflets; bud scales few. Nut with thin brittle shell and sweet kernel. Many varieties grown on commercial scale throughout the South. |
| Bitter pecan (*Hicoria texana*). | Along rivers from Arkansas to Texas. | Leaves of 7 to 13 leaflets. Nut flattened with bitter kernel. |
| Bitternut hickory (*Hicoria cordiformis*). | Eastern United States to Great Plains. | Leaves of 7 to 9 long-pointed leaflets. Nut broad, thin-husked, with bitter kernel. |
| Nutmeg hickory (*Hicoria myristicaeformis*). | Coastal plain region, South Carolina west to Texas. | Leaves of 7 to 9 leaflets, silvery and shiny below. Nut 4-ridged, 1½ inches long. |
| Water hickory (*Hicoria aquatica*). | South Atlantic and Gulf coastal region. Mississippi Valley. | Nut flattened, 4-ridged, thin husk, bitter kernel. Leaves of 7 to 13 leaflets. |
| Shagbark hickory (scaly bark hickory) (*Hicoria ovata*). | Eastern United States (exclusive of southern coastal region). | Bark loosening in narrow strips. Leaves of 5 large leaflets. Nut thick-shelled, with sweet kernel. |
| Southern shagbark hickory (*Hicoria carolinea septemtrionalis*). | Southern Appalachian region largely on limestone soils. | Leaves small, mostly of 5 slender leaflets. Nut 4-angled, thin-shelled, with sweet kernel. |
| Bigleaf shagbark hickory (shellbark hickory) (*Hicoria laciniosa*). | Eastern United States, exclusive of New England. | Leaves large, 15 to 20 inches long, mostly of 7 leaflets. Nut large, with sweet kernel. |
| Mockernut hickory (white or big-bud hickory) (*Hicoria alba*). | Southeastern quarter of United States and a little northward. | Winter buds large. Leaves broad, of 7 to 9 leaflets, strong-scented, hairy. Nut thick-shelled, small sweet kernel. |
| (Swamp) pignut hickory (*Hicoria leiodermis*). | Arkansas, Mississippi, Louisiana. | Leaves of 7 long-pointed leaflets. Nut smooth, shell thick, small sweet kernel. |
| Hickory (*Hicoria mollissima*). | Mississippi, Louisiana, and Texas. | Leaves like above but velvety or hairy. |
| (Sand) pignut hickory (*Hicoria pallida*). | Atlantic and Gulf coastal region. | Leaves of 7 narrow, finely toothed, fragrant, long-pointed leaflets. Nut white, with sweet kernel. |
| Pignut hickory (*Hicoria glabra*). | Vermont to Michigan and south in Appalachian Mountains and foothills. | Nut smooth, thick-shelled, sweet kernel, rounded or pear-shaped. Leaves of 5 pointed leaflets. |
| (Hammock) hickory (*Hicoria ashei*). | Florida and adjacent coastal regions. | Branchlets bright red-brown, smooth. Leaves variable, of 3 to 9 leaflets. Nut in tight, thin husk, with sweet kernel. |

**(Continued)**

## *Appendix VI (Continued)*

### SPECIES COMMON TO EASTERN UNITED STATES

| Name of Tree | Where the Tree Grows | Descriptive Notes |
|---|---|---|
| (Red) pignut hickory (*Hicoria ovalis*). | Pennsylvania west to Illinois, south in mountains and foothills. Common and widely distributed, along with pignut hickory. | Branchlets stout, reddish. Leaves usually of 7 leaflets, with reddish leafstalks. Nut small, thin-husked, small sweet kernel. |
| (Scrub) hickory (*Hicoria floridana*). | Northern and central Florida. | Leaves small, usually of 5 leaflets. Nut ½ inch diameter, pointed at base. |
| (Black) hickory (*Hicoria buckleyi*). | Central States, Indiana to Louisiana and eastern Texas. | Leaves 8 to 12 inches long, usually of 7 shiny leaflets. Nut pointed, 4-angled, with sweet kernel. |
| Pignut hickory (black hickory) (*Hicoria villosa*). | Illinois, Missouri, Arkansas, Oklahoma. | Resembling the above, but lower side midrib often fuzzy and with longer hair clusters. |
| Wax myrtle (*Myrica cerifera*). | Coastal region, New Jersey to Texas. | Wax coated berries in clusters. Leaves broader at outer end, fragrant. |
| Wax myrtle (*Myrica inodora*). | Florida to Louisiana. | Leaves not toothed; little odor. |
| Corkwood (*Leitneria floridana*). | Gulf Coast region and lower Mississippi Valley. | Lightest of all native woods. Leaves 4 to 6 inches long, shiny. Fruit ¾ inch long, podlike. |
| Aspen (popple) (*Populus tremuloides*). | Northern United States; south in Rocky Mountains. Nearly across Canada. | Leaves broad, finely toothed; leafstalks flat and long. |
| Largetooth aspen (*Populus grandidentata*). | Maine west to North Dakota, south in mountains to North Carolina. | Leaves coarsely toothed, broad, with flattened leafstalks. |
| Swamp cottonwood (*Populus heterophylla*). | Atlantic and Gulf Coasts, central Mississippi. | Leaves broadly oval, 4 to 7 inches long, with rounded leafstalks, finely woolly when young. Buds resinous. |
| Balsam poplar (balm-of-Gilead) (*Populus balsamifera*). | Across northern United States and Canada. | Leaves dull-toothed; leafstalks rounded. Winter buds ½ inch long, shiny, resinous. |
| Eastern cottonwood (Carolina poplar) (*Populus deltoides*). | Eastern half of United States. | Leaves triangular, coarsely toothed, fragrant, with flattened stems. Buds resinous. |
| Cottonwood (*Populus palmeri*). | Southwestern Texas. | Leaves finely toothed; leafstalks flattened. |
| Cottonwood (*Populus texana*). | Northwestern Texas (Panhandle). | Leaves coarsely toothed; leafstalk flattened. |
| Black willow (*Salix nigra*). | Eastern half of United States, along streams, not in swamps. | Leaves slender, long-pointed, finely toothed. Branchlets reddish. Largest of the willows. |
| Harbinson willow (*Salix harbinsonii*). | Coast, Virginia to Florida. | Leaves whitish below, on short stems. |
| Peachleaf willow (*Salix amygdaloides*). | Northern United States, south in Rocky Mountains. | Leaves long, pointed (peachleaf), pale below. |
| Willow (*Salix longipes*). | North Carolina to Florida. | Leaves lance-shaped; leafstems hairy. |
| Shiny willow (*Salix lucida*). | Northeastern quarter of United States. | Leaves shiny above, pale below, ovate. |

(Continued)

## Appendix VI (Continued)

### SPECIES COMMON TO EASTERN UNITED STATES

| Name of Tree | Where the Tree Grows | Descriptive Notes |
|---|---|---|
| Sandbar willow (*Salix longifolia*). | Eastern and Rocky Mountain regions. | Leaves 4 inches long, smooth. |
| Balsam willow (*Salix pyrifolia*). | Extreme northern New England. | Leaves broad, plum-shaped. |
| Missouri River willow (*Salix missouriensis*). | Central Mississippi River Basin. | Branchlets hairy. |
| Pussy willow (*Salix discolor*). | Northeastern quarter of United States. | Leaves, broad, shiny, and silky below. |
| (Bebbs) willow (*Salix bebbiana*). | Northern United States, south in Rocky Mountains. | Leaves elliptical, silvery white below. |
| Blue beech (water beech) (*Carpinus caroliniana*). | United States east of the Great Plains. | Trunk fluted with ridges, bluish gray. Leaflike wing attached to seed. |
| Hophornbeam (ironwood) (*Ostrya virginiana*). | United States and Canada east of the Great Plains. | Thin brown scaly bark. Fruit resembling hops, each seed in bag. Leaves doubly toothed. |
| Sweet birch (black birch) (*Betula lenta*). | Maine to Michigan, Appalachian Mountains to Georgia and Alabama. | Young inner bark aromatic (source of wintergreen flavoring). Fruit of all birches is of 2 kinds of catkin borne on same tree. Timber tree. |
| Yellow birch (*Betula lutea*). | Maine to Minnesota, south in mountains to Georgia. | Bark peeling in yellow-brown curls. Leaves rounded in outline. Timber tree. |
| River birch (red birch) (*Betula nigra*). | Southern New England, west to Minnesota, south to Texas. Along streams. | Bark red-brown, peeling in tough layers. Leaves oval, 2 to 3 inches long, narrowed at base, doubly toothed. |
| Gray birch (*Betula populifolia*). | New England, New York, Pennsylvania, and Delaware. | Trunks small, dull gray bark. Twigs drooping; leaves triangular, long-pointed, shiny. Small, short-lived tree. |
| Blueleaf birch (*Betula coerulea*). | Scattered in northern New England. | Leaves dull blue-green above, yellow-green below, oval, long-pointed. |
| Paper birch (canoe birch) (*Betula papyrifera*). | New England across the northern states to Pacific, south in Appalachians. | Bark pure white to light gray, separating in thin sheets. Leaves thick rounded at base. |
| Seaside alder (*Alnus maritima*). | Delaware, Maryland, Oklahoma. | Flowers opening in fall. |
| Beech (*Fagus grandifolia*). | Eastern half of United States. A widely ranging tree. | Leaves toothed, flat, thin, firm. Triangular edible nuts. |
| Chinkapin (*Castanea pumila*). | Pennsylvania to Florida and Texas. | Leaves smaller than above, shallow teeth. Burs of all chinkapins have 1 nut each. |
| Chinkapin (*Castanea ashei*). | Lower Atlantic and Gulf Coast regions. | Leaves densely woolly beneath. Fruit spines stout. |
| Chinkapin (*Castanea alnifolia floridana*). | Coastal region, North Carolina to Louisiana. | Leaves rounded at end, narrowed at base. Bur with sparse spines. |
| Chinkapin (*Castanea floridana margaretta*). | Gulf States region, Alabama to Arkansas. | Leaves shiny beneath. |

(Continued)

## Appendix VI (Continued)

### SPECIES COMMON TO EASTERN UNITED STATES

| Name of Tree | Where the Tree Grows | Descriptive Notes |
| --- | --- | --- |
| (Ozark) chinkapin (*Castanea ozarkensis*). | Northwestern Arkansas, southwestern Missouri, eastern Oklahoma. | Leaves 5 to 10 inches long, long-pointed, toothed. Bur large with much-prized nut. Good-sized tree. |
| Chinkapin (*Castanea alabamensis*). | Northwestern Alabama. | Leaves large, nearly smooth below. Spines fuzzy. |
| Chestnut (*Castanea dentata*). | Northeastern States and Appalachian region to Florida. | Leaves long, coarsely toothed, pointed. Spiny bur with edible nuts. Trees mostly killed back by blight disease. |
| Northern red oak (*Quercus borealis*). | Northeastern quarter of United States, south in Appalachian Mountains and cool locations along streams. (Variety. *Maxima* important in southern Appalachian region.) | Acorn large, in flat, shallow cup. Leaves mostly with 7 to 11 uniform lobes, 6 to 9 inches long, dull above, green below. High-grade timber tree. (Beginning the black oak group which has pointed leaf lobes and requires 2 seasons to mature the acorns.) |
| Pin oak (*Quercus palustris*). | Eastern United States. | Leaves small, deeply (mostly 5) lobed, with hair clusters in axils of veins and midrib. Acorn small, in saucer-shaped cup. Branches numerous, drooping. |
| Georgia oak (*Quercus georgiana*). | Central northern Georgia. | Leaves 3- to 5-lobed. Acorn ½ inch long, in flat cup. |
| Texas red oak (*Quercus texana*). | Central and western Texas. | Leaves 3 inches long, 5- or 7-lobed. Acorn ¾ to 1 inch long in deep cup. |
| Shumard red oak (*Quercus shumardii*). | Southeastern quarter of United States. | Leaves deeply or shallowly lobed, leafstalks slender. Acorn in shallow cup. |
| Graves oak (*Quercus gravesii*). | Southwestern Texas. | Similar to Texas red oak, but the leaves have sharp-pointed lobes and the acorns small cups. |
| Jack oak (*Quercus ellipsoidalis*). | Michigan to Iowa and Minnesota. | Leaves shiny, deeply and roundly lobed, 3 to 5 inches long. Acorn top shaped, often striped. |
| Scarlet oak (*Quercus coccinea*). | Northeastern United States. Maine to Missouri, mountains to Georgia. | Leaves with deep, rounded sinuses, lobes pointed. Acorn large, often striped, in medium cup. |
| Black oak (*Quercus velutina*). | Eastern half of United States, except Lake States region. | Leaves mostly 7-lobed, the lower ones rather full, others more deeply lobed. Acorn deeply enclosed in scaly cup. Inner bark orange. |
| Smoothbark oak (*Quercus leiodermis*). | Missouri and northward. | Leaves smaller, narrower, and smoother than black oak. |
| Turkey oak (*Quercus catesbaei*). | Coastal plain, Virginia to Louisiana. | Leaves of few prominent curved lobes. Acorn, full rounded in flat cup. |
| Bear oak, (scrub oak) (*Quercus ilicifolia*) (*Quercus nana*). | Northeastern United States, south in Mountains. | Leaves small, thick, silvery below. Small tree or shrub. |
| Southern red oak (*Quercus rubra*). | Southeastern United States. Abundant. | Leaves urn-shaped at base, with finger-like lobes or a 3-pointed outer end. Acorn ½ inch long in flat cup. Important timber tree. |

(Continued)

## Appendix VI (Continued)

### SPECIES COMMON TO EASTERN UNITED STATES

| Name of Tree | Where the Tree Grows | Descriptive Notes |
|---|---|---|
| Nuttall oak (Red River oak) (*Quercus nuttallii*). | Mississippi delta region, first and second bottoms. | Bark smooth and tight, light to dark grayish-brown. Leaves dull, dark green, usually 5 to 7 lobes. Acorn oblong-ovoid, ¾ to 1¼ inches long and usually striped. |
| Blackjack oak (*Quercus marilandica*). | Eastern United States, except New England. | Leaves full, thick, dark green, shiny. Acorn small, in medium cup. |
| Water oak (*Quercus nigra*). | Southeastern United States. | Leaves nearly evergreen, oblong with narrowing base, not toothed, but sometimes 3-lobed. Acorn small in shallow cup. |
| (Arkansas) water oak (*Quercus arkansana*). | Southwestern Arkansas. | Leaves resembling above, but broader at outer end. Acorn ⅓ inch long. |
| Water oak (*Quercus obtusa*). | Southeastern United States. | Leaves not lobed or toothed, widest beyond the middle, end rounded, narrowed at base. |
| Willow oak (*Quercus phellos*). | Atlantic and Gulf coastal region, New York to Texas. | Leaves narrow, willowlike, smooth, 2 to 5 inches long. Acorn small, striped lengthwise, in shallow cup. |
| Laurel oak (*Quercus laurifolia*). | Coastal plain, North Carolina to Louisiana. | Leaves glossy, dark green, elliptical, 3 to 4 inches long, smooth on lower surface, evergreen. Bark dark, rather smooth (black oak group). |
| Blue-jack oak (upland willow oak) (*Quercus cinerea*). | Coastal plain, Virginia to Texas. | Small tree with blue-green leaves, densely woolly below. Acorn small, striped, soft, hairy. |
| Shingle oak (*Quercus imbricaria*). | Central eastern United States. | Leaves without lobes, dark green, hairy below. Acorn in deep, thin cup. |
| Myrtle oak (*Quercus myrtifolia*). | On coast and islands, South Carolina to Mississippi. | Leaves with broad, rounded outer ends, thick, leathery, shiny, evergreen. |
| Live oak (*Quercus virginiana*). | South Atlantic and Gulf Coasts, Virginia to Texas. | Leaves oblong, edges smooth but incurved, thick, pale, fuzzy below, evergreen. Bark grayish. Acorn borne on long stem (peduncle). (Beginning the white oak group, whose leaf lobes are rounded and whose acorns mature in 1 season.) |
| Shin oak (*Quercus vaseyana*). | Western Texas. | Leaves with small lobes, wavy margins. |
| Shin oak (*Quercus mohriana*). | Western Texas and Oklahoma. | Leaves narrow, gray-green, thick. Acorn in deep cup. |
| Shin oak (*Quercus laceyi*). | Western Texas. | Leaves wavy-edged or 3-lobed. Acorn in shallow cup. |
| Shin oak (*Quercus annulata*). | Central and western Texas. | Leaves variable. Acorn in rounded cup. |
| Durand white oak (*Quercus durandii*). | Southern Gulf region, Georgia to Texas. | Leaves widening toward apex where slightly lobed. Acorn in flat cup. |
| Chapman white oak (*Quercus chapmanii*). | Southeastern United States, South Carolina to Florida. | Leaves oblong, wavy margin. Acorn without stem (sessile). |
| White oak (forked-leaf white oak) (*Quercus alba*). | Eastern half of United States. | Leaves deeply and wavy lobed. Acorn in low flat cup. Important timber tree. |

(Continued)

## *Appendix VI (Continued)*

### SPECIES COMMON TO EASTERN UNITED STATES

| Name of Tree | Where the Tree Grows | Descriptive Notes |
|---|---|---|
| Post oak (*Quercus stallata*). | Central and southern United States, Massachusetts to Texas. | Leaves like Maltese cross, thick, leathery, woolly below. Acorn close to branchlet, in deep cup. |
| Bastard white oak (*Quercus austrina*). | Southern United States, South Carolina to Mississippi. | Leaves 5-lobed, shiny, smooth below. Acorn in deep cup. |
| Bur oak (*Quercus macrocarpa*). | Northeastern and North Central United States. | Leaves deeply lobed and notched, broadest toward apex. Acorn enclosed in mossy or scaly cup. |
| Overcup oak (*Quercus lyrata*). | Atlantic and Gulf Coasts, New Jersey to Texas. Near water. | Leaves narrow with shallow lobes; acorn nearly enclosed in fringed cup. |
| Swamp white oak (*Quercus bicolor*). | Northeastern quarter of United States. In low or cool ground. | Leaves notched and lobed, whitish below. Acorn large in heavy cup. |
| Swamp chestnut oak (basket oak), (cow oak) (*Quercus prinus*). | Central and southern United States, New Jersey to Missouri. Borders of streams or swamps. | Leaves large, coarsely notched, often silvery below. Acorn large, shiny. |
| Chestnut oak (rock oak) (*Quercus montana*). | Northeastern and central United States. | Leaves coarsely notched. Acorn large, shiny, in warty cup. Bark extensively used for tanning leather. |
| Chinkapin oak (*Quercus muehlenbergii*). | Central part of eastern United States. | Leaves oblong, sharply notched, silvery on lower side. Acorn sweet, edible (if roasted). |
| Dwarf chinkapin oak (scrub oak) (*Quercus prinoides*). | Central part of eastern United States. | Leaves smaller than the above, teeth shorter. |
| American elm (white elm) (*Ulmus americana*). | Eastern half of United States to the Great Plains. | Leaves doubly and sharply toothed, smooth above. Wings of seed with tiny hairs. Large tree with drooping branches. Extensively planted. |
| Rock elm (*Ulmus racemosa*). | Belt across northeastern States to Kansas. | Branchlets often with corky wings. Leaves smooth above, soft hairy below. Winged seeds hairy. |
| Winged elm (wahoo) (*Ulmus alata*). | Southeastern quarter of United States. | Leaves small, variable in size. Seeds winged, hairy. Young twigs often corky. Planted for shade and ornament in South. |
| Slippery elm (*Ulmus fulva*). | Eastern United States. | Leaves rough, hairy above, soft downy below. Winged seeds, not hairy on edges. Inner bark muscilagenous. |
| Cedar elm (*Ulmus crassifolia*). | Mississippi, southern Arkansas, across central and southern Texas. | Leaves 1 to 2 inches long, coarsely toothed, rough above. Flowers and fruit late. |
| Red elm (*Ulmus serotina*). | Kentucky south to Georgia and west into Missouri, Arkansas, and Oklahoma. | Flowers in late summer. Seeds ripen late fall, hairy. Tree upright in habit of growth. |
| Planer tree (water elm) (*Planera aquatica*). | Southern United States. | Leaves resembling those of elms. Fruit small, nutlike. |
| (Roughleafed) hackberry (*Celtis occidentalis*). | Most of northeastern United States. | Leaves oval, thin, broad near base, long pointed. Seed in a purple berry. |

**(Continued)**

## *Appendix VI (Continued)*

### SPECIES COMMON TO EASTERN UNITED STATES

| Name of Tree | Where the Tree Grows | Descriptive Notes |
|---|---|---|
| Sugarberry (southern hackberry) (*Celtis laevigata*). | Southeastern quarter of United States. | Leaves long, narrow, smooth on edges. Fruit nutlike, red or orange. |
| Palo blanco (*Celtis lindheimerii*). | Southern Texas. | Leaves smaller than those of sugarberry. Fruit red-brown. |
| Hackberry (*Celtis pumila georgiana*). | Central part of southeastern United States. | Leaves 2 inches long, thin, rough above. Fruit red-purple with bloom. |
| (Name?) (*Trema mollis*). | Southern Florida (tropical). | Leaves in 2 rows, 3 to 4 inches long. |
| Red mulberry (*Morus rubra*). | Eastern United States. | Leaves thin, variably heart-shaped, sharply toothed. Fruit red or black. |
| Osage-orange (bois d'arc) (*Toxylon pomiferum*). | Arkansas, Oklahoma, Texas. Widely spread by planting. | Leaves smooth, shiny, 3 to 5 inches long, deep green. Fruit a multiple orange with milky flesh. Twigs thorny. Wood very durable in ground. |
| Golden fig (*Ficus aurea*). | Southern Florida (tropical). | Leaves oblong, leathery, evergreen. Fruit rounded. |
| Wild fig (*Ficus brevifolia*). | do. | Leaves broader than above, thin. |
| Whitewood (*Schoepfia chrisophylloides*). | do. | Leaves elliptical, 1 to 3 inches long. Fruit small, with stone seed. |
| Tallowwood (*Ximenia americana*). | do. | Leaves oblong, shiny. Fruit round, yellow. |
| Seagrape (*Coccolobis uvifera*). | do. | Leaves round, 4 to 5 inches in diameter. |
| Pigeon-plum (*Coccolobis laurifolia*). | do. | Leaves oval, thick. Fruit clustered. |
| Blolly (*Torrubia longifolia*). | do. | Leaves small. Fruit bright red, clustered. |
| Evergreen magnolia (*Magnolia grandiflora*). | South Atlantic and Gulf Coasts (widely planted for ornament). | Leaves thick, glossy, 5 to 8 inches long, evergreen. Fruit, head of many bright red seeds. Flowers large, white. |
| Sweet bay (*Magnolia virginiana*). | Coastal region. Massachusetts to Florida and Texas. | Leaves oblong, pale green, whitish below. Seeds scarlet. Flowers white, sweet. |
| Cucumber magnolia (*Magnolia acuminata*). | Central and Southern States, Ohio to Georgia and Arkansas. | Leaves oblong, wavy edges. Head of scarlet seeds. Flowers greenish. Large timber tree. |
| Yellow-flowered magnolia (*Magnolia cordata*). | North Carolina, Georgia, Alabama. Rare, mostly in cultivation. | Flowers bright canary yellow. Leaves broad, rounded, thick; branchlets hairy. |
| Bigleaf magnolia (*Magnolia macrophylla*). | Southern end of Appalachian Mountains, Gulf States. | Leaves 20 to 30 inches long, heart-shaped at base. Flowers large, white, fragrant. |
| (Florida) magnolia (*Magnolia ashei*). | Western Florida. | Resembles bigleaf magnolia, but with smaller flowers, fruit, and twigs. |
| Umbrella magnolia (umbrella-tree) (*Magnolia tripetala*). | Southeastern quarter of United States. | Leaves 14 to 22 inches long, crowded at ends of branches. Flowers ill-scented. |
| Mountain magnolia (*Magnolia fraseri*). | Southern Appalachian Mountains, Virginia to Alabama. | Leaves eared at base, 10 to 12 inches long, crowded. Flowers pale yellow. |

**(Continued)**

## *Appendix VI (Continued)*

### SPECIES COMMON TO EASTERN UNITED STATES

| Name of Tree | Where the Tree Grows | Descriptive Notes |
|---|---|---|
| Mountain magnolia (*Magnolia pyramidata*). | Gulf Coast region of Georgia, Florida, Alabama. | Leaves very narrow and eared at base, 5 to 8 inches long. Flowers white. |
| Yellow poplar (tulip poplar), (tuliptree) (*Liriodendron tulipifera*). | Southern New England to Michigan and Southern States. | Leaves squared, with lobe on sides. Flowers greenish-yellow, tulip-shaped. Fruit a cone of winged seed. Important timber tree. |
| Papaw (*Asimina triloba*). | Eastern United States, except northern portion. | Leaves narrowed toward base, 8 to 10 inches long. Fruit pulpy, edible. |
| Pond-apple (*Anona glabra*). | Southern Florida (tropical). | Leaves leathery. Fruit pear-shaped, fleshy. |
| Red bay (*Persea borbonia*). | South Atlantic and Gulf Coasts to Texas. | Leaves evergreen, oblong, thick, bright green, orange-colored·midrib. Fruit fleshy, nearly black. |
| Swamp bay (*Persea pubescens*). | Coast of Southern States. | Leaves elliptical, 5 inches long, evergreen. |
| Lancewood (*Ocotea catesbyana*). | Southern Florida (tropical). | Leaves narrowed at both ends, leathery, shiny, evergreen. Fruit dark blue, round. |
| Sassafras (*Sassafras variifolium*). | Eastern United States. | Leaves variable in shape. Leaves, twigs, and especially inner bark on roots aromatic. Close relative of camphor-tree of Asia. |
| (Name?) (*Misanteca triandra*). | Southern Florida (tropical). | Leaves elliptical, evergreen. Fruit olive-shaped. |
| Caper tree (*Capparis jamaicensis*). | do. | Leaves 2 to 3 inches long, rounded at ends, leathery, shiny. Fruit, long pod. |
| Caper tree (*Capparis cynophallophora*). | do. | Leaves scaly. Fruit pulpy. |
| Witch hazel (*Hamamelis virginiana*). | Eastern United States. | Leaves deeply veined, with wavy margin. Flowering in fall. |
| (Southern) witch hazel (*Hamamelis macrophylla*). | Gulf Coast region (Georgia to Texas), Oklahoma. | Leaves rounded, wavy-edged, hairy. Flowers, December to February. |
| Sweet gum or red gum (*Liquidambar styraciflua*). | Southeastern quarter of United States. | Leaves star-shaped, aromatic. Fruit a spiny ball of many capsules with seeds. Large tree. Important timber tree. |
| Sycamore (*Platanus occidentalis*). | Eastern half of United States. Moist or cool locations. | Bark gray, flaking off. Leaves large, broad, lobed. Balls single, hanging by slender stem over winter. Largest of all hardwood trees—up to 10 feet in diameter and 170 feet in height. |
| Narrowleaf crab apple (*Malus angustifolia*). | Southeastern United States, except in mountains. | Leaves oblong, bluntly toothed, firm. Fruit round, yellow-green, fleshy. (Most of the crab apples have sharp spines on branchlets.) |
| Crab apple (*Malus glaucescens*). | Appalachian Mountains and Plateau. | Leaves toothed, coarsely notched, whitish below. Fruit pale yellow. |
| Crab apple (*Malus glabrata*). | Western North Carolina. | Leaves triangular, sharply lobed, toothed. |

**(Continued)**

## Appendix VI (Continued)

### SPECIES COMMON TO EASTERN UNITED STATES

| Name of Tree | Where the Tree Grows | Descriptive Notes |
| --- | --- | --- |
| Sweet crab apple (*Malus coronaria*). | Central eastern United States. | Leaves oval, finely toothed. Fruit yellow-green. |
| Crab apple (*Malus bracteata*). | Kentucky to Missouri, southward. | Leaves oval, pointed, toothed. Fruit round. |
| Crab apple (*Malus platycarpa*). | Central Appalachian region. | Leaves rounded ovate, finely toothed. Fruit flattened. |
| Lanceleaf crab apple (*Malus lancifolia*). | Central eastern United States. | Leaves broadly lance-shaped, thin. |
| Crab apple (*Malus ioensis*). | Central Mississippi Basin. | Leaves fuzzy beneath, notched and toothed. |
| Soulard crab apple (*Malus soulardii*). | Minnesota to Texas (not abundant). | Leaves oval, or elliptical, hairy on lower surface. Fruit 2 inches in diameter. |
| Mountain-ash (*Sorbus americana*). | Northeastern United States. Widely planted for ornament. | Leaves of 13 to 17 leaflets, sharply toothed. Fruit in cluster, bright orange-red. |
| Serviceberry (shadbush) (*Amelanchier canadensis*). | Eastern half of United States. | Flowers white, appearing before the leaves. Leaves thin, oval, finely toothed. |
| Serviceberry (*Amelanchier laevis*). | Maine to Wisconsin, southward. | Flowers appearing after the leaves. Berries pulpy, sweet. |
| Hawthorn, haw, thorn, thorn apple, apple, or thorn (*Crataegus* species) (178 different species recognized in the United States). | Eastern United States, with 175 species (most numerous in Southern States); 3 species in western United States. | Small trees, mostly with stiff crooked branchlets, armed with sharp spines. Leaves mostly rounded, broader toward apex, sharply toothed or slightly lobed. Flowers in showy clusters, mostly white with some rose shading. Fruit rounded apple, scarlet, orange, red, yellow, blue, or nearly black. |
| Canada plum (*Prunus nigra*). | New England, west through northern tier of states to North Dakota. | Leaves broadly ovate, doubly toothed. Fruit red. (All species of *Prunus* have bitter taste or smell, flowers in clusters, and stone in fruit.) |
| Wild plum (hog or red plum) (*Prunus americana*). | Eastern United States and Rocky Mountain region to Utah and New Mexico. | Leaves sharply toothed, wedge-shaped at base, oval, 3 to 4 inches long. Fruit 1 inch diameter, bright red. |
| Wild plum (*Prunus lanata*). | North and South Central States. | Leaves oval, hairy below. Plum with whitish bloom. |
| Wild goose plum (*Prunus hortulana*). | Central States. | Leaves shiny, pointed. Fruit red or yellow. |
| Wild goose plum (*Prunus munsonia*). | Central Mississippi Valley, Oklahoma, and Texas. | Leaves long elliptical or lance-shaped, thin, shiny. Fruit red, good quality. |
| Mexican plum (*Prunus mexicana*). | Kansas to Louisiana and Texas. | Fruit purplish red; ripens late summer. |
| Chickasaw plum (*Prunus angustifolia*). | Native probably in Oklahoma and Texas. Now found widely distributed through South. | Leaves broadly lance-shaped, thin, shiny, finely toothed. Fruit red or yellow, much used for food. |
| Allegheny sloe (*Prunus alleghaniensis*). | Connecticut, south (in mountains), to North Carolina. | Leaves long, pointed, finely toothed. Fruit purple, with bloom. |

(Continued)

## *Appendix VI (Continued)*

### SPECIES COMMON TO EASTERN UNITED STATES

| Name of Tree | Where the Tree Grows | Descriptive Notes |
|---|---|---|
| Black sloe (*Prunus umbellata*). | Southern States. | Leaves broadly ovate. Fruit, various colors. |
| Texas sloe (*Prunus tenuifolia*). | Texas. | Leaves thin. Fruit oblong, with flat stone. |
| Pin cherry (bird or wild red cherry) (*Prunus pennsylvanica*). | Across northern United States, south in Appalachian Mountains. | Leaves long, pointed, finely toothed. Flowers in flat clusters (umbels). Cherry red, each on long stem. Spreads rapidly on burned-over forest lands. |
| Choke cherry (*Prunus virginiana*). | Northeastern quarter of United States, south in Appalachian Mountains, west to northern Rockies. | Leaves broadly oval, sharp-pointed, shiny. Flowers in long clusters (racemes). Cherry dark red. |
| Georgia wild cherry (*Prunus cuthbertii*). | Georgia, range not well known. | Leaves smooth, firm, twigs hairy. Fruit red. |
| Black cherry (*Prunus serotina*). | Eastern half of United States to the Great Plains. | Leaves shiny, long-pointed. Flowers in long clusters (racemes). Cherry black, pleasant flavor. Timber tree. |
| Alabama cherry (*Prunus alabamensis*). | Low mountains of central Alabama. | Leaves broadly oval, thick, firm, up to 5 inches long. Fruit red or dark purple. |
| Cherry (*Prunus australis*). | Conecuh County, southern Alabama. | Leaves broadest near middle. Fruit purple. |
| Laurel cherry (mockorange) (*Prunus caroliniana*). | South Atlantic and Gulf coastal region. | Leaves evergreen, thick, shiny, 2 to 4 inches long. Fruit black, shiny, holding over winter. Planted as ornamental tree. |
| West Indian cherry (*Prunus myrtifolia*). | Southern Florida (tropical). | Leaves pointed, firm, yellow-green above, 2 to 4 inches long. Fruit orange-brown. |
| Coco-plum (*Chrysobalanus icaco*). | do. | Leaves broad, much rounded at end. |
| Florida catclaw (*Pithecolobium unguis-cati*). | do. | Leaves of two pairs of leaflets, each rounded, thin. Pod 2 to 4 inches long. |
| Huajillo (wa-hil-yo) (*Pithecolobium brevifolium*). | Lower Rio Grande Valley of Texas. | Leaves doubly compound of many leaflets. Pods straight, 4 to 6 inches long. |
| Texas ebony (*Pithecolobium flexicaule*). | Gulf Coast of Texas. | Leaves very small, twice compound, broad. Pod thick, 4 to 6 inches long. |
| Wild tamarind (*Lysiloma bahamensis*). | Southern Florida (tropical). | Leaves compound of many pairs of leaflets. Pod 1 inch broad, 4 to 5 inches long. |
| Huisache (acacia) (*Acacia farnesiana*). | Cental and western Texas. | Leaves doubly compound, very small, bright green. Pods cylindrical. Flowers in round heads. Widely planted for its fragrant flowers. |
| Catclaw (*Acacia tortuosa*). | Southwestern Texas. | Leaves tiny, compound. Pod slender, beadlike. |
| Catclaw (*Acacia wrightii*). | Western Texas. | Leaves compound, tiny, on long stems. |

(Continued)

## Appendix VI (Continued)

### SPECIES COMMON TO EASTERN UNITED STATES

| Name of Tree | Where the Tree Grows | Descriptive Notes |
|---|---|---|
| Catclaw (Acacia emoriana). | Southern Texas. | Leaflets tiny. Pod much narrowed at base. |
| (Mimosa) (Leucaena greggii). | Southern Texas. | Leaves doubly compound. Pods narrow. |
| (Mimosa) (Leucaena pulverulenta). | Southern Texas (Gulf Coast). | Leaves doubly compound. Pods 8 inches long. |
| (Mimosa) (Leucaena retusa). | Southern Texas and New Mexico. | Leaves featherlike compound of many leaflets. |
| Honey mesquite (Prosopis glandulosa). | Kansas to California and southward. | Leaves generally similar to above, 9 inches long, leaflets often 2 inches long. |
| Redbud (Cercis canadensis). | Eastern United States (south and west of New York). | Leaves heart-shaped, thin. Flowers bright purplish red, in clusters. Pods pink, 2 to 3 inches long. |
| Texas redbud (Cercis reniformis). | Eastern Texas. | Leaves kidney-shaped, firm, shiny. |
| Coffeetree (Gymnocladus dioicus). | Central portion of eastern United States. | Leaves doubly compound, 2 to 3 feet long, of rounded pointed leaflets. Pods 8 inches long. |
| Honeylocust (Gleditsia triacanthos). | Central portion of eastern United States (extended widely by planting). | Leaves doubly compound of small elliptical leaflets. Pods 10 to 18 inches long, twisted, sweet pulp. Tree usually spiny. |
| Texas honeylocust (Gleditsia texana). | Central Mississippi Valley (Indiana to Texas). | Leaves compound of very small leaflets. Pods small, flattened, thin, straight. Trees spiny. |
| Waterlocust (Gleditsia aquatica). | Coastal region (South Carolina to Texas), Mississippi Valley. | Leaves single or doubly compound. Pods short, with 1 to 3 seeds. Tree spiny. |
| Border paloverde (Cercidium floridum). | Southern Texas (mouth of Rio Grande) (small tree). | Leaves tiny, twice compound. Bark bright green. Pods 2 inches long, pointed. straight. |
| Coralbean (Sophora affinis). | Mississippi River to California. | Leaves compound, 13 to 19 leaflets. Pods beaded. |
| Yellowwood (Cladrastis lutea). | Southern Appalachian Mountains west to Arkansas. | Leaves of 7 to 11 rounded leaflets, 3 to 4 inches long. Pods small, pointed, in clusters. Wood, yellow. |
| Black locust (yellow locust) (Robinia pseudacacia). | Appalachian Mountain region. Widely cultivated and naturalized over United States. | Leaves compound of 7 to 17 rounded leaflets. Flowers white, sweet-scented. Pods 3 inches long with tiny seeds. Wood very durable. |
| Clammy locust (Robinia viscosa). | Southern Appalachian Mountains. | Leaves compound. Leafstalks sticky, hairy (clammy). |
| Jamaica dogwood (Ichthyomethia piscipula). | Southern Florida (tropical tree). | Leaves of 5 to 11 rounded leaflets, dropping early. Pods with 4 crinkly wings. |
| Lignumvitae (Guajacum sanctum). | Southern Florida (tropical). | Leaves of 6 to 8 leaflets. Pod tiny, orange. |
| (Soapbush) (Porliera angustifolia). | Southern Texas. | Leaves of 8 to 12 narrow leaflets. Flowers purple, sweet-scented. |

**(Continued)**

## *Appendix VI (Continued)*

### SPECIES COMMON TO EASTERN UNITED STATES

| Name of Tree | Where the Tree Grows | Descriptive Notes |
|---|---|---|
| (Name?) (*Byrsonima lucida*). | Southern Florida (tropical). | Leaves opposite, wedge-shaped, evergreen. |
| Hercules' club (prickly ash) (*Xanthoxylum clavaherculis*). | South Atlantic and Gulf coastal regions, Arkansas, Oklahoma, Texas. | Leaves 5 to 8 inches long, of 6 to 18 pointed leaflets, on spiny stems. Fruit small in terminal clusters. This is not the Devil's-walking-stick, sometimes called "Hercules' club." |
| Florida boxwood (*Schaefferia frutescens*). | Southern Florida (tropical). | Leaves alternate, 2 inches long by 1 inch wide, narrow at base. Rounded fruit with stone. |
| (Name?) (*Maytenus phyllanthoides*). | do. | Leaves leathery. Fruit, 4-angled, red capsule. |
| Bladdernut (*Staphylea trifolia*). | Great Lake States and south to Georgia and Oklahoma. | Leaves opposite, of 3 leaflets, 2 leaf bracts at base of stem. Fruit pod with bony seeds. |
| Mountain maple (*Acer spicatum*). | Northeastern United States, south in mountains. | Leaves opposite, 8-lobed, coarsely toothed, red leaf stems. Flowers (racemes) and keys (fruit) in long clusters. |
| Striped maple (moosewood) (*Acer pennsylvanicum*). | Northeastern United States, south in mountains. | Leaves opposite, drooping, rounded, 3-lobed at apex. Bark striped, greenish, smooth. |
| Sugar maple (*Acer saccharum*). | Eastern United States to Kansas and Oklahoma. | Leaves opposite, pale and smooth below, 5-lobed, rounded sinuses. Keys ripen late. Tree yields sweet sap. |
| Black maple (*Acer nigrum*). | Centers in region from Ohio to Iowa. | Leaves opposite, dull green (black), yellow downy below, thick, drooping. |
| Whitebark maple (*Acer leucoderme*). | Lower Appalachian Mountains to Arkansas and northern Louisiana. | Leaves opposite, small, 3-lobed, light yellow-green, and densely downy beneath. |
| Southern sugar maple (*Acer floridanum*). | Southeastern Virginia to eastern Texas. | Leaves opposite, with 3 rounded lobes, dark green, pale or fuzzy below, strongly veined. |
| Silver maple (white maple) (*Acer saccharinum*). | Eastern United States, especially in central Mississippi Basin. | Leaves opposite, deeply lobed, toothed, silvery below. Flowers before leaves. Keys fall early. |
| Red maple (soft maple) (*Acer rubrum*). | Eastern United States. | Leaves opposite, small, 3- or 5-lobed on red stems. Flowers red, opening before the leaves. Keys fall early. |
| Box elder (ashleaf maple) (*Acer negundo*). | Eastern half of United States, northern Rocky Mountain. | Leaves opposite, thin, mostly compound of 3, 5, or 7 leaflets. Greenish twigs. |
| Ohio buckeye (*Aesculus glabra*). | Pennsylvania, south and west to Missouri and Texas. | Leaves of 5 leaflets, on slender stems, opposite. Flowers yellow. Fruit with prickles. |
| Georgia buckeye (*Aesculus neglecta lanceolata*). | North Carolina to western Florida. | Leaves opposite, of 5 leaflets. Flowers red or yellow. No prickles on fruit. |
| Red buckeye (*Aesculus pavia*). | Southeastern United States. | Leaves opposite. Flowers red. No prickles on fruit. |

**(Continued)**

## *Appendix VI (Continued)*

### SPECIES COMMON TO EASTERN UNITED STATES

| Name of Tree | Where the Tree Grows | Descriptive Notes |
|---|---|---|
| Yellow buckeye (*Aesculus octandra*). | Pennsylvania to Illinois, south mostly in mountains. | Leaves opposite, 5 to 7 leaflets, sharply toothed. Flowers yellow (rarely red). Fruit without prickles. |
| Woolly buckeye (*Aesculus discolor*). | Georgia to Missouri and Texas. | Leaves woolly beneath, opposite. Flowers rose and yellow. |
| Scarlet buckeye (*Aesculus austrina*). | Southern central United States. | Flowers scarlet. Leaves opposite. |
| Wingleaf soapberry (*Sapindus saponaria*). | Southern Florida (tropical). | Leaves of 4 to 9 leaflets rounded at ends, brown leaf stem winged. 1-seeded, round fruit. |
| Soapberry (*Sapindus marginatus*). | Georgia, Florida. | Leaflets, 7 to 13. No wings on leaf stem. Fruit yellow. |
| Inkwood (*Exothea paniculata*). | Southern Florida (tropical). | Leaves of 4 leaflets, each 4 to 5 inches long, dark green. Fruit, 1-sided, dark orange. |
| White ironwood (*Hypelate trifoliata*). | Florida Keys. | 3 leaflets, 1 to 2 inches long, rounded at ends. Round fruit with round stone. |
| (Name?) (*Cupania glabra*). | Southern Florida (tropical). | Leaves of 6 to 12 toothed leaflets. |
| Varnish leaf (*Dodonaea microcarpa*). | Long Pine Key, Florida (tropical). | Leaves wedge-shaped, sticky. Fruit a capsule. |
| Bluewood (*Condalia obovata*). | Western Texas. | Branches spine-tipped. Leaves small. |
| Red ironwood (*Reynosia septentrionalis*). | Southern Florida (tropical). | Leaves opposite, thick, dark green, notched end. Dark, edible purple "plum." |
| Black ironwood (*Krugiodendron ferreum*). | do. | Leaves bright green, shiny, opposite, persistent, 1 inch across. Fruit round, black, 1 seed. |
| Yellow buckthorn (*Rhamnus caroliniana*). | Southeastern United States. | Leaves elliptical, slightly toothed, dark yellow-green, strongly veined. Round, black fruit. |
| Soldierwood (*Colubrina reclinata*). | Southern Florida (tropical). | Leaves thin, smooth, yellow-green, 2 to 3 inches long. Fruit 3-lobed, red-orange. Smooth trunk. |
| Nakedwood (*Colubrina cubensis*). | do. | Leaves thick, dull green, densely fuzzy. |
| Nakedwood (*Colubrina arborescens*). | do. | Leaves thick and leathery, reddish, fuzzy beneath. |
| (Smooth) basswood (*Tilia glabra*). | Maine to Michigan and south to Ohio River, west to Nebraska. | Leaves coarsely toothed, smooth except tufts of hairs on upper surface. Flower stalks smooth. |
| Basswood (*Tilia porracea*). | Western Florida. | Leaves fuzzy below, oblique at base. |
| (White-fruited) basswood (*Tilia leucocarpa*). | Alabama to Arkansas and Texas. | Leaves coarsely toothed, not hairy tufted. Flower stalk densely hairy. |
| Basswood (*Tilia venulosa*). | Southwestern North Carolina. | Branchlets bright red and stout. |
| Basswood (*Tilia littoralis*). | Southeastern Georgia. | Leaves finely toothed. Branchlets slender. |

**(Continued)**

## *Appendix VI (Continued)*

### SPECIES COMMON TO EASTERN UNITED STATES

| Name of Tree | Where the Tree Grows | Descriptive Notes |
|---|---|---|
| Basswood (*Tilia crenoserrata*). | Southwestern Georgia and Florida. | Leaves roundedly toothed, smooth on lower surface. |
| Basswood (*Tilia australis*). | Northeastern Alabama. | Leaves smooth below, thin. |
| (Southern) basswood (*Tilia floridana*). | North Carolina, south and west to Oklahoma and Texas. | Leaves thin, coarsely toothed. Summer twigs not pubescent. |
| Basswood (*Tilia cocksii*). | Southwestern Louisiana. | Leaves blue-green, shiny below in early summer. |
| (Hairy) basswood (*Tilia neglecta*). | New England south, in mountains to Mississippi, west to Missouri. | Leaves with short, fine hairs on lower surface. |
| (Carolina) basswood (*Tilia caroliniana*). | North Carolina, Georgia, and west to Texas. | Leaves square at base, sparsely hairy below, smooth above. Branchlets smooth. |
| (Texas) basswood (*Tilia Texana*). | Southeastern Texas. | Leaves, heart-shaped base. Branchlets smooth. |
| Basswood (*Tilia phanera*). | South-central Texas. | Leaves rounded, deeply heart-shaped at base. |
| Basswood (*Tilia eburnea*). | Western North Carolina to Florida. | Leaves obliquely squared at base. Branchlets hairy. |
| Basswood (*Tilia lata*). | Northwestern Alabama. | Leaves oval, long-pointed, heart-shaped at base. Branchlets reddish. |
| White basswood (*Tilia heterophylla*). | Pennsylvania to Missouri and south into Gulf States. | Leaves densely woolly below, squared or heart-shaped at base. Branchlets slender. |
| White basswood (*Tilia monticola*). | Appalachian Mountains (meeting of Virginia, North Carolina, and Tennessee). | Leaves white, woolly below, squared at base. Branchlets stout. |
| (Georgia) basswood (*Tilia georgiana*). | South Carolina to Florida. Arkansas. | Leaves pale, woolly below. Branchlets fine, hairy. Winter buds hairy. |
| Loblolly-bay (*Gordonia lasianthus*). | South Atlantic and Gulf coastal region. | Leaves thick, shiny, smooth, 4 to 5 inches long, narrow at base, persistent on branch. Related to the tea plant of Asia. |
| Franklinia (*Franklinia altamaha*). | Altamaha River, Ga. (originally), but now known only in cultivation. | Leaves 5 inches long, oblong, narrowed at base, shiny. Flowers showy white, 3 inches across. Planted for ornament. |
| Cinnamon bark (*Canella winterana*). | Southern Florida (tropical). | Leaves elliptical, rounded at ends, thick, shiny. Inner bark, the cinnamon of commerce. |
| Papaya (*Clarica papaya*). | Eastern coast of southern Florida (tropical). | Leaves very large, much lobed; 3 to 5 inches long, edible. Cultivated for fruit. |
| Tree cactus (*Cephalocereus deeringii*). | Southern Florida (tropical). | No leaves. Branches usually 10-ribbed, spiny. Flowers inconspicuous, dark red. |
| Mangrove (*Rhizophora mangle*). | Coast of lower Florida peninsula (tropical). | Leaves opposite, thick, evergreen, elliptical, 4 inches long. Fruit, a berry germinating on the tree. |

**(Continued)**

## *Appendix VI (Continued)*

### SPECIES COMMON TO EASTERN UNITED STATES

| Name of Tree | Where the Tree Grows | Descriptive Notes |
|---|---|---|
| Gurgeon stopper (*Eugenia buxifolia*). | Southern Florida (tropical). | Leaves opposite, rounded at end, thick, 1 inch long. Flower clusters (racemes) in leaf axil. |
| White stopper (*Eugenia axillaris*). | East coast of Florida (tropical). | Leaves opposite, 2 inches long, narrow, blunt pointed. |
| Red stopper (*Eugenia rhombea*). | Florida Keys (tropical). | Leaves opposite. Flowers in bunches (fascicles). |
| Red stopper (*Eugenia confusa*). | Southern Florida (tropical). | Leaves opposite, long-pointed. Flowers as above. |
| Naked stopper (*Eugenia dicrana*). | do. | Leaves opposite. Flowers 3-flowered, open clusters. |
| Stopper (*Eugenia simpsonii*). | do. | Leaves larger than above. Doubly 3-flowered. |
| Stopper (*Eugenia longipes*). | do. | Leaves opposite, evergreen. Flowers white, fragrant. |
| Stopper (*Eugenia bahamensis*). | do. | Leaves rounded. Fruit black. Flowers sweet. |
| White spicewood (*Calyptranthes pallens*). | do. | Leaves opposite, long-pointed, 2 to 3 inches long. Flowers minute, in compound clusters (panicles). |
| Spicewood (*Calyptranthes zuzygium*). | do. | Leaves opposite, elliptical, rounded; branchlets smooth. Flowers small, in sparse clusters (cymes). |
| (Name?) (*Tetrazygia bicolor*). | do. | Leaves opposite. Flowers showy, white. |
| Black olive tree (*Bucida buceras*). | do. | Leaves in whorls, 2 to 3 inches long, rounded at ends. Flowers in spikes. |
| Buttonwood (*Conocarpus erecta*). | do. | Flowers in heads. Fruit in cones. |
| White buttonwood (*Laguncularia racemosa*). | do. | Leaves opposite, short, rounded, thick, leathery. Flowers minute, borne on hairy clusters (spikes). |
| Devil's walking stick (Hercules' club) (*Aralia spinosa*). | Most of eastern half of United States. | Spiny, aromatic tree or shrub. Leaves doubly compound, 3 to 4 feet long at end of branches. |
| Black gum (sour gum) (*Nyssa sylvatica*). | do. | Leaves oblong, broadest above the middle, thick. Fruit small, stone slightly marked (ribbed). |
| Swamp black gum (*Nyssa biflora*). | Coastal acid swamps, Maryland to Texas. | Leaves narrower than those of black gum (1 inch wide). Fruit small, stone prominently marked (ribbed). |
| Sour tupelo gum (*Nyssa ogeche*). | Coastal region South Carolina to Florida (not abundant). | Fruit red (plum), large (1 inch long), single. Leaves 4 to 6 inches long. |
| Tupelo gum (*Nyssa aquatica*). | Coastal fresh water or "deep" swamps, Virginia to Texas, up Mississippi River. Not found in stagnant swamps. | Fruit large (1 inch), purple (plum), single on long stem. Leaves broadly elliptical, 5 to 7 inches long. |
| Dogwood (flowering dogwood) (*Cornus florida*). | Eastern half of United States. | Leaves opposite, oval, pointed. Flowers small, in dense head with showy white bracts. Fruit red. |

**(Continued)**

## *Appendix VI (Continued)*

### SPECIES COMMON TO EASTERN UNITED STATES

| Name of Tree | Where the Tree Grows | Descriptive Notes |
| --- | --- | --- |
| Blue dogwood (*Cornus alternifolia*). | Northeastern States and Appalachian Mountains. | Leaves alternate (otherwise similar to *Cornus florida*). Flowers small, without showy scales. |
| Roughleaf dogwood (*Cornus asperifolia*). | Eastern United States. | Leaves opposite. Flowers in loose heads, not showy. Fruit white. |
| (Name?) (*Elliottia racemosa*). | Southeastern Georgia. | Flowers with 4 petals, in long clusters. |
| Great rhododendron (*Rhododendron maximum*). | New England, Ohio, south in the Appalachian Mountains. | Leaves thick, evergreen, 4 to 12 inches long, clustered at ends of branches. Flowers showy in large clusters. |
| Catawba rhododendron (*Rhododendron catawbiense*). | Appalachian Mountains, Virginia south to Georgia and Alabama. | Leaves 4 to 6 inches long, broad, thick. Calyx lobes of flowers sharp-pointed. |
| Mountain-laurel (*Kalmia latifolia*). | New England to Indiana and south to Gulf. | Leaves elliptical, thick, evergreen, 3 inches long. Flowers in clusters (corymbs), showy. |
| Sourwood (*Oxydendrum arboreum*). | Appalachian Mountains, west to Louisiana. | Leaves elliptical, finely toothed. Flowers bell-shaped in long compound clusters (panicles). |
| (Name?) (*Lyonia ferruginea*). | South Atlantic Coast. | Flower clusters in leaf axils. |
| Tree huckleberry (*Vaccinium arboreum*). | Coast, Virginia to Texas, northward in Mississippi River Basin. | Leaves elliptical, thin, 2 inches long. Flowers in open clusters (racemes). |
| Marlberry (*Icacorea paniculata*). | Southern Florida (tropical). | Leaves thick with numerous resin dots. Blackberries in clusters. |
| (Name?) (*Rapanea guianensis*). | do. | Leaves oblong. Fruit round. |
| Joewood (*Jaquinia keyensis*). | do. | Leaves sometimes opposite. Flower terminal. |
| Satinleaf (*Chrysophyllum oliviforme*). | do. | Leaves soft, hairy below, 2 to 3 inches long. Fruit oval, fleshy, purple. |
| Mastic (*Sideroxylon foetidissimum*). | do. | Leaves elliptical, thin. Flowers minute. |
| Bustic (*Dipholis salicifolia*). | do. | Leaves narrow, shiny. Flowers minute. |
| Tough buckthorn (*Bumelia tenax*). | South Atlantic Coast, southwestern Georgia. | Leaves thin, oblong, silky below. Fruit round, sweet, edible. |
| Gum elastic (*Bumelia lanuginosa*). | Coastal region Georgia to Texas, Mississippi Basin. | Leaves with soft brown hairs curved backward. Fruit oblong, in leaf axils. |
| Buckthorn (*Bumelia monticola*). | Southern and western Texas. | Leaves thick, shiny. Branchlets often ending in stout spines. |
| Buckthorn (*Bumelia lycoides*). | Southeastern States. | Leaves thin, oblong. Fruit oblong, fleshy. |
| Saffron plum (*Bumelia angustifolia*). | Southern Florida (tropical). | Leaves leathery, 1 inch long, evergreen. Fruit small with sweet flesh. |
| Wild dilly (*Mimusops parvifolia*). | Florida Keys (tropical). | Leaves clustered at branch ends, notched. |
| Persimmon (*Diospyros virginiana*). | Eastern United States, except northern portion. | Leaves oval (widest below middle), firm. Fruit fleshy, edible, stone seed. Close relative of ebony tree of the tropics. |

**(Continued)**

# *Appendix VI (Continued)*

## SPECIES COMMON TO EASTERN UNITED STATES

| Name of Tree | Where the Tree Grows | Descriptive Notes |
|---|---|---|
| Black persimmon (*Diospyros texana*). | Southern and southwestern Texas. | Leaves rounded at end, narrow at base, 1 inch long. Fruit black. |
| Sweetleaf (*Symplocos tinctoria*). | Delaware to Florida, west to Arkansas and Texas. | Leaves pointed, good for browse. Fruit small, in close clusters. |
| Silverbell (Lily-of-the valley tree) (*Halesia carolina*). | Southern Appalachian Mountain region. | Flowers about ½ inch long, in small clusters (fascicles). Fruit 4-winged. Leaves elliptical. |
| Mountain silverbell (*Halesia monticola*). | Southern Appalachian Mountains, west to Oklahoma. | Fruit as above. Flowers 2 inches long in fascicles. Leaves 8 to 11 inches long. |
| Little silverbell (*Halesia parviflora*). | Southern Georgia, northern Florida, Alabama. | Fruit club-shaped, 1 inch long. Flowers minute, in fascicles. Leaves 3 inches long. |
| Two-wing silverbell (*Halesia diptera*). | Coastal plain of Georgia west to eastern Texas. | Fruit 2-winged. Flowers in clusters (racemes). Leaves 3 to 5 inches long. |
| Snowbell (*Styrax grandifolia*). | South Atlantic and Gulf Coast region. | Leaves broadly oval, 2 to 5 inches long. Flowers white, in terminal clusters (racemes). |
| Blue ash (*Fraxinus quadrangulata*). | Michigan to Iowa, south to Tennessee and Oklahoma. | Branchlets square; leaves opposite, 5 to 11 leaflets on short stems. Flowers without calyx, perfect. |
| Black ash (*Fraxinus nigra*). | Northeastern United States. (Cold swamps, along streams and lakes.) | Leaves opposite, of 7 to 11 leaflets without stems (sessile). Branchlets round. Flowers without calyx, polygamous. |
| Water ash (*Fraxinus caroliniana*). | South Atlantic and Gulf Coast region. Deep swamps and river bottoms. | Leaves opposite, leaflets 5 or 7 on stems. Flowers with calyx, 2 kinds on separate trees. Fruit often 3-winged. |
| (Gulf) water ash (*Fraxinus pauciflora*). | Southern Georgia, Florida. Deep swamps and river bottoms. | Leaves opposite, leaflets 3 or 5, more pointed than above. Flowers like above. Fruit 2-winged. |
| White ash (*Fraxinus americana*). | Eastern half of United States. | Leaves opposite, of 5 to 9 leaflets each, broadly oval, usually smooth and whitish below. Flowers of 2 kinds on separate trees. Important timber tree. |
| Biltmore white ash (*Fraxinus biltmoreana*). | Central portion of eastern United States. | Leaves and branchlets fuzzy, 7 to 9 leaflets, whitish below. Leaves opposite. Wing of fruit mostly terminal. |
| Texas ash (*Fraxinus texensis*). | Texas, except southern portion. | Leaves opposite, mostly of 5 rounded leaflets. |
| Mexican ash (*Fraxinus berlandieriana*). | Western Texas. | Leaves opposite, of 3 or 5 long, narrow leaflets. Wing extending halfway on fruit body. |
| Red ash (*Fraxinus pennsylvanica*). | Most of the eastern United States. (See Green ash.) | Leaves opposite, of 7 or 9 tapering, long-stemmed leaflets, slightly fuzzy (also branchlets), green below. Wing extending part way up the fruit body. Flowers (2 kinds) on separate trees. Important timber tree. |

**(Continued)**

## *Appendix VI (Continued)*

### SPECIES COMMON TO EASTERN UNITED STATES

| Name of Tree | Where the Tree Grows | Descriptive Notes |
|---|---|---|
| Green ash (*fraxinus pennsylvanica lanceolata*). | Eastern United States; west in the Rocky Mountains. (Important variety of Red ash species.) | Same as Red ash except smooth leaflets and branchlets. Very difficult to distinguish from red ash. A very common ash. Important timber tree. |
| Pumpkin ash (*Fraxinus profunda*). | Scattered, mostly east of the Mississippi River. | Leaves large, opposite, of mostly 3 leaflets, soft, fuzzy below and on stem. |
| Swamp privet (*Forestiera acuminata*). | Central portion of eastern half of United States. | Leaves opposite, elliptical, 2 to 4 inches long. Flowers without petals, small. |
| Fringetree (*Chionanthus virginica*). | Pennsylvania south to Florida and west to Texas. | Leaves opposite, thick, smooth, oblong. Flowers of 4 drooping white petals. |
| Devilwood (*Osmanthus americanus*). | South Atlantic and Gulf Coasts. | Resembling fringetree, except flowers small, tube-shaped, and leaves evergreen. |
| (Florida) devilwood (*Osmanthus floridana*). | Southern Florida. | Differs from *Osmanthus americanus* in hairy flower clusters and large yellow-green fruit. |
| Geiger-tree (*Cordia sebestena*). | Southern Florida (tropical). | Leaves 5 inches long. Flowers orange color. |
| Strongback (*Bourreria ovata*). | do. | Leaves oval. Flowers white. Fruit orange-red. |
| Anaqua (*Ehretia elliptica*). | Southern and western Texas. | Leaves oblong, downy below. Flowers tiny. |
| Fiddlewood (*Citharexylong fruiticosum*). | Southern Florida (tropical). | Leaves opposite, 3 to 4 inches long, narrow. Flowers in long cluster. |
| Blackwood (*Avicennia nitida*). | Gulf Coast to Louisiana. | Leaves opposite, leathery, evergreen, 6 inches long. |
| Potato tree (*Solanum verbascifolium*). | Southern Florida (tropical). | Leaves rank smelling, oval, 5 to 7 inches long. Small flowers. Yellow berries. |
| Common catalpa (*Catalpa bignonioides*). | Central portion of Southern States. | Leaves opposite, broadly heart-shaped, 4 to 6 inches long. Flowers in crowded clusters. Pods slender, thin-walled. |
| Hardy catalpa (*Catalpa speciosa*). | Central Mississippi River Basin. Widely planted for its straight trunk. | Leaves opposite, longer pointed than those of common catalpa. Flowers in few-flowered clusters. Pods thick-walled, relatively large in diameter. |
| Black calabash-tree (*Enallagma cucurbitina*). | Southern Florida (tropical). | Leaves 6 to 8 inches long, thick, shiny. Fruit fleshy. |
| Fever tree (*Pinckneya pubens*). | South Atlantic Coast (rare). | Leaves opposite. Fruit 2-celled capsule. |
| Princewood (*Exostema caribaeum*). | Southern Florida (tropical). | Flowers long, tubular. Heavy, handsome wood. |
| Buttonbush (*Cephalanthus occidentalis*). | Eastern United States, across southern New Mexico and Arizona to California. | Broadly elliptical leaves, opposite, on stout stems. Flowers in round heads or balls. |
| Seven-year apple (*Genipa clusiifolia*). | Southern Florida (tropical). | Leaves bunched near ends of branches. Flowers small, white, clustered. |
| (Name?) (*Hamelia patens*). | do. | Dry, pulpy. Leaves opposite. |
| Velvetseed (*Guettarda elliptica*). | do. | Leaves opposite, broadly oval, thin. |

**(Continued)**

# Appendix VI (Continued)

## SPECIES COMMON TO EASTERN UNITED STATES

| Name of Tree | Where the Tree Grows | Descriptive Notes |
|---|---|---|
| Roughleaf velvetseed (*Guettarda scabra*). | Southern Florida (tropical). | Leaves opposite, leathery, stiff, hairy, and harsh to touch. |
| Balsamo (*Psychotria nervosa*). | Northeastern Florida. | Leaves opposite, oval to lance-shaped. |
| (Name?) (*Psychotria undata*). | Southern Florida (tropical). | Leaves opposite, thin, elliptical. Fruit bright red. |
| Florida elder (*Sambucus simpsonii*). | Eastern Florida. | Leaves opposite, of 5 leaflets. Shiny black berries in clusters (cymes). |
| Nannyberry (*Viburnum lentago*). | Northeastern United States west into northern Rocky Mountains. | Leaves opposite, on winged leaf stems. Winter buds long-pointed. |
| Blackhaw (*Viburnum prunifolium*). | Connecticut to Georgia, narrowing belt to Kansas. | Leaves opposite, smooth leaf stems, flowers on short stalks. Winter buds blunt-pointed. |
| Rusty blackhaw (*Viburnum rufidulum*). | Virginia to Florida west to Kansas, Oklahoma, and Texas. | Leaves opposite. Winter buds and stems of early leaves reddish, fuzzy. |
| (Name?) (*Viburnum obovatum*). | Central Atlantic States. | Leaves thick, shiny. Flowers white. |
| Groundsel tree (*Baccharis halimifolia*). | Atlantic and Gulf Coasts (salty flats and marshes). | Leaves broadly wedge-shaped, resinous. Flowers on female (pistillate) tree showy white. |
| (Groundsel tree) (*Baccharis glomeruliflora*). | Coast region. North Carolina to Florida. | Flowers and fruit in much crowded clusters. Leaves not resinous. |
| Wild lime tree (*Xanthoxylum fagara*). | Tropical parts of Florida and Texas. | Leaves 3 to 4 inches long, of 7 to 9 rounded leaflets. Bark bitter, pungent. |
| Satinwood (*Xanthaxylum flavum*). | Southern Florida (tropical). | Leaves of 3 to 5 leaflets, evergreen. |
| Hercules' club (*Xanthoxylum coriaceum*). | do. | Leaves small, leathery, compound, without terminal leaflet, evergreen. Fruit in dense terminal cluster. |
| Baretta (*Helietta parvifolia*). | Texas (along the Rio Grande). | Leaves opposite, small, mostly three-foliate. |
| Hoptree (*Ptelea trifoliata*). | Eastern United States, Southern Rocky Mountain region. | Leaves three-divided, alternate on stem. Seed enclosed in thin, papery, circular wing. |
| Torchwood (*Amyris elemifera*). | Southern Florida (tropical). | Leaves usually opposite, of three leaflets. Fruit black. |
| Balsam torchwood (*Amyris balsamifera*). | do. | Leaves compound of 3 to 5 leaflets. Fruit with small, hard seed. |
| Paradise tree (*Simarouba glauca*). | do. | Leaves of 12 rounded leaflets. Stone fruit. |
| Bitterbush (*Picramnia pentandra*). | do. | Bark bitter, medicinal. Fruit fleshy. |
| (Name?) (*Alvaradoa amorphoides*). | do. | Tree with bitter juice. Fruit three-winged. |
| Bay cedar (*Suriana maritima*). | Coast of southern Florida (tropical). | Leaves fleshy, long, wedge-shaped. Flowers yellow. |
| Gumbo limbo (*Bursera simaruba*). | Southern Florida (tropical). | Large tree. Smooth bark. Leaves compound. |

**(Continued)**

## *Appendix VI (Continued)*

### SPECIES COMMON TO EASTERN UNITED STATES

| Name of Tree | Where the Tree Grows | Descriptive Notes |
|---|---|---|
| Mahogany (*Swietenia mahogani*). | Southern Florida (tropical) (nearly exterminated). | Tree producing true mahogany wood. Leaves of 6 to 8 leaflets. Fruit hood-shaped. |
| Guiana plum (*Drypetes lateriflora*). | Southern Florida (tropical). | Leaves pointed and narrow. Fruit red, in small clusters. |
| Big Guiana plum (*Drypetes diversifolia*). | Florida Keys (tropical). | Leaves hold for 2 years, broadly elliptical, thick. Fruit white, 1 inch long. |
| Crabwood (*Gymnanthes lucida*). | Southern Florida (tropical). | Fruit scarce, small, nearly black. |
| Manchineel (*Hippomane mancinella*). | do. | Sap very poisonous. Apple-shaped fruit with a stone. |
| Savia (*Savia bahamensis*). | do. | Leaves evergreen. Flowers green, of two kinds. |
| American smoketree (chittamwood) (*Cotinus americanus*). | Kentucky to western Texas. | Leaves rounded, scarlet or orange in fall. Fruit on stalks with purple hairs. |
| Poisonwood (*Metopium toxiferum*). | Shores and hammocks of southern Florida (tropical). | Bark exuding gum with caustic properties. Leaves compound, borne in terminal clusters. |
| Staghorn sumac (*Rhus hirta*). | Northeastern United States, south in mountains. | Leaves of 11 to 31 leaflets. Stems and branchlets velvety. Fruit red, dense head. |
| Dwarf sumac (*Rhus copallina*). | Eastern half of United States. | Leaves of 9 to 21 leaflets. Leaf stalks winged. Fruit in open head. |
| Poison sumac (*Rhus vernix*). | Much of eastern United States. | Leaves of 7 to 13 leaflets with scarlet midribs. Fruit white, in open clusters in leaf axils. |
| Texas pistache (*Pistacia texana*). | Southwestern Texas. | Leaves compound. Flowers tiny, clustered. |
| Swamp ironwood (leatherwood) (*Cyrilla racemiflora*). | Coast region, Virginia to Texas and somewhat inland. | Leaves narrow, clustered near ends of branches. Fruit small in long, slender clusters. |
| Titi (*Cliftonia monophylla*). | Coast, South Carolina to Texas. | Forming "titi" swamps. Leaves shiny. Fruit winged. |
| Holly (*Ilex opaca*). | Southeastern United States, north along coast to Massachusetts. | Leaves evergreen, stiff, spiny. Flowers of 2 kinds on separate trees. Fruit (on female tree) red berry. Christmas evergreen. |
| Dahoon (*Ilex cassine*). | Coast, South Carolina to Louisiana. | Leaves narrow, smooth on edges. Fruit small, red. |
| Krugs holly (*Ilex krugiana*). | Southern Florida (tropical). | Leaves oval, pointed. Fruit brownish purple. |
| Yaupon (*Ilex vomitoria*). | Southeastern Coast region, Virginia to Texas. | Leaves oblong-elliptical, coarsely toothed, thick, shiny, used for tea. Berries red. |
| Winterberry (Christmas berry) (*Ilex decidua*). | Southeastern States, except in mountains. | Leaves dropping in fall. Berries showy, orange or scarlet. |
| Mountain holly (*Ilex montana*). | Tree size only in Great Smoky Mountains of North Carolina and Tennessee. | Leaves dropping in fall, rounded at base, pointed, toothed, up to 5 inches long. Fruit, red berry. |

**(Continued)**

## Appendix VI (Continued)

### SPECIES COMMON TO EASTERN UNITED STATES

| Name of Tree | Where the Tree Grows | Descriptive Notes |
|---|---|---|
| Eastern wahoo (burningbush) (*Euonymus atropurpureus*). | Northeastern States westward, to Montana, south in central Mississippi River Basin. | Leaves broad in middle, long-pointed, toothed. Fruit 4-lobed, fleshy, purple. |
| False boxwood (*Gyminda latifolia*). | Southern Florida (tropical). | Leaves opposite, rounded, thick, finely toothed. |
| (Name?) (*Rhacoma crossopetalum*). | do. | Leaves alternate or opposite. Stone fruit. |

### SPECIES COMMON TO WESTERN UNITED STATES

| | | |
|---|---|---|
| Whitebark pine (*Pinus albicaulis*). | Northern Rocky Mountains, eastern Washington to California. | Bark usually thin. Leaves 5 in cluster 1 to 3 inches long, persisting for 5 to 8 years. Small tree. |
| Mexican white pine (*Pinus strobiformis*). | Western Texas to southeastern Arizona. | Leaves 5 in cluster, slender, 4 to 6 inches long. Cone scales turning backward. |
| Parry pinon (*Pinus parryana*). | Southern California. | Leaves usually 4 in cluster. Cone small, irregular. Small tree. |
| Mexican pinon (*Pinus cembroides*). | Central and southern Arizona, western Texas. | Leaves 2 or 3 in cluster, 1 to 2 inches long. Cone much like above. Small tree. |
| Pinon (nut pine) (*Pinus edulis*). | Dry foothills of southern Rocky Mountain region, Utah to California. | Leaves mostly 2 in cluster, 1 to 2 inches long. Cone 1 to 2 inches long. Seeds large, edible. |
| Singleleaf pinon (*Pinus monophylla*). | Utah, northern Arizona, central and southern California. | Leaves occurring singly (occasionally 2), 1 to 2 inches long. Cone irregular. Seeds edible. Sprawling tree. |
| Foxtail pine (*Pinus balfouriana*). | High mountains of northern and central California. | Leaves in fives, thick, stiff, dark green, 1 inch long. Cone with thick scales. |
| Bristlecone pine (*Pinus aristata*). | High southern Rocky Mountains, Utah to southern California. | Leaves in fives, 1 to 2 inches long. Cone with long, slender prickles. |
| Torry pine (*Pinus torreyana*). | San Diego County and Santa Rosa Island, Calif. Range very limited. | Leaves in fives, clustered at ends of branches, 9 to 12 inches long. Cone with thick scales. |
| Arizona pine (*Pinus arizonica*). | Southern parts of New Mexico and Arizona. | Leaves in threes to fives, stout, 5 to 7 inches long. Cone about 2 inches long. |
| Ponderosa pine (western yellow pine) (*Pinus ponderosa*). | Mountains of western United States. Often forms extensive pure stands in southern Rockies. | Leaves in clusters of 3, tufted, 5 to 10 inches long. Cone on short stem (if any), 3 to 6 inches long, with prickles. Important timber tree. |
| Apache pine (Arizona longleaf pine) (*Pinus apacheca*). | Central and southwestern New Mexico, southern Arizona. | Leaves very long (8 to 15 inches), dark green, stout. Cone 1-sided. |
| Jeffrey pine (*Pinus jeffreyi*). | Southern Oregon south through California. | Leaves 5 to 9 inches long, in threes, stiff. Cone 6 to 15 inches long, with large seeds. |
| Chihuahua pine (*Pinus leiophylla*). | Mountains of Arizona, southwestern New Mexico. | Leaves in threes, slender, gray-green. Cone small, ripening in 3 years. |

(Continued)

## *Appendix VI (Continued)*

### SPECIES COMMON TO WESTERN UNITED STATES

| Name of Tree | Where the Tree Grows | Descriptive Notes |
|---|---|---|
| Lodgepole pine (*Pinus contorta*). | Mountains of western United States; most abundant in northern Rockies. | Leaves in twos, 1 to 3 inches long. Cone remaining closed for several years. Tree used for crossties and poles. |
| Digger pine (*Pinus sabiniana*). | Foothills of the Sierra Nevadas in central California. | Leaves in threes, blue-green, drooping, 8 to 12 inches long. Cone large, sharp, spiny, with edible seeds or nuts. |
| Coulter pine (*Pinus coulteri*). | Mountains of southern California (scattering). | Leaves in threes, thick, dark blue-green, 7 to 10 inches long. Cone is largest of all native pines, 10 to 14 inches long, with strong curved spines. |
| Monterey pine (*Pinus radiata*). | Narrow strip of coast in central California. | Leaves mostly in threes. Cone often remaining closed on trees for many years. |
| Knob-cone pine (*Pinus attenuata*). | Dry mountain slopes, Oregon and California. | Leaves pale green, 3 in bundle. Cone 1-sided at the base. |
| Bishop pine (*Pinus muricata*). | Coast mountains of California. | Leaves in twos, 3 to 5 inches long. Cone spiny, often staying closed for years. |
| Western larch (*Larix occidentalis*). | Mountains of northwestern United States. | Leaves 1 inch long, closely crowded, falling in winter. Cone with bracts extending beyond scales. Important for timber and crossties. |
| Alpine larch (*Larix lyallii*). | High northern Rocky Mountains. | Resembling above except leaves 4-angled. |
| White spruce (*Picea glauca*). The common western variety is *Albertiana*. | Northern Rocky Mountain region, including the Black Hills (S. Dak.) and Washington. Alaska. | Leaves 4-sided, pale blue-green, sharp. Cone scale rounded. |
| Englemann spruce (*Picea englemannii*). | Extensive over Rocky Mountain region; Washington and Oregon. | Leaves 4-sided, 1 inch long. Cone brown, shiny, with thin notched scales. Pulpwood and timber tree. |
| Blue spruce (*Picea pungens*). | Central Rocky Mountains. | Leaves stiff, sharp-pointed, curved, blue-green. |
| Sitka spruce (*Picea sitchensis*). | Coast region of northern California to Washington. Alaska. | Leaves flattened, sharp. Cone with scales notched toward ends. Important timber tree. |
| Weeping spruce (*Picea breweriana*). | High mountains near timber line extreme northern California and southwestern Oregon. | Leaves flattened, blunt. Branchlets hairy, light brown. |
| Western hemlock (*Tsuga heterophylla*). | Pacific Coast and northern Rocky Mountains. | Leaves flat, blunt, shiny, twisted on branch to form two rows. Cone 1 inch long, without stem. Important timber tree. |
| Mountain hemlock (*Tsuga mertensiana*). | High altitudes northwestern United States. | Leaves rounded or grooved above, curved. Cone with short bracts. |
| Douglas fir (*Pseudotsuga taxifolia*). | Western United States (except Nevada). Largest size and most abundant in coast forests of western Washington and Oregon. | Leaves straight, flat, rounded near end, soft, flexible, about 1 inch long. Cone 2 to 4 inches long with bracts extended between the scales. Up to 380 feet in height. Important timber tree. |

**(Continued)**

## Appendix VI (Continued)

### SPECIES COMMON TO WESTERN UNITED STATES

| Name of Tree | Where the Tree Grows | Descriptive Notes |
|---|---|---|
| Bigcone spruce (*Pseudotsuga macrocarpa*). | Mountain slopes of southern California. | Resembling the above, but cone 4 to 6 inches long. |
| Alpine fir (*Abies lasiocarpa*). | High Rocky Mountains; west into Oregon and Washington. Alaska. | Leaves flat and grooved above, pale green, 1 inch long. Cone purple. Bark hard. Note that cones on all true firs stand erect on branches. |
| Corkbark fir (*Abies arizonica*). | Highest mountain tops of Arizona and New Mexico. | Bark soft, corky, ashy white. Leaves and cones resembling above. |
| Lowland white fir (*Abies grandis*). | Northern Rocky Mountains, coast forest south to California. | Leaves flat, dark green, shiny above. Cone green. Pulpwood tree. |
| White fir (*Abies concolor*). | Central and southern Rockies, southwestern Oregon to southern California. Of all firs, it grows in warmest and driest climate. | Same as above, except leaves pale blue-green or whitish, and often 2 to 3 inches long. Cone 3 to 4 inches long, purple. Pulpwood tree. |
| Silver fir (*Abies amabilis*). | Coast forest of Washington and Oregon, Cascade Mountains. | Leaves flat, dark green, shiny, pointing forward on sterile branches. Cone deep purple, with broad scales. Pulpwood tree. |
| Noble fir (*Abies nobilis*). | Coast mountains, Washington to California; Cascade Mountains of Washington and Oregon. | Leaves often 4-sided, blue-green, smooth. Cone purple, bracts much longer than cone scales, green. Pulpwood tree. |
| California red fir (*Abies magnifica*). | Sierra Nevadas of California, Cascade Mountains of southern Oregon. | Leaves on sterile branches, 4-sided. Cone purplish brown, slender tips of bracts same length as scales. Pulpwood tree. |
| Bristlecone fir (*Abies venusta*). | Santa Lucia Mountains, Monterey County, Calif. | Cone bracts many times longer than cone scales. |
| Sierra redwood, or big tree (*Sequoia washingtoniana*) (*S. gigantea*). | Western slopes of the Sierra Nevadas in central eastern California. | Leaves tiny, scalelike. Cone 2 to 3 inches long, much larger than those of coast redwood, ripening in 2 years. Bark very thick. Up to 320 feet in height and 35 feet in diameter. Trees mostly protected from cutting. |
| Coast redwood, or redwood (*Sequoia sempervirens*). | Low mountains of Pacific Coast, from southern Oregon to Monterey County, Calif. | Leaves small, ½ inch long, thin, flat, spreading in 2 ranks. Cone small, about 1 inch long, ripening in 1 year. Up to 364 feet in height and about 25 feet in diameter. Important timber tree. A tree logged in Humboldt County, California, scaled 361,366 board feet of lumber. |
| Incense cedar (*Libocedrus decurrens*). | Oregon (Mount Hood) through the mountains of California. | Resinous, aromatic tree with scaly bark. Leaves variable, up to ½ inch long; cone ½ inch long, maturing in 1 season. Wood used for making pencils. |
| Western red cedar (*Thuja plicata*). | Coast of Washington, Oregon, northern California; inland to Montana. Alaska. | Leaves and fruit smaller than those of incense cedar. Soft, reddish-brown wood, used for lumber and shingles. |

(Continued)

## *Appendix VI (Continued)*

### SPECIES COMMON TO WESTERN UNITED STATES

| Name of Tree | Where the Tree Grows | Descriptive Notes |
| --- | --- | --- |
| Monterey cypress (*Cupressus macrocarpa*). | Coast of southern California. | Leaves scalelike, dark green, ¼ to ½ inch long, dull pointed. |
| Sargent cypress (*Cupressus sargentii*). | Coast region of central California. | Leaves scalelike, dark green, glandular-pitted. |
| Gowen cypress (*Cupressus goveniana*). | Mendocino and Monterey Counties, Calif. | Leaves dark green, sharp-pointed. Cones ½ inch diameter; seed dark. |
| Macnab cypress (*Cupressus macnabiana*). | Southwestern Oregon and northwestern California. | Cone ½ to 1 inch in diameter, often with whitish bloom. |
| Tecate cypress (*Cupressus forbesii*). | San Diego County, Calif. | Leaves pale bluish-green. Bark smooth, shiny. Branchlets bright red. |
| Arizona cypress (*Cupressus arizonica*). | Mountains of southern Arizona and New Mexico. | Leaves scalelike, pale bluish-green. Bark separating into narrow fibers. |
| Smooth cypress (*Cupressus glabra*). | Mountains of southern Arizona. | Differing slightly from the above. |
| Alaska cedar (yellow or Sitka cypress) (*Chamaecyparis nootkatensis*). | Oregon and Washington. | Bark thin. Branchlets stout. Leaves bluish-green, scalelike. Wood fragrant. Important timber tree. |
| Port Orford cedar (*Chamaecyparis lawsoniana*). | Coast, southern Oregon and northern California. | Bark thick. Branchlets slender. Wood fragrant and easily worked. Important timber tree. |
| Dwarf juniper (*Juniperus communis*). | Across northern United States. Rocky Mountain and northern Pacific regions. | Leaves short, ½ inch long. Sweet aromatic berries, ripening in 3 seasons. |
| California juniper (*Juniperus californica*). | Mountains and foothills of central and southern California. | Berries reddish brown, ripening in 1 season. Leaves in clusters of 3. |
| Utah juniper (*Juniperus utahensis*). | Desert regions, Wyoming to New Mexico. | Bark falling in strips. Berry large, ripening in 1 season. Leaves opposite. |
| Alligator juniper (*Juniperus pachyphloea*). | Desert ranges Texas west to Arizona. | Bark in nearly square plates. Berry large, ripening in 2 seasons. |
| Western juniper (*Juniperus occidentalis*). | Sierra Nevadas of California and Cascade Mountains of Oregon. | Berries dark blue, small, maturing in 1 season. Bark thin. Leaves rough. Heavy branches. Tree up to 10 feet in diameter and 60 feet in height. |
| One-seeded juniper (cedro) (*Juniperus monosperma*). | Extensive areas over foothills of Rocky Mountains. | Berry small, 1-seeded. Branchlets and leaves very small; leaves rough. Berries ripening in 1 season. |
| Rocky Mountain red cedar (*Juniperus scopulorum*). | Rocky Mountains. | Berries ripening in 2 seasons. Wood red, fragrant, resembling eastern red cedar. |
| California nutmeg (*Tumion californicum*). | Coast Mountains and the Sierra Nevadas of California. | Leaves over 1 inch long, shiny. Fruit dark purple, 1 inch long. All of tree pungent and aromatic. |
| Pacific yew (*Taxus brevifolia*). | Pacific Coast region east to northern Montana. Alaska. | Leaves less than 1 inch long, holding on for 5 to 12 years. Fruit nearly enclosed in thick cup. |
| California palm (*Washingtonia filifera*). | Southern California. | Leafstalks armed with spines. Fruit berrylike. Leaves fan-shaped. Widely planted for ornament. |

**(Continued)**

## Appendix VI (Continued)

### SPECIES COMMON TO WESTERN UNITED STATES

| Name of Tree | Where the Tree Grows | Descriptive Notes |
|---|---|---|
| Mohave yucca (*Yucca mohavensis*). | Northwestern Arizona across Mohave Desert to Pacific Coast. | Flower part (style) short. |
| Spanish bayonet (*Yucca torreyi*). | Western Texas to Arizona. | Leaves smooth, 1 to 2 feet long. |
| Spanish bayonet (*Yucca schottii*). | Southern Arizona. | Leaves 2 to 3 feet long, 1 to 2 inches wide, concave, smooth, light green. |
| Joshua tree (*Yucca brevifolia*). | Southwestern Utah through Mohave Desert to California. | Leaves stiff, blue-green, sharply toothed, pointed, crowded in dense clusters. |
| Soapweed (*Yucca elata*). | Texas to southern Arizona. | Flower stalks 3 to 7 feet long. |
| Little walnut (*Juglans rupestris*). | Texas, New Mexico, Arizona. | Leaves small, of 9 to 23 leaflets. Nuts grooved, up to 1 inch in diameter. |
| California walnut (*Juglans californica*). | Southern California, coast region. | Leaves 8 inches long, of 11 to 15 leaflets. Nuts less than 1 inch in diameter. |
| Hinds walnut (*Juglans kindsii*). | Central California, coast region. | Leaves compound. Nuts up to 2 inches diameter. |
| Pacific wax myrtle (*Myrica californica*). | Coast region, California to Washington. | Leaves sharply toothed, narrow at base, shiny. Fruit waxy, dark purple. |
| Aspen (quaking aspen) (*Populus tremuloides*) (varieties: *Vancouveriana* and *Aurea*). | Northeastern and all western United States. | Leaves broad, finely toothed, leafstalks flat and long. |
| Balsam poplar (Balm-of-Gilead) (*Populus balsamifera*). | Across northern United States. | Leaves dull-toothed, leafstalks round. Winter buds ½ inch long, shiny, resinous. |
| Black cottonwood (*Populus trichocarpa*). | California Mountains and foothills. | Leaves broad, wedge-shaped at base, whitish below. Buds resinous. |
| Lanceleaf cottonwood (*Populus acuminata*). | Rocky Mountains and foothills. | Leaves long-pointed, narrow, 3 inches long, on long stalks. Buds resinous. |
| Narrowleaf cottonwood (*Populus angustifolia*). | Rocky Mountains and foothills. | Leaves 2 to 3 inches long, narrow, tapering, sharp-pointed. Buds very resinous. |
| Arizona cottonwood (*Populus arizonica*). | Southern New Mexico and Arizona. | Leaves with flattened stalks, thick, coarsely toothed. |
| Cottonwood (*Populus sargentii*). | Rocky Mountain foothills to Plains. | Resembles the above species. |
| (Fremont) cottonwood (*Populus fremontii*). | States west of the Rocky Mountains. | Leaves coarsely toothed, 2 to 2½ inches long and broad. Leafstems flattened. |
| (Wislizenus) cottonwood (*Populus wizlizenii*). | Texas, New Mexico, western Colorado. | Leaves broadly delta-shaped (triangular), coarsely toothed, thick, firm. |
| MacDougal cottonwood (*Populus macdougalii*). | Southern Arizona, southeastern California. | Leaves 1 to 2 inches long, square at base, toothed. Branchlets fuzzy. |
| Dudley willow (*Salix gooddingii*). | Western Texas to California, north in State. | Branchlets yellow-green. Fruit hairy. |
| Peachleaf willow (*Salix amygdaloides*). | Northern United States, south in Rocky Mountains. | Leaves long, pointed (peachleaf), pale below. |
| Red willow (*Salix laevigata*). | Arizona, Utah, California. | Fruit (capsules) on long stalks. |
| Willow (*Salix bonplandiana toumeyi*). | Arizona and New Mexico. | Fruit (capsule) short-stalked. |

**(Continued)**

## *Appendix VI (Continued)*

### SPECIES COMMON TO WESTERN UNITED STATES

| Name of Tree | Where the Tree Grows | Descriptive Notes |
| --- | --- | --- |
| Western black willow (*Salix lasiandra*). | Central Rocky Mountains. Pacific Coast. | Leaves whitish below, stems with glands. |
| Sandbar willow (*Salix sessilifolia*). | Western Washington and Oregon. | Stamens 2. Leaves small, with stems. |
| Narrowleaf willow (*Salix exigua*). | Western United States. | Leaves white, silky below. |
| Yewleaf willow (*Salix taxifolia*). | Western Texas to Arizona. | Leaves 1 inch long. |
| White willow (*Salix lasiolepis*). | California, southern Arizona. | Leaves slightly toothed, pale below. |
| (Diamond) willow (*Salix mackenzieana*). | Northern Rocky Mountains, California. | Leaves 4 inches long, narrow-pointed. |
| (Bebbs) willow (*Salix bebbiana*). | Northern United States, south in Rocky Mountains. | Leaves elliptical, silvery white below. |
| Scouler willow (*Salix scouleriana*). | Western United States. | Leaves broadest beyond middle. |
| Willow (*Salix hookeriana*). | Oregon and Washington. | Leaves broadly oval, fuzzy beneath. |
| Silky willow (*Salix sitchensis*). | Pacific Coast States. | Leaves densely silky below. |
| Western hop-hornbeam (*Ostrya knowltonii*). | Colorado River in Arizona and Utah. | Leaves 1 to 2 inches long, broad, rounded, sharply toothed. Fruit hoplike. |
| Paper birch (*Betula papyrifera*). | Northern United States, across the continent. | Bark pure white to light gray, separating into thin sheets. Leaves thick, rounded at base. |
| Red birch (*Betula fontinalis*). | Rocky Mountains, Pacific Coast. | Bark firm, shiny. Leaves small. |
| Sitka alder (*Alnus sinuata*). | Northwestern Coast States, Montana. Alaska. | Flowers opening with or after the leaves. All alders have two kinds of flowers (aments) on same tree. |
| Red alder (*Alnus rubra*). | Pacific Coast. Alaska. | Flowers opening before leaves. |
| Mountain alder (*Alnus tenuifolia*). | Rocky Mountain region. | Flowering as above. Leaves thin. |
| White alder (*Alnus rhombifolia*). | Idaho and Pacific States. | Leaves broadly oval, rounded at ends. |
| Mexican alder (*Alnus oblongifolia*). | Arizona, southern New Mexico. | Leaves oblong and pointed. |
| Golden chinkapin (*Castanopsis chrysophylla*). | Pacific Coast region, south to southern California. | Leaves thick, evergreen. Nut in prickly golden burr, ripe in 2 seasons. |
| Tan oak (*Lithocarpus densiflora*). | California into southern Oregon. | Acorn set in flat, hairy cup. Leaves toothed, evergreen, heavily veined. Acorn ripening in 2 seasons. |
| California black oak (*Quercus kelloggii*). | Western Oregon, through mountains of California. | Acorn in deep, thin cup. (Beginning of the black oak group whose leaves have pointed lobes, if any, and whose acorns require 2 seasons to mature.) |
| Whiteleaf oak (*Quercus hypoleuca*). | Western Texas to Arizona. | Leaves hairy below, narrow, acorn in fuzzy cup. |
| Highland live oak (*Quercus wislizenii*). | California, lower mountain slopes and foothills. | Leaves thick, shiny, dark green. Acorn deeply enclosed in cup. |

**(Continued)**

# Appendix VI (Continued)

## SPECIES COMMON TO WESTERN UNITED STATES

| Name of Tree | Where the Tree Grows | Descriptive Notes |
| --- | --- | --- |
| Coast live oak (*Quercus pricei*). | Coast of Monterey County, Calif. | Leaves similar to above. Acorn with saucer-shaped cup. |
| Coast live oak (*Quercus agrifolia*). | Coastal mountains and valleys of California. | Leaves evergreen, thick, with sharp teeth, dull green, 1 to 3 inches long. |
| Canyon live oak (*Quercus chrysolepis*). | Southern Oregon, California, southern Arizona. | Leaves long, thick, leathery, evergreen. Acorns 2 inches long, in densely hairy cup. |
| Huckleberry oak (*Quercus vaccinifolia*). | High Sierra Nevadas of California. | Leaves small, with smooth margins. Acorn cup mossy. (Often low shrub.) |
| Island live oak (*Quercus tomentella*). | Islands off coast of southern California. | Leaves 3 or 4 inches long, broadly elliptical, toothed, thick, hairy below, evergreen. |
| Emory oak (*Quercus emoryi*). | Mountains, western Texas to southern Arizona. | Leaves very shiny, flat, stiff. Acorns shiny black, much used for food. (Beginning of white oak group, whose leaves have rounded lobes, if any, and whose acorns require only 1 season to mature.) |
| California scrub oak (*Quercus dumosa*). | California, Sierra Nevadas and Coast Mountains. | Leaves mostly 1 inch long, with shallow lobes. Acorn broad, in deep cup. |
| Netleaf oak (*Quercus reticulata*). | Southern parts of New Mexico and Arizona. | Leaves coarsely and deeply veined, yellow fuzzy below. Acorn on long stems. |
| Toumey oak (*Quercus toumeyi*). | Southeastern Arizona. | Leaves tiny. Acorn in thin cup. |
| Arizona white oak (*Quercus arizonica*). | Southern New Mexico and Arizona. | Leaves broad, thick, firm, blue-green. Acorn striped, in deep cup. |
| Mexican blue oak (*Quercus oblongifolia*). | Western Texas to southern Arizona. | Leaves elliptical, blue-green. Acorn small, in shallow cup. |
| Evergreen white oak (*Quercus engelmannii*). | Southern California, belt along the coast. | Leaves resembling the above, or with coarse teeth on edge. |
| California blue oak (*Quercus douglasii*). | Southern half of California, low mountains. | Leaves blue-green, mostly 2 to 5 inches long, deeply notched or lobed. Acorn broad above base. Good-sized tree. |
| Valley white oak (*Quercus lobata*). | Western and southern California. | Leaves deeply lobed. Acorn conical, long, in rather deep cup. |
| Oregon white oak (*Quercus garryana*). | Pacific Coast region south to central California. | Leaves 4 to 6 inches long, lobed, smooth above, hairy below. |
| Rocky Mountain white oak (*Quercus utahensis*). | Central and southern Rocky Mountain region. | Leaves 3 to 7 inches long, regularly lobed. Acorn with half-round cup. Common, abundant oak. |
| Rocky Mountain white oak (*Quercus leptophylla*). | Colorado and New Mexico. | Leaves resembling above, but smooth below. Acorns small. Large spreading tree. |
| Wavyleaf shin oak (*Quercus undulata*). | Colorado, New Mexico, Arizona, and a little northward. | Leaves lyre-shaped, lobed. Acorn set in shallow scaly or warty cup. Small tree. |
| Palo blanco (*Celtis reticulata*). | Oklahoma and Texas to southern Arizona. | Leaves green on lower surface. Berry orange-red. |

(Continued)

## Appendix VI (Continued)

### SPECIES COMMON TO WESTERN UNITED STATES

| Name of Tree | Where the Tree Grows | Descriptive Notes |
|---|---|---|
| Douglas hackberry (*Celtis douglasii*). | Rocky Mountain region, Canada to Mexico. | Leaves ovate, heart-shaped at base, coarsely toothed, rough above. |
| (Western) mulberry (*Morus microphylla*). | Texas, southern parts of New Mexico and Arizona. | Leaves small, rounded, coarsely toothed. Fruit nearly black, sweet. |
| California-laurel (*Umbellularia californica*). | Oregon and through foothills of California. | Leaves long, elliptical, 2 to 5 inches, evergreen. Fruit rounded, 1 inch long, in clusters. |
| California sycamore (*Platanus racemosa*). | Southern half of California. | Fruit balls in string of 3 to 5. Leaves with 3 to 5 pointed lobes. |
| Arizona sycamore (*Platanus wrightii*). | Arizona, southwestern New Mexico. | Leaves with 5 to 7 deep lobes. Fruit balls in string 6 to 8 inches long. |
| (Name?) (*Vauquelinia californica*). | Southern New Mexico and Arizona. | Leaves narrow, toothed, hairy beneath. |
| Santa Cruz ironwood (*Lyonothamnus floribundus*). | Islands off coast of southern California. | Leaves willowlike, or deeply divided (pinnae), about 4 to 8 inches long. |
| Oregon crab apple (*Malus fusca*). | Northern California, western Oregon, and Washington. Alaska. | Leaves broadly oval, sharply toothed. Fruit oblong, yellow-green to nearly red. |
| Pacific mountain-ash (*Sorbus sitchensis*). | California, Oregon, Washington, Idaho. Alaska. | Leaflets shiny, thin, narrow. Fruit red. |
| Alpine mountain-ash (*Sorbus occidentalis*). | Near timber line in northern Rocky Mountains. Alaska. | Flowers fragrant. Berries pear-shaped, purplish. |
| Christmasberry (*Photinia salicifolia*). | Southern half of California. | Leaves elliptical, sharply but finely toothed, shiny, evergreen. Scarlet berries in clusters. |
| Pacific serviceberry (*Amelanchier florida*). | Rocky Mountains to north Pacific Coast region. Alaska. | Leaves rounded, coarsely toothed above middle. Small clusters of blue berries. |
| Willow thorn (*Crataegus saligna*). | Colorado, in mountains, valleys, and foothills. | Leaves oval or squared, 1 to 2 inches long, finely toothed. Fruit very shiny, blue-black. Small tree. |
| Black hawthorn (*Crataegus douglasii*). | Pacific Coast region south to California. Northern Rocky Mountains to Wyoming. | Leaves thick, shiny, squared, notched, and finely toothed. Many short stout spines. Clusters of black berries. Small tree. |
| Thorn (*Crataegus rivularis*). | Rocky Mountains. | Leaves without lobes, thinner than above, pointed, dull green. Spines few. |
| Bigleaf mountain-mahogany (*Cercocarpus traskiae*). | Santa Catalina Island, Calif. | Leaves rounded, coarsely toothed toward end, woolly below. Flowers in cluster. Flowers singly on stem. (All mahoganies have long silky threads to the seeds.) Small tree. |
| Curlleaf mountain-mahogany (*Cercocarpus ledifolius*). | Northern Rocky Mountains south to Colorado. Eastern and southern California. | Leaves small, narrow, up to 1 inch long, pointed at both ends. Small tree. |
| Birchleaf mountain-mahogany (*Cercocarpus betuloides*). | Coast Mountains of California. | Leaves small, 1 inch long, finely toothed, wider beyond middle. Flowers in cluster. Small tree. |

(Continued)

## Appendix VI (Continued)

### SPECIES COMMON TO WESTERN UNITED STATES

| Name of Tree | Where the Tree Grows | Descriptive Notes |
|---|---|---|
| Alderleaf mountain-mahogany (*Cercocarpus alnifolius*). | Santa Catalina and Santa Cruz Islands. | Leaves oval, long toothed, smooth below. Flowers on long stems in cluster. Small tree. |
| Hairy mountain-mahogany (*Cercocarpus paucidentatus*). | Western Texas, New Mexico, Arizona. | Leaves 1 inch long, broader toward end, smooth or slightly toothed. Flowers singly. Small tree. |
| Cliffrose (*Cowania stansburiana*). | Colorado, Utah, and South. | Long feathery thread from each seed. |
| Wild plum (hog or red plum) (*Prunus americana*). | Eastern United States, central and southern Rocky Mountains. | Leaves oval, sharply toothed, 3 to 4 inches long. Fruit 1 inch in diameter, bright red. Usually only a shrub in this region. |
| Pacific plum (*Prunus subcordata*). | Central Oregon to California. | Leaves broadly ovate. Fruit red or yellow. |
| Bitter cherry (*Prunus emarginata*). | Rocky Mountains and westward. | Fruit small, bright red, shiny, bitter. |
| Pin cherry (*Prunus pennsylvanica*) (variety *saximontana*). | Across northern United States, northern Rocky Mountains to Colorado. | Leaves long, pointed, finely toothed. Flowers in clusters (umbels), cherries red, each on long stem, spreads rapidly on burned-over forest lands. |
| Western choke cherry (*Prunus demissa*). | Southwestern New Mexico, southern California. | Leaves often heart-shaped at base, and fine-hairy below. |
| Black choke cherry (*Prunus melanocarpa*). | Southern Rocky Mountains. | Leaves thicker and fruit darker than above. |
| Southwestern black cherry (*Prunus virens*). | Western Texas, New Mexico, Arizona. | Leaves small, elliptical, finely toothed. Fruit purplish black, in long clusters. |
| Hollyleaf cherry (*Prunus ilicifolia*). | Coast mountains of southern California. | Leaves broadly oval, coarsely and sharply toothed, leathery. Fruit dark purple. |
| Catalina cherry (*Prunus lyonii*). | Coast islands, including Santa Catalina, Calif. | Leaves thick, shiny, slightly toothed. Fruit purple to nearly black. |
| (Name?) (*Lysiloma watsoni*). | Southern Arizona. | Leaves small of leaflets, densely hairy. Flowers in round head. Pods 1 inch wide. |
| Catclaw (una-de-gato) (*Acacia greggii*). | Western Texas, southern New Mexico, Arizona. | Leaves small, of 1 to 3 pairs of leaf clusters (pinnae). Pods flat, twisted, 2 to 4 inches long. |
| Mimosa (*Leucaena retusa*). | Southern parts of Texas and New Mexico. | Leaves featherlike compound of many leaflets. |
| Mesquite (*Prosopis juliflora*). | Texas, Oklahoma, New Mexico, Arizona, California. | Leaves doubly compound (mostly 2 pinnae) each with 12 to 22 leaflets. Pods flattened, in small clusters, remaining closed. |
| Honey mesquite (*Prosopis glandulosa*). | Kansas to California and southward. | Leaves generally similar to above, 9 inches long, leaflets often 2 inches long. |
| Velvet mesquite (*Prosopis velutina*). | Southern Arizona. | Leaves similarly compound, 5 to 6 inches long, finely hairy. |
| Screwbean (*Strombocarpa odorata*). | Western Texas to California, Utah, Nevada. | Leaves smaller than above. Pods small, spirally twisted or screwed. |

**(Continued)**

## Appendix VI (Continued)

### SPECIES COMMON TO WESTERN UNITED STATES

| Name of Tree | Where the Tree Grows | Descriptive Notes |
|---|---|---|
| California redbud (*Cercis occidentalis*). | Coast ranges and lower slopes of Sierras, California, Utah. | Leaves broad, rounded, heart-shaped at base. Flowers rose color. |
| Jerusalem-thorn (*Parkinsonia aculeata*). | Texas, Arizona. | Leaflets 50 to 60, small. Spiny stems. |
| Littleleaf horsebean (*Parkinsonia microphylla*). | Southern parts of Arizona and California. | Leaves tiny, of few pairs of leaflets. Flowers pale yellow. |
| Paloverde (*Cercidium torreyanum*). | Southern parts of Arizona and California. | Leaves 1 inch long, of few, tiny leaflets. Branches with yellow-green bark. |
| Mescalbean (*Sophora secundiflora*). | Southern parts of Texas and New Mexico. | Leaves 4 to 6 inches long, of 7 to 9 rounded leaflets. Pods narrowed between seeds. |
| Coralbean (*Sophora affinis*). | Southern California east to Mississippi River. | Leaves of 13 to 19 leaflets. Pods bearded. |
| (Name?) (*Eysenhardtia polystachia*). | Western Texas to Arizona. | Leaves of 20 to 46 leaflets, terminal. |
| Smokethorn (*Parosela spinosa*). | Deserts of Arizona, California. | Branches spiny. Leaves soon dropping. |
| New Mexican locust (*Robinia neo-mexicana*). | Southern Rocky Mountain region. | Leaves of 15 to 21 broad leaflets. Flowers rose to white. Pods 3 inches long. |
| Tesota (*Olneya tesota*). | Deserts of Arizona, California. | Leaves tiny, compound. Flowers purple. |
| Hoptree (*Ptelea trifoliata*). | Eastern United States, southern Rocky Mountains. | Leaves 3-divided, alternate on stem. Seed enclosed in thin, papery, circular wing. |
| (Name?) (*Bursera microphylla*). | Arizona, southern California. | Leaves of tiny leaflets. Fruit 3-angled. |
| Mahogany sumach (*Rhus integrifolia*). | Coast region of southern California. | Leaves not compound, edges prickly. Thick fruit in terminal clusters. |
| Laurel sumach (*Rhus laurina*). | Arizona, southern California. | Leaves not compound, evergreen, aromatic. |
| Canotia (*Canotia holacantha*). | do. | Tree leafless. Twigs ending in spines. |
| Bigleaf maple (*Acer macrophyllum*). | Coast of California, Oregon, and Washington. Alaska. | Leaves opposite, 10 inches across, on long stems, 3 large and 2 small lobes. |
| Vine maple (*Acer circinatum*). | Pacific Coast region. | Low tree, almost vinelike, in thickets, leaves opposite, rounded, with 7 to 9 lobes. |
| Rocky Mountain maple (*Acer glabrum*). | Plains and western mountains. | Leaves opposite, rounded, 3-lobed or parted, toothed. |
| Douglas maple (*Acer douglasii*). | Northern Rocky Mountain and northern Pacific regions. Alaska. | Leaves 3-lobed. Keys with erect, broad wings. |
| Southwestern maple (*Acer brachypterum*). | Southern New Mexico. | Leaves hairy, small. Keys short. |
| Bigtooth maple (*Acer grandidentatum*). | Rocky Mountains, from Montana and Idaho to Mexico. | Leaves opposite, thick, firm, green, shiny above, fuzzy below, 3-lobed. |
| Box elder (*Acer negundo var. violaceum*). | Eastern half of United States; this variety in northern Rocky Mountains. | Leaves opposite, thin, mostly compound of 3, 5, or 7 leaflets. Twigs greenish. |

**(Continued)**

## Appendix VI (Continued)

### SPECIES COMMON TO WESTERN UNITED STATES

| Name of Tree | Where the Tree Grows | Descriptive Notes |
|---|---|---|
| Inland box elder (*Acer interius*). | Rocky Mountain region (Canada to Mexico). | Leaves compound, opposite, thick not densely hairy. Young twigs smooth. Keys spreading. Hardiest box elder and widely planted. |
| California box elder (*Acer californicum*). | Southern half of eastern California. | Leaves thick, opposite, mostly compound, densely hairy below. Young twigs velvety. Keys parallel. |
| California buckeye (*Aesculus californica*). | Southern half of California, in mountains. | Leaves of 4 to 7 leaflets, opposite. Flowers white or pale red. Winter buds resinous. |
| Western soapberry (*Sapindus drummondii*). | Southern Rocky Mountain region and eastward. | Leaflets 8 to 18, dropping in fall, leaf stem not winged. Fruit black. |
| Mexican buckeye (*Ungnadia speciosa*). | Eastern Texas to New Mexico. | Leaflets 7, shiny, dark green, pointed. |
| Hollyleaf buckthorn (*Rhamnus crocea*). | Southern mountain ranges of Arizona and California. | Leaves rounded, 1 inch across, sharp spiny teeth, dark yellow beneath. |
| Cascara (*Rhamnus purshiana*). | Western Rocky Mountain and Pacific Coast States. | Leaves 5 inches long, broadly elliptical, strongly veined. Fruit black, round with 2- or 3-coffee berry seeds. Bark medicinal. |
| Island myrtle (*Ceanothus arboreus*). | Islands off coast of southern California. | Leaves 3-ribbed, broad, fuzzy. Flowers pale blue, in dense clusters. Fruit 3-lobed. |
| Blue myrtle (*Ceanothus thyrsiflorus*). | Western California. | Leaves narrowed at base, 3-ribbed, smooth. |
| Spiny myrtle (*Ceanothus spinosus*). | Coast of southern California. | Branchlets spiny-pointed. Leaves with midrib. |
| Flannelbush (*Fremontodendron californicum*). | Entire eastern California, southern Arizona. | Leaves thick, 3-lobed, red on lower surface. Flowers yellow. |
| Allthorn (*Koeberlinia spinosa*). | Southern Texas west to Arizona. | Almost leafless, spiny. Bark green. |
| Giant cactus (*Carnegiea gigantea*). | Central and southern Arizona. | Tree cactus, with spines and bristles but no leaves. Flowers large, white. |
| Cholla (*Opuntia fulgida*). | Southern Arizona. | Cactus. Leaves pale green. Flowers pink. |
| Tasajo (*Opuntia spinosior*). | do. | Cactus. Spines white. Flowers yellow. |
| Cholla (*Opuntia versicolor*). | do. | Cactus. Spines brown. Flowers green. |
| Pacific dogwood (*Cornus nuttallii*). | Pacific Coast, Washington to southern California. | Leaves opposite. Flower head enclosed by showy white bracts. Fruit red. |
| Tasseltree (*Garrya elliptica*). | Coast, Oregon and California. | Leaves opposite, leathery, woolly beneath. |
| Pacific madrone (manzanita) (*Arbutus menziesii*). | Pacific Coast region, inland in eastern California. | Leaves oblong, thick, 3 to 5 inches long. Bark reddish brown. |
| Texas madrone (*Arbutus texana*). | Western Texas. | Leaves narrow oval, thick, firm. |
| Arizona madrone (*Arbutus arizonica*). | Southern Arizona. | Leaves 2 to 3 inches long, narrow, pointed, firm. Bark ashy gray. |

(Continued)

## *Appendix VI (Continued)*

### SPECIES COMMON TO WESTERN UNITED STATES

| Name of Tree | Where the Tree Grows | Descriptive Notes |
|---|---|---|
| Fragrant ash (*Fraxinus cuspidata*). | Southwestern Texas and adjacent New Mexico. | Leaves opposite (like all ashes), compound of narrow leaflets. Flowers with pistil and stamens (perfect). |
| Littleleaf ash (*Fraxinus greggii*). | Western Texas. | Leaves opposite, rounded at end. Flowers with calyx, no corolla. |
| Singleleaf ash (*Fraxinus anomala*). | Western Colorado, Utah, and southward. | Leaves opposite, not compound (simple). Flowers polygamous, with calyx, no corolla. |
| Ash (*Fraxinus lowellii*). | Northern Arizona. | Leaves opposite, small, mostly of 5 leaflets. Branchlets 4-sided. |
| Ash (*Fraxinus standleyi*). | Western New Mexico, Arizona. | Leaves opposite, of 5 or 7 leaflets, smooth above. |
| Red ash (*Fraxinus pennsylvanica*) (Green ash var. *lanceolata*). | Eastern half of United States, Rocky Mountains. | Leaves opposite, of 7 or 9 smooth-pointed, long-stemmed leaflets. Branchlets smooth. |
| Velvet ash (*Fraxinus velutina*). | Southern New Mexico, Arizona. | Leaflets 3 or 5, small, broadly oval. Branchlets hairy. |
| Toumey ash (*Fraxinus toumeyi*). | Arizona and New Mexico. | Leaves of 5 to 7 narrow, pointed, toothed leaflets. |
| Leatherleaf ash (*Fraxinus coriacea*). | Utah, Nevada, and southeastern California. | Leaflets thicker and coarsely toothed. Branchlets nearly smooth. |
| Oregon ash (*Fraxinus oregona*). | Pacific Coast region of Washington, Oregon, California. | Leaflets mostly 5 or 7, closely attached (sessile), finely hairy, broadly oblong. |
| Anacahuita (*Cordia boissieri*). | Texas and southern New Mexico. | Leaves broadly oval, 4 to 5 inches long. Flowers white. Fruit partly enclosed. |
| Desert willow (*Chilopsis linearis*). | Western Texas to southern California. | Leaves 6 to 12 inches long, narrow, opposite or alternate. Pods slender. |
| Buttonbush (*Cephalanthus occidentalis*). | Eastern United States, across New Mexico and Arizona to California. | Broadly elliptical and opposite leaves, on stout stems. Flowers in round heads or balls. |
| Blueberry elder (*Sambucus coerulea*). | Western United States, east to the Great Plains. | Leaves opposite, of 5 to 9 leaflets. Berries with blue bloom, sweet, juicy. |
| Velvet elder (*Sambucus velutina*). | High mountains of eastern California, Nevada. | Leaves opposite, leaflets soft, hairy below. |
| Redberry elder (*Sambucus callicarpa*). | Northern California through Oregon and Washington. | Flowers and fruit in oval (not flat) clusters. Berries red. |
| Nannyberry (*Viburnum lentago*). | Northeastern United States west into northern Rocky Mountains. | Leaves opposite, on winged leaf stems. Winter buds long-pointed. |

(Adapted from U.S.D.A. Miscellaneous Publication 217)

## AGENCIES IN THE SOUTH HAVING RESPONSIBILITIES IN RANGE AND WILDLIFE PROGRAMS

| State | Organization | Activity[1] T | R | E/A | Discipline[2] R | W | P-B | Range Type[3] P-W | H-B | L-S | M |
|---|---|---|---|---|---|---|---|---|---|---|---|
| Alabama | Auburn Univ., Auburn | X | X | X | | X | | | X | X | |
| | Dept. Conserv. & Nat. Res., Montgomery | | X | X | | X | | | X | X | X |
| | Soil Conserv. Serv., Auburn | | | X | | X | | | X | X | |
| Arkansas | Game & Fish Comm., Little Rock | | | X | X | X | | | X | | |
| | Soil Conserv. Serv., Little Rock | | | X | X | X | | | X | | |
| | Univ. Arkansas, Fayetteville | X | X | X | X | | | | X | | |
| Florida | Game & Fish Comm., Tallahassee | | | X | | X | | X | | | |
| | Soil Conserv. Serv., Gainesville | | | X | X | X | | X | | | X |
| | Southeast. For. Exp. Stn., Lehigh Acres & Marianna | | X | | X | X | | X | | | |
| | Univ. of Florida, Gainesville | X | X | X | X | X | | X | | | X |
| Georgia | Coastal Plain Exp. Stn., Tifton | | | X | | X | | X | | | |
| | Game & Fish Div., Macon | | X | X | | X | | X | | X | |
| | Soil Conserv. Serv., Athens | | | X | | X | | X | | X | |
| | Univ. Ga., Athens | X | X | X | X | X | | X | | X | |
| Louisiana | Dept. of Conserv., Baton Rouge | | | X | | X | X | | X | X | X |
| | La. State Univ., Baton Rouge | X | X | X | | X | X | | X | X | X |
| | Soil Conserv. Serv., Alexandria | | | X | X | X | X | | | X | |
| | Southern For. Exp. Stn., Pineville | | X | | X | X | X | | | X | |

(Continued)

## Appendix VII (Continued)

| State | Organization | Activity[1] | | | Discipline[2] | | Range Type[3] | | | | |
|---|---|---|---|---|---|---|---|---|---|---|---|
| | | T | R | E/A | R | W | P-B | P-W | H-B | L-S | M |
| Mississippi | Game & Fish Comm., Jackson | | | X | | X | X | | | X | |
| | Miss. State Univ., Mississippi State | X | X | X | | X | X | | | X | X |
| | Soil Conserv. Serv., Jackson | | | X | | X | X | | | X | X |
| N. Carolina | N.C. State Univ., Raleigh | X | X | X | X | X | | | | X | X |
| | Soil Conserv. Serv., Raleigh | | | X | | X | | | | X | X |
| | Wildlife Resources Comm., Raleigh | | | X | | X | | | | X | X |
| S. Carolina | Clemson Univ., Clemson | X | X | X | | X | | | | X | X |
| | Soil Conserv. Serv., Columbia | | | X | | X | | | | X | |
| Tennessee | Game & Fish Comm., Nashville | | | X | | X | | | X | X | |
| | Soil Conserv. Serv., Nashville | | | X | | X | | | X | X | |
| Texas | Soil Conserv. Serv., Temple | | | X | X | X | | | X | X | X |
| | Southern For. Exp. Stn., Nacogdoches | | X | | X | X | X | | X | | |
| | Stephen F. Austin State Univ., Nacogdoches | X | X | | X | X | X | | X | | |
| | Texas A & M Univ., College Station | X | X | X | X | X | | | X | X | X |
| Virginia | Game & Inland Fish Comm., Richmond | | | X | | X | | | X | X | |
| | Soil Conserv. Serv., Richmond | | | X | X | X | | | X | X | |
| | Southeast. For. Exp. Stn., Blacksburg | | X | | X | X | | | X | | |
| | Va. Polytech. Institute, Blacksburg | X | X | X | | X | | | X | X | |

[1]T = Teaching; R = Research; E/A = Extension/Assistance.
[2]R = Range Management; W = Wildlife.
[3]P-B = Pine-bluestem; P-W = Pine-wiregrass; H-B = Hardwood-bluestem; L-S = Loblolly-shortleaf; M = Marshes.

(From Bulletin N.S. 9, *Range Resources of the South*, by the Southern Section, Society of Range Management; Georgia Agricultural Experiment Station; and University of Georgia, College of Agriculture)

## Appendix VIII

# AVERAGE WEIGHTS OF SOME COMMERCIALLY IMPORTANT WOODS

| Species | Weight, Cu. Ft., Sawn, 12 Per Cent Moisture Content | Weight, 1,000 Bd. Ft., Air Dry, 12 Per Cent Moisture Content | Species | Weight, Cu. Ft., Sawn, 12 Per Cent Moisture Content | Weight, 1,000 Bd. Ft., Air Dry, 12 Per Cent Moisture Content |
|---|---|---|---|---|---|
| | .... pounds .... | | | .... pounds .... | |
| Alder, red | 28 | 2,330 | Hickory, true[5] | 51 | 4,250 |
| Ash, black | 34 | 2,830 | Larch, western | 36 | 3,000 |
| Ash, commercial white[1] | 41 | 3,420 | Locust, black | 48 | 4,000 |
| Aspen | 26 | 2,170 | Magnolia, cucumber | 33 | 2,750 |
| Bald cypress | 32 | 2,670 | Magnolia, evergreen | 35 | 2,920 |
| Basswood | 26 | 2,170 | Maple, red | 38 | 3,170 |
| Beech | 45 | 3,750 | Maple, sugar | 44 | 3,670 |
| Birch[2] | 44 | 3,670 | Oak, red[6] | 44 | 3,670 |
| Birch, paper | 38 | 3,160 | Oak, white[7] | 47 | 3,920 |
| Butternut | 27 | 2,250 | Pine, lodgepole | 29 | 2,420 |
| Cherry, black | 35 | 2,930 | Pine, eastern white | 25 | 2,080 |
| Chestnut | 30 | 2,500 | Pine, red | 34 | 2,830 |
| Cottonwood, eastern | 28 | 2,330 | Pine, ponderosa | 28 | 2,330 |
| Cottonwood, northern | | | Pines, southern yellow: | | |
| black | 24 | 2,000 | Loblolly | 36 | 3,000 |
| Douglas fir (coast region) | 34 | 2,830 | Longleaf | 41 | 3,420 |
| Douglas fir ("Inland Em- | | | Shortleaf | 36 | 3,000 |
| pire" region) | 31 | 2,580 | Pine, sugar | 25 | 2,080 |
| Douglas fir (Rocky | | | Pine, western white | 27 | 2,250 |
| Mountain region) | 30 | 2,500 | Red cedar, eastern | 33 | 2,750 |
| Elm, American | 35 | 2,920 | Red cedar, western | 23 | 1,920 |
| Elm, rock | 44 | 3,670 | Redwood | 28 | 2,330 |
| Elm, slippery | 37 | 3,080 | Redgum | 34 | 2,830 |
| Fir, balsam | 25 | 2,080 | Spruce, eastern[8] | 28 | 2,330 |
| Fir, commercial white[3] | 27 | 2,250 | Spruce, Engelmann | 23 | 1,920 |
| Gum, black | 35 | 2,920 | Sugarberry | 36 | 3,000 |
| Gum, tupelo | 35 | 2,920 | Sycamore | 34 | 2,830 |
| Hackberry | 37 | 3,080 | Walnut, black | 38 | 3,170 |
| Hemlock, eastern | 28 | 2,330 | White cedar, northern | 22 | 1,830 |
| Hemlock, western | 29 | 2,420 | White cedar, southern | 23 | 1,920 |
| Hickory, pecan[4] | 45 | 3,750 | Yellow poplar | 28 | 2,330 |

[1]Average of Biltmore white ash, blue ash, green ash, and white ash.
[2]Average of sweet birch and yellow birch.
[3]Average of lowland white fir and white fir.
[4]Average of bitternut hickory, nutmeg hickory, water hickory, and pecan.
[5]Average of bigleaf shagbark hickory, mockernut hickory, pignut hickory, and shagbark hickory.
[6]Average of black oak, laurel oak, pin oak, red oak, scarlet oak, southern red oak, swamp red oak, water oak, and willow oak.
[7]Average of bur oak, chestnut oak, post oak, swamp chestnut oak, swamp white oak, and white oak.
[8]Average of black spruce, red spruce, and white spruce.

(Source: Yearbook of Agriculture, *Trees*)

## *Appendix IX*

## STATE FORESTS IN THE SOUTH ADMINISTERED BY STATE FORESTRY AGENCIES

| State | Name of State Forest | County | Acreage |
|-------|---------------------|--------|---------|
| **Alabama** | Geneva | Geneva | 7,120 |
| | Choccolocco Corridor | Calhoun | 4,517 |
| | Little River | Monroe and Escambia | 2,210 |
| | Weogufka | Coosa | 240 |
| | Mobile | Mobile | 172 |
| | Panther Creek | Covington | 40 |
| | St. Stephens | Washington | 20 |
| | George Washington | Covington | 20 |
| | Baldwin | Baldwin | 240 |
| **Arkansas** | Poison Spring | Nevada and Ouachita | 19,400 |
| **Florida** | Blackwater River | Okaloosa and Santa Rosa | 183,112 |
| | Withlacoochee | Citrus, Hernando, Sumter, and Pasco | 113,265 |
| | Pine Log | Washington and Bay | 6,911 |
| | Cary | Nassau and Duval | 3,414 |
| **Georgia** | Dixie Memorial | Ware and Brantley | 35,879 |
| **Kentucky** | Kentucky Ridge | Bell | 11,937 |
| | Kentenia | Harlan | 3,738 |
| | Dewey Lake | Floyd | 7,350 |
| | Tygarts | Carter | 800 |
| | Olympia | Bath | 785 |
| | Knobs | Nelson | 4,000 |
| | Pennyrile | Hopkins, Christian, and Caldwell | 16,424 |
| **Louisiana** | Alexandria | Rapides Parish | 8,000 |
| **Mississippi** | Kurtz | Green | 1,760 |
| **North Carolina** | Bladen Lakes | Bladen | 36,000 |
| **South Carolina** | Cassatt | Kershaw | 462 |
| | Harbison | Richland | 2,188 |
| | Manchester | Sumter | 28,830 |
| | Sand Hills | Chesterfield and Darlington | 92,000 |
| **Tennessee** | Bledsoe | Bledsoe, White, Cumberland, and Van Dunn | 6,656 |
| | Chuck Swan | Campbell and Union | 24,300 |
| | Chickasaw | Chester and Hardeman | 13,104 |

(Continued)

## *STATE FORESTS IN THE SOUTH (Continued)*

| State | Name of State Forest | County | Acreage |
|-------|----------------------|--------|--------:|
| **Tennessee** | Franklin | Franklin and Marion | 6,941 |
| **(Continued)** | Cedars of Lebanon | Wilson | 6,943 |
| | Lewis | Lewis | 1,257 |
| | Madison | Madison | 38 |
| | Lone Mountain | Morgan | 3,597 |
| | Natchez Trace | Carroll, Benton, Decatur, | |
| | | and Henderson | 35,904 |
| | Pickett | Pickett and Fentress | 10,887 |
| | Prentice Cooper | Marion, Sequatchie, | |
| | | and Hamilton | 25,802 |
| | Scott | Scott and Fentress | 3,182 |
| | Standing Stone | Overton and Clay | 8,445 |
| | Stewart | Stewart | 4,000 |
| **Texas** | E. O. Siecke | Newton | 1,821 |
| | I. D. Fairchild | Cherokee | 2,944 |
| | J. H. Kirby | Tyler | 600 |
| | W. G. Jones | Montgomery | 1,633 |
| **Virginia** | Buckingham-Appomattox | Buckingham and | |
| | | Appomattox | 19,687 |
| | Prince Edward-Gallion | Prince Edward | 6,957 |
| | Cumberland | Cumberland | 16,466 |
| | Conway Robinson | Prince William | 400 |
| | Paul | Augusta | 173 |
| | Lesesne | Nelson | 421 |
| | Pocahontas | Chesterfield | 5,313 |
| | Whitney | Fauquier | 148 |

(Courtesy Southeastern Area, State and Private Forestry, U.S. Forest Service)

*Appendix X*

## PARTIAL LIST OF MANUFACTURERS
## OF WOOD PRESERVATIVES

The inclusion of manufacturers in this listing does not imply an endorsement of their products or a guarantee of the quality of those products. Information as to brands and methods of use may be obtained by writing those manufacturers listed. No discrimination in any manner is intended.

### CREOSOTE AND TAR PRODUCERS

Allied Chemical Corporation
Plastics Division
40 Rector Street
New York, New York 10006

American Creosote Works, Inc.
1305 Dublin Street
New Orleans, Louisiana 70150

American Tar Company
Foot of Wallingford Avenue
Seattle, Washington 98111

Bernuth Lembcke Company, Inc.
420 Lexington Avenue
New York, New York 10017

C-A-Wood Preserves Company
3622 Dover Place
St. Louis, Missouri 63166

Crown Tar and Chemical Works, Inc.
900 Wewatta Street
Denver, Colorado 80201

Crowley Tar Products Company
271 Madison Avenue
New York, New York 10016

Koppers Company, Inc.
Tar Products Division
1202 Koppers Building
Pittsburgh, Pennsylvania 15219

Mutual Chemical and Supply Company
629 North Cassaday Avenue
Columbus, Ohio 43216

Phoenix Oil Company
625 5th Street
Augusta, Georgia 30903

Reilly Tar and Chemical Company
Merchants Bank Building
Indianapolis, Indiana 46204

Standard Tar Products Company
2546 Cornell Street
Milwaukee, Wisconsin 53201

Tar Distilling Company, Inc.
500 Fifth Avenue
New York, New York 10036

U.S. Steel Corporation
524 William Penn Place
Pittsburgh, Pennsylvania 15230

Western Tar Products Corporation
2525 Prairie Road
Terre Haute, Indiana 47808

### PENTACHLOROPHENOL PRODUCERS

American Chemet Corporation
P.O. Box 437
400 County Line Road
Deerfield, Illinois 60015

Androc Chemical Company
7301 West Lake Street
Minneapolis, Minnesota 55804

Barada and Page Incorporated
2812 Center Street
Houston, Texas 77008

B. Preise and Company, Inc.
416 West Washington Street
Charleston, West Virginia 25321

Chapman Chemical Company, Inc.
528 Terminal Sales Building
Portland, Oregon 97208

Chapman Chemical Company, Inc.
P.O. Box 9158
Memphis, Tennessee 38109

Chemical Research Products Company
235 West Olney Road
Norfolk, Virginia 25301

Continental Chemical Company
Cayce, South Carolina 29033

Daly-Herring Company
P.O. Box 237
Kingston, North Carolina 28501

Delta Oil Products Company
Teutonia Avenue and Mill Road
Milwaukee, Wisconsin 53201

Extermital Chemicals, Inc.
1026 Wayne Avenue
Dayton, Ohio 45401

Garthol Chemical Company
406 Tussing Building
Lansing, Michigan 48901

Kentucky Color and Chemical Company
600 North 34th Street
Louisville, Kentucky 40201

Louisiana Agricultural Supply Company
1175 Choetau Road
Baton Rouge, Louisiana 70821

Osmose Wood Preserving Company
of America, Inc.
980 Ellicott Street
Buffalo, New York 14209

Pennsylvania Salt Manufacturing
Company of Washington
P.O. Box Route 6
Montgomery, Alabama 36101

Pennsylvania Salt Manufacturing
Company of Washington
Bryan, Texas 77801

Pennsylvania Salt Manufacturing
Company of Washington
Tacoma, Washington 98401

Penta Products Company
1114 Fourteenth Avenue
Oakland, California 94604

Reasor-Hill Corporation
Arkansas Ordinance Plant
Jacksonville, Arkansas 72076

Souford Products Corporation
P.O. Box 8471
Jackson, Mississippi 39205

Tesco Chemicals, Inc.
P.O. Box 173, Station C
Atlanta, Georgia 30309

Triangle Chemical Company
P.O. Box 529
Macon, Georgia 31202

Waltham Chemical Company
817 Moddy Street
Waltham, Massachusetts 02154

Ward Chemical and Supply Company
1710 South Main Street
Tulsa, Oklahoma 74101

Wood Treating Chemicals Company
716 South Orleans
Tampa, Florida 33601

Wood Treating Chemicals Company
5137 Southwest Avenue
St. Louis, Missouri 63166

## SUPPLIERS OF OTHER WOOD-PRESERVING CHEMICALS

### Copper Sulfate

Allied Chemical Corporation
61 Broadway
New York, New York 10004

Mountain Copper Company
Martinez, California 94553

Phelps Dodge Refining Corporation
300 Park Avenue
New York, New York 10022

Tennessee Corporation
1330 West Peachtree
Atlanta, Georgia 30309

### Disodium Arsenate

Allied Chemical Corporation
61 Broadway
New York, New York 10004

Chipman Chemical Company
Bound Brook, New Jersey 08805

Saltcake Sales
230 Park Avenue
New York, New York 10017

The Sherwin-Williams Company
General Chemical Division
260 Madison Avenue
New York, New York 10016

### Sodium Chromate

Allied Chemical Corporation
Solvay Process Division
61 Broadway
New York, New York 10004

Diamond Alkali Company
300 Union Commerce Building
Cleveland, Ohio 44115

Harshaw Chemical Company
1945 East 97th Street
Cleveland, Ohio 44106

### Sodium Fluoride

Allied Chemical Corporation
205 South 16th Street
Milwaukee, Wisconsin 53233

Mallinckrodt Chemical Works
Second and Mallinckrodt Streets
St. Louis, Missouri 63107

Olin Mathieson Chemical Corporation
120 West Ogden Avenue
Chicago, Illinois 60607

Source of this list is the Forest Products Laboratory, U.S. Forest Service. No endorsement as to quality of service or cost is implied.

NOTE: Copper sulfate is widely distributed and is carried in stock by a large number of dealers. The nearest dealer in industrial chemicals should be contacted. Suppliers of copper sulfate are also often the source of sodium chromate. Any of the companies listed above can furnish the addresses of their distributors.

*Appendix XI*

**CHARACTERISTICS OF
COMMON RANGE GRASSES OF THE SOUTH**

*Appendix XI—CHARACTERISTICS OF*

| Species | | Range and Prevalence |
|---|---|---|
| BLUESTEMS | ANDROPOGON SPP. | |
| Pinehill bluestem | A. divergens | Fla. to eastern Tex. Very common from western Ala. to eastern Tex. |
| Elliott b. | A. elliottii | Throughout coastal plains. Gets up into southern Ind., Ill., and Mo. |
| Big b. | A. gerardii | Scattered throughout South. Never very abundant. |
| Bushy b. | A. glomeratus | Common. Shows a marked preference for the sites with extra moisture. |
| Little b. | A. scoparius | Common in the west portion of the Piedmont and Okla. and Ark. |
| Creeping b. | A. stolonifer | Very common from west Ala. to the east. Important in S. Ga. and Fla. |
| Slender b. | A. tener | Likes drier sites. Is found throughout coastal plains, but is abundant only where overstory is light. |
| Paintbrush b. | A. ternarius | Scattered. Rarely found in pure stands, but common throughout South. |
| Broomsedge b. | A. virginicus | Common throughout. Very conspicuous in old fields and disturbed areas. |
| PANICUMS | PANICUM SPP. | |
| Cutthroat grass | P. abscissum | Extends from S.C. south to the Keys. Not common in S.C., but important south. |
| Beaked panicum | P. anceps | Found on moist sites throughout the South. |

Footnote on last page of table.

## COMMON RANGE GRASSES OF THE SOUTH[1]

| Season of Most Use | Response to Heavy Grazing and Prescribed Burning | Palatability Preference During Season of Most Use | | |
|---|---|---|---|---|
| | | High | Med. | Low |
| Early spring, summer, and fall—some all year. | Will maintain itself with burns every three years and 50 per cent use. | X | | |
| Grows with and used about the same as pinehill. | Will increase with burns more often than three-year interval. | | X | |
| Early spring through July. Becomes coarse in the fall. | Cannot take heavy use. Fire more frequent than once in three years will cause this grass to decrease in occurrence. | X | | |
| February through May. Is only important on large marshy areas. | Rarely grazed-out on site to which best adapted. Response to burning unknown. | | | X |
| April thru July. Some use made of this in winter. Cures well on the stem in Okla. and Ark. | Will thrive with use to as high as 50 per cent. Yearly burns will kill it. | X | | |
| Summer and early fall. | Stands up well to heavy grazing and burning. Exceeds over other bluestems under same grazing pressure. | X | | |
| The earliest of the southern bluestems to head out, spring and summer. | Increases with prescribed burning. Is grazed heavily when young and tender. | X | | |
| Late spring and summer into fall. Among the latest of the bluestems to flower. | Not so susceptible to smothering as other bluestems. Increases with heavy grazing. | | | X |
| March to June with open winters. Considerable use made of this in December and January. | Rarely grazed closely except in mild winters on heavily stocked range. Generally underrated as forage in the South. | | X | |
| Spring and summer. | Rarely burned because wet site will generally not support fire. Stands up well under heavy grazing. | | X | |
| Spring and summer. | Shows quick recovery when tender, young shoots are taken in early spring. | X | | |

**(Continued)**

## CHARACTERISTICS OF COMMON

|  | Species | Range and Prevalence |
|---|---|---|
| Narrowleaf p. | *P. angustifolium* | Throughout the South. One of the more important of the low panicums. |
| Maidencane | *P. hemitomon* | Common on wet sites of the coastal states. Important forage in Fla. |
| Woolly panicum | *P. lanuginosum* | Common throughout the South. One of the better low panicums. |
| Spreading p. | *P. rhizomatum* | Confined generally to the coastal states. Likes extra moisture. |
| Roundseed p. | *P. sphaerocarpon* | Common in the Southeast. One of the first to head in the spring. |
| Switchgrass | *P. virgatum* | Throughout. Sometimes locally abundant but generally least common of the important panicums. |
| PASPALUMS | PASPALUM SPP. | |
| Fringeleaf p. | *P. ciliatifolium* | Throughout the South. Very common. Will withstand moderately heavy grazing. |
| Florida p. | *P. floridanum* | Largely confined to the Southeast. Common throughout. |
| Brownseed p. | *P. plicatulum* | Found in all coastal plains states. Common on more moist sites. |
| DROPSEEDS | SPOROBOLUS SPP. | |
| Curtiss d. | *S. curtissii* | Largely confined to the wiregrass ranges of southern Ga., Ala., and Fla. |

Footnote on last page of table.

# RANGE GRASSES (Continued)

| Season of Most Use | Response to Heavy Grazing and Prescribed Burning | Palatability Preference During Season of Most Use | | |
|---|---|---|---|---|
| | | High | Med. | Low |
| February thru May. | Tends to increase under heavy use. One of the best of the low panicums. | | | X |
| Winter and spring. Provides a real need for livestock when most other grasses are dormant. | Will decrease under continued heavy grazing and be replaced with cordgrass and carpetgrass. | X | | |
| Early winter thru April. | Will increase under heavy grazing. Continued heavy grazing will find it replaced with annuals. | | X | |
| March through September. | Very much like beaked panicum in both sites occupied and grazing response. Heavy seeder. | X | | |
| Used from February thru May, and again in the late fall. | Takes close grazing well. Used heavily on fresh burns in early spring. Tolerant of fire. | | X | |
| Becomes coarse with maturity. March through July. | A decreaser under heavy grazing. Difficult to keep in stand even with moderate grazing. | X | | |
| Spring and summer. | Will increase with continued heavy grazing. Moderately tolerant of fire. | X | | |
| Early in spring and summer. | Will decrease under heavy grazing and increase slowly with light grazing. | | X | |
| Late summer into winter. | Often grazed heavily in spring along road ditches and other wet sites. Bluestem easily exceeds on uplands. Increaser on moist sites. | | X | |
| Late fall and winter. | Burning will decrease the amount of Curtiss dropseed in the total cover. Tolerant of heavy grazing and shade. Increases on unburned sites. | | X | |

**(Continued)**

## CHARACTERISTICS OF COMMON

| | Species | Range and Prevalence |
|---|---|---|
| Pineywoods d. | S. junceus | Extends all along the coastal plain from Tex. to Fla. and up into Va. Common. |
| **THREE-AWNS** | ARISTIDA SPP. | |
| Arrowfeather t. | A. purpurascens | Throughout the Southeast. Range extends into the Midwest and New England. |
| Pineland t. | A. stricta | Coastal plains from Miss. east to N.C. Common in southern Ga., Ala., and Fla. |
| Trinius t. | A. virgata | Has about the same range as pineland three-awn. Not so common, however. |
| **LOVEGRASSES** | ERAGROSTIS SPP. | |
| Elliott l. | E. elliottii | N.C. to east Tex. Shows preference for wetter sites. |
| Coastal l. | E. refracta | Limited to the coastal plains states. More common in Fla. and Ga. |
| Purple l. | E. spectabilis | Common everywhere east of the 100th meridian. Very showy in fall. |
| **INDIAN GRASSES** | SORGHASTRUM SPP. | |
| Slender i. | S. elliottii | Throughout the South on sandy soil. More common in the east. |
| Yellow i. | S. nutans | Eastern U.S. west to the Rocky Mountain Range. |
| Lopside i. | S. secundum | Largely confined to wiregrass types in Fla., southern Ga., Ala., and coastal S.C. |

## OTHER IMPORTANT AND COMMON GRASSES

| | Species | Range and Prevalence |
|---|---|---|
| Goobergrass | Amphicarpum muhlenbergianum | Fla., Ga., and S.C.; very common in southern Fla. |
| Green silkyscale | Anthaenantia villosa | Throughout the South. |
| Giant cane | Arundinaria gigantea | Throughout the South. |

Footnote on last page of table.

## RANGE GRASSES (Continued)

| Season of Most Use | Response to Heavy Grazing and Prescribed Burning | Palatability Preference During Season of Most Use | | |
|---|---|---|---|---|
| | | High | Med. | Low |
| Spring and early summer and during the winter. | Tolerant of fire and grazing. Frequent fire will decrease amount of this in the stand. | | | X |
| On fresh-burned range in spring. | Increaser. Comes close to being an invader. Very tolerant of fires. | | | X |
| On fresh-burned range in spring. Some use during winter. | Can be maintained in stand if moderately grazed. Increases with fire. | | X | |
| On fresh-burned range in spring and winter. | Heavy grazing will cause it to decrease. Tolerant of fire. | | | X |
| Early spring. Most abundant in Fla. | Increaser. Shows a good tolerance of fire. | | | X |
| Early spring. | Increaser. The most palatable of the perennial lovegrasses. | | X | |
| Early spring. | Increases with heavy grazing and frequent burns. A sand lover. | | | X |
| Late spring and summer. | Decreaser. Does not have rhizomes but is deep rooted. | X | | |
| Late spring and summer. | Can't take heavy grazing. Hot burns damage rhizomes. | X | | |
| April, May, and June. Seedstalks readily eaten in late summer and fall. | Decreaser. | X | | |

### OF THE SOUTH AND SOUTHEAST

| | | | | |
|---|---|---|---|---|
| Summer and fall. Some used year-long. | Increaser. Shows good response to discing or roller cutter. | | X | |
| Summer. | Increaser. Moderately tolerant to fire. | | X | |
| May to January. | Decreaser. Burning followed by heavy grazing will kill it. | X | | |

(Continued)

## CHARACTERISTICS OF COMMON

| Species | | Range and Prevalence |
|---|---|---|
| Switchcane | *A. tecta* | Mainly east of Mississippi River. |
| Common carpetgrass | *Axonopus awnis* | Coastal plains. |
| Toothachegrass | *Ctenium aromaticum* | Coastal plains. Mainly wetter sandy sites. |
| Skeleton grass | *Gymnopogon ambiguus* | Coastal plains north to Ohio River. |
| Cutover muhly | *Muhlenbergia expansa* | Coastal plains, eastern Tex. to Fla. and Va. Common on infrequently burned sites. |
| Pine barrens tridens | *Tridens ambiguus* | Coastal plains, Tex. to Fla., and S.C.—mainly on poorly drained soils. |
| Purpletop | *Tridens flavus* | Eastern U.S. Most prevalent on moderately to heavily wooded sites. |
| Longleaf uniola | *Uniola sessiliflora* | Coastal plains, Piedmont and into eastern Tex. and Okla. |

[1]Adapted from Forestland Grazing, U.S. Forest Service, S. & P. Forestry, Southeastern Area, July 1967.

# RANGE GRASSES (Continued)

| Season of Most Use | Response to Heavy Grazing and Prescribed Burning | Palatability Preference During Season of Most Use | | |
|---|---|---|---|---|
| | | High | Med. | Low |
| May to January. | Decreaser. Shows same response to grazing and fire as above. | X | | |
| Spring and summer. | Must be grazed to stay in stand. Will tolerate heavy grazing. An invader species. | X | | |
| Early spring after fresh burn. | Because of site, rarely killed by fire. Tolerate moderate shade and litter. Will increase on unburned sites. | | X | |
| Fresh growth after a burn. Becomes very coarse. | Fire tolerant—will increase with heavy use following disturbance. | | | X |
| Late fall and winter. Is closely cropped in spring on fresh burns. | Decreases under heavy use and frequent burns. | | X | |
| Spring and early summer. | Increases with burning. Can't tolerate heavy, rough or dense shade. | | | X |
| Summer and early fall. | Decreaser under heavy grazing. Tolerant of fire. | | X | |
| Spring and early summer. | Decreaser. One of the most shade tolerant grasses in the South and somewhat tolerant to litter buildup. | | | X |

## Appendix XII

## SAMPLE SALE AGREEMENT FORMS

### Form A

STATE OF _____

COUNTY (PARISH) OF _____

### PROPOSED
### FOREST PRODUCTS SALE AGREEMENT

In which each tree is designated by the Seller and
payment is made by the Buyer on the basis of
measurements on each tree

This agreement is made and entered into by and between _____

_____ hereinafter

called the Seller, and _____

of _____ hereinafter called the Buyer.

Article 1. The Buyer agrees to buy from the Seller, and the Seller agrees
to sell to the Buyer, upon the terms and conditions hereinafter stated, all the
trees which have been marked or designated by the Seller or his representatives and described hereinafter.

The sale area on which the timber will be felled is located in the

_____ Survey in the County (Parish) of _____

(state), from which the Seller is empowered to cut and/or sell forest
products. Further description follows:

_____

_____

Article 2. The Buyer agrees to pay the Seller for all timber cut under
this contract at the following rate:

| Species | Price per _____ <br>( M bd. ft., cd., unit, or piece ) | Unit of Measurement <br>( log rule, cord, etc. ) |
|---|---|---|
| _____ | _____ | _____ |
| _____ | _____ | _____ |
| _____ | _____ | _____ |
| _____ | _____ | _____ |

Payment shall be made _____
<br>( describe where, when, and how )

Article 3. The Buyer further agrees to cut and remove the above-described trees in accordance with the following conditions:

1. Trees felled shall be limited to those that have been marked or designated by the Seller with two spots of _____ paint: one
<br>color
<br>spot near the ground line, the other 4 or more feet high on the trunk.

2. Unmarked pine or pine and hardwood merchantable trees, if cut or unnecessarily destroyed, shall be paid for at the rate per tree shown below:

| Diameter in inches inside <br> bark 12″ above ground | Price per tree |
|---|---|
| 7 | $ 0.90 |
| 8 | 2.00 |
| 9 | 2.50 |
| 10 | 5.00 |
| 11 | 6.75 |
| 12 | 9.00 |
| 13 | 11.75 |
| 14 | 15.00 |
| 15 | 18.50 |
| 16 | 22.25 |
| 17 through 19 | 29.50 |
| 20 through 24 | 59.00 |

3. Unless specifically mentioned in Article 1, such terms as slabs, edgings, tops, and sawdust that result from cutting operations will remain the property of the Seller.

4. All trees shall be utilized to the lowest possible top diameter for
_____ material.
(define whether sawtimber, pulp, etc.)

5. Stumps of trees shall be cut no higher than _____
inches above the average ground level, except for those trees wherein wire,
nails, or visible defects including fork or excessive flare necessitate cutting
higher than the above stated limit.

6. Young and unmarked trees shall be protected against unnecessary injury during cutting and hauling operations. Skid trails shall be located,
insofar as possible, to protect young trees and the residual stand from
damage.

7. The Buyer assumes responsibility for the prevention and suppression of all forest fires and agrees to pay for the damage resulting from
fires caused by him and/or his agents or employees.

8. The Buyer agrees to repair at his own expense damages to gates,
fences, bridges, culverts, and other improvements caused by his operations,
on the described area and to remove logging debris from existing roads.

9. Except for negligence that might be attributable to the Seller,
his agents, servants, or employees, Buyer agrees to hold Seller harmless from
any injury to person or property occurring in connection with this agreement and on the premises herein described.

10. At all times during the performance of this agreement Buyer
shall protect and hold harmless the Seller from any liability for any claims of
persons performing services or furnishing materials to the Buyer for the use
in the performance of this Agreement and shall pay all such claims so as to
prevent the filing of any lien against the property of the Seller by reason of
the furnishing of any such material or the performance of any such work.
In the event that any mechanic's lien or other lien shall be filed against the
property of Seller, by virtue of Buyer's activities under this Agreement,
Buyer shall immediately satisfy any and all such liens.

Article 4. It is mutually understood and agreed by and between the
parties hereto as follows:

1. This agreement shall terminate _____
(give date)
unless extended in writing.

2. Any marked trees which are uncut and any forest products
which are not removed at the date this agreement terminates become the
property of the Seller.

3. This agreement may be assigned in whole or in part only with
the written consent of the Seller.

4. The Seller hereby guarantees to the Buyer, his successors and assigns, that he will forever warrant and defend the title to said forest products and privileges herein granted against all lawful claims at his expense. The Seller retains and the Buyer grants a vendor's lien on all forest products cut or removed under this agreement until payment in full is made.

5. The Buyer and his agents shall have free ingress and egress upon the sale area and adjacent property of the Seller for the purpose of cutting and removing the forest products, but the Seller reserves the right to designate or approve the location of any haul roads across cleared land.

6. A portable sawmill may be set upon this tract of land to cut this timber. Sawmill sites selected by the Buyer shall be approved in advance of installation by the Seller.

7. The Seller reserves the right of checking the operation at any time to determine whether the provisions of this agreement are being carried out.

8. In case of dispute over the execution of the terms of this agreement, final decision shall rest with an arbitration board of three persons, one to be selected by each party to this agreement, and a third to be a graduate forester acceptable to the Seller and the Buyer.

Article 5. The Buyer agrees to post a performance bond in the amount of $_____ at the time this agreement is executed, with said performance bond to be returned to the Buyer within 14 days after the removal of the timber or the termination of this agreement, whichever occurs first.

In witness whereof the parties hereto have set their hands and seal.

Witness_____        Buyer:_____

                                    By:_____

                                    Date:_____

Witness_____        Seller:_____

                                    By:_____

                                    Date:_____

Sworn to and subscribed before me by the above person(s) and firm(s) this _____ day of _____, 19_____, _____ _____, Notary Public, County (Parish) of _____,

State _____.

## *Form B*

STATE OF _____

COUNTY OF _____

### TIMBER DEED
(Lump Sum Sale Agreement)

BE IT KNOWN that the following contract and agreement has this day been made and entered into by and between _____

_____

_____

_____

a resident(s) of _____and hereinafter designated
                            (county & state)
as "Vendor," whether one or more; and _____

_____, a _____corporation,
                                                (state)
domiciled in _____, hereinafter
                            (county & state)
designated and known as the "Vendee," witnesseth:

The Vendor declared and acknowledged that, for the price and consideration and upon the terms and conditions hereinafter set out and expressed, he has sold, transferred, and delivered and does by his act, sell, transfer, and deliver, free from all liens, mortgages, or other encumbrances, with full and complete warranty of title and with full and complete subrogations of all rights of actions of warranty against all prior Vendors or owners unto the Vendee, all and singular the following described property, to-wit: (Property Legal Description)

The price and consideration for which this sale is made is the sum of _____DOLLARS ($_____) cash, receipt of which is hereby acknowledged.

It is understood and agreed that the Vendee, its heirs and assigns, shall have _____in which to cut and remove said
                    (time period)
timber from the above-stated lands.

The act of Vendee in cutting over said lands shall not constitute a forfeiture of the rights of Vendee, but Vendee may enter the premises and cut and remove merchantable timber herein conveyed as many times as it sees fit; however, the Vendee shall not enter upon the premises and cut or remove any timber after _____,

(cutting completion date)

which date shall be known as termination date.

It is further understood and agreed that the Vendee shall have free right of ingress and egress to and from the lands for its managers, laborers, teams, or trucks or other motive power used in cutting and removing the timber from the lands.

This sale is made subject to the following conditions:

1. For the period of the sale agreement, the Vendee and its agents shall have free ingress and egress upon the sale area for the purpose of cutting and removing designated forest products. Vendee shall, wherever possible, use existing haul roads and fence gaps across property.

2. Trees felled shall be limited to those pine trees that have been marked by Vendor's agent for Vendor, with two yellow spots of paint; young and unmarked pine trees shall be protected against needless and unnecessary injury; skidding trails, roads, and loading docks shall be located (insofar as possible) to protect the remaining pine stand. Unmarked pine trees deliberately and needlessly cut, damaged or destroyed shall be paid for at three times the bid price (on a thousand board feet basis). All hardwood trees, which have been cut, unnecessarily damaged or destroyed, will be paid for at the rate of $_____ per thousand board feet. All penalty volumes shall be determined by a third party mutually agreed upon by the Vendor and Vendee.

3. The Vendee agrees to repair, at its own expense, damages caused by its operations to existing improvements, including fences, gaps, buildings, roads and drainages. Repair shall be at least as good as original condition. Care should be exercised for power lines, drainage tile, fence, etc., near the house.

4. Vendee will do all reasonable things in its power to prevent and suppress forest fires on or threatening the sale area during its harvesting operations and Vendee will be responsible for damages resulting from fires caused by Vendee's agents.

5. The Vendee agrees to assist Vendor in salvaging insect-attacked timber during the sale agreement period at a mutually agreed upon stumpage price.

6. The Vendor reserves the right of checking operations from time to time.

7. The failure on the part of the Vendee to comply with the conditions of this contract shall result in the termination of same provided, however, that the Vendee will be reimbursed by the Vendor for sawlog portions of trees conveyed to the Vendee under this contract which have not been cut and removed from the premises at the price that the Vendee paid the Vendor for the sawlogs conveyed under this contract less 15 per cent for value reduction due to volume reduction.

The effective date of this instrument shall be the _____ day of _____.

VENDOR _____

VENDEE _____

DONE AND SIGNED by the parties hereto in the presence of the undersigned witnesses on this the _____ day of _____.

WITNESSES:

_____

_____

STATE OF _____

COUNTY OF _____

DONE AND SIGNED by _____ in the presence of the undersigned attesting witnesses on this _____ day of _____.

WITNESSES:

_____        By:    _____

_____

## Appendix XIII

## MISCELLANEOUS TABLES USED IN FORESTRY

### LENGTH AND AREA CONVERSION FACTORS

| Linear Measure | | | Area Measure | | |
|---|---|---|---|---|---|
| 1 inch | = | .0833 feet | 1 sq. foot | = | 144 sq. inches |
| 1 link | = | 7.92 inches | 1 sq. yard | = | 9 sq. feet |
| 1 foot | = | 12 inches | 1 sq. rod | = | 30.25 sq. yards |
| 1 vara | = approx. | 33 inches | 1 sq. chain | = | 16 sq. rods |
| 1 vara | = approx. | 2.75 feet | 1 sq. chain | = | 4,356 sq. feet |
| 1 yard | = | 3 feet | 1 acre | = | 10 sq. chains |
| 1 rod | = | 25 links | 1 acre | = | 4,840 sq. yards |
| 1 chain | = | 100 links | 1 acre | = | 43,560 sq. feet |
| 1 rod | = | 16.50 feet | 1 sq. mile | = | 640 acres |
| 1 rod | = | 5.50 yards | 1 sq. mile | = | 1 section |
| 1 chain | = | 66 feet | 1 township | = | 36 sq. miles |
| 1 mile | = | 80 chains | 1 township | = | 6 miles sq. |
| 1 mile | = | 320 rods | | | |
| 1 mile | = | 5,280 feet | | | |
| 1 mile | = | 1,760 yards | | | |

| To Change | Metric Equivalents<br>To | Multiply By |
|---|---|---|
| Acres | Hectares | .4047 |
| Centimeters | Inches | .3937 |
| Centimeters | Feet | .03281 |
| Feet | Meters | .3048 |
| Hectares | Acres | 2.4710 |
| Inches | Centimeters | 2.5400 |
| Meters | Feet | 3.2808 |
| Meters | Yards | 1.0936 |
| Miles | Kilometers | 1.6093 |
| Rods | Meters | 5.029 |
| Square Feet | Square Meters | .0929 |
| Square Kilometers | Square Miles | .3861 |
| Square Meters | Square Yards | 1.1960 |
| Square Miles | Square Kilometers | 2.5900 |
| Square Yards | Square Meters | .8361 |
| Yards | Meters | .9144 |
| Gallons | Liters | 3.7854 |
| Liters | Gallons | .2642 |
| Kilograms | Pounds | 2.2046 |
| Pounds | Kilograms | .4536 |
| Short Tons | Metric Tons | .9072 |
| Short Tons | Kilograms | 907.1847 |
| Metric Tons | Kilograms | 1000.0 |

(Source: Adapted from *American Heritage Dictionary of the English Language*.)

## RATIOS FOR CUSTOMARY MAP SCALES

| Scale 1 to— | Inches per Mile | Miles per Inch | Feet per Inch | Meters per Inch | Feet per ⅟₂₅ Inch | Acres per Square Inch | Square Miles per Square Inch |
|---|---|---|---|---|---|---|---|
| 600 | 105.6 | 0.0095 | 50 | 15.2 | 2 | 0.06 | 0.0001 |
| 1,200 | 52.8 | .0189 | 100 | 30.5 | 4 | .23 | .0004 |
| 2,500 | 25.344 | .0395 | 208 | 63.5 | 8.3 | 1.00 | .0016 |
| 4,800 | 13.2 | .0758 | 400 | 121.9 | 16 | 3.67 | .0057 |
| 5,280 | 12 | .0833 | 440 | 134.1 | 17.6 | 4.44 | .0069 |
| 10,000 | 6.336 | .1578 | 833 | 254.0 | 33.3 | 15.94 | .0249 |
| 15,840 | 4 | .25 | 1,320 | 402.3 | 52.8 | 40.00 | .0625 |
| 20,000 | 3.168 | .3157 | 1,667 | 508.0 | 66.7 | 63.77 | .0996 |
| 24,000 | 2.64 | .3788 | 2,000 | 609.6 | 80 | 91.83 | .1435 |
| 25,000 | 2.534 | .3946 | 2,083 | 635.0 | 83.3 | 99.64 | .1557 |
| 31,680 | 2 | .5 | 2,640 | 804.7 | 105.6 | 160 | .2500 |
| 45,000 | 1.408 | .7102 | 3,750 | 1,143.0 | 150 | 323 | .5044 |
| 63,360 | 1 | 1 | 5,280 | 1,609.3 | 211.2 | 640 | 1.00 |
| 90,000 | .704 | 1.4205 | 7,500 | 2,286.0 | 300 | 1,291 | 2.02 |
| 96,000 | .66 | 1.5152 | 8,000 | 2,438.4 | 320 | 1,469 | 2.30 |
| 125,000 | .507 | 1.9729 | 10,417 | 3,175.0 | 416.7 | 2,491 | 3.89 |
| 500,000 | .127 | 7.8914 | 41,667 | 12,700.0 | 1,666.7 | ............ | 62.3 |
| 1,000,000 | .063 | 15.7828 | 83,333 | 25,400.1 | 3,333.3 | ............ | 249 |
| 2,500,000 | .025 | 39.4571 | 208,333 | 63,500.1 | 8,333.3 | ............ | 1,557 |

## GRADE PER CENT AND EQUIVALENT DEGREE OF SLOPE[1]

| Grade (per cent) | Slope in Degrees | Grade (per cent) | Slope in Degrees | Grade (per cent) | Slope in Degrees | Grade (per cent) | Slope in Degrees |
|---|---|---|---|---|---|---|---|
| | ° ′ | | ° ′ | | ° ′ | | ° ′ |
| 1 | 0 34.4 | 11 | 6 16.6 | 21 | 11 51.6 | 55 | 28 48.6 |
| 2 | 1 8.7 | 12 | 6 50.6 | 22 | 12 24.4 | 60 | 30 57.8 |
| 3 | 1 43.1 | 13 | 7 24.4 | 23 | 12 57.2 | 65 | 33 1.4 |
| 4 | 2 17.4 | 14 | 7 58.2 | 24 | 13 29.7 | 70 | 34 59.5 |
| 5 | 2 51.7 | 15 | 8 31.8 | 25 | 14 2.2 | 75 | 36 52.2 |
| 6 | 3 26.0 | 16 | 9 5.4 | 30 | 16 42.0 | 80 | 38 39.6 |
| 7 | 4 0.3 | 17 | 9 38.9 | 35 | 19 17.4 | 85 | 40 21.9 |
| 8 | 4 34.4 | 18 | 10 12.2 | 40 | 21 48.1 | 90 | 41 59.2 |
| 9 | 5 8.6 | 19 | 10 45.5 | 45 | 24 13.7 | 95 | 43 31.9 |
| 10 | 5 42.6 | 20 | 11 18.6 | 50 | 26 33.9 | 100 | 45 0 |

[1] Equivalents of customary expressions of grade are as follows:
Grades and slopes: 1 foot per chain = 1.515 per cent; 1 foot per mile = 0.018939 per cent; 1 millimeter per meter = 0.1 per cent; 1 foot per thousand = 0.1 per cent; 1 per cent grade = 633.6 inches per mile = 52.8 feet per mile = 10 millimeters per meter = 10 feet per thousand feet = 1 foot per 1.515 chains = 0.66 feet per chain.

## DEGREE OF SLOPE AND EQUIVALENT GRADE PER CENT[1]

| Degree of Slope | Grade (per cent) | Degree of Slope | Grade (per cent) | Degree of Slope | Grade (per cent) | Degree of Slope | Grade (per cent) |
|---|---|---|---|---|---|---|---|
| ° ′ | | ° ′ | | ° ′ | | ° ′ | |
| 0 30 | 0.873 | 5 | 8.749 | 9 30 | 16.734 | 18 | 32.492 |
| 1 | 1.746 | 5 30 | 9.629 | 10 | 17.633 | 19 | 34.433 |
| 1 30 | 2.619 | 6 | 10.510 | 11 | 19.438 | 20 | 36.397 |
| 2 | 3.492 | 6 30 | 11.394 | 12 | 21.256 | 22 30 | 41.421 |
| 2 30 | 4.366 | 7 | 12.278 | 13 | 23.087 | 25 | 46.631 |
| 3 | 5.241 | 7 30 | 13.165 | 14 | 24.933 | 30 | 57.735 |
| 3 30 | 6.116 | 8 | 14.054 | 15 | 26.795 | 35 | 70.021 |
| 4 | 6.993 | 8 30 | 14.945 | 16 | 28.675 | 40 | 83.910 |
| 4 30 | 7.870 | 9 | 15.838 | 17 | 30.573 | 45 | 100.0 |

[1] See footnote 1, preceding table.

## SCALE OF VELOCITY EQUIVALENTS OF THE
## BEAUFORT SCALE OF WIND

| Beaufort Scale No. | Description | Indicators of Velocity | Velocity | |
|---|---|---|---|---|
| | | | Meters per Second | Miles per Hour |
| 0 | Calm........................ | Calm air; smoke rises vertically. | Less than 0.3..... | Less than 1 |
| 1 | Light air.................... | Direction of wind shown by smoke drift, but not by wind vanes. | 0.3 to 1.5........... | 1 to 3 |
| 2 | Slight breeze............... | Wind felt on face; leaves rustle; ordinary vane moved by wind. | 1.6 to 3.3........... | 4 to 7 |
| 3 | Gentle breeze.............. | Leaves and small twigs in constant motion; wind extends light flag. | 3.4 to 5.4.......... | 8 to 12 |
| 4 | Moderate breeze......... | Raises dust and loose paper; small branches are moved. | 5.5 to 7.9......... | 13 to 18 |
| 5 | Fresh breeze............... | Small trees in leaf sway; crested wavelets form on inland waters. | 8.0 to 10.7....... | 19 to 24 |
| 6 | Strong breeze.............. | Large branches in motion; whistling heard in telegraph wires; umbrellas used with difficulty. | 10.8 to 13.8..... | 25 to 31 |
| 7 | High wind.................. | Whole trees in motion; inconvenience felt when walking against wind. | 13.9 to 17.1..... | 32 to 38 |
| 8 | Gale......................... | Breaks twigs off trees; wind generally impedes progress. | 17.2 to 20.7..... | 39 to 46 |
| 9 | Strong gale................. | Slight structural damage occurs to signs; branches broken. | 20.8 to 24.4..... | 47 to 54 |
| 10 | Whole gale.... ........... | Trees uprooted or broken; considerable structural damage occurs. | 24.5 to 28.4..... | 55 to 63 |
| 11 | Storm........................ | Very rarely experienced; accompanied by widespread damage; forests windthrown or broken off. | 28.5 to 33.5..... | 64 to 75 |
| 12 | Hurricane................. .... | .................................................................... | 33.6 or above.... | Above 75 |

## APPROXIMATE[1] EQUIVALENTS OF FOREST PRODUCTS

| Cubic Feet | Board Feet | Cords | Cubic Meters (steres) |
|---|---|---|---|
| 1 ............................................... | 6[2] | — | 0.0283 |
| 200[3] ......................................... | 1,000 | 2 | 7.25 |
| 90[4] ........................................... | 500 | 1 | 2.5 |
| 35 ............................................. | 138 | 0.25 | 1 |

[1]Most of these volumetric units are not capable of absolute conversion because of the character of the product and the manner of its utilization.

[2]The board foot per cubic foot ratio varies greatly, depending upon usage. Theoretically, 1 cubic foot contains 12 board feet. For average values 6 should be used, though 10 is a convenient figure for approximations. When the conversion applies to trees, ratios of 3 to 8 should be applied.

[3]The number of cubic feet of wood per thousand board feet varies as between softwoods and hardwoods. In softwoods, conversion factors vary from 160 to 220 cubic feet (working average about 183), and in hardwoods, from 220 to 250 (working average 242).

[4]Standard cord is 4 by 4 by 8 feet and contains 128 cubic feet gross volume (3.625m³). Because of methods of piling, character of material, etc., a cord contains from 75 to 115 cubic feet of solid wood. A rough conversion figure of 90 cubic feet is generally applicable.

## APPROXIMATE QUANTITIES OF FOREST PRODUCTS REPRESENTED BY 1,000 FEET OF TIMBER BOARD MEASURE (1 M FEET B. M.)

| Product | Quantity | Product | Quantity |
|---|---|---|---|
| Shingles | 10,000 | Tight heading, sets | 250 |
| Lath | 5,000 | Fence posts | 200 |
| Hoops | 3,000 | Round timber (ratio, 6:1) | |
| Slack staves | 3,000 | cubic feet | 166.667 |
| Tight staves | 1,000 | Sawed material (ratio, 12:1) | |
| Slack heading, sets | 500 | cubic feet | 83.333 |
| | | Poles (telephone) | 16.667 |

## NUMBER OF TREES PER ACRE BY VARIOUS METHODS OF SPACING

| Spacing (feet) | Trees | Spacing (feet) | Trees | Spacing (feet) | Trees |
|---|---|---|---|---|---|
| | Number | | Number | | Number |
| 2×2 | 10,890 | 7×9 | 691 | 12×15 | 242 |
| 3×3 | 4,840 | 7×10 | 622 | 12×18 | 202 |
| 4×4 | 2,722 | 7×12 | 519 | 12×20 | 182 |
| 4×5 | 2,178 | 7×15 | 415 | 12×25 | 145 |
| 4×6 | 1,815 | 8×8 | 681 | 13×13 | 258 |
| 4×7 | 1,556 | 8×9 | 605 | 13×15 | 223 |
| 4×8 | 1,361 | 8×10 | 544 | 13×20 | 168 |
| 4×9 | 1,210 | 8×12 | 454 | 13×25 | 134 |
| 4×10 | 1,089 | 8×15 | 363 | 14×14 | 222 |
| 5×5 | 1,742 | 8×25 | 218 | 14×15 | 207 |
| 5×6 | 1,452 | 9×9 | 538 | 14×20 | 156 |
| 5×7 | 1,245 | 9×10 | 484 | 14×25 | 124 |
| 5×8 | 1,089 | 9×12 | 403 | 15×15 | 194 |
| 5×9 | 968 | 9×15 | 323 | 15×20 | 145 |
| 5×10 | 871 | 10×10 | 436 | 15×25 | 116 |
| 6×6 | 1,210 | 10×12 | 363 | 16×16 | 170 |
| 6×7 | 1,037 | 10×15 | 290 | 16×20 | 136 |
| 6×8 | 908 | 10×18 | 242 | 16×25 | 109 |
| 6×9 | 807 | 11×11 | 360 | 18×18 | 134 |
| 6×10 | 726 | 11×12 | 330 | 18×20 | 121 |
| 6×12 | 605 | 11×15 | 264 | 18×25 | 97 |
| 6×15 | 484 | 11×20 | 198 | 20×20 | 109 |
| 7×7 | 889 | 11×25 | 158 | 20×25 | 87 |
| 7×8 | 778 | 12×12 | 302 | 25×25 | 70 |

## SCRIBNER DECIMAL C LOG RULE

[In tens—i.e., 0 omitted]

| Diameter (inches)[1] | Contents in Board Feet of Logs of Length Indicated in Feet | | | | | | | | | |
|---|---|---|---|---|---|---|---|---|---|---|
| | 6 | 8 | 10 | 12 | 14 | 16 | 18 | 20 | 22 | 24 |
| 6 | 0.5 | 0.5 | 1 | 1 | 1 | 2 | 2 | 2 | 3 | 3 |
| 7 | .5 | 1 | 1 | 2 | 2 | 3 | 3 | 3 | 4 | 4 |
| 8 | 1 | 1 | 2 | 2 | 2 | 3 | 3 | 3 | 4 | 4 |
| 9 | 1 | 2 | 3 | 3 | 3 | 4 | 4 | 4 | 5 | 6 |
| 10 | 2 | 3 | 3 | 3 | 4 | 6 | 6 | 7 | 8 | 9 |
| 11 | 2 | 3 | 4 | 4 | 5 | 7 | 8 | 8 | 9 | 10 |
| 12 | 3 | 4 | 5 | 6 | 7 | 8 | 9 | 10 | 11 | 12 |
| 13 | 4 | 5 | 6 | 7 | 8 | 10 | 11 | 12 | 13 | 15 |
| 14 | 4 | 6 | 7 | 9 | 10 | 11 | 13 | 14 | 16 | 17 |
| 15 | 5 | 7 | 9 | 11 | 12 | 14 | 16 | 18 | 20 | 21 |
| 16 | 6 | 8 | 10 | 12 | 14 | 16 | 18 | 20 | 22 | 24 |
| 17 | 7 | 9 | 12 | 14 | 16 | 18 | 21 | 23 | 25 | 28 |
| 18 | 8 | 11 | 13 | 16 | 19 | 21 | 24 | 27 | 29 | 32 |
| 19 | 9 | 12 | 15 | 18 | 21 | 24 | 27 | 30 | 33 | 36 |
| 20 | 11 | 14 | 17 | 21 | 24 | 28 | 31 | 35 | 38 | 42 |
| 21 | 12 | 15 | 19 | 23 | 27 | 30 | 34 | 38 | 42 | 46 |
| 22 | 13 | 17 | 21 | 25 | 29 | 33 | 38 | 42 | 46 | 50 |
| 23 | 14 | 19 | 23 | 28 | 33 | 38 | 42 | 47 | 52 | 57 |
| 24 | 15 | 21 | 25 | 30 | 35 | 40 | 45 | 50 | 55 | 61 |
| 25 | 17 | 23 | 29 | 34 | 40 | 46 | 52 | 57 | 63 | 69 |
| 26 | 19 | 25 | 31 | 37 | 44 | 50 | 56 | 62 | 69 | 75 |
| 27 | 21 | 27 | 34 | 41 | 48 | 55 | 62 | 68 | 75 | 82 |
| 28 | 22 | 29 | 36 | 44 | 51 | 58 | 65 | 73 | 80 | 87 |
| 29 | 23 | 31 | 38 | 46 | 53 | 61 | 68 | 76 | 84 | 91 |
| 30 | 25 | 33 | 41 | 49 | 57 | 66 | 74 | 82 | 90 | 99 |
| 31 | 27 | 36 | 44 | 53 | 62 | 71 | 80 | 89 | 98 | 106 |
| 32 | 28 | 37 | 46 | 55 | 64 | 74 | 83 | 92 | 101 | 110 |
| 33 | 29 | 39 | 49 | 59 | 69 | 78 | 88 | 98 | 108 | 118 |
| 34 | 30 | 40 | 50 | 60 | 70 | 80 | 90 | 100 | 110 | 120 |
| 35 | 33 | 44 | 55 | 66 | 77 | 88 | 98 | 109 | 120 | 131 |
| 36 | 35 | 46 | 58 | 69 | 81 | 92 | 104 | 115 | 127 | 138 |
| 37 | 39 | 51 | 64 | 77 | 90 | 103 | 116 | 129 | 142 | 154 |
| 38 | 40 | 54 | 67 | 80 | 93 | 107 | 120 | 133 | 147 | 160 |
| 39 | 42 | 56 | 70 | 84 | 98 | 112 | 126 | 140 | 154 | 168 |
| 40 | 45 | 60 | 75 | 90 | 105 | 120 | 135 | 150 | 166 | 181 |
| 41 | 48 | 64 | 79 | 95 | 111 | 127 | 143 | 159 | 175 | 191 |
| 42 | 50 | 67 | 84 | 101 | 117 | 134 | 151 | 168 | 185 | 201 |
| 43 | 52 | 70 | 87 | 105 | 122 | 140 | 157 | 174 | 192 | 209 |
| 44 | 56 | 74 | 93 | 111 | 129 | 148 | 166 | 185 | 204 | 222 |
| 45 | 57 | 76 | 95 | 114 | 133 | 152 | 171 | 190 | 209 | 228 |
| 46 | 59 | 79 | 99 | 119 | 139 | 159 | 178 | 198 | 218 | 238 |
| 47 | 62 | 83 | 104 | 124 | 145 | 166 | 186 | 207 | 228 | 248 |
| 48 | 65 | 86 | 108 | 130 | 151 | 173 | 194 | 216 | 238 | 260 |
| 49 | 67 | 90 | 112 | 135 | 157 | 180 | 202 | 225 | 247 | 270 |
| 50 | 70 | 94 | 117 | 140 | 164 | 187 | 211 | 234 | 257 | 281 |
| 51 | 73 | 97 | 122 | 146 | 170 | 195 | 219 | 243 | 268 | 292 |
| 52 | 76 | 101 | 127 | 152 | 177 | 202 | 228 | 253 | 278 | 304 |
| 53 | 79 | 105 | 132 | 158 | 184 | 210 | 237 | 263 | 289 | 316 |
| 54 | 82 | 109 | 137 | 164 | 191 | 218 | 246 | 273 | 300 | 328 |
| 55 | 85 | 113 | 142 | 170 | 198 | 227 | 255 | 283 | 312 | 340 |
| 56 | 88 | 118 | 147 | 176 | 206 | 235 | 264 | 294 | 323 | 353 |
| 57 | 91 | 122 | 152 | 183 | 213 | 244 | 274 | 304 | 335 | 365 |
| 58 | 95 | 126 | 158 | 189 | 221 | 252 | 284 | 315 | 347 | 379 |
| 59 | 98 | 131 | 163 | 196 | 229 | 261 | 294 | 327 | 359 | 392 |
| 60 | 101 | 135 | 169 | 203 | 237 | 270 | 304 | 338 | 372 | 406 |

[1]Diameter given is for the small end of the log, measured inside bark.

## THE INTERNATIONAL LOG RULE
[Saw kerf ¼ inch][1]

| Diameter (inches) | Volume in Board Feet of Logs of Indicated Length in Feet | | | | | | | Diameter (inches) |
|---|---|---|---|---|---|---|---|---|
| | 8 | 10 | 12 | 14 | 16 | 18 | 20 | |
| 4 | — | 5 | 5 | 5 | 5 | 5 | 10 | 4 |
| 5 | 5 | 5 | 10 | 10 | 10 | 15 | 15 | 5 |
| 6 | 10 | 10 | 15 | 15 | 20 | 25 | 25 | 6 |
| 7 | 10 | 15 | 20 | 25 | 30 | 35 | 40 | 7 |
| 8 | 15 | 20 | 25 | 35 | 40 | 45 | 50 | 8 |
| 9 | 20 | 30 | 35 | 45 | 50 | 60 | 70 | 9 |
| 10 | 30 | 35 | 45 | 55 | 65 | 75 | 85 | 10 |
| 11 | 35 | 45 | 55 | 70 | 80 | 95 | 105 | 11 |
| 12 | 45 | 55 | 70 | 85 | 95 | 110 | 125 | 12 |
| 13 | 55 | 70 | 85 | 100 | 115 | 135 | 150 | 13 |
| 14 | 65 | 80 | 100 | 115 | 135 | 155 | 175 | 14 |
| 15 | 75 | 95 | 115 | 135 | 160 | 180 | 205 | 15 |
| 16 | 85 | 110 | 130 | 155 | 180 | 205 | 235 | 16 |
| 17 | 95 | 125 | 150 | 180 | 205 | 235 | 265 | 17 |
| 18 | 110 | 140 | 170 | 200 | 230 | 265 | 300 | 18 |
| 19 | 125 | 155 | 190 | 225 | 260 | 300 | 335 | 19 |
| 20 | 135 | 175 | 210 | 250 | 290 | 330 | 370 | 20 |
| 21 | 155 | 195 | 235 | 280 | 320 | 365 | 410 | 21 |
| 22 | 170 | 215 | 260 | 305 | 355 | 405 | 455 | 22 |
| 23 | 185 | 235 | 285 | 335 | 390 | 445 | 495 | 23 |
| 24 | 205 | 255 | 310 | 370 | 425 | 485 | 545 | 24 |
| 25 | 220 | 280 | 340 | 400 | 460 | 525 | 590 | 25 |
| 26 | 240 | 305 | 370 | 435 | 500 | 570 | 640 | 26 |
| 27 | 260 | 330 | 400 | 470 | 540 | 615 | 690 | 27 |
| 28 | 280 | 355 | 430 | 510 | 585 | 665 | 745 | 28 |
| 29 | 305 | 385 | 465 | 545 | 630 | 715 | 800 | 29 |
| 30 | 325 | 410 | 495 | 585 | 675 | 765 | 860 | 30 |
| 31 | 350 | 440 | 530 | 625 | 720 | 820 | 915 | 31 |
| 32 | 375 | 470 | 570 | 670 | 770 | 875 | 980 | 32 |
| 33 | 400 | 500 | 605 | 715 | 820 | 930 | 1045 | 33 |
| 34 | 425 | 535 | 645 | 760 | 875 | 990 | 1110 | 34 |
| 35 | 450 | 565 | 685 | 805 | 925 | 1050 | 1175 | 35 |
| 36 | 475 | 600 | 725 | 855 | 980 | 1115 | 1245 | 36 |
| 37 | 505 | 635 | 770 | 905 | 1040 | 1175 | 1315 | 37 |
| 38 | 535 | 670 | 810 | 955 | 1095 | 1245 | 1390 | 38 |
| 39 | 565 | 710 | 855 | 1005 | 1155 | 1310 | 1465 | 39 |
| 40 | 595 | 750 | 900 | 1060 | 1220 | 1380 | 1540 | 40 |
| 41 | 625 | 785 | 950 | 1115 | 1280 | 1450 | 1620 | 41 |
| 42 | 655 | 825 | 995 | 1170 | 1345 | 1525 | 1705 | 42 |
| 43 | 690 | 870 | 1045 | 1230 | 1410 | 1600 | 1785 | 43 |
| 44 | 725 | 910 | 1095 | 1290 | 1480 | 1675 | 1870 | 44 |
| 45 | 755 | 955 | 1150 | 1350 | 1550 | 1755 | 1960 | 45 |
| 46 | 795 | 995 | 1200 | 1410 | 1620 | 1835 | 2050 | 46 |
| 47 | 830 | 1040 | 1255 | 1475 | 1695 | 1915 | 2140 | 47 |
| 48 | 865 | 1090 | 1310 | 1540 | 1770 | 2000 | 2235 | 48 |
| 49 | 905 | 1135 | 1370 | 1605 | 1845 | 2085 | 2330 | 49 |
| 50 | 940 | 1185 | 1425 | 1675 | 1920 | 2175 | 2425 | 50 |
| 51 | 980 | 1235 | 1455 | 1745 | 2000 | 2265 | 2525 | 51 |
| 52 | 1020 | 1285 | 1545 | 1815 | 2080 | 2355 | 2625 | 52 |
| 53 | 1060 | 1335 | 1605 | 1885 | 2165 | 2445 | 2730 | 53 |
| 54 | 1100 | 1385 | 1670 | 1960 | 2245 | 2540 | 2835 | 54 |
| 55 | 1145 | 1410 | 1735 | 2035 | 2330 | 2640 | 2945 | 55 |

Footnote on last page of table.                                                                    (Continued)

## THE INTERNATIONAL LOG RULE (Continued)

### [Saw kerf ¼ inch][1]

| Diameter (inches) | Volume in Board Feet of Logs of Indicated Length in Feet | | | | | | | Diameter (inches) |
|---|---|---|---|---|---|---|---|---|
| | 8 | 10 | 12 | 14 | 16 | 18 | 20 | |
| 56 | 1190 | 1495 | 1800 | 2110 | 2420 | 2735 | 3050 | 56 |
| 57 | 1230 | 1550 | 1865 | 2185 | 2510 | 2835 | 3165 | 57 |
| 58 | 1275 | 1605 | 1930 | 2265 | 2600 | 2935 | 3275 | 58 |
| 59 | 1320 | 1660 | 2000 | 2345 | 2690 | 3040 | 3390 | 59 |
| 60 | 1370 | 1720 | 2070 | 2425 | 2785 | 3145 | 3510 | 60 |

[1]Scale for seasoned lumber with $\frac{1}{16}$-inch shrinkage per 1-inch board, and saws cutting a ¼-inch kerf, or for green lumber, for saws cutting a $\frac{5}{16}$-inch kerf. For saws cutting a ⅛-inch kerf add 10.5 per cent.

Formula: $((D^2 \times 0.22) - 0.71D) \times 0.904762$ for 4-foot sections.

Taper allowance: ½ inch per 4 feet lineal.

NOTE.—The International log rule gives consistent results under good milling practice. It is the most fair rule for all classes of timber and logs and should be used for second-growth material particularly. For this reason the International volume tables are recommended.

## GROSS VOLUME OF TREE, SCRIBNER LOG RULE

### FORM CLASS 78

| Tree Diameter (inches) | Volume (board feet) by Number of Usable 16-Foot Logs | | | | | | | | | | |
|---|---|---|---|---|---|---|---|---|---|---|---|
| | 1 | 1½ | 2 | 2½ | 3 | 3½ | 4 | 4½ | 5 | 5½ | 6 |
| 10 | 28 | 36 | 44 | 48 | 52 | | | | | | |
| 11 | 38 | 49 | 60 | 67 | 74 | | | | | | |
| 12 | 47 | 61 | 75 | 85 | 95 | 100 | 106 | | | | |
| 13 | 58 | 76 | 94 | 107 | 120 | 128 | 136 | | | | |
| 14 | 69 | 92 | 114 | 130 | 146 | 156 | 166 | | | | |
| 15 | 82 | 109 | 136 | 157 | 178 | 192 | 206 | | | | |
| 16 | 95 | 127 | 159 | 185 | 211 | 229 | 247 | | | | |
| 17 | 109 | 146 | 184 | 215 | 246 | 268 | 289 | | | | |
| 18 | 123 | 166 | 209 | 244 | 280 | 306 | 331 | | | | |
| 19 | 140 | 190 | 240 | 281 | 322 | 352 | 382 | | | | |
| 20 | 157 | 214 | 270 | 317 | 364 | 398 | 432 | 459 | 486 | | |
| 21 | 176 | 240 | 304 | 358 | 411 | 450 | 490 | 523 | 556 | | |
| 22 | 194 | 266 | 338 | 398 | 458 | 504 | 549 | 588 | 626 | | |
| 23 | 214 | 294 | 374 | 441 | 508 | 558 | 607 | 652 | 698 | | |
| 24 | 234 | 322 | 400 | 484 | 558 | 611 | 665 | 718 | 770 | | |
| 25 | 258 | 355 | 452 | 534 | 617 | 678 | 740 | 799 | 858 | | |
| 26 | 281 | 388 | 494 | 585 | 676 | 745 | 814 | 880 | 945 | | |
| 27 | 304 | 420 | 536 | 636 | 736 | 811 | 886 | 959 | 1,032 | | |
| 28 | 327 | 452 | 578 | 686 | 795 | 877 | 959 | 1,040 | 1,120 | 1,190 | 1,261 |
| 29 | 354 | 491 | 628 | 746 | 864 | 953 | 1,042 | 1,132 | 1,222 | 1,306 | 1,389 |
| 30 | 382 | 530 | 678 | 806 | 933 | 1,028 | 1,124 | 1,224 | 1,325 | 1,421 | 1,517 |
| 31 | 411 | 571 | 731 | 871 | 1,011 | 1,117 | 1,223 | 1,328 | 1,434 | 1,541 | 1,648 |
| 32 | 440 | 612 | 784 | 936 | 1,089 | 1,206 | 1,322 | 1,432 | 1,543 | 1,661 | 1,779 |
| 33 | 469 | 654 | 838 | 1,001 | 1,164 | 1,289 | 1,414 | 1,534 | 1,654 | 1,783 | 1,912 |
| 34 | 498 | 695 | 892 | 1,066 | 1,239 | 1,373 | 1,507 | 1,636 | 1,766 | 1,906 | 2,046 |
| 35 | 530 | 742 | 954 | 1,141 | 1,328 | 1,473 | 1,618 | 1,757 | 1,896 | 2,044 | 2,192 |
| 36 | 563 | 789 | 1,015 | 1,216 | 1,416 | 1,572 | 1,728 | 1,877 | 2,026 | 2,182 | 2,338 |
| 37 | 596 | 836 | 1,075 | 1,290 | 1,506 | 1,670 | 1,835 | 1,998 | 2,160 | 2,324 | 2,488 |
| 38 | 629 | 882 | 1,135 | 1,366 | 1,596 | 1,769 | 1,942 | 2,118 | 2,295 | 2,466 | 2,637 |
| 39 | 666 | 935 | 1,204 | 1,449 | 1,694 | 1,881 | 2,068 | 2,251 | 2,434 | 2,616 | 2,799 |
| 40 | 703 | 988 | 1,274 | 1,532 | 1,791 | 1,993 | 2,195 | 2,384 | 2,574 | 2,768 | 2,961 |

(Courtesy U.S. Forest Service [Mesavage-Girard])

## GROSS VOLUME OF TREE, DOYLE LOG RULE
## FORM CLASS 78

| Tree Diameter (inches) | Volume (board feet) by Number of Usable 16-Foot Logs | | | | | | | | | | |
|---|---|---|---|---|---|---|---|---|---|---|---|
| | 1 | 1½ | 2 | 2½ | 3 | 3½ | 4 | 4½ | 5 | 5½ | 6 |
| 10 | 14 | 17 | 20 | 21 | 22 | | | | | | |
| 11 | 22 | 27 | 32 | 35 | 38 | | | | | | |
| 12 | 29 | 36 | 43 | 48 | 53 | 54 | 56 | | | | |
| 13 | 38 | 48 | 59 | 66 | 73 | 76 | 80 | | | | |
| 14 | 48 | 62 | 75 | 84 | 93 | 98 | 103 | | | | |
| 15 | 60 | 78 | 96 | 108 | 121 | 128 | 136 | | | | |
| 16 | 72 | 94 | 116 | 132 | 149 | 160 | 170 | | | | |
| 17 | 86 | 113 | 140 | 161 | 182 | 196 | 209 | | | | |
| 18 | 100 | 132 | 164 | 190 | 215 | 232 | 248 | | | | |
| 19 | 118 | 156 | 194 | 225 | 256 | 276 | 297 | | | | |
| 20 | 135 | 180 | 225 | 261 | 297 | 322 | 346 | 364 | 383 | | |
| 21 | 154 | 207 | 260 | 302 | 344 | 374 | 404 | 428 | 452 | | |
| 22 | 174 | 234 | 295 | 344 | 392 | 427 | 462 | 492 | 521 | | |
| 23 | 195 | 264 | 332 | 388 | 444 | 483 | 522 | 558 | 594 | | |
| 24 | 216 | 293 | 370 | 433 | 496 | 539 | 582 | 625 | 668 | | |
| 25 | 241 | 328 | 414 | 486 | 558 | 609 | 660 | 709 | 758 | | |
| 26 | 266 | 362 | 459 | 539 | 619 | 678 | 737 | 793 | 849 | | |
| 27 | 292 | 398 | 505 | 594 | 684 | 749 | 814 | 877 | 940 | | |
| 28 | 317 | 434 | 551 | 650 | 750 | 820 | 890 | 961 | 1,032 | 1,096 | 1,161 |
| 29 | 346 | 475 | 604 | 714 | 824 | 902 | 980 | 1,061 | 1,142 | 1,218 | 1,294 |
| 30 | 376 | 517 | 658 | 778 | 898 | 984 | 1,069 | 1,160 | 1,251 | 1,339 | 1,427 |
| 31 | 408 | 562 | 717 | 850 | 983 | 1,080 | 1,176 | 1,273 | 1,370 | 1,470 | 1,570 |
| 32 | 441 | 608 | 776 | 922 | 1,068 | 1,176 | 1,283 | 1,386 | 1,488 | 1,600 | 1,712 |
| 33 | 474 | 654 | 835 | 994 | 1,152 | 1,268 | 1,385 | 1,497 | 1,609 | 1,734 | 1,858 |
| 34 | 506 | 700 | 894 | 1,064 | 1,235 | 1,361 | 1,487 | 1,608 | 1,730 | 1,866 | 2,003 |
| 35 | 544 | 754 | 964 | 1,149 | 1,334 | 1,472 | 1,610 | 1,743 | 1,876 | 2,020 | 2,163 |
| 36 | 581 | 808 | 1,035 | 1,234 | 1,434 | 1,583 | 1,732 | 1,878 | 2,023 | 2,173 | 2,323 |
| 37 | 618 | 860 | 1,102 | 1,318 | 1,534 | 1,694 | 1,854 | 2,013 | 2,172 | 2,332 | 2,492 |
| 38 | 655 | 912 | 1,170 | 1,402 | 1,635 | 1,805 | 1,975 | 2,148 | 2,322 | 2,491 | 2,660 |
| 39 | 698 | 974 | 1,250 | 1,498 | 1,746 | 1,932 | 2,118 | 2,298 | 2,479 | 2,662 | 2,844 |
| 40 | 740 | 1,035 | 1,330 | 1,594 | 1,858 | 2,059 | 2,260 | 2,448 | 2,636 | 2,832 | 3,027 |

(Courtesy U.S. Forest Service [Mesavage-Girard])

# Glossary[1]

**Abney level.** A hand surveying instrument designed to measure angles of elevation or depression, expressed in degrees or per cent.

**Acclimation.** The physiological and behavioral adjustments of an organism to changes in its immediate environment.*

**Acid, acetic.** A colorless liquid, obtained commercially in the destructive distillation of wood.

**Acre.** A unit of land measurement, 43,560 square feet or 10 square chains, or a square 208.7 feet on the side.*

**Adaptation.** A change in structure or habit of an organism that produces better adjustment to the environment.*

**Advance growth.** See Growth, advance.

**Aerobic.** Refers to life or processes that can occur only in the presence of oxygen.*

**Afforestation.** Establishment of a forest on an area not previously forested.

**Age class.** One of the intervals into which the range of ages of vegetation is divided for classification and use.

**Age, rotation.** The age at which the stand is considered ready for harvesting under the adopted plan of management.

**Age, stand.** The average age of the trees which compose a stand.

**Age, tree.** The number of years elapsed since the germination of the seed, or the budding of the sprout or root sucker.

**Air pollution.** The presence of contaminants in the air in concentrations that prevent the normal dispersive ability of the air and that interfere directly or indirectly with the health, safety, or comfort of humans or with the full use and enjoyment of their property.*

**Alidade.** An instrument used in fire towers to locate forest fires. The alidade is equipped with sights for determining the direction of the fire.*

**All-aged.** Applies to a stand in which theoretically trees of all ages up to and including those of the felling age are found. See also Even-aged and Uneven-aged.

**Ammate.** A plant-killing chemical, ammonium sulfamate, usually applied in crystalline form in cups cut at the base of an undesirable tree or stump.

**Anaerobic.** Refers to life or processes that occur in the absence of oxygen.*

**Annual ring.** See Ring, annual.

**Area, cutting.** A portion of woodland upon which timber is being cut or will be cut.*

---

[1]Definitions, except for those indicated by asterisks, were taken in whole or in part from *Forest Terminology*, a publication of the Society of American Foresters.

**Area, virgin.** An area in which there has been virtually no disturbance of the natural vegetation.

**Artificial reproduction.** See Reproduction.

**Aspect.** The direction toward which a slope faces. Syn. "Exposure."

**Auger, soil.** An instrument or tool used for boring holes in soil and taking samples thereof.

**Back-fire.** In fire suppression, a fire set along the inner side of a control line to destroy the fuels on a strip sufficiently wide to check an advancing fire.

**Bar, planting.** A hand tool used in making a slit-hole in which trees are planted.

**Bark, inner.** The physiologically active layer of tissues between the cambium and the last-formed periderm.

**Bark, outer.** The layer of dead tissue, of a dry corky nature, outside the last-formed periderm.

**Bearing (of a line).** Direction or course of a line in relation to the cardinal points of the compass.*

**B.F.** Abbreviation for "board feet."

**Biomass.** Weight of complete trees, including roots, stump, stem, limbs, branches, and leaves.*

**Blaze.** A mark placed on a standing tree to call special attention to the tree.

**B.M.** Abbreviation for "board measure," meaning board feet.

**Board foot.** See Foot, board.

**Bolt.** Any short log, such as a pulpwood or veneer bolt.

**Borer, increment.** An augerlike instrument with a hollow bit, used to extract cores from trees for the determination of growth and age.

**Breast high.** Four and a half feet high; the point on a tree where diameter measurements are taken.

**Broadleaf.** See Hardwood.

**Burning, controlled.** Any burning that has been started intentionally by a landowner to accomplish some particular purpose, and over which that person exercises some surveillance or control.

**Burning, prescription.** The application of fire to land under such conditions of weather, soil moisture, time of day, and other factors as presumably will result in the intensity of heat and spread required to accomplish specific silvicultural, wildlife, grazing, or fire-hazard reduction purposes.

**Butt cut.** The first log above the stump. Syn. "Butt log."

**Caliper (or Calipers), tree.** An instrument used to measure diameters of trees or logs. It consists of a graduated rule with two arms, one fixed at right angles to one end of the rule, the other sliding parallel to the fixed arm.

**Cambium.** A usually laterally disposed sheath of generative tissues between xylem and phloem. It gives rise to secondary xylem (wood) and phloem, a part of inner bark.

**Canopy.** See Cover, crown.

**Capacity, grazing.** In range management, the ability of a range unit, exclusive of severe drought years, to give adequate support to a constant number of livestock for a stated period each year without deteriorating with respect to this or other proper land use; expressed in number of livestock per acre of given kind or kinds, or in number of acres per specified animals.

**Capital, forest.** The lands, timber, reproduction, and physical improvements, such as roads and fire towers, which make up a forest property.

**Cast, leaf.** A premature shedding of leaves.

**Cast, needle.** The leaf cast of needle-bearing conifers.

**Catface.** A scar on the surface of a log, generally elliptical in shape, resulting from wounds which have not healed over; also a fire scar at the base of a tree.

**Cellulose.** A complex carbohydrate occurring in wood and all other vegetable matter.

**Chain.** A unit of measure 66 feet or 4 rods long.*

**Charcoal.** One of the principal products of the destructive distillation of wood.

**Check.** A lengthwise separation of the wood, which usually extends across the rings of annual growth, commonly resulting from stresses set up in wood during seasoning.

**Chips.** Hogged wood ready for cooking into pulp. In turpentining, particles of wood or bark fallen into the cups.

**Chlorophyll.** The green coloring matter in plants necessary for photosynthesis.*

**Chlorosis.** Yellowing or whitening of normally green plant parts. It can be caused by disease organisms, lack of oxygen or nutrients in the soil, or by various air pollutants.*

**Class, age.** One of the intervals into which the range of ages of vegetation is divided for classification and use.

**Class, crown.** A designation of trees in a forest with crowns of similar development and occupying similar positions in the crown cover. Differentiation into crown classes is intended for application to even-aged stands and within small even-aged groups in which trees in an uneven-aged stand are often arranged. The following four crown classes are commonly recognized: dominant, codominant, intermediate, and overtopped (suppressed).

**Class, diameter.** One of the intervals into which the range of diameters of trees in a forest is divided for purposes of classification and use.

**Clean-boled.** Free or cleared of branches; used to designate timber with a satisfactory length of clear bole.

**Cleaning.** A cutting operation in a young stand not past the sapling stage to provide better growing conditions for crop trees by eliminating trees of similar age but of less desirable species or form which are overtopping or likely to overtop the crop trees. Syn. "Disengagement cutting; Weeding."

**Clearcutting.** An area on which the entire timber stand has been cut. See Cutting, methods of.

**Clinometer.** An instrument for measuring vertical angles or slopes.*

**Codominant.** Trees with crowns forming the general level of the crown cover and receiving full light from above, but comparatively little from the sides; usually the medium-sized crowns more or less crowded on the sides.

**Collar, root.** The transition zone between stem and root. Usually recognizable in trees and seedlings by the presence of a slight swelling.

**Combustion.** Burning. Technically, a rapid oxidation accompanied by the release of energy in the form of heat and light.*

**Compass, staff.** An instrument used to determine direction and which is placed on a Jacob staff for stability.*

**Conifer.** A tree belonging to the order Coniferae, usually evergreen, with cones and needle-shaped leaves, and producing wood known commercially as "softwood."

**Conk.** A definite, individual, woody spore-bearing structure of a wood-destroying fungus, which projects beyond the bark.

**Conky.** Name applied to a log or tree bearing sporophores of wood-rotting fungi.

**Conservation.** A relatively new word that describes natural resources. Gifford Pinchot, a turn-of-the-century forester, fabricated the word to describe a natural resource process. It meant "wise use." Through the years it has taken on an extended meaning that really means "Wise use over a period of time." The time factor forces one to consider the consequence of current use compared to future use. This removes the element of exploitation which could occur under the "wise-use" concept alone.*

**Control, biological.** Control of plants, diseases, and animal pests by the use of natural enemies.

**Control, fire.** All activities concerned with the protection of wild land and forest growth from fire.

**Controlled burning.** See Burning, controlled.

**Cooperage, slack and tight.** Containers consisting of two round heads and a body composed of one or more staves held together with hoops. In slack cooperage, used as containers for non-liquid products, the staves may be made from one or more sheets of rotary-cut veneer. In tight cooperage, used as containers for liquids, the numerous staves fit snugly together and are held tightly with hoops.

**Cord.** A volume measure of stacked wood. A standard cord is 4×4×8 feet, or 128 cubic feet of space. A long cord (unit) contains 160 cubic feet of space and is 4×5×8 feet. Since round wood cannot be stacked to give solid volume, actual wood volume varies between 70 and 90 cubic feet per cord.

**Core, increment.** That part of the cross-section of a tree extracted by an increment borer. Used to determine age and data on growth.

**Corewood or core.** The inner layer or layers of plywood or coreboard, usually of low-quality material.

**Cover, crown.** The canopy of green leaves and branches formed by the crowns of all trees in a forest. Syn. Leaf canopy.

**Creosote, coal-tar (solution).** A preservative mixture of coal-tar creosote commonly used for treating crossties and certain other timbers; may contain up to 50 per cent coal tar.

**Creosote, coal-tar (solution).** A preservative mixture of coal-tar creosote commonly used for treating crossties and certain other timbers; may contain up to 50 per cent coal tar.

**Creosote, petroleum (solution).** A preservative mixture of petroleum and coal-tar creosote, commonly used for treating crossties. The proportion of petroleum, which serves as a diluent for the creosote, may range from 30 to 70 per cent.

**Creosote, wood-tar.** A distillate oil derived from wood-tar produced as a by-product in the destructive distillation of either hardwoods or softwoods.

**Crook.** A defect in logs and poles or piling, consisting of an abrupt bend.

**Crop.** In turpentine orcharding, a working unit comprising the number of cups worked by a chipper; or, technically, 10,000 cups or faces.

**Crop rotation.** See Rotation.

**Crop tree.** See Tree, crop.

**Crosscut.** To cut a board, timber, or log at right angles to the general direction of the fibers. Syn. Buck.

**Crosshaul.** A method of loading log-transportation vehicles. One end of a line is passed over the load, around the log to be loaded, and made fast to the load. Power applied to the other end of the line imparts a rolling motion to the log.

**Crosstie.** Cross member, either hewn or sawed, supporting railroad rails.

**Crotch.** The fork of a tree or branch; a small sled, without a tongue, often made from the natural fork of a tree and used as an aid in skidding logs on stony or bare ground. Syn. Crazy dray; Go-devil; Lizard.

**Crown.** The branches and foliage of a tree; the upper portion of a tree.

**Crown class.** See Class, crown.

**Crown density.** See Density, crown.

**Crown fire.** See Fire, crown.

**Cubic foot.** See Foot, cubic.

**Cull.** A tree or log of merchantable size rendered unmerchantable because of poor form, limbyness, rot, or other defect.

**Cup.** A cut or notch made in the base of a tree or stump with an axe for the purpose of holding ammate or other such chemicals.

**Cupping.** In turpentining, the installation of a container and chipping of a tree for production of oleoresin.

**Cutting area.** See Area, cutting.

**Cutting cycle.** See Cycle, cutting.

**Cutting, improvement.** A cutting made in a stand past the sapling stage for the purpose of improving its composition and character, by removing trees of less desirable species, form, and condition in the main crown canopy.

**Cutting, methods of:**

1. **Clearcutting.** Removal of the entire stand in one cut; an area on which the entire stand has been so removed.

2. **Seed-tree.** Removal of the mature timber in one cut, except for a small number of seed trees left singly or in small groups; called a group cutting when the seed trees are left in groups; also a reserve cutting when specially selected seed trees are left for growth as well as to furnish seed.

3. **Selection.** Removal of mature timber, usually the oldest or largest trees, either as single scattered trees or in small groups at relatively short intervals, commonly 5 to 20 years, repeated indefinitely. By this means, a continuous establishment of natural reproduction is encouraged and an uneven-aged stand is maintained.

4. **Shelterwood.** Removal of the mature timber in a series of cuttings, which extend over a period of years usually equal to not more than one-quarter and often not more than one-tenth of the time required to grow the crop. The establishment of natural reproduction under the partial shelter of seed trees is encouraged.

**Cuttings, intermediate.** Cuttings made in a stand between the time of its formation and its major harvest.

**Cycle, cutting.** The planned interval between major felling operations in the same stand.

**Damage, ice.** Breakage of tops and branches and of stems in young stands; in juvenile conifer stands, the stripping of branches and needles from trees by an ice storm.

**Danger, fire.** The resultant of both constant and variable factors, which determines whether fires will start, spread, and do damage, and determines the difficulty of control.

**Deciduous.** Term applied to trees which drop their leaves in the fall.*

**Decimal Scale.** A log scale graduated and marked in tenths of board feet.

**Deck, log.** The platform in a sawmill upon which logs are held previous to sawing. Syn. Mill deck.

**Decomposition.** Reduction of net energy level and change in chemical composition of organic matter because of the actions of aerobic or anaerobic microorganisms.*

**Defect.** Any irregularity or imperfection in a tree, log, piece, product, or in lumber that reduces the volume of sound wood or lowers its durability, strength, or utility value.

**Dendrology.** The identification and systematic classification of trees.

**Density, crown.** The compactness of the crown cover of the forest, dependent upon (1) the distance apart and (2) the compactness of the individual crowns. A loose term combining the meanings of crown closure and shade density.

**Density, stand.** Density of stocking expressed in number of trees, basal area, volume, or other criteria.

**Diameter breast high.** The diameter of a tree at 4.5 feet above average ground level; in National Forest practice it is measured from the highest ground level. Abbreviated "**d.b.h.**" The abbreviations "**d.o.b.**" and "**d.i.b.**" are used to designate diameter measured outside and inside the bark, respectively, usually at the small end of the log.

**Diameter class.** All trees in a stand whose diameters are within prescribed limits.

**Diameter tape.** A tape, based on relationship of circumference to diameter, for measuring the diameters of trees directly.

**Dibble.** A metal tool used to make a hole for planting of seedlings.*

**Dioecious.** Male and female flowers produced on separate plants.

**Dominant.** Trees with crowns extending above the general level of the crown cover and receiving full light from above and partly from the side; larger than the average trees in the stand, and with crowns well developed but possibly somewhat crowded on the sides.

**Dote.** An early stage of decay usually characterized by a change in color of the wood in patches or streaks which may be lighter or darker than normal. See Rot.

**Drill.** A shallow trench in a nursery bed in which seeds are planted.

**Duff.** Forest litter and other organic debris in various stages of decomposition on top of the mineral soil, typical of coniferous forests in cool climates where rate of decomposition is slow, and where litter accumulation exceeds decay.

**Durability.** As applied to wood, the lasting qualities or permanence in service, with particular reference to decay. Syn. Decay resistance.

**Ecology.** The science which deals with the relation of plants and animals to their environment and to the site factors that operate in controlling their distribution and growth.

**Ecosystem.** The interacting system of a biological community and its non-living environment.*

**Entomology, forest.** The science that deals with insects and their relation to forests and forest products.

**Epidemic.** A widespread high level of insect or disease incidence beyond normal proportions, and usually accompanied by increased damage.

**Even-aged.** Applied to a stand in which relatively small age differences exist between individual trees. The maximum difference in age permitted in an even-aged stand is usually 10 to 20 years, though where the stand will not be harvested until it is 100 to 200 years old, larger differences up to 25 per cent of the rotation age may be allowed.

**Excelsior.** Shavings utilized for packing material.

**Exotic.** Not native, foreign.*

**Extraction, seed.** Process of removing seed from fruit.

**Farm, tree.** An area, privately owned, dedicated by the owner to the production of timber crops.

**Fire, crown.** A fire which runs through the tops of living trees, brush, or chaparral.

**Fire, ground.** A fire that not only consumes all the organic materials of the forest floor but also burns into the underlying soil itself; for example, a peat fire. (Usually combined with, but not to be confused with, a surface fire.)

**Fire line.** See Line, fire.

**Fire, surface.** A fire which runs over the forest floor and burns only the surface litter, the loose debris, and the smaller vegetation. See Fire, ground.

**Firebreak.** An existing barrier, or one constructed before a fire occurs, from which all or most of the inflammable materials have been removed; designed to stop or check creeping or running but not spotting fires, or to serve as a line from which to work and facilitate the movement of firefighters and equipment in fire suppression.

**Flash point.** The temperature at which material will burst into flame.*

**Foot, board.** A unit of measurement represented by a board 1 foot long, 1 foot wide, and 1 inch thick (144 cubic inch). Abbr. Ft. b.m.; bd. ft. In finished or surface lumber, the board-foot measure is based on the measurement before surfacing or other finishing. In practice the working unit is 1,000 board feet. Abbr. M bd. ft.; M B.M.; M B.F.

**Foot, cubic.** A cube 12 inches on a side. A cubic foot of wood is considered to contain from 6 to 10 board feet.

**Forage.** In range management, unharvested plant material of any kind available for animal consumption. When cut, it becomes feed.

**Forb.** A non-grass-like herbaceous plant; same as herb or weed in the range stock producer's language. Syn. Broadleaved herb.

**Forest, multiple use.** The practice of forestry which combines two or more objectives, such as production of wood or wood-derivative products, forage and browse for domestic livestock, proper environmental conditions for wildlife, landscape effects, protection against floods and erosion, recreation, production and protection of water supplies, and national defense.

**Forest type.** See Type, forest.

**Forest utilization.** See Utilization, forest.

**Forest, virgin.** A mature or overmature forest growth essentially uninfluenced by human activity.

**Forestation.** The establishment of forest naturally or artificially upon areas where it has been absent or insufficient.

**Fungicide.** A pesticide chemical that kills fungi or prevents them from causing diseases, usually on plants of economic importance.*

**Fungus.** A plant without chlorophyll which derives its nourishment from the organic matter of other plants.*

**Gall.** A pronounced, localized swelling of greatly modified structure which occurs on plants from irritation by a foreign organism.

**Gallery.** A passage, burrow, or mine bored or excavated by an insect under bark or in wood for feeding or egg-laying purposes.

**Germination.** Botanically, the growth of a seed or spore.

**Girdle.** To encircle the stem of a living tree with cuts that completely sever bark and cambium and often are carried well into the outer sapwood, for the purpose of killing the tree by preventing the passage of nutrients or by admitting toxic materials.

**Grade.** To assort lumber of logs and classify according to quality. Syn. Cull.

**Grain.** The direction, size, arrangement, appearance, or quality of the fibers in wood. To have a specific meaning, the term must be qualified.

**Ground fire.** See Fire, ground.

**Growing stock.** All the trees growing in a forest or in a specified part of it, generally expressed in terms of "number" or "volume."

**Growth, advance.** Young trees which have become established naturally in a forest before cutting or regeneration operations are begun. Syn. Advance reproduction.

**Growth rate.** See Rate, growth.

**Growth, second.** Forests that originate naturally after removal of a previous stand by cutting, fire, or other cause. A loosely used term for young stands.

**Habit.** The general form of arrangement of stem, roots, and branches, or of the entire plant, possessed in common by a species in a given habitat.

**Habitat.** The unit-area of environment, practically synonymous with site; the kind of place in which the plant or animal lives.

**Hardwood.** Generally, one of the botanical group of trees that have broad leaves, in contrast to the needle-bearing conifers; also wood produced by broad-leaved trees regardless of texture or density.

**Harvest.** See Cutting, methods of.

**Heartwood.** The inner core of a woody stem, wholly composed of non-living cells and usually differentiated from the outer enveloping layer (sapwood) by its darker color. Syn. Duramen.

**Heavy metals.** Metallic elements with high molecular weights, generally toxic in low concentrations to plant and animal life.*

**Heel-in.** To store young trees prior to planting by placing them in a trench and covering the roots with soil.

**Height, merchantable.** The length of the tree stem from the top of the stump to the top end of the last merchantable section. Usually expressed in feet or number of logs or bolts of some standard length.

**Herbicide.** A pesticide chemical used to destroy or control the growth of weeds, trees, shrubs, or other undesirable plants.*

**High-grading.** The removal from the stand of only the best trees.

**Hog.** A device used to reduce waste pieces of lumber and slabs, or small stems, to chip form.

**Hot-and-cold bath.** See Preservation, methods of.

**Humidity, relative.** The ratio of the actual mass of water vapor per unit of volume to the mass of water vapor that would saturate that volume at the same temperature and pressure, or roughly the per cent saturation of the space.

**Humus.** The plant and animal residues of the soil, litter excluded, which are undergoing decomposition.

**Hypsometer.** An instrument used to measure the heights of trees, employing geometric or trigonometric principles. Variety of instruments used.

**Ignite.** To burn; to burst into flames.

**Improvement cutting.** See Cutting, improvement.

**Incising.** Making slit-like holes in the lateral surface of timbers that are resistant to treatment, so deeper and more uniform penetration of a preservative may be obtained.

**Increment.** An increase in the diameter, basal area, height, volume, quality, or value of individual trees or stands in relation to time.

**Increment borer.** See Borer, increment.

**Intermediate.** Referring to trees shorter than those in the dominant or codominant classes, but with crowns either below or extending into the crown cover formed by codominant and dominant trees, receiving a little direct light from above, but none from the sides; usually with small crowns considerably crowded on the sides.

**Interplant.** To set seedlings among existing forest growth, planted or natural.

**Intolerance.** The incapacity of a tree to develop and grow in the shade of and in competition with other trees.

**Kerf, saw.** The width of cut made by a saw.

**Kiln, dry.** A structure heated by gas or electricity, in which lumber is seasoned artificially or pine cones are dried and opened.

**Kiln-dry (or kiln-dried).** A term applied to wood dried in a kiln.

**Knee.** A round or spurlike growth rising from the roots of some swamp trees such as bald cypress and tupelo.

**Length, clear.** The portion of the stem of a tree free from limbs, from the ground to the lowest branch or branch stub.

**Limit, diameter.** The smallest, and occasionally the largest, size to which trees or logs are to be measured, cut, or used. The points to which the limit usually refers are stump, breast height, or top.

**Line, fire.** The narrow portion of a control line from which inflammable materials have been removed by scraping or digging down to mineral soil.

**Litter.** The uppermost layer of the organic debris composed of freshly fallen or slightly decomposed organic materials. Commonly designated by the letter L.

**Log.** To cut and deliver logs; tree segment suitable for lumber and other products; tree segment 8 to 16 feet in length.

**Log rule.** See Rule, log.

**Log scale.** See Stick, scale.

**Logger.** Anyone who is engaged in a logging operation; locally, anyone who hauls logs to landings or skidways.*

**Logging, selective.** See Cutting, methods of: Selection.

**Lookout.** A station or post used primarily in the detection of fires. A permanent lookout is generally equipped with a lookout tower, or structure erected to enable the tower observer to get above nearby obstructions; this may be either a lookout house equipped for living quarters or merely a lookout observatory.

**Lop.** To chop branches, tops, or small trees after felling, so that the slash will lie close to the ground; to cut the limbs from a felled tree.

**Lumber, green.** Lumber with the moisture content greater than that of air-dried lumber. Unseasoned lumber.

**Machine, planting.** Mechanical equipment which opens a hole or furrow, closes it again, and firms the soil about a tree seedling usually inserted in the furrow by hand.

**Management, forest.** The application of business methods and technical forest principles to the operation of a forest property.

**Management plan.** See Plan, management.

**Management, range.** Application of business methods and technical principles to the handling of the range.

**Many-aged.** See All-aged.

**Marking, timber.** Selecting and indicating, usually by a blaze or paint spot, trees to be cut or retained in a cutting operation. Syn. Spotting.

**Maturity.** For a given species or stand, the approximate age beyond which growth declines or decay begins to increase at a rate likely to assume economic importance.

**Measure, board (B.M.).** A unit of measurement of the volume in board feet of logs or lumber.

**Mensuration, forest.** A science dealing with the measurement of the volume, growth, and development of individual trees and stands, and the determination of the various products obtainable from them.

**Merchantable.** Trees or stands of a size and quality suitable for marketing and utilization. They may or may not be so located as to be accessible for logging. Also a specific grade of southern yellow pine timbers.

**Mill, portable.** A small sawmill that can be readily moved from one place to another. The usual daily capacity ranges from 3 M to 10 M board feet.

**Mill, stationary.** A sawmill which has a permanent location as contrasted with a portable sawmill which may be moved at frequent intervals.

**Mill tally.** See Tally, lumber.

**Moisture, soil.** In forest description, the relative amount of moisture in the soil, usually applied to A and B horizons and occasionally to humic material.

**Monoecious.** Unisexual flowers of both sexes produced on the same plant.

**Mortality.** Death or destruction of forest trees as a result of competition, disease, insect damage, drought, wind, fire, and other factors.

**National forests.** Administered by the National Forest System, national forests differ from national parks in that recreation is not their only use. On most forest land, timber, water, wildlife, recreation, and grazing are compatible resources, and these are managed for productive and sustained yields according to the land's capability. There are more acres of wilderness areas in national forests than in national parks. The National Forest System administers 154 forests and 19 grasslands.*

**National parks.** Established by Congress, the National Park Service promotes and regulates the use of national parks, monuments, and reservations and conserves the scenery, the natural and historic objects, and the wildlife therein. The Park Service administers 195 separate areas and manages some areas for historical or recreational uses. Each of the 35 national parks was established to preserve a unique natural area for enjoyment and study. National parks are sometimes confused with national forests.*

**Naval stores.** Turpentine and resin derived from the distillation of oleoresins from slash and longleaf pine.

**Non-inflammable.** Not capable of being ignited.*

**Normal growing stock.** The maximum volume which any given site is capable of maintaining in relation to economic conditions and the desires of the operator.

**Notch.** See Undercut.

**Nursery, forest trees.** An area in which young trees are grown for forest planting. May be characterized as seedling or transplant, temporary or permanent.

**Old growth.** Describes virgin forests, or forests with trees over 100 years of age.*

**One-lick method.** See Suppression, fire.

**Outplant.** Planting nursery-grown stock in a field. See Transplant.

**Overgrazing.** Grazing so heavy as to impair future forage production and cause range deterioration through consequential damage to plants or soil or both.

**Overmaturity.** That period in the life cycle of trees and stands when growth or value is declining. See Maturity.

**Overrun.** The excess of the amount of lumber actually sawed from logs over the estimated volume or log scale, usually expressed in per cent of log scale.

**Overstocked.** A condition of the stand or forest indicating more trees than normal or full stocking would require. Dominants in such stands have narrow growth rings indicating suppression.

**Overstocking.** The placing of more animals on a range area than the range will support or maintain through the grazing period without overgrazing. Contrast overgrazing.

**Overstory.** That portion of the trees in a stand forming the upper crown cover.

**Overtopped.** Trees with crowns entirely below the general level of the crown cover receiving no direct light either from above or from the sides. Syn. Suppressed.

**Palatability.** The relative relish with which forage plants are consumed by domestic livestock or other animals. This may vary with composition of the plant cover or the season of grazing.

**Partial cut.** Any method of cutting mature trees, such as shelterwood cut, selection cut, or seed tree cut.*

**Particulates.** Finely divided solid or liquid particles in the air or in an emission. Particulates include dust, smoke, fumes, mist, spray, and fog.*

**Pathology, forest.** The science that pertains to diseases of forest trees or stands, and to the deterioration of forest products by organisms.

**Pen.** A loose, rectangular stack of fuelwood or pulpwood in layers of two pieces each laid at right angles to the ends of the previous two sticks. Pens vary in height and width.

**Per cent, growth.** The ratio of current or periodic annual increment, usually in terms of volume, to the quantity at the beginning or middle of the period in question.

**Percolation.** The movement of water through the soil.

**Piling.** Round timbers to be driven into the ground to support other structures.

**Pitch.** A term applied to the resin occurring in the wood of certain conifers.

**Pitch pocket.** See Pocket, pitch.

**Plan, management.** A written plan for the operation of a forest property using forestry principles. It usually records data and prescribes measures designed to provide optimum use of all forest resources.

**Planer, green.** A planing mill in which green lumber is surfaced.

**Plant.** To set out young trees or cuttings, to establish a forest crop. Sometimes used loosely to include direct seeding. Trees may be set out as bare-root stock, or with roots within a ball of earth, or in earth within a container (pot).

**Plantation.** An artificially reforested area established by planting or by direct seeding.

**Planting bar.** See Bar, planting. See Dibble.

**Plot, sample.** An area laid out for the purpose of experimentation or of mensuration; may be permanent or temporary, Syn. Study plot.

**Plow, fire.** A heavy duty, usually specialized machine either of the share or of the disc type, designed solely for the abusive work in the woods and pulled with horses, tractors, or jeeps to construct firebreaks and fire lines.

**Plywood.** An assembly product constructed of three or more layers of veneer joined with glue and usually laid with the grain of adjoining plies at right angles to one another. Usually an odd number of plies are used to give balanced construction.

**Pocket, pitch.** A well defined, lens-shaped opening between or within annual growth layers of coniferous wood, usually either solid or liquid containing pitch; bark may also be present in the pocket. Syn. Gum check.

**Pole.** A young tree 4 inches d.b.h. or more. The maximum size of poles is usually, though not invariably, taken to be some d.b.h. between 8 and 12 inches. See Sapling.

**Poles.** Timbers in the round, usually used to support power or telephone lines.

**Precipitation.** Deposits of atmospheric moisture in liquid or solid form, including rain, snow, hail, dew, or hoarfrost.

**Preframing.** In a framing mill or otherwise, fashioning each piece of wood to the final shape and dimension required in the finished structure before treatment.

**Preheating.** A practice followed at certain wood-treating plants, in which timbers resistant to impregnation are steeped in a hot preservative (creosote) before pressure is applied.

**Prescription burning.** See Burning, prescription.

**Preservation.** In natural resources, "preservation," other than wood preservation, is a term related to land use. The meaning stems from nineteenth century land reserves wherein areas and resources were set aside for limited or restricted use and development. Preservation often restricts land to recreation or scientific study. Preservation may be contrasted to the principle of multiple use which rather intensively develops one or more of an area's resources.*

**Preservation, wood.** Wood preservation is the art of protecting timber and wood products against the action of destructive living organisms, especially fungi, insects, and marine borers. Compare with "protection." It usually refers to the treatment of wood with chemical substances (preservatives) which reduces its susceptibility to deterioration by organisms.

**Preservation, methods of.** Ordinary methods of wood preservation by impregnating the wood with chemical preservatives are of two orders—non-pressure and pressure—depending on whether the impregnation process is aided by artificial pressure.

    1. **Brush, spray, or pouring.** Application of one or more coats of coal-tar creosote or similar oils.

    2. **Dipping.** A superficial open-tank method of treating seasoned wood by immersing it for several minutes in a bath of creosote or other preservative oil or sash preservative oil or sash preservative (chlorinated phenol solution).

3. **Hot-and-cold bath.** Immersion of seasoned wood for several hours or longer in successive baths of hot and relatively cool preservative—preservative oils or water-soluble salts may be used, but commonly coal tar and mixtures of creosote and other oils are employed. Known also as open-tank process.

4. **Open-tank process.** See no. 3: Preservation, methods of.

5. **Steeping.** An open-tank treatment in which the wood is submerged, usually in a water solution, for a period of days.

6. **Pressure treatment.** The most widely used pressure treatment is that in which the wood is placed in a closed treating cylinder or retort, usually 6 feet in diameter and 30 to 180 feet long, and impregnated with preservative under considerable pressure.

**Preservative.** A chemical substance which, when suitably applied to wood, makes it resistant to attack by fungi, insects, or marine borers.

**Preserve.** In wildlife management, a game shooting area on which game species are propagated, released, or otherwise maintained.

**Prevention, fire.** Those fire-control activities concerned with the attempt to reduce the number of fires through education, hazard reduction, and law enforcement.

**Properties, mechanical.** Those properties inherent in wood which determine its capacity to resist the action of applied forces that tend to change its size and shape.

**Protection, forest.** The activities connected with the prevention and control of damage to living forests from fire, insects, disease, and other injurious and destructive agencies.

**Pruning.** The removal of live or dead branches from standing trees. This may be done artificially or naturally. Natural pruning results from such causes as deficiency of light, also decay, snow, ice, etc. Syn. Self-pruning.

**Pubescent.** Bearing fine, woolly hairs such as on leaves, twigs, or buds.*

**Pulp, wood.** Mechanically ground or chemically digested wood used in the manufacture of paper and allied products. Bleached and purified chemical wood pulp is also widely employed for rayon and other chemical uses.

**Pulpwood.** Wood cut or prepared primarily for manufacture into wood pulp, for subsequent manufacture into paper, fiberboard, or other products, depending largely on the species cut and the pulping process.

**Punky.** A soft, weak, often spongy wood condition caused by decay.

**Pure stand.** See Stand, pure.

**Quarter-sawed.** Wood so sawed that the growth rings form an angle of 45 to 90 degrees with the surface of the piece.

**Radial (surface).** A longitudinal surface or plane extending wholly or in part from the pith to the bark.

**Range.** Land not under cultivation which produces forage suitable for grazing by livestock. Includes forest land producing forage.

**Range, open.** An extensive grazing area on which the free movement of livestock is unrestricted.

**Range yearlong.** Range suitable for grazing use at any time of the year.

**Ranger.** An administrative officer in charge of a unit of forest land, usually a subdivision of a public forest or park. Various classifications are recognized, as forest ranger, park ranger, and county ranger.

**Rate, growth.** With reference to wood, the rate at which the wood substance has been added to the tree at any particular point; usually expressed in terms of number of rings per inch.

**Ray.** In wood anatomy, a ribbon-shaped strand of tissue formed by the cambium and extending in a radial direction across the grain.

**Reforestation.** The natural or artificial restocking of an area with forest trees; most commonly used in reference to the latter.

**Reproduction.** The process by which a forest or range is renewed.
  1. **Artificial.** Renewal by direct seeding or planting. Syn. Reforestation.
  2. **Natural.** Renewal by self-sown seeds, sprouts, rhizomes, etc. Syn. Regeneration. (See Cutting, methods of.) Also seedings or saplings of any origin. Syn. Young growth.

**Reproduction, advance.** See Growth, advance.

**Reproduction, cutting.** See Cutting, methods of.

**Reseeding, range.** Sowing of seed on range lands to restore or increase forage production.

**Residual stand.** That portion of trees left after any partial cut.*

**Resins.** A class of inflammable, amorphous, vegetable substances secreted by certain plants or trees, and characterizing the wood of many coniferous species.

**Restocking.** Applied to an area on which the forest is being re-established by natural means.

**Ring, annual.** The growth layer of one year, as viewed on the cross section of a stem, branch, or root.

**Ring, false annual.** One of the growth rings of a multiple annual ring.

**Ring, growth.** Any growth layer as viewed on the cross section of a stem, branch, or root.

**Root collar.** See Collar, root.

**Root sucker.** See Sucker.

**Rot.** Wood in a state of decay.

**Rot, dry.** A decay of the brown root type, caused by specialized fungi able to conduct moisture from an available source and extend their attack to wood previously too dry to decay. Found chiefly in buildings. The term is open to the misinterpretation that wood will rot when dry, which is not true.

**Rot, heart.** A decay characteristically confined to the heartwood. It usually originates in the living tree.

**Rotation.** The period of years required to establish and grow timber crops to a specified condition of maturity.

**Rule, log.** A table showing the estimated or calculated amount of lumber which can be sawed from logs of given length and diameter.
  1. **Doyle rule.** A simple formula rule used in the eastern and southern United States. It underestimates the volume of small logs and overestimates logs over 28 inches in diameter.
  2. **Doyle-Scribner rule.** A combination rule derived by using Doyle rule values for logs up to 28 inches in diameter and Scribner rule for logs larger than 28 inches.
  3. **International rule.** A formula rule allowing ½-inch taper for each 4 feet of length and ⅛-inch shrinkage for each 1-inch board. Closely approximating the green-chain lumber tally, in one form it assumes a ⅛-inch kerf; in modified form it assumes a ¼-inch kerf.

    4. **Scribner rule.** A diagram rule, one of the oldest in existence. It assumes 1-inch boards and ¼-inch kerf, makes a liberal allowance for slabs, and disregards taper. Official rule in many parts of the United States.

    5. **Scribner decimal C rule.** The Scribner rule modified by rounding off the last digit to the nearest 10 and dropping the cypher. Cypher added to total of volumes.

**Runoff, subsurface.** Runoff through subsurface streams.

**Runoff, surface.** The rate at which water is discharged from a drainage area, usually expressed in cubic feet per square mile of drainage area.

**Sample plot.** See Plot, sample.

**Sample tree.** See Tree, sample.

**Sapling.** A young tree less than 4 inches d.b.h. The minimum size of saplings is usually, though not invariably, placed at 2 inches d.b.h.

**Sapwood.** The light-colored wood which appears on a cross section of wood. The sapwood is composed of living cells and serves to conduct water and minerals to the crown.*

**Sawmill.** A plant at which logs are sawed into salable products. It includes all the machinery and buildings necessary for the operation of the plant.

**Sawtimber.** Trees that yield logs suitable in size and quality for the production of lumber.

**Scale.** The estimated sound contents in terms of a given log rule of a log or group of logs; to estimate the sound contents of a log or group of logs. See Rule, log.

**Scar, fire.** A healing or healed-over injury or wound caused or accentuated by fire in the trunk or other large woody part of a tree.

**Scrub.** Stunted trees or brush, often in dense stand.

**Season.** To dry lumber, either in the open or in a kiln.

**Season, fire.** The period or periods of the year during which fires are likely to occur, spread, and do sufficient damage and otherwise warrant organized fire control.

**Seasoning.** The process of drying (curing) lumber or other forms of wood for better utilization, by natural seasoning (air or underground drying), or artificial seasoning (kiln drying, electrical drying, oil drying, etc.).

**Second growth.** See Growth, second.

**Section.** A unit of land measure, 640 acres, or 6,400 square chains, one mile, or 80 chains square.*

**Section, cross.** A section of a stem taken at right angles to its longitudinal axis. Syn. Transverse section.

**Seedbed.** In natural reproduction, the soil or forest floor on which seed falls; in nursery practice a prepared area in which seed is sown.

**Seedling.** A tree grown from seed. Usually the term is restricted to trees smaller than saplings.

**Seed spot.** See Spot, seed.

**Seed-tree.** A tree that produces seed: usually trees reserved in a cutting operation to supply seed. See also Cutting, methods of.

**Seed year.** See Year, seed.

**Selection.** See Cutting, methods of: Selection.

**Shake.** A lengthwise separation of wood, which usually occurs between and parallel to the growth layers. Shake is usually wind-caused. Also section split from a bolt of wood and used for roofing or siding, or a shingle manufactured to imitate it.

**Shelterbelt.** A wind barrier of living trees and shrubs maintained for the purpose of protecting farm fields. As applied to individual farmsteads, termed "windbreak." Syn. Belt.

**Shelterwood.** See Cutting, methods of: Shelterwood.

**Shrinkage.** The contraction of wood caused by drying the material below the fiber saturation point. Shrinkage values are usually expressed as a percentage of some specific dimensions (or the volume) of the wood when green.

**Shrub.** A woody perennial plant differing from a perennial herb by its persistent and woody stems, and from a tree by its low stature and habit of branching from the base.

**Silvics.** The life history and general characteristics of forest trees and stands, with particular reference to environmental factors.

**Silvicultural system.** See Cutting, methods of.

**Silviculture.** The art of producing and tending a forest; the application of the knowledge of silvics in the treatment of a forest; the theory and practice of controlling forest establishment, composition, and growth. See also Thinning.

**Site.** An area, considered as to its ecological factors with reference to capacity to produce forests of other vegetation; the combination of biotic, climatic, and soil condition of an area.

**Skid.** To pull logs from the stump to the skidway, landing, or mill.

**Skidway.** Two skids laid parallel to right angles to a road, usually raised above the ground at the end nearest the road. Logs are usually piled upon at skidway, as they are brought from the stump for loading upon sleds, wagons, or cars.

**Slab.** The exterior portion of a log removed in sawing timber.

**Slash.** Branches, bark, tops, chunks, cull logs, uprooted stumps, and broken or uprooted trees left on the ground after logging; also, a large accumulation of debris after wind or fire.

**Snag.** A standing, dead tree from which the leaves and most of the branches have fallen, or a standing section of the stem of a tree broken off at a height of 20 feet or more. If less than 20 feet, properly termed a "stub."

**Softwood.** One of the botanical group of trees that generally have needle or scalelike leaves—the conifers. Also, the wood produced by such trees regardless of texture or density.*

**Species (of trees).** Subordinate to a genus; trees having common characteristics. In common language, a kind or variety.*

**Spot, seed.** A prepared spot in which tree seeds are sown.

**Springwood.** The less dense, larger-celled, first-formed part of a growth layer.

**Spud.** A hand tool used in stripping bark from felled trees.

**Staff compass.** See Compass, staff.

**Stain, blue.** A fungous discoloration, predominantly bluish but sometimes grayish, blackish, or brownish in appearance; confined almost exclusively to sapwood.

**Stand.** An aggregation of trees or other growth occupying a specific area and sufficiently uniform in composition (species), age, arrangement, and conditions as to be distinguishable from the forest or other growth on adjoining areas.

**Stand, fully stocked.** A forest stand in which all growing space is effectively occupied but having ample room for the development of crop trees.

**Stand, mixed.** A stand in which less than 75 per cent of the trees in the main crown canopy are of a single species.

**Stand, pure.** A stand in which at least 75 per cent of the trees in the main crown canopy are of a single species.

**Stem.** The trunk of a tree. It may extend to the top of the tree as in some conifers, or it may be lost in the ramification of the crown, as in most broadleaf trees. Syn. Bole; Trunk; Shaft. Also the principal axis of a plant from which buds and shoots are developed.

**Stick, Biltmore.** A rule graduated in such a way that the diameter of a standing tree may be estimated when the stick is held tangent to the surface at right angles to the main axis of the tree, and at a distance from the eye for which the stick is graduated.

**Stick, scale.** A graduated stick for measuring the diameters and contents of logs; both measures are stamped on the stick.

**Stock, growing.** The sum (in number and volume) of all the trees in a forest.

**Stores, naval.** A term applied to resin and turpentine obtained in the distillation of oleoresin.

**Stratification.** The operation or method of burying seeds, often in alternate layers, in a moist medium such as sand or peat to overcome dormancy or for storage.

**Strip, sample.** A long narrow strip used as a sampling unit in surveys.

**Stumpage.** The value of timber as it stands uncut in the woods; in a general sense, the standing timber itself.

**Stump-wood.** Resinous stump and root of longleaf or slash pine. Also called lighter pine.*

**Succession.** The progressive development of the vegetation toward its highest ecological expression, the climax. The replacement of one plant community by another.

**Succession, primary.** Plant succession on newly formed soils or upon surfaces, exposed for the first time, which have never borne vegetation.

**Succession, secondary.** Plant succession which is subsequent to the destruction of a part or all of the original vegetation.

**Sucker.** A shoot from the lower portion of a stem or especially from the root. Syn. Sprout.

**Summerwood.** The denser, smaller-celled, later-formed part of a growth layer.

**Suppressed tree.** See Overtopped.

**Suppression, fire.** All the work of extinguishing a fire following its detection.

1. **Direct.** A method whereby the edge of the fire is extinguished directly.
2. **Indirect.** A method whereby the control line is located along a favorable firebreak and the intervening strip between the fire and the firebreak is backfired.
3. **One-lick.** A system of managing personnel on a fire whereby an entire crew constructing the control line moves forward without the workers changing their relative position in the line. As they move forward, they do one lick of work, then advance one or more steps. The number of steps is controlled primarily by the number of persons engaged, and the consequent proper spacing of licks in order that the control line may be completed and the fire extinguished when the last worker has passed over the line.

**Survey, forest.** An inventory of forest land to determine area, condition, timber volume, and species, for specific purposes such as timber purchase and forest management, or as a basis for forest policies and programs.

**Sustained yield.** Continuous yield of forest products on a given area.

**Swamp.** To clear the ground of underbrush, fallen trees, and other obstructions to facilitate such subsequent logging operations as skidding.

**Swatter, fire.** A fire suppression tool consisting usually of a flap of belting fabric attached to a long wooden handle, used in direct attack on grass or similar light-fuel fires.

**Sweep.** A gradual bend in a log, pole, or piling, considered as a defect.

**Swell-butted.** As applied to a tree, greatly enlarged at the base. Syn. Bottle-butted; Churn-butted.

**Systemic pesticide.** A pesticide chemical that is carried to other parts of a plant or animal after it is injected or taken up from the soil or body surface.*

**Table, stand.** A summary table showing the number of trees by species and diameter class for any given area.

**Table, volume.** A table showing for a given species the average contents of trees of given sizes in a specified unit of volume.

**Tally.** The count of trees, logs, or other products; to count trees, logs, or other products; to record products, distances, etc., as measured.*

**Tally, lumber.** A record of lumber giving the number of boards or pieces by size, grade, and species. Syn. Mill tally.

**Tally person.** One who makes a record of units being counted or measured.*

**Tape, diameter.** A tape based on relationship of circumference to diameter, for measuring the diameters of trees directly.

**Taper.** The gradual diminution of diameter in a stem of a tree or a log from the base to the top. Syn. Rise.

**Taproot.** The main root of a tree which strikes downward with or without heavy branching until it either reaches an impenetrable layer or one so lacking in oxygen or moisture that further downward growth is impossible.

**Technology, wood.** The study of wood in all its aspects; the science of wood, including its anatomy, chemistry, properties, and treatment.

**Texture.** In wood anatomy, the sizes, distribution, and proportional volumes of the cellular elements of which wood is composed; often used interchangeably with grain.

**Thinning.** Cutting in an immature stand to increase its rate of growth, to foster quality growth, to improve composition, to promote sanitation, to aid in litter decomposition, to obtain greater total yield, and so recover and use material that would be lost otherwise.

**Thinning, natural.** Death of trees in a stand as a result of competition.

**Timber.** A term loosely applied to forest stands or their products; often applied to wood in forms suitable for heavy construction, as for houses, ships, and bridges.

**Timber, merchantable.** A tree or stand of trees which may be disposed of at a profit through conversion to salable products.

**Tolerance.** The capacity of a tree to develop and grow in the shade of and in competition with other trees; a general term for the relative ability of a species to survive a deficiency of an essential growth requirement, such as light, moisture, or nutrient supply.

**Tool, council or rich.** A long-handled combination rake and cutting tool, the blade of which is constructed of mowing-machine sickle-cutter sections fastened to a piece of angle iron.

**Toughness.** A quality of wood which permits the material to undergo considerable deformation before breaking. When broken, the wood is splintery.

**Tower, lookout.** See Lookout.

**Tower observer.** A lookout stationed at a tower.

**Toxicity.** The power of acting as a poison.

**Transpiration.** The process by which water vapor leaves a living plant and enters the atmosphere.

**Transplant.** To replant a nursery seedling in another part of the nursery for further development. See Outplant.

**Tree.** A woody plant having one well-defined stem and a more or less definitely formed crown, usually attaining a height of at least 8 feet.

**Tree, crop.** A tree selected in a young stand or planation because of rate of growth or position, to be carried through to maturity. The growth of such trees is made the object of frequent thinnings or other cuttings.

**Tree, cull.** A live tree of merchantable size but which is unmerchantable now or prospectively because of defects or decay.

**Tree, den.** A hollow tree used as a home by a mammal or other animal.

**Tree farm.** See Farm, tree.

**Tree, sample.** A representative or average-sized tree. A tree chosen for detailed measurement of condition, size, growth, or quality.

**Tree, weed.** A tree of a species with relatively little or no value.

**Tree, wolf.** A tree occupying more space than its silvicultural value warrants, curtailing better neighbors. A term usually applied to broad-crowned, short-stemmed trees.

**Turpentine.** The liquid product resulting from the distillation of oleoresin.

**Turpentine, gum.** The gum exuded from living pine trees.

**Type, forest.** A descriptive term used to group stands of similar character as regards composition and development due to certain ecological factors, by which they may be differentiated from other groups of stands.

**Underbrush.** The brush growing in a forest.

**Undercut.** In logging, the notch cut in a tree to govern the direction in which the tree is to fall and to prevent splitting.

**Undergrowth.** Small trees and shrubby plants growing under a forest canopy.

**Understory.** That portion of the trees in a forest stand below the overstory.

**Uneven-aged.** Applied to a stand in which there are considerable differences in the age of the trees and in which three or more age classes are represented. See also All-aged.

**Unit.** A long cord containing 160 cubic feet. Sticks are also usually cut 5 feet long as compared to 4-foot sticks in a standard cord.

**Unit, animal.** A measure of livestock numbers by which kinds, classes, sizes, and ages are converted to an approximate common standard in relation to feed and forage resources based on the equivalent of a mature cow (approximately 1,000 lbs., live weight). In the western range territory, an animal unit is roughly one head of cattle, one horse, one mule, five sheep, five swine, or five goats.

**Upperstory.** See Overstory.

**Utilization, forest.** That branch of forestry concerned with the operation of harvesting and marketing the forest crop and other resources of the forest.

**Value, forage.** The relative importance for grazing purposes of a range plant or plants as a whole on a range.

**Value, nutritive.** A term usually prefixed by "high," "low," etc., to indicate relative quality of a given forage or feed to furnish elements valuable for livestock nutrition.

**Variety.** A subdivision of a species having some heritable characteristics distinctly different from the typical. Partial syn., Race.

**Veneer.** A thin sheet of wood cut on a veneer machine. There are three kinds of veneers: sawed, sliced, and rotary cut.

**Virgin forest.** See Forest, virgin.

**Volume, merchantable.** The amount of wood in a single tree or stand considered salable.

**Volume table.** See Table, volume.

**Water, available.** The amount of moisture in the soil in excess of the wilting coefficient or the wilting per cent.

**Water, hygroscopic.** Suspended water adhering to the surface of solid particles which molecular attraction of solid for liquid can hold against root absorption and evaporation. It does not move as a liquid but may in the form of vapor.

**Watershed.** A drainage area; an area from which the run-off flows into a given stream.*

**Wedge.** In logging, to drive a wedge into the saw cut to prevent the saw from binding and to direct the fall of the tree.

**Weed tree.** See Tree, weed.

**Wilderness.** In the strictest sense, an area that has never been developed by humans. A 1964 Wilderness Act defined it thus: "A Wilderness, in contrast with those areas where man and his own works dominated landscape, and is hereby recognized as an area where the earth and its community of life are untrammelled by man, where man himself is a visitor and does not remain." In more common use the word is associated with these undeveloped areas and those set aside with a little development. In some cases, manufactured items are dismantled to reduce the area to a primitive state. Under these broader uses, some roadless areas are considered wildernesses when the access is limited to hiking, canoeing, or horsebacking, and the use is set aside for recreation. To most of the general public, wilderness experiences are gained in a number of settings involving wild but not necessarily true wilderness areas.*

**Wildfires.** Fires burning out of control, regardless of how or why they started.

**Wilding.** A seedling naturally reproduced outside of a nursery used in forest planting.

**Windbreak.** A wind barrier of living trees and shrubs maintained for the purpose of protecting the farm home, other buildings, garden, orchard, or feedlots.

**Windfall.** A tree uprooted or broken off by wind; an area on which the trees have been thrown by wind. Syn. Blowdown; Wind slash.

**Wind-firm.** Able to withstand heavy wind.

**Wolf tree.** See Tree, wolf.

**Wood.** The lignified water-conducting, strengthening, and storage tissue of branches, stems, and roots. Syn. Xylem.

**Wood, early.** See Springwood.

**Wood, late.** See Summerwood.

**Wood, rough.** Unpeeled cordwood.

**Wood technology.** See Technology, wood.

**Woodland, farm.** The wooded portion of a farm or ranch, or the wooded land operated in connection with a farm or ranch.

**Woodlot.** In the South, a shady enclosure for domestic livestock; an enclosure near the house for the winter woodpile.

**Yard.** A place where logs, pulpwood, or other timbers are collected; to collect logs in a yard, landing, or skidway.

**Year, seed.** A year in which a given species produces (over a considerable area) a seed crop greatly in excess of the normal. Applied usually to trees of irregular or infrequent seed production.

**Yield, sustained.** As applied to a policy, method, or plan of forest management, implies continuous production with the aim of achieving, at the earliest practicable time, an approximate balance between net growth and harvest, either by annual or somewhat longer periods.

# Index